Perspectives on Methodology in Consumer Research

Perspectives on Methodology in Consumer Research

Edited by
David Brinberg and Richard J. Lutz

With 32 Figures

Springer-Verlag
New York Berlin Heidelberg
London Paris Toyko

David Brinberg
Department of Marketing
State University of New York at Albany
Albany, New York 12222

Richard J. Lutz
Department of Marketing
University of Florida
Gainesville, Florida 32611

Library of Congress Cataloging in Publication Data
Main entry under title
Perspectives on methodology in consumer research
Includes bibliographies and indexes.
1. Consumers—Research—Addresses, essays, lectures.
2. Marketing research—Addresses, essays, lectures.
3.Motivation research (Marketing)—Addresses, essays,
lectures. I. Brinberg, David. II. Lutz, Richard
John, 1947– .
HF5415.3.P464 1986 658.8'34 85-26047

Typeset by Publishers Service, Bozeman, Montana.
Printed and bound by R.R. Donnelley, Harrisonburg, Virginia.
Printed in the United States of America.

9 8 7 6 5 4 3 2 1

ISBN 0-387-96238-7 Springer-Verlag New York Berlin Heidelberg
ISBN 3-540-96238-7 Springer-Verlag Berlin Heidelberg New York

Preface

Methodological advances in consumer behavior are increasing rapidly. We can characterize these advances by work in two logically separate but functionally related areas: (a) the philosophical underpinnings of our methods, and (b) the analytic strategies for examining the phenomena of interest in the field. An important aspect in communicating these advances is the demonstration of their use on focal problems in consumer behavior.

Current research strategies and analytic techniques in the field of consumer research reflect the dominant logical empiricist epistemology. The development of new epistemologies (e.g., scientific relativism, hypothetical realism), however, is likely to modify the dominant logical empiricist approach and is also likely to influence the analytic strategies used to conduct research. For instance, with the increased awareness of scientific relativism and hypothetical realism, greater emphasis is anticipated for idiographic rather than nomothetic designs, for observational rather than experimental designs, for process rather than static analyses, and for more sophisticated techniques for summarizing findings across studies.

The major theme underlying this volume is that conceptual, analytic, and substantive diversity are essential for consumer behavior research to advance. Collectively, the chapters we present in this volume are a diverse set of perspectives for the study of consumer behavior.

This volume is organized into three parts: (1) philosophical orientations toward consumer behavior research, (2) analytic strategies for consumer behavior research, and (3) applications of these orientations and strategies to current research areas.

The first part contains two chapters that focus on alternative approaches toward science and new epistemological approaches toward marketing and consumer behavior. In the first chapter, Belk contrasts art versus science as ways of generating and testing hypotheses. He describes how literature, comics, painting, photography, grave goods, music, film, and poetry all can be used to provide some understanding of materialism. The basic premise of his chapter is that multiple orientations are essential for a thorough understanding of a phenomenon.

Moreover, Belk argues that to limit research strategies to experimental methods severely and unnecessarily restricts what the researcher is able to learn about the focal problem.

Ryan contrasts the traditional logical empiricist philosophy of science with the more current work in relativism and the "new physics." He argues that buyer behavior researchers have been preoccupied with social psychological theories that are embedded in logical empiricist philosophy. An illustration is presented in the form of a reconceptualization of the variable ordering controversy in cognitive response models. That illustration highlights how the "new physics" can alleviate problems arising from an empirical bias and can lead to richer concepts and theories. In particular, the role of the scientist is viewed as more proactive and, to some extent, inseparable from the phenomena under study.

In Part II, we present four chapters that describe recent analytic advances. Jaccard and Wood examine the limitations of nomothetic (aggregate) level analyses and present a detailed analysis of consumer decision making at an idiothetic (individual) level. In their application of idiothetic designs to consumer decision making, Jaccard and Wood describe a systematic and thorough analysis of: (1) an individual's preference structure among a set of options and (2) the perceptual structure among the attributes associated with each option. The implications of their approach for attitude and behavioral change are presented.

In his chapter, Dillon discusses issues in the use of latent variables in consumer behavior research. After a short introduction to causal modeling, and in particular, the influential LISREL model, Dillon applies this technique to an analysis of the attitude-behavior relation. He highlights the need to consider both the convergent and discriminant validity of theoretical concepts when using LISREL and the problems associated with collinearity among latent variables. In that discussion, Dillon identifies a number of issues concerning the limitations associated with the application of LISREL to consumer behavior research. Further, Dillon describes a sequence of steps for the use of LISREL when analyzing a multitrait-multimethod matrix.

Brinberg and Jaccard summarize the numerous meta-analytic techniques that have been proposed for the quantitative integration of a set of empirical findings. Initially, these authors describe the strengths and weaknesses associated with a literature review. As they note, a reviewer can increase his/her understanding of a focal problem by partitioning the set of findings across a number of facets. The facets described in their chapter focus on substantive, methodological, and conceptual issues. The quantitative techniques for summarizing and contrasting a set of findings are then presented and sample data are described to illustrate the use of these techniques.

Moore describes the use of both procedural and analytic strategies to study several areas in consumer behavior that involve dyadic interaction (e.g., buyer-seller interaction and couple decision making). As Moore notes, these research areas are traditionally examined using only static approaches (e.g., self-report questionnaires), although the phenomena are clearly both interactive and dynamic. Moore discusses the strengths and weaknesses of the various coding procedures used to examine social interaction data and he presents a variety of analytic techniques that can be used to extract information from these data.

In Part III, we present two chapters that describe current research areas in consumer behavior that use the epistemological or analytic techniques discussed in Parts I and II. Hirschman and Holbrook examine the problem of experiential consumption from an epistemology embedded in a relativistic tradition. These authors describe the relation among thought, emotion, activity, and values and relate each of these concepts to the consumption experience. Several methodological approaches for the study of consumption experience consistent with the relativistic epistemology are described (e.g., role-taking and introspection). The application of these techniques to the consumption experience is then illustrated.

Meyer describes a theory and an approach for examining the learning of multiattribute preferences. Consistent with a relativistic and an idiographic approach, the focus of this chapter is on an individual rather than an aggregate level analysis. Meyer argues that evaluations are formed through a directed search across a schematically organized knowledge base. The proposed structure described in his chapter provides a unified framework for explaining a diversity of empirical findings in product impression formation, learning, and inference.

In our selection of topics for this volume, we are not taking the position that any single researcher needs to use all the perspectives described by the set of authors. We do take the position, however, that the field of consumer research collectively, needs to approach the study of a substantive problem from a wide variety of perspectives in order to increase the field's understanding of that problem. For example, the use of diverse approaches to study the same focal problem can be found in the chapters by Ryan, Jaccard and Wood, and Dillon. A common theme across these three chapters is the focus on information processing, and more specifically, the relation between attitudes and behavior. Ryan discusses the relation between attitude and behavior by examining the epistemological assumptions associated with "traditional" research in that area. Jaccard and Wood examine the attitude-behavior relation from an experimental, idiothetic perspective, while Dillon examines the same relation through the use of causal modeling. These chapters each offer a new perspective on the study of the attitude-behavior relation.

We have several objectives for this volume: (a) to summarize, integrate, and evaluate important methodological advances, (b) to provide a comprehensive, though not exhaustive, discussion of epistemological issues and analytic strategies, (c) to illustrate their application for research on current focal problems in consumer behavior, and (d) to provide a sourcebook for researchers interested in current perspectives on methodology in consumer research.

We would like to thank the following people for their insightful and thorough reviews: Russell Belk, Jim Bettman, William Dillon, Wes Hutchinson, Jim

Jaccard, R. Krishnan, John Lynch, Danny Moore, Alan Sawyer, and Peter Wright. Each of these reviewers helped us to improve this volume.

Methodological advances in consumer research are likely to occur when the field is willing to use a diversity of perspectives to study the focal problems of the field. This volume is an attempt to make salient research perspectives that can help add new insights into our understanding of consumer behavior.

David Brinberg, State University of New York, Albany
Richard J. Lutz, University of Florida, Gainesville

Contents

Contributors

RUSSELL W. BELK, College of Business Administration, University of Utah, Salt Lake City, Utah 84112.

DAVID BRINBERG, Department of Marketing, State University of New York at Albany, Albany, New York 12222.

WILLIAM R. DILLON, Department of Marketing, Baruch College, City University of New York, New York 10010.

ELIZABETH C. HIRSCHMAN, Department of Marketing, New York University, New York, New York 10003.

MORRIS B. HOLBROOK, Department of Marketing, Columbia University, New York, New York 10027.

JAMES JACCARD, Department of Psychology, State University of New York at Albany, Albany, New York 12222.

RICHARD J. LUTZ, Department of Marketing, University of Florida, Gainesville, Florida 32611.

ROBERT J. MEYER, Graduate School of Management, University of California, Los Angeles, California 90024.

DANNY L. MOORE, Strategic Business Development, Burke Marketing Services, Inc., Cincinnati, Ohio 45202.

MICHAEL J. RYAN, Graduate School of Business Administration, University of Michigan, Ann Arbor, Michigan 48109.

GREGORY WOOD, Department of Psychology, State University of New York at Albany, Albany, New York 12222.

Part I Philosophical Orientations

1
Art Versus Science as Ways of Generating Knowledge About Materialism

RUSSELL W. BELK

Traditional Antipathy of Art and Science

Love (which includes poetry)
Is to science
As the free & beautiful
Catchings of a child are
To the vile & unreturning
Throes of the hangman.
Kenneth Patchen (1967)*

As Patchen's poem clearly implies, there is often an assumption that art and science represent not only opposite, but mutually hostile approaches to revealing the world around us. Art traditionally sees science as overly cold, rational, and devoid of humanitarianism. It is seen as destroying the beautiful rainbow by logically dismissing it as so much light reflected and refracted in air-suspended droplets of water.

This apparent antipathy is neither new nor restricted to the view of the artist. In the tenth book of *The Republic*, Plato warned that "poetry has no serious value or claim to truth" (1974, p. 439). In this ancient version of the quarrel between science and art, philosophy (Plato's science) sees art as frivolous fantasy and mysticism that promotes emotion over logic. Plato adds, "We can fairly take the poet and set him beside the painter. He resembles him both because his works have a low degree of truth and also because he deals with a low element of the mind" (1974, p. 435).

The distinction between art and science is perpetuated in the separation of university programs into liberal arts—thought to provide sound bases for appreciating and enjoying life during leisure—and the sciences—thought to provide more practical bases for understanding and enhancing life during work.

While the public may recognize both art and science as the fruits of civilization, generally there is thought to be little or no overlap in their domains, objectives, or accomplishments. In the traditional view art is created to give vent to feelings and is consumed in order to remind us of basic human feelings, to make us forget worldly cares, entertain us, or help us escape into a more ethereal realm. Science is instead seen as being pursued ("created" is too artistic and therefore too tainted a word) for the sake of knowledge and is consumed for the sake of learning about natural or manmade phenomena. Art is seen to seek beauty while science is seen to seek truth (Hospers, 1946; Johnson, 1949), and in order to achieve these ends, art is seen as deriving from intuition and inspiration while science is seen to be the product of logic and reasoning. Thus art is seen to be preoccupied with form while science is seen to focus on substance.

There is, however, some recent indication that these views may be changing and that art and science, while remaining distinct approaches, are beginning to be seen as less antagonistic. In their book on approaches to science, Mitroff and Kilmann (1978) distinguish four types of scientific styles that can be arrayed in the two-dimensional space shown in Figure 1.1. Of the four types of scientists described in this classification, the *Analytic Scientist* comes closest to the traditional (logical positivist) view of science. For such a scientist, the controlled experiment is thought to be the best approach to knowledge because it allows objective testing of logical premises. The other scientific types move away from thinking and sensing toward feeling and intuiting, each moves at least part of the way from the traditional methods of science to the traditional methods of art. In fact, the *Conceptual Humanist*, who shifts on both dimensions, comes very close to the traditional perspective of the artist. For the Conceptual Humanist, knowledge is seen as best pursued through the passionate cultivation of speculative and subjective insight. The arts are seen by such a scientist to be higher ways of gaining knowledge. Mitroff and Kilmann (1978) stress that there is a need in science for *both* the Analytic Scientist and the Conceptual Humanist. Both are needed for our knowledge to advance.

Ways of Knowing

After exemplifying the ways in which various art forms can contribute to knowledge, I will return the discussion to a question that Mitroff and Kilmann (1978) fail to address: Is the knowledge generated by the conceptual humanist or artist preliminary to and more tentative than the knowledge generated by the analytic scientist? To simplify, the essence of the question: Can art only suggest hypotheses for science to test, or can the knowledge generated by art and science have equal claims to presenting the truth. The question is not a new one, and it is important to consider the context that prevails when it is answered. As Walsh (1969) notes, there was once a time when a poet's reference to the moon as a goddess was taken as a direct threat to astronomy. We no longer interpret such a poetic reference in a way that would threaten scientists, because science is held in such high esteem that the literal truth of such a reference would not be enter-

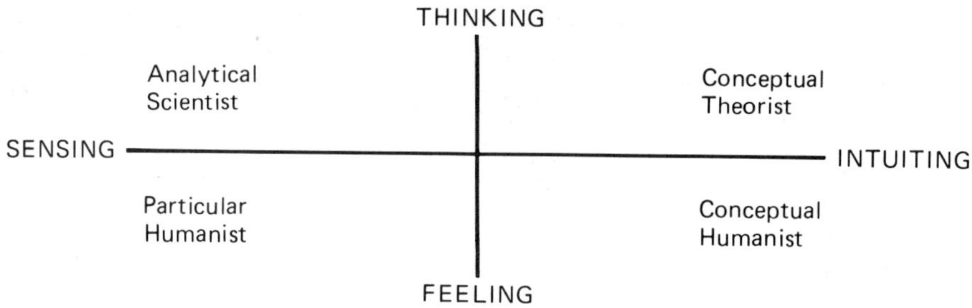

FIGURE 1.1. Mitroff and Kilmann's scientific styles.

tained. However, as Berman (1981) points out, until the 16th century art and science were held in similar esteem as ways of knowing.

The present intellectual climate in science is increasingly skeptical of claims of logical positivists that so-called scientific method leads to rational and defensible truth (e.g., Anderson, 1983; Peter & Olson, 1983). The alternative position of relativism is much less predisposed to view one method as generating the truth or to dismiss others as irrelevant. But because virtually all consumer behavior research to date has been carried on within the logical positivist framework, this narrow but traditional view of science has been maintained throughout most of the following comments. It is from this perspective that this paper seeks to evaluate whether art can contribute to knowledge and, if so, how.

Materialism Context and Issues

Art may contribute to knowledge in ways that are potentially different when considering the types of knowledge of concern to various physical and behavioral sciences: Therefore, the illustrations and much of the discussion of this paper is restricted to knowledge about consumer behavior. Because this still leaves a nearly limitless number of applications, the illustrative scope is further restricted to issues involving consumer materialism. While narrower definitions of materialism have been given (Belk, 1984b), the present paper construes materialism to mean the relationship between people and things or, more accurately, the relationship between people as mediated by things (Isaacs, 1935). As an illustration of the sorts of issues posed by consumer materialism, Belk (1984a) lists the following five:

1. Is materialism healthy?
2. How do consumers make tradeoffs between money, durables, and discretionary nondurables?
3. What roles do consumption objects play in interpersonal relationships?
4. What roles does consumption play in self-identity, self-maintenance, and self-enhancement?
5. What is marketing's influence on materialism and satisfaction in life?

There is very little in the way of behavioral theory and research bearing on these important issues. While it might be possible to gain a few insights into these questions by using existing general theoretical perspectives such as attribution theory and attitude models, what really is needed are fresher and broader vantage points to provide significant answers to such questions.

Applications of Art to Materialism

Literature

One nontraditional vantage point bearing on the fourth issue above, for instance, is literature. In order to see how science and literature are capable of providing similar insights into the issue of how consumption objects may affect our identities, consider first the following passage by novelist Henry James:

> When you've lived as long as I you'll see that every human being has his shell and that you must take the shell into account. By the shell I mean the whole envelope of circumstances. There's no such thing as an isolated man or woman; we're each of us made up of a cluster of appurtenances. What shall we call our "self"? Where does it begin? Where does it end? It overflows into everything that belongs to us—and then it flows back again. I know that a large part of myself is in the clothes I choose to wear. I've got a great respect for *things*! One's self—for other people—is one's expression of one's self; and one's house, one's furniture, one's garments, the books one reads, the company one keeps—these things are all expressive. (Madame Merle to Isabel Archer, *Portrait of a Lady*, 1881, p. 200)

Now consider the very similar scientific conclusion of Henry James' brother William who is arguably the father of modern psychology:

> A man's self is the sum total of all that he CAN call his, not only his body and his psychic powers, but his clothes and his house, his wife and his children, his ancestors and friends, his reputation and works, his lands, and yacht and bank-account. All these things give him the same emotions. If they wax and prosper, he feels triumphant; if they dwindle and die away, he feels cast down—not necessarily in the same degree for each thing, but in much the same way for all. (*The Principles of Psychology*, Vol. 1, 1890, pp. 291–292)

The parallel notions of self extended to include possessions are remarkable. It is possible, of course, that these two brothers merely shared their ideas, but given William's disdain for brother Henry's novels, it is doubtful that he would borrow his brother's ideas. It seems more likely that two brothers raised in the same environment came to some of the same conclusions about human nature, but chose to express them in different ways—one in science and the other in art. The fact that their father, Henry James Sr., was obsessed with religious asceticism, may well have sensitized both sons to materialism (King, 1983).

The views of Henry James on extended self are actually more complete and complex than those of his brother William. Not only is self expressed through possessions a frequent theme in many of Henry James' novels, in *Portrait of a Lady* the point is debated by Isabel Archer who disagrees with Madame Merle and contends that "nothing that belongs to me is any measure of me." Rather than the cultural universal that William James had suggested, Henry James' treatments suggest that certain people are more likely than others to invest self in possessions. This view has recently been supported in a study by Rochberg-Halton (Csikszentmihalyi & Rochberg-Halton, 1981) in which people were asked to describe their most treasured possessions and explain why they are valued.

It would be possible to explore parallels in Henry and William James' work further and to examine materialism treatments in literary works by other authors including F. Scott Fitzgerald, John Dos Passos, Horatio Alger, John Steinbeck, and Theodore Dreiser. However, the present intent is only to illustrate literary contributions to a knowledge of materialism, and not to undertake a thorough analysis. The potential for literature to contribute to knowledge has been well recognized in other fields as well, as the following examples of titles suggest:

Travuchis and Goode, *The Family Through Literature*
Spradley and McDonough, *Anthropology Through Literature*
Fernandez, *Social Psychology Through Literature*
Coser, *Sociology Through Literature*
Rabkin, *Psychopathology and Literature*
Merriam, *Themes of Adulthood Through Literature*
Sharpless, *Symbol and Myth in Modern Literature*
London, *The World of Law, Volume I, The Law in Literature*
Green and Walzer, *The Political Imagination in Literature*
Meyer and Subbiondo, *Borrowed Time: Literature on Man and His Environment*
Felman, *Literature and Psychoanalysis*
Trautmann and Pollard, *Literature and Medicine*
Meyerhoff, *Time in Literature*
Ross, *Literature and Philosophy*
Gardner, *Religion and Literature*.

In examining literature (or other art forms) for their potential contributions to knowledge, two basic approaches may be taken. One views literature as a source of explanations and a second, less common view, treats literature as data. When examining literature as a source of explanations, its assertions and implications about a phenomenon are treated as hypotheses or theories. For example, consider a portion of John Donne's Meditation XVII (1623):

> No man is an island, entire of itself; every man is a piece of the continent, a part of the main. If a clod be washed away by the sea, Europe is the less, as well as if a promontory were, as well as if a manor of thy friend's or of thine own were. Any man's death diminishes me because I am involved in mankind, and therefore never send to know for whom the bell tolls; it tolls for thee.

In this eloquent statement that a brotherhood of man does or should exist, the perplexing question of selfishness and egoism versus empathy and altruism surfaces. While some may argue with Donne's optimism about the human condition, the knowledge imparted in this passage goes beyond the hypothesis advanced, by suggesting a powerful series of metaphors. Man does not exist as an isolated island, but shares a common destiny with others who make up the mainland. Thus others' losses are our losses and their deaths take something from us. Such a rich metaphor goes considerably beyond the simple hypothesis that our well-being is affected by the well-being of others. It *re*-presents the phenomenon being considered, using a different vantage point that allows it to be seen afresh in different ways than before. Thus besides contentions of fact about egoism versus altruism, Donne's prose provides a metaphorical model that recasts the issue in a way capable of generating further implied hypotheses. Jessup (1965) notes that Wittgenstein's "scientific" treatment of language hinges on a rich metaphor of language as cities, suburbs, houses, and streets. Langer (1963,xi) maintains that such metaphors are essential to the advancement of knowledge: "Really new concepts, having no names in current language, always make their earliest appearance in metaphorical statements; therefore, the beginning of any theoretical structure is inevitably marked by fantastic inventions." Or as Geiger (1973, p. 316) concludes, "Indeed it would appear that our ability to communicate what we know—or possibly . . . even to understand what we know—is a function of the literariness of our expression."

In the second major use of literature and other arts, as data, a work of art is potentially both a reflection of dominant cultural values and a shaper of cultural values. Because artworks provide a record of past, even prehistoric, peoples, they serve as important indices of culture. By content analyses of, say, the literature characteristic of a place and time, inferences about cultural values can be reached that may not be possible in other ways. Ultimately questions of whether the art form is a cause or an effect of cultural values and distinctions between high culture and popular culture may emerge, but these are merely additional considerations that affect the interpretation of the data.

In regarding works of art as data, analyses may be either qualitative or quantitative. An example of treating Henry James' works via qualitative data analysis is the work of Agnew (1983). His analysis of James' materialism and consumption themes reaches some of the same conclusions about the communication value of possessions that anthropologists have reached. It is interesting for instance that Douglas and Isherwood (1979), who draw on Henry James more to illustrate their hypotheses, also conclude that the primary power of commodities is to serve as communication symbols that allow and express class membership and social ties.

Comics

Turning from the sublime to the ridiculous in literature (and from high culture to popular culture), it is also possible to glean insights about materialism from comic books and strips. Both qualitative data analysis (e.g., Berger, 1973; Braun, 1971; Inge, 1979; Luciano, 1982; McAllister, 1983; Paymans, 1976; Perebinossoff, 1974; Powers, 1980; Sanders, 1974; Schecter 1977; Streicher, 1974; Summer, 1981) and quantitative data analysis (e.g., Barcus, 1961; Gallyer, 1951; Kassarjian, 1983) are relatively abundant using comic material. While there is little that focuses on materialism per se, I am now engaged in a longitudinal content analysis of materialistic themes in comics portraying wealth (e.g., *Uncle Scrooge* (Barks, 1948), *Richie Rich* (Harvey Publications, 1960), Veronica Lodge in *Archie* (Goldwater, 1942).

An an example of the hypothesis and theory generation potential of the comics, consider the story of the Land of Tra La La contained in *Uncle Scrooge*, 6 (1954). Briefly, the story begins with Scrooge (originally taken from Dickens' character) besieged by requests for his money and with an array of business problems including a threat by an oil sultan to nationalize Scrooge's oil wells unless he is placated with favors. In the face of this pressure Scrooge has a breakdown and seeks to escape money which he concludes "has brought me nothing but work, labor, toil, & jeers." His physician tells of a land that has no money, envy, greed, or possessiveness. The parallel to the Garden of Eden is intriguing. Scrooge decides to go there, accompanied as always by Donald Duck and his three nephews. After the nephews' boy scout ingenuity helps locate Tra La La (the paradise), Scrooge hires a plan to fly them into the cloud-enshrouded dormant volcano where Tra La La is located in the Himalayas. The reluctant pilot dives into the clouds after Scrooge offers him twice the value of the plane. Just before the ducks parachute into the valley Uncle Scrooge opens a last bottle of nerve medicine and the bottle cap falls innocently out of the plane. When the ducks arrive they are given meaningful work and find the idyllic life of happiness Scrooge expected. Soon however another worker finds Scrooge's errant bottle cap in his rice paddy. When he shows the unusual object to another he is offered a sheep for it. As others find out, the bidding increases and as the bottle cap gets traded around it goes for as much as a year's labor. Just as Scrooge is about to pour out his last bottles of nerve medicine on the presumption that he no longer needs them, the natives learn that he is the "rich" possessor of five bottle caps. Thoroughly unnerved by the ensuing lust for the caps, he orders Donald to take Sherpas and hike out of the valley to order a billion bottle caps to be flow in and dropped on the village in order to sate their acquisitive desires and get them back to work (which has stopped in order to pursue the bottle caps as the only real form of wealth).

Just as Donald returns, the first plane load of a million bottle caps rain down on the village. At first the villagers are ecstatic, but they soon learn that everyone has a "fortune" in bottle caps and that they are now worthless. By the time the second plane load arrives it is clear that there is a snake in the garden. The falling bottle caps destroy rice crops and so pollute the land that the sheep cannot find grass to eat. The ducks are brought to trial and would be put to death except that the nephews convince the magistrate that the only way to stop the destruction is to send them out of the valley to stop the planes from dropping more bottle caps. They leave the valley for India and civilization and Scrooge's need for nerve tonic is reinitiated when the nephews ask for their wage of 30¢ per hour.

What hypotheses might be derived from this story? A few possibilities include:

1. The wealthy have problems because of their wealth (or is this a rationalization like dumb blondes?).

2. Invidious distinction-seeking is natural whenever there is a scarcity of something; that is, greed is a function of scarcity.
3. The simple pleasures are the most rewarding (see Scitovsky, 1976).
4. When *having* becomes the means to distinction, *doing* suffers (what Albee [1977] calls the paradox of the Protestant Ethic).
5. Tampering with the economic system of third world countries can only do harm (see Dorfman & Mattelart, 1975; Dorfman, 1983).

These are only a few of the possible hypotheses that might be taken from this deceptively simple story. Interestingly, there is a very parallel story in the South African film *The Gods Must Be Crazy* (Uys, 1980) in which a Coca Cola bottle falls from a plane to a Bushman tribe. To a greater extent than with high culture however, the comics offer an opportunity to consider the power of mass media to influence the attitudes and hypotheses that shape a society's values. It is unlikely that Uncle Scrooge alone could have such an effect in modern Western society, but as a part of a broader set of mass media messages it may have a significant role. This makes quantitative content analyses all the more important.

Painting

Turning back to high culture, painting offers a convenient historical record of material life that in many cases predates written historical records (Pfeiffer, 1982). Berger, Blomberg, Fox, Dibbs, and Hollis (1972) for instance have analyzed the increased depiction of possessible material objects in paintings of 16th to 18th century Europe. They also point to works like Hans Holbein's *The Ambassadors* (1533) that shows two ambassadors posed with the riches they have obtained abroad along with the instruments of science, music, and religion that have allowed them to do so. The manifest destiny and paternalistic colonial views of these ambassadors is evident without words. What makes the painting especially interesting is the fact that Holbein painted a mysterious surrealistically elongated skull in the foreground as a reminder that death is inevitable and, in a more recent vernacular, that you can't take it with you.

Berger et al. (1972) also point out the proprietary attitude toward property that is evident in Thomas Gainsborough's *Mr. and Mrs. Andrews* (1755), in which the subjects display a haughty attitude, posed before the fields of their estate. This is actually a genre painting of lord, lady, and land, and is repeated in such works as Arthur Dervis' *Van Hartels Family* (1749) and *Horace Walpole* (c. 1750), Johann Zoffany's *Family Group* (c. 1800), and Gainsborough's *Richard Savage and His Sister* (c. 1750). It is useful to bear in mind that these family portraits were painted at a time when the position of the aristocracy was thought to be God-given and the violation of this order was unthinkable. Attitudes toward the sanctity of aristocratically owned land were also well entrenched. The penalty for stealing a potato was public flogging and the penalty for poaching was deportation.

Interestingly, while Berger chronicled the rise of 16th to 17th century European materialism as seen in paintings for a BBC television series in the early

1970s (Berger et al., 1972) there has just recently been a spate of historical treatments reaching the same conclusion (Boorstin, 1973; Braudel, 1973; Lears, 1983; McCracken, 1985; McKendrick, Brewer, & Plumb, 1982; Mukerji, 1983; Williams, 1981). Inasmuch as family portraits were done primarily for the aristocracy and the newly wealthy merchant class, a more complete perspective is obtained by examining the inexpensive pictoral prints that were popular at the same time. Mukerji(1983) has provided just such an analysis and finds that there is also evidence for increasingly materialistic attitudes among the common man in 15th and 16th century Europe. (For a criticism of this analysis see McCracken, in press.) She notes for instance that "Major forms of property, from land to homes to jewelry and decorative objects were central images in these [prints]" (Mukerji, 1983, p. 71). As Praz (1971) notes, these trends are paralleled by trends in novels like those of Henry James:

> It seems as if the pleasure of inventorying and mustering a universality of things is behind both the accumulation of furnishings. . . and the cummulative representation of a whole family in a painting, as well as the minute—and often superfluous and cumbersome—descriptions of milieux in novels. (Praz 1971, p. 23)

While aristocratic and common materialism may have peacefully coexisted in sixteenth century Europe, by the eighteenth century the unquestioned extravagance of the aristocracy began to be questioned. Besides the French Revolution consider Pietro Longhi's *Masked Women in Venice* (c. 1750). The painting shows a public scene with finely dressed women using handheld masquerade ball masks to hide their identities, and a finely dressed man with a long black overgarment to hide his finery. Both methods were apparently used in 18th century Venice to allow one to dress well but avoid provoking the envy of others (Schoeck, 1966). These practices were quite common at the time and preserved conspicuous consumption for a private circle of peers while circumventing guilt from the presence of the poor (Braudel, 1979, p. 489)

Other historical insights about materialism can also be gained from paintings. For example, the changing nature of private museum collections is evident in paintings and suggests changing attitudes toward the material objects of art and science. Frans Franken II's study of a collector (1610) shows an early private museum that makes little distinction between art, science, and religion. Paintings of saints, landscapes, and aristocrats are hung together with shells of crabs and mollusks, manuscripts, scientific instruments like armillory spheres, and bibles. Jan Bruegel's *Allegory of the Sense of Sight* (1618) shows a similar encyclopedic accumulation of the riches of the world, with a similar disregard for distinctions between art, science, and religion. As Berman (1981) points out, science has not yet divorced itself from nature and taken a rarefied and abstract view of the world. It was still an era when a great artist like Leonardo da Vinci (1452–1519) could also be a great engineer. Nor is the split between art and science evident in the *Wunderkammern* pictured in the *Collection of Fernando Cospi* (Anonymous, 1677). Praz (1964, pp. 138–139) notes that such a collection held a variety of curiosities including:

lamps and ink wells made of shells
musical and mathematical instruments
stuffed serpents
a peg made from the cedars of Lebanon and used in Solomon's temple
a coconut mounted in silver
automata
mosaics of hummingbirds' wings
Mexican curios
objects of ivory and coral
elephants' tusks and sharks' teeth
a length of rope with which Judas hanged himself
ostrich eggs
carved cherry pits
a male and female mandrake set on a bed of blue taffeta
and portraits of famous jurists and beautiful women.

A century later, however, when Lorenzo Pécheau painted the *Marchese Rocapadali* (1776) with her collection, the scope of private collections had begun to narrow. Her collection was not dissimilar to what might be found in a natural history museum today. It included butterflies, sea shells, stuffed animals, and models of prehistoric man. There was some ancient Egyptian art and reproductions, but these were displayed more as archaeological artifacts than as works of art or mere curiosities whatever their nature might be. Just as the Marchese's collection was more of a specialized science collection, Zoffany's painting of *Charles Towneley and His Friends in His Library* (1790) shows a specialized art collection. Actually the several dozen sculptures from the Villa Hadrian have been portrayed by the artist in a single room even though they were really from several rooms of Towneley's manor. But the painting clearly shows the more specialized nature of later collections and the separation of art and science that had occurred.

Beyond showing the separation of art and science, painting can also convey the state of scientific knowledge of early periods. For instance, Klein (1978) has analyzed Pieter Bruegel the Elder's paintings and finds rare evidence of the states of science and technology 400 years ago. Machines of industry and warfare, concepts of time, theories of physical movement, methods of accounting, and principles of medicine are all inferred from Bruegel's paintings in Klein's analysis.

Historical paintings can also provide a rare glimpse of consumer lifestyles during earlier periods. Contrast, for instance, Hieronymous Janssen's *Interior with Family* (1650) with the monogramist "R.W.'s" *Dutch Interior of the 17th Century* (c. 1650). Both paintings are of the main hall which was still where the family ate, slept, and received guests (Tuan, 1982). Although both portray a similar social class in a similar region at the same point in history, the former room shows some warmth and luxury in its paintings, embellished cabinets, sculpture, and tables, while the latter is a cold and functional hall devoid of decoration and warmth. The expressions and clothing of occupants portray largely the same impression.

Photography

If painting is a convenient and useful historical record of early consumption, photography provides such a record of later consumption. As several authors have pointed out, a potential problem with using past photographic records as data archives rather than as sources of hypotheses (and the same can be said of so-using paintings, even more clearly), is that the photographs we retain in family albums tend to be largely fictional histories (Sontag, 1973; Milgram, 1976, 1977a, 1977b; Krieger, 1979; Musello, 1979). That is, we pose our personal and professional photographs to capture the happy moments of life and selectively retain only the best renderings of the way we would like to remember our pasts. Nevertheless, such photos can still provide a valuable unobtrusive record of material life. Even though people may display their best clothing in family photos, household furnishings, interior and exterior home design, and the knick-nacks and memorabilia of life are unlikely to be selected for a photograph. Furthermore, the problem of bias is a lesser concern in documentary and artistic photography (Lesy, 1976; Peters & Mergen, 1977; Wagner, 1979).

Examinations of material lifestyles in the home are aided by several historic collections of such photographic subjects (see Peters & Mergen, 1977). One such collection is Seale's (1981) *The Tasteful Interlude: American Interiors through the Camera's Eye, 1860–1917*. From the more than 250 residential interiors in this collection any number of aspects of material life might be analyzed. For instance, American attitudes toward nature during the late 19th and early 20th century may be examined from the abundance of indoor plants and animal skins, horns, and mounted heads that are jointly present in a variety of households from Idaho and Alaska territories' cabins to mainline Philadelphia estates and elegant Manhattan apartments. It is evident that these artifacts were popular and seem to suggest trophies of man's overcoming and defeating nature. It is unlikely that a similar survey today would find positive covariance between bearskin rugs and indoor plants, given a less combative attitude toward nature and the current association of indoor plants, but not animal remains, with ecological responsibility.

One pair of photos in the Seale collection (numbers 213 and 214) are useful to illustrate the sort of hypotheses photographs may yield. The photos are of the living room of a Boston house in approximately 1912. The most striking feature of the room is that it conspicuously displays literally dozens of artifacts and photographs from a trip to India. The prominent display of these souvenirs suggests that we may attempt to tangibilize transient travel experiences in a way that will recall these experiences to the participants and communicate something about the events to others. Unlike the more common form of conspicuous consumption in which only the possession of material goods is the status symbol, in the case of souvenirs, the doing of intangible experiences is recounted in commodities. This tendency has been noted by others both in the context of travel (e.g., MacCannell, 1976; Greenwood, 1977) and in the context of tangibilizing museum patronage (Kelly, 1977, in press).

To a greater degree than any of the other art forms considered, besides yielding hypotheses and serving as data, photography also offers a method for collecting data. While this use of photography is well established in the physical sciences of astronomy, medicine, and micrography, it is less well established in the behavioral sciences. A pioneering example of its potential is the use of photos in the book *Nonverbal Communication* by Ruesch and Kees (1959). Among the many interesting aspects of materialism they analyze via photographs are their studies of lifestyles as expressed in the object arrangements and interior decoration of six homes. Both the differences in lifestyles and the similarities in the orderly arrangements and framing of treasured objects are telling in these pictures. While the houses of "the Bohemian," "the aristocrat," and "the intellectual" are readily distinguished from each other, there are consistencies in repetitive and balanced arrangements and in leading the eye to treasured objects.

Such intentionally gathered photographs might also be used to test a priori behavioral theories of interior design (e.g., Kron, 1983; Hansen & Altman, 1976). However, one shortcoming in the innovative Ruesch and Kees photographic data is that it failed to supplement the mute testimony of the photographs with interpretation and commentary by the owners of the items photographed. Owens' (1973) insightful photo-essay on suburbia is a step in this direction. Better examples are the work of Goldberg (1985), Heisley and Levy (1985), and Wallendorf (1984) which illustrate the added richness that such personal explanations of item significance and symbolism can provide. For instance, Wallendorf asked families and cohabiting couples to pose ("coincidentally") by items they had indicated were especially meaningful or important to them. With reasons given for the items' significance (e.g., "my daughter made it") a much more enlightened analysis is possible than with the item alone.

The photograph and photography have also come to be used in the emerging field of phototherapy (e.g., Krauss, 1981a, 1981b, 1982; Entin, 1982). Using patient's photographs as projective stimuli or diagnostic tools has allowed these therapists to analyze relationships between people, between people and things, and between people and pets. For example, one telling photo from a family seen by Alan Entin one year before their divorce shows the mother with the family dog and the father with the children (Meer, 1984). Predictably, after the divorce she got custody of the dog and he got custody of the children.

Grave Goods

If photographs are an art form applicable to learning about materialism in recent times, grave goods are artifacts applicable to learning about materialism in prehistoric times. While grave goods are frequently objects of art (e.g., ornaments, jewelry, clothing), they are also frequently utilitarian objects (e.g., tools, weapons, utensils). But since many items in these latter categories show evidence of artistic embellishments and decorations, I shall not distinguish between objects of art, craft, and manufacture in the following discussion.

In studying people with no written history or descendant population, physical traces such as grave goods are the primary means by which the archaeologist is able to learn of the material culture and, by inference, the abstract culture of the group. When grave goods are buried with the dead, one immediate inference might be that these people had a belief in an afterlife in which these items were thought to be needed (Grolnick & Langyel, 1978). However, as Griffin (1956) points out, there are alternate interpretations of the widespread practice of burying grave goods with the deceased. One explanation, particularly relevant to the study of materialism, is that the goods were seen as "belonging" to the deceased or as contaminated by the spirit of the deceased so that use of these objects by others would bring bad luck. Contemporary explanations of grave goods by so-called primitive peoples support such an explanation, as do applications of contamination theory to the purchase of used clothing (O'Reilly et al., 1984).

A variety of other inferences related to materialism might be made based on grave goods. Besides obvious inferences about the level of technology, leisure pursuits, sex roles, and wealth in a culture during various points in time and location, inferences about more subtle behavioral patterns may be possible. For instance, Rowlett and Schneider (1974) use Neanderthal grave goods to argue that Neanderthals were much more advanced than previously thought. Their analysis finds evidence of compassion, care, education, and protection of the young, crippled, and aged, for instance, rather than the harsh survival of the fittest mentality attributed frequently to the Neanderthals. Pfeiffer's (1982) analysis of prehistoric cave paintings suggests the development of conspicuous accumulation in the Upper Paleolithic. Alekshin (1983) used grave goods to examine the relative status of men and women over time in prehistoric Europe. He found that while there were always sex role differences (e.g., women were buried with more cooking utensils, and men were buried with more weapons), the absolute quantity and presumed value of graved goods did not differ by sex until about the third mellenium B.C., when men began to have considerably more grave goods than women and a greater difference between "rich" and "poor" graves in quantity and quality of grave goods arose. This suggested to Alekshin greater social and sexual stratification arising as former hunters and gatherers established reasonably fixed-location agriculture. While there is other evidence that societies became more patriarchal and hierarchical at about this time, it is not clear that this is the explanation for the differences in grave goods. As Lee (1979) illustrates, possessions can be a burden for nomadic peoples and there may be a disadvantage to accumulating possessions under such conditions. This could explain the difference in grave goods among more settled populations without invoking an interpretation involving earlier egalitarianism.

Given the lack of modern grave goods, such artifacts are less useful in more recent times. However, practices such as the burning of elaborate paper facsimilies of cars, houses, yachts, and televisions are still performed during the *Hungry Ghosts Festivals* in Singapore and China in order to provide for the needs of dead relatives in the afterlife (Hodgson, 1981). Furthermore, there is evidence of conspicuous consumption in the funerals and monuments for certain social classes (Kephart, 1950; Pine & Phillips, 1970). The artwork on cemetery headstones forms yet another artistic medium that might be analyzed for evidences of materialism over different groups of people and periods of time (e.g., Dethlefsen, 1981).

Music

Shifting from visual to auditory art loses some dimensions of meaning, retains the verbal dimension of meaning where words (lyrics) are present, and adds the effects of tunes, melodies, and other expressive aspects of music. As an example of the ability of lyrics to suggest hypotheses, consider two of the many popular songs about motor vehicles during the 1960s: *409*, The Beach Boys (Wilson & Usher, 1962) and *The Motorcycle Song*, Arlo Guthrie (Guthrie, 1967). These songs both esteem and personalize their respective vehicles. They refer to *my* 409 (Chevrolet) and *my* motorcycle. The male youthful ego identity with such vehicles is evident (Holtz, 1975; Stone, 1966; Weiland, 1955). Furthermore, these songs both value the objects they revere because of what these objects allow them to *do*—"When I take *her* to the drags, she really shines. Giddy-up, giddy-up, 409," and "I just want to ride on *my* motorcycle." As Csikszentmihalyi and Rochberg-Halton (1981) find, this attitude of valuing things for their uses is characteristic of the "instrumental materialism" of teenagers.

Contrast these vehicle songs with three others: *Crazy 'Bout an Automobile*, Ry Cooder (William R. Emerson, 1980), *Mercedes Benz*, Janis Joplin (Joplin & McClure, 1971), and *A.M. World*, Louden Wainwright III (Wainwright III, 1973). These songs fail to personalize the car—*an* automobile, Cadillac*s*, Ford*s*, *a* Mercedes Benz, *a* limousine—and clearly revere these objects as either status *symbols* or sex *symbols* (see Stein, 1985). Particularly in the last two songs, such values are also belittled and ridiculed. This is not as much evident in the lyrics themselves as through the music that accompanies them. Joplin's voice and Wainwright's discordant guitar make it clear that they are mocking the values that the lyrics might seem to tout. This is the added dimension that distinguishes music from poetry (Cole, 1971; Denisoff & Levine, 1972; Riesman, 1950). Thus Wainwright is ridiculing himself when he sings "I've got three guitars, I've got credit cards, I've got more money than you!" What these songs are mocking is the "terminal materialism" (Csikszentmihalyi & Rochberg-Halton, 1981) thought to be more characteristic of adults.

Besides generating such hypotheses, music can also be analyzed as data reflecting or potentially changing cultural values. There have been a number of content analyses of popular music to investigate such changes (e.g., Anderson, Hesbacher, Etzkorn, & Denisoff, 1980; Belz, 1972; Chalfant & Beckley, 1977; Cole, 1971; Cooper & Haverkos, 1973; Day, 1985; Edmonds, 1980; Gritzner, 1978; Hamm, 1975; Martin, 1979; Mohrmann & Scott, 1976; Mooney, 1968; Reagon, 1974; Ryder, 1976; Shepherd, Virden, Vulliam, & Wishart, 1977; Staats, 1979; Stone, 1966; Titon, 1977; Whetmore, 1979). One such example of particular relevance to the study of materialism is Friedman's (1984) analysis of the frequency with which brands were mentioned in the lyrics of popular 1946 to 1980 American songs. Based on the increased frequency of such mentions (and comparable findings in analyses of popular novels and plays over the same period), he concludes that there is increasing commercial influence on formerly noncommercial spheres of life. He also found this to be especially true with value-expressive products such as automobiles (Munson & Spivey, 1981).

Film

By combining the dimensions of sound and sight, motion pictures are able to convey still more information. This is seen for instance in the rock video, "Living in the Material World" by Madonna (Rogers, 1985). While the lyrics are clearly promaterialism, the video turns them into a mild satire in which the heroine rejects worldly goods for love, but still winds up with wealth.

Arguably, a novel that is made into a motion picture is capable of communicating considerably more than the original novel, despite limitations on length (Sobchack, 1979). There is no question that adapting a novel to the screen is a creative process that is far removed from a mere mechanical transference (Carringer, 1978). However, it is not unusual that when a novel is the basis for a film, the critics bemoan its lack of faithfulness to the original. For example, John Ford's (1940) adaptation of John Steinbeck's *The Grapes of Wrath* has been seen as conveying a very different sort of message (Sobchack, 1979). The novel is political, harsh, and emphasizes the land as a source of identity and humanity. The film, however, is apolitical, nostalgic, and emphasizes a family alienated from the land. For example, Steinbeck (1939, pp. 50–51) includes such dialogue as:

> If a man owns a little property, that property is him, its part of him, and it's like him. If he owns property only so he can walk on it and handle it and be sad when it isn't doing well, and feel fine when the rain falls on it, that property is him, and in some way he's bigger because he owns it.*

There is no such dialogue in Ford's movie.

Another movie with a materialism theme from the same era is Orson Welles' (1941) *Citizen Kane*. In this case the film version is credited with developing a much stronger message about materialism than the original screen play roughly based on the life of William Randolph Hearst (Carringer, 1978). Starting with the opening lines from Samuel Taylor Coleridge's (1797) *Kubla Khan*, Welles presents a portrait of the newspaper empire building of Charles Foster Kane and his transformation of his wealth into a new Xanadu in which he collects the treasures of the world in acres of rooms, parks, zoos, and gardens. His last word at death, however, is "Rosebud," the name of his sled during a much simpler childhood before wealth and power were thrust upon him. There is a two-sided message about materialism here. The more obvious half is that Kane acquired all the valuable and sought-after material goods of the world only to find that they did not bring the satisfaction of a single possession associated with the happy experiences of his childhood. On the other hand, Rosebud was still a material

---

*From *The Grapes of Wrath* by John Steinbeck. Copyright 1939, renewed © 1967 by John Steinbeck. Reprinted by permission of Viking Penguin, Inc.

possession, rather than a person, experience, or inner belief, that was thought by Kane to be the most important thing in his wide-ranging life. Nevertheless, the film theme that money cannot buy happiness is clear and unchallenged.

It is not difficult to find themes of the happy poor-but-honest in films. A recent example analyzed by Wallendorf (1984) is Carl Reiner's (1979) *The Jerk*. After acquiring a fortune from a simple invention, Mavis Johnson (played by comedian Steve Martin) loses it all due to a class action product liability suit. He ultimately finds love and happiness again in his rural home with a poor but honest hard working family that has invested the money he sent them and become prosperous. Again there are two-sided messages about materialism however. The wealthy Mavis Johnson is ostentatiously nouveau riche and lacking in refined taste. But the poor Mavis Johnson is either an ignorant hick or a shiftless bum. Happiness seems a rural pleasure where consumption is limited but resources are abundant. Still not even this message is unequivocal. Johnson's girl (played by Bernadette Peters) laments their loss of wealth: "Its not the money that I'll miss. Its all the stuff." There is a clearer message in the film about the role of possessions in securing one's identity. When Mavis Johnson is financially ruined he tries to indicate his inner strength of character by leaving and saying he doesn't need any of the former possessions of his wealthy life. But he turns to say *except*. . . , and goes on to grasp almost anything he can find—television remote control tuner, ashtray, chair, lamp, and other useless objects. While these items may not be functionally useful to him, he seems to cling to the hope that they will symbolically help him secure a new sense of self without having to literally start from scratch. The similarity to the contentions about self by William and Henry James is clear.

While it is not difficult to find films condemning wealth or regarding wealth and material possessions ambiguously, it is difficult to find films suggesting the hypothesis that wealth and material possessions are good. One of the rare films to do so is Ingmar Bergman's (1982) *Fanny and Alexander*. The film centers on Emilie Ekdahl (played by Ewa Fröling) who, after her husband dies, goes from the rich and opulently Victorian Ekdahl household to live in the cold and austere castle of the local bishop whom she remarries. The bishop requires that neither she nor her children Fanny and Alexander bring furnishings, clothing, jewelry, toys, or any other trappings from their former lifestyle to his castle. Not only is life in the bishop's castle austere in terms of lack of possessions, the people are also severe and there is little happiness or warmth. The joy of childhood is taken from Fanny and Alexander and they are virtually prisoners in the castle until the bishop dies by fire in a bizarre accident and they and their mother Emilie are restored to the richness and the loving warmth of the Ekdahl household. The contrast between abundance and happiness on one hand and austerity and unhappiness on the other is not restricted to the people and settings, the lighting and richness or starkness of surfaces is also contrasted by cinematographer, Sven Nykvist (Block, 1984). The contrast is as strikingly apparent as between the paintings by Janssen and R. W. discussed earlier. Bergman seems to be saying that if possessions can make the world magical and add childlike joy to life, this is preferable to the harsh and severe life of the ascetic who avoids the possessions and pleasures of life. Furthermore, the magic is seen to be introduced by *things*, just as props helped to create the magic of the theatre run by the Ekdahl family.

Like other art media, films can be analyzed as data in addition to their role in suggesting hypotheses (e.g., Blewett, 1974; Chappell, 1978; Cripps, 1975; Isenberg, 1975, 1976; Jennings, 1980; Kliman, 1978; Leob, 1973; O'Guinn, Faber, & Marshall, 1985; O'Guinn, Lee, & Faber, in press; Shain, 1974; Valenti, 1979; Zynda, 1979). In addition, film, like still photography, can be used to collect data. As in interpreting films as historical data however, some attention must be devoted to the potential overt or covert biases of the film maker (Gillette, 1977; Isenberg, 1973; Loy, 1977; O'Connor, 1973; Rollins, 1974).

Poetry

Since this paper began with a poem and a discussion of Plato's arguments against poetry, it is only appropriate to end with examples of poetry's contributions to knowledge about materialism. Examples of materialistic themes can be found in the poetry of Stephen Dobyns.

Covetousness

Keep your toys and small possessions;
I only want your hands.
Everything I touch feels like it's mine.

He does his shopping in the houses of his friends.

I dreamt I was you, sleeping with your wife,
dreaming you were me, sleeping with mine.

Dobyns (1976)*

Greed

I come to your house and paint it grey;
I come into your room and make it smaller:
your television is smaller, the bed squeaks.
The man next door has a nicer fedora.
Were you happy? Were you content?
Your dog needs a rhinestone collar.

You flatter yourself with presents;
it's the thought that counts—
golf shoes, wedding rings—
like a tree holding sunlight,
a sieve holding water.

He was born with small hands, deep pockets

Dobyns (1976)*

Covetousness (or envy) is three separate thoughts showing that both people and their possessions can be envied. The center thought, "He does his shopping in the houses of his friends," illustrates the power of a few words to convey a rich and telling description of this motivation. And the last couplet shows the grass-is-always-greener mutuality of envy and thus its inevitability and fruitlessness.

Greed is written in the first stanza as greed speaking, showing the power of greed to make people envious and discontent. The last thought in this poem is again a telling line about people who can't get enough—"He was born with small hands, deep pockets." The second stanza hypothesizes a tendency of people to attempt to bolster their self-image by buying themselves things, a tendency that has also been supported in the child development literature (Mischel, Coates, & Raskoff, 1968; Moore, Clyburn, & Underwood, 1976; Underwood, Moore, & Rosenhan, 1973). This stanza also concludes that the attempt to bolster ego in this way is in vain. Similar thoughts were expressed by John Webster (1613):

Vain the ambition of Kings,
Who seek by trophies and dead things
To leave a living name behind,
And weave but nets to catch the wind.

A final Stephen Dobyns poem, written about Balthus' (1937–1938) painting *The Greedy Child* serves both to illustrate one art medium inspiring themes for another, and the depth of meaning that art can convey:

The Greedy Child

Gripping the mantle with thick fingers,
the maid's greedy Baby reaches for fruit
in the glass and silver bowl. The baby
violently wants to become the fruit, to absorb
the fruit into his fat, transparent body.
A glass of white wine stands next to the bowl,
while nearby the nearly full bottle is reflected
in a baroque mirror with an ornate gilt frame.
But the baby has no interest in the aesthetics
of his surroundings. Instead he thrusts his hand
toward the fruit as if the bowl itself might
feel his desire and slide across the white marble,
allow the baby to suck it in, bowl and all.
Then he would tumble back, a round white heap,
and with puckered lips he would try sucking
the room toward him: he sucks and sucks until
bits of paper begin fluttering through the air,
until a gray hat rolls across the carpet, then
a pair of felt slippers, until table and chairs
crash to the floor, begin also to creep toward him;
then the Persian carpet pops its tacks and
the whole house finds itself being sucked inward,
until even people passing on the street feel a tug

as if a hand were tugging them toward the seemingly
innocuous street door of the house already half
devoured by the greedy baby in the way a worm can
devour a pear from the inside, while the baby
sits on a floor as gleaming and polished as a plate
licked clean, and he bangs his little fists
and purses his lips, and sucks and sucks,
wants to suck in all the rich and tasty world.

Dobyns (1982)*

This is certainly a strong and evocative description of greed. Dealing with an infant as it does (see Balthus' painting), the poem suggests the state that Freud (1914) called primary narcissism. According to Freud, the child is born into such a state in which there is an inability to distinguish self from others and environment, and the whole world is seen to exist solely for self-satisfaction. But the poem goes beyond this and suggests the later Freudian oral stage of development. This was seen by Freud to be the stage during which the child is nursing and when any characteristic deprivation would produce an adult who is greedy. While the seeking/taking character of this trait is evident both in Freud's writings and Balthus' painting, the exaggerated characterization by Dobyns is the most elaborated and fully developed by far.

The ability of poetry to suggest hypotheses and theories is also seen in Lewis Hyde's insightful work entitled *The Gift: Imagination and the Erotic Life of Property* (1983). Hyde skillfully blends the anthropological work of Mauss (1967) with the poetry of Ezra Pound and Walt Whitman to develop some truly new ideas about gift giving; something that anthropology has been unable to do since Mauss' original work in the early 1920s. As with other media, poetry also may serve as data for analyzing materialism and other trends over time (e.g., Day, 1979; Downs, 1979; Pino, 1973; Wepman, Newman, & Binderman, 1974). But because of the somewhat lesser tendency for poetry to be faithfully representative of material phenomena (e.g., versus painting, photography, and film), it is probably less commonly used for this purpose.

How Do Art and Science Differ as Approaches to Knowledge?

While the preceding examples have not included some forms of art such as dance, sculpture, architecture, and instrumental music, they are perhaps sufficient to illustrate that art does indeed have something valuable to say about materialism. This is certainly not to say that art is just like science or that they follow the same precepts however. Figure 1.2 suggests some of the major ways in which art and

Art	*Science*
Subjective	Objective
Feeling	Thinking
Qualitative	Quantitative
Fanciful	Practical
Particular	General
Personal	Impersonal
Re-presentational	Analytical
Symbolic	Factual
Interested	Disinterested

FIGURE 1.2. Some differences in the approaches to knowing things by art and science.

science differ. Both portraits are overdrawn. The relativist position for instance would claim that scientists are just as ego involved and prejudiced in their work as artists are in theirs (e.g., Peter & Olson, 1983). In addition, some art is undoubtedly intended to expand intellect and thinking rather than merely to convey feeling (Holbrook & Zirlin, 1985). Nevertheless, as generalizations these contrasts tend to be mostly true of art versus science. For instance, art is commonly intended to reveal the particular and personal whereas science is intended to convey more generally applicable and impersonal truths. Art requires the perceiver to suspend disbelief while science expects skepticism unless compelling logical and often quantitative evidence can create tentative acceptance. Art attempts to "re-present" an experience in a new and unique way while science seeks to analyze the common essential part of the experience that is shared.

It is interesting to note that the list of art versus science differences in Figure 1.2 is quite parallel to the list of "hard" versus "soft" modes of thinking shown in Figure 1.3. This list also relates to what Freud (1911) called primary process thinking versus secondary process thinking. He maintained that both processes were necessary for creative success, but that primary process thinking is the first stage that results in the genesis of the idea while secondary process thinking is the second stage that verbalizes and refines the idea so that it can be successfully communicated to others. This would suggest that art is more useful for generating hypotheses and science is more useful for refining and testing these ideas. While there is some truth in this assertion in light of the differences shown in Figures 1.2 and 1.3, the question of whether this is *all* that art is good for with regard to knowledge production brings us back to the issue that I noted in the first section of this paper and that Mitroff and Kilmann (1978) failed to address: Can art and science have equal claims to presenting the truth?

Art's Potential Contributions to Consumer Behavior

The earlier positions granting art some social worth tended to maintain that while science seeks truth, art seeks beauty (e.g., Cadden & Brostowin, 1964) or feeling (Johnson, 1949). While the idea that art might convey behavioral insights (e.g., Shakespeare's lessons about human nature) were occasionally entertained (e.g.,

"Soft"	*"Hard"*
Primary	Secondary
Eros	Logos
Right Brain	Left Brain
Dream	Reason
Childlike	Adult
Metaphor	Logic
Intuitive	Proven
Feeling	Thinking
Ambiguous	Consistent
Fuzzy	Precise
Play	Work
Fantasy	Reality
Humor	Seriousness
Indirect	Direct
Subjective	Objective
Open	Critical
Inductive	Deductive
Nonverbal	Verbal

FIGURE 1.3. Two modes of thought.*

Stoll, 1933), such contentions could always be dismissed when "science" provided contradictory evidence. The assumption was that science always provides a superior method for gaining understanding (Hospers, 1946).

A somewhat more charitable position regarding art was raised by Gadamer (1975, p. 87) who asked:

> Is there to be no knowledge in art? Does not the experience of art contain a claim to truth which is certainly different from that of science, but equally certainly is not inferior to it? And is not the task of aesthetics precisely to provide a basis for the fact that artistic experience is a mode of knowledge of a unique kind, certainly different from that sensory knowledge which provides science with the data from which it constructs the knowledge of nature, and certainly different from all moral rational knowledge and indeed from all conceptual knowledge, but still knowledge, i.e., the transmission of truth?

The position taken by Gadamer is similar to the conclusion of Walsh (1969). She maintains (based on Langer, 1963) that science is able to convey knowledge *about* a phenomenon, but art (her examples are restricted to literature) is able to convey knowledge *of* an experience. That is, short of the experience itself, perceptively experienced and appreciated, only art is able to convey the specific, personal, and experiential knowledge (Holbrook & Hirschman, 1982) of, say, a day in Victorian England, in a way that approaches the intensity and intimacy of the actual experience. It is the sort of knowledge that Berman (1981) calls noncognitive knowing. Given the cognitive orientation of present scientific knowledge of psychology and consumer behavior, the noncognitive contributions of art should be especially provocative. As Kenneth Patchen says in his novel *The Journal of Albion Moonlight* (1941, p. 7), "Think enough and you won't know anything."

*After von Oech (1983) and Hanks and Parry (1983).

It is this potential contribution of art that led Barzun (1964, p. 228) to conclude that "Art is like life and science the antithesis of life." Just as Berman (1981) observed that science has distanced man from nature, and as McGuire (1973) warned that social science has lost touch by observing data rather than people, we may say that science tries to distance the scientist and audience from phenomena, whereas art tries to immerse the artist and audience in phenomena.

While these conclusions go beyond the view that art seeks beauty rather than truth, they stop short of a full recognition of the potential contributions of art to knowledge. The contributions in Figure 1.4 provide a somewhat more complete perspective. While it is maintained that art is a potential source of hypotheses, this is hardly its only use. The hypotheses derived from the *Uncle Scrooge* story summarized here are just one example of the sorts of hypotheses about materialism that might be derived from comics and other forms of art. Furthermore, the comparison of insights from William and Henry James demonstrates that science has no claim to superiority or primacy in its ability to generate hypotheses. In light of the creative environment of art (e.g., Figures 1.2 and 1.3), it is likely that art may often suggest innovative hypotheses that are unlikely to occur to the analytical scientist (Mitroff & Kilmann, 1978). Thus a would-be conceptual theorist seeking inspiration for theory in consumer behavior would do well to become immersed in art.

The use of art to provide a more gestalt picture of consumer behavior is related to the point that art can provide noncognitive knowledge. An example of this might be the combination of Balthus' (1937–1938) painting and Dobyn's (1982) poem, *The Greedy Child*. Together, or even separately, the painting and poem provide a clear and extensive portrayal of greed. While Dobyn's poem may not provide a literal description of what impels the child to reach longingly toward the bowl of fruit, the hyperbole graphically conveys the emotional strength of the desire rather than the simple fact of the striving toward a goal as a goal-directed behavior. Because science is a simplified abstraction to explain an action, and art is an embellished elaboration of an experience, we can often rely on art to provide the more complete and multidimensional multisensory perspective to help us understand rather than simply explain. The point was made by sociologist and novelist Richard Sennett who wrote, "One can learn more about the complexity of motives and mutal perception from a reasonably good novel than from a 'solid' piece of social-science research" (1980, p. 9). The same conclusion is echoed by psychologist Zick Rubin who suggests that, "The most illuminating writing about

1. Source of hypothesis
2. A more gestalt picture
3. Thicker description
4. Data from the past
5. Data for the future
6. Validation

FIGURE 1.4. Ways in which art can help generate knowledge about consumer behavior.

close relationships has come from storytellers and playwrights, not from psychologists and sociologists" (quoted in Davis, 1985, p. 30).

The third use of art to provide thicker description (Geertz, 1973) is an amplification of this point. Scientific data and scientific writing is precise, but at the expense of richness or thickness of description of the phenomena under study. Consider for example the portrayal of opulence and ascetic deprivation depicted in the movie *Fanny and Alexander* (Bergman, 1982). In the three hours of the film (the European television version was six hours), more is conveyed about these lifestyles than could be conveyed in any scientific description that might be envisioned. Because some of the film's knowledge is noncognitive and cannot be verbalized, an art work or an artistic mode of "data" storage and retrieval is the only way of communicating this knowledge to others. In addition, because we are willing to surrender our disbelief and empathize in attending art, we can grasp the emotional aspects of a phenomenon much more readily than is likely in any scientific presentation.

This is not to suggest that art strives to faithfully represent the details of daily life. Although some suggest that this should be the purpose of art and that abstract art is a mistake (Gowans, 1973), the more general consensus is that art should not try to imitate life in superficial detail (e.g., Danto, 1973; Fiet, 1976). As Langer (1963, pp. 250–251) notes:

> A painter of no insight, judgment, or imagination worth mentioning might follow Goethe's suggestion for a picture, find a graceful and perfect model to impersonate a noble character, and depict with faithful accuracy . . . and produce a picture that might hang in every parlor, but mean exactly nothing to the sensibilities of any real artist.

In place of this sort of faithfulness to detail in portraying a subject, what good art can do is reveal the essence of that which it concerns. As Highwater (1981) notes, this is like "primitive" representations of the world and the modern art that these primitive images inspired. It is the view represented in the American Indian Black Elk's reflection that "Whether it happened so or not I do not know; but if you think about it you can see that it is true" (Neihardt, 1974). That is, it is not the literal truthfulness of a thing that art is normally concerned with, but the essential truth. This, perhaps more than Geertz realized, is what thick description can convey.

The fourth use of art to serve as data from the past points out that art forms not only a convenient unobtrusive historical record of consumption events, but also that these records may often be the *only* records of the mundane consumption events of the past that may interest not only the consumer researcher but also the so-called new historian (e.g., Fernand Braudel). The paintings of land-owning aristocracy, cave paintings, and, of course, grave goods provide good examples of rare records preserved in art. In considering these records as data we must be concerned with how representative they are likely to be, but at least we know that they have not been created or preserved to intentionally bias our research interests (Mukerji, 1978). And if we desire to know what attitudes toward property were in 18th century France or how close families were during the Mousterian prehistoric period in Europe, few alternative sources of data are available.

Within this use of art more than the others, it should be recognized that not all art may be suitable. Jessup (1965) gives the example of the poem "Sing-Song":

Mother shake the cherry-tree,
  Susan catch a cherry;
Oh how funny that will be,
  Let's be merry!

While Jessup concludes that this poem has little to do with truth, there may be some sense in which even such a shallow poem could be a useful datum. For instance, as part of a historical sample, it might contribute to a knowledge of what leisure activities were regarded as fun at a particular time and place. While such a poem may have little to do with truth in the sense of thick description, it may have much to do with truth in the sense of what we might call thin or superficial description. It follows that those art works that best provide thick description of a phenomena may sometimes do least well in providing thin, superficial but factually faithful, description. A work like Lewis Carroll's (Charles L. Dodgson's, 1865) *Alice in Wonderland* provides such an example.

Besides providing data from the past, the intentional use of artistic media to collect data provides records for the future of the same elusive sorts of events that are unlikely to survive as traditional scientific data. Wallendorf's (1984) photographic study of people and their favorite possessions is one good example of what might be done. The emerging field of phototherapy also suggests the potential consumer use of artistic objects as projective stimuli in gathering data. While photography and films suggest themselves most readily for consumer data collecting and for communicating these data to others, the consumer researcher seeking insight and inspiration could do worse than to attempt to create prose, poetry, or visual art on the subject of interest. And given the miniaturization and price decreases in home videotaping equipment, the ability to gather film data on consumers may open new horizons in seeking consumer behavior knowledge. Rook (1985) demonstrates through his analysis of Christmas home movies, that consumers themselves may provide potentially rich archives of such data.

The last use of art listed for consumer behavior is that of validation. This is a useful transposition of the roles of art and science suggested by the first purpose listed by hypothesis generation. Whereas in its role as hypothesis generator art provides initial insights that may be pursued by science, in the validation role of art, science provides the tentative findings and art attempts to test these findings. This is a role suggested by Donald Campbell (1978), although he was speaking more generally of qualitative research without specific reference to art. An example of such a validation would be to examine the evidence from introspective novels depicting purchase decisions to attempt to support or refute information processing theories of consumer choice. Or we could take Csikszentmihalyi and Rochberg-Halton's (1981) findings that the young tend to value *doing* things, middle aged people value *having* things, and older generations value things for the interpersonal memories they evoke, and test them via the music popular with each age group and via photos showing people with their favorite possessions (e.g., Wallendorf, 1984).

Conclusion

This paper has been necessarily a limited exploration of the thesis that art can be a useful way of generating knowledge about consumer materialism. Hopefully it has made the point that art has much to contribute to consumer behavior and should be used more by consumer researchers. Since it has been suggested that potential uses of art range from the derivation of hypotheses through the collection and dissemination of data to the validation of hypotheses and theories, art may be seen to provide an attractive alternative to more traditional "scientific" means of consumer research. While a major use of art should continue to be to suggest and inspire hypotheses and theories, art is not just for hypothesis generation any more. In fact, for those who perceive the other functions of art, it has never been just that. The common uses of art to set the tone for a chapter or article or to illustrate a point are normally more than attempts to show that one is well-read or erudite. They are attempts to draw on art as data for evidence to validate a point or to provide a thicker, richer description.

References

Agnew, J.-C. (1983). The consuming vision of Henry James. In R. W. Fox & T. J. J. Lears (Eds.), *The culture of consumption: Critical essays in American history, 1880–1980* (pp. 65–100). New York: Pantheon.

Albee, G. W. (1977). The protestant ethic, sex, and psychotherapy. *American Psychologist, 32*, 150–161.

Alekshin, V. A. (1983). Burial customs as an anthropological source. *Current Anthropology, 24*, 137–150.

Anderson, B., Hesbacher, P., Etzkorn, P. K., & Denisoff, S. R. (1980). Hit record trends, 1940–1977. *Journal of Communication, 30*(2), 31–43.

Anderson, P. F. (1983). Marketing, scientific progress, and scientific method. *Journal of Marketing, 47* (Fall), 18–31.

Anonymous (author) (1677). Collection Of Fernando Cospi [engraving], frontispiece of the *Mseo Cospiano*, Bologna.

Balthus (painter) (1937–1938). *The greedy child* [painting]. Rome: the French Academy.

Barks, C. (originator) (1948, 1952–1967). *Uncle Scrooge* [comic], Poughkeepsie, New York: Western Publishing Company.

Barzun, J. (1964) . *Science: The glorious entertainment*. New York: Harper & Row.

Barcus, F. E. (1961). A content analysis of trends in Sunday comics, 1900–1959. *Journalism Quarterly, 38* (2), 171–180.

Belk, R. W. (1984a). Manifesto for a consumer behavior of consumer behavior. In P. F. Anderson & M. F. Ryan (Eds.), *1984 AMA Winter Educators Conference*. Chicago: American Marketing Association.

Belk, R. W. (1984b). Three scales to measure constructs related to materialism: Reliability, validity, and relationships to measures of happiness. In T. Kinnear (Ed.), *Advances in Consumer Research: Vol. 11* (pp. 291-297). Provo, UT: Association for Consumer Research.

Belz, C. (1972). Rock as folk art. In J. B. Hall & B. Utanov (Eds.), *Modern Culture and the Arts* (pp. 106–114). New York: McGraw-Hill Book Company.

Berger, A. A. (1973). *Pop culture*. Dayton, OH: Pflaum/Standard.

Berger, J., Blomberg, S., Fox, C., Dibb, M., & Hollis, R. (1972). *Ways of seeing*. London: British Broadcasting Corporation.

Bergman, I. (1982). *Fanny and Alexander* (A. Blair, Trans.). New York: Pantheon Books.

Berman, M. (1981). *The reenchantment of the world*. Ithaca: Cornell University Press.

Blewett, M. (1974). Women in history: A history through film approach. *Film and History, 4* (4), 12–15, 20.

Block, B. A. (1984). Sven Nykvist, ASC, and Fanny and Alexander. *American Cinematographer, 65* (4), 50–58.

Boorstin, D. J. (1973). *The Americans: The democratic experience*. New York: Random House.

Braudel, F. (1973). *Capitalism and material life, 1400–1800* (S. Reynolds, Trans.). New York: Harper & Row.

Braudel, F. (1979). *The wheels of commerce: Civilization and capitalism* (S. Reynolds, Trans.). New York: Harper & Row.

Braun, S. (1971, May). Shazam! Here comes captain relevant. *New York Times Magazine*, pp. 32–55.

Bruegel, J. (painter) (1618). *Allegory of the sense of sight* [painting], Madrid: Prado.

Cadden, J. J. & Brostowin, . R. (Eds.) (1964). *Science and literature: A reader.* Boston: D. C. Heath and Company.

Campbell, D. T. (1978). Qualitative knowing in action research. In M. Brenner, P. Marsh, & M. Brenner (Eds.), *The Social Contexts of Method* (pp. 184–209). London: Croom Helm.

Carringer, R. L. (1978). The scripts of Citizen Kane. *Critical Inquiry, 5* (2), 369–400.

Chalfant, H. P. & Beckley, R. E. (1977, July). Beguiling and betraying: The image of alcohol use in country music. *Journal of Studies on Alcohol, 38*, 1428–1433.

Chappell, F. (1978). The image of the south in film. *Southern Humanities Review, 12* (4), 303–311.

Cole, R. R. (1971). Top songs in the sixties. *American Behavioral Scientist, 14*, 389–400.

Coleridge, S. T. (poet) (1797). Kubla Khan [poem]. In E. Schneider (Ed.), *Coleridge, opium, and Kubla Khan* (pp. v-vi). Chicago: University of Chicago Press (1953).

Cooper, B. L. & Haverkos, L. S. (1973). The image of American society in popular music: A search for identity and values. *Social Studies, 64* (7), 319–322.

Coser, L. A. (Ed.) (1963). *Sociology through literature*. Englewoods Cliffs, NJ: Prentice-Hall.

Cripps, T. (1975). The movie Jew as an image of assimilationism. *Journal of Popular Film, 4* (3), 190–207.

Csikszentmihalyi, M. & Rochberg-Halton, E. (1981). *The meaning of things: Domestic symbols and the self.* Cambridge: Cambridge University Press.

Danto, A. C. (1973). Artworks and real things. *Theoria, 39*, 1–15.

Davis, K. E. (1985, February). Near and dear: Friendship and love compared. *Psychology Today*, 22–30.

Day, E. (1985). Accounting for musical tastes, preferences, and attendance patterns.

In R. W. Belk (Ed.), *Advances in nonprofit marketing* (pp. 295–329). Greenwich, CT: JAI Press.

Day, R. D. (1979). Sport in poetry: A nineteenth century study of Catham, Ontario journals. *Canadian Journal of the History of Sport and Physical Education*, *10* (1), 62–82.

Denisoff, R. S. & Levine, M. H. (1972, December). Youth and popular music: A test of the taste culture hypothesis. *Youth and Society*, *4*, 237–255.

Dervis, A. (painter) (1749). *Van Hartels family* [painting]. Banbury, Oxfordshire: Upton House.

Dervis, A. (painter) (c. 1750). *Horace Walpole* [painting]. Wimpole, Cambridgeshire: Collection of Mrs. George Bambridge.

Dethlefsen, E. S. (1981). The cemetery and culture change: Archaeological focus and ethnographic perspective. In R. A. Gould & M. B. Schiffer (Eds.), *Modern material culture: The archaeology of us* (pp. 137–159). New York: Academic Press.

Dobyns, S. (1976). *Griffon*. New York: Atheneum.

Dobyns, S. (1982). *The Balthus poems*. New York: Atheneum.

Dodgson, C. L. (a.k.a. Lewis Carroll) (1865). *Alice's adventures in wonderland*. In P. C. Blackburn and L. White (Eds.), *The complete works of Lewis Carroll* (pp. 79–144). Garden City, NY: Anchor Books (1942).

Donne, J. (1623–1624). Meditation XVII. In M. H. Abrams (Ed.), *The Norton anthology of English literature* (pp. 794–796). New York: W. W. Norton & Company.

Dorfman, A. (1983). *The empire's old clothes: What the Lone Ranger, Barbar, and other innocent heroes do to our minds*. New York: Pantheon Books.

Dorfman, A. & Mattelart, A. (1975). *How to read Donald Duck: Imperialist ideology in the Disney comics*. New York: International General.

Douglas, M. & Isherwood, B. (1979). *The world of goods: Towards an anthropology of consumption*. New York: W. W. Norton and Company.

Downs, V. (1979). Folk poetry in gravestone verse. *Kentucky Folklore Record*, *25* (1–2), 28–36.

Edmonds, A. O. (1980). Popular music in the 1950s and the contemporary American family. *Indiana Social Studies Quarterly*, *33* (2), 93–100.

Emerson, W. R. (composer) (1980). *Crazy 'Bout an Automobile* [song]. Conrad Music Corporation, BMI.

Entin, A. D. (1982, Winter). Family photo albums: Icons of the family. *Photo Therapy*, *3*, 7–10.

Felman, S. (Ed.) (1982). *Literature and psychoanalysis*. Baltimore: Johns Hopkins University Press.

Fernandez, R. (Ed.) (1972). *Social psychology through literature*. New York: John Wiley & Sons.

Fiet, L. A. (1976). 'The Tragic Fallacy' revisited. *Journal of Aesthetic Education*, *10*, 61–74.

Ford, J. (director) (1940). *Grapes of wrath* [film]. Los Angeles: Universal.

Franken II, F. (painter) (1610). *Study of a collector* [painting]. Rome: M. Goffi collection.

Friedman, M. (1984). Are we creating a 'brand' new language? A content analysis of commercial expressions in the lyrics of popular American songs in the postwar era. Working paper, Ypsilanti, MI: Eastern Michigan University, Department of Psychology.

Freud, S. (1958). Formulations on the Two Principles of Mental Functioning. *The Standard Edition of the Complete Psychological Works of Sigmund Freud*, Vol. 12. London: Hogarth. (Original work published 1911)

Freud, S. (1914). On narcissism. In E. Jones (Ed.), *Sigmund Freud, Collected Papers: Vol. 4*. London: Hogarth.
Gadamer, H.-G. (1975). In G. Barden & J. Cumming (Eds), *Truth and method* (G. Barden & J. Cummings, Trans.). New York: Seabury Press.
Gainsborough, T. (painter) (1755). *Mr. and Mrs. Andrews* [painting]. London: National Gallery.
Gainsborough, T. (painter) (c. 1750). *Richard Savage and his sister* [painting]. Washington, DC: collection of Mrs. Paul Mellon.
Gallyer, L. (1951). A report of comic book reading by pupils of grades IV–VII (pp. 1–20). Salt Lake City: Salt Lake City School District.
Gardner, H. (1971). *Religion and literature*. London: Faber and Faber.
Geertz, C. (1973). Thick description: Toward an interpretation theory of culture. In C. Geertz (Ed.), *The Interpretation of Cultures*. New York: Basic Books.
Geiger, D. (1973). Poetic realizing as knowing. *Quarterly Journal of Speech*, *59*, 311–318.
Gillette, H. (1977). Film as artifact: The city. *American Studies*, *18* (2), 71–85.
Goldberg, J. (1985). *Rich and poor*. New York: Random House.
Goldwater, J. (originator) (1942-present). *Archie* [comic]. New York: Archie Publications.
Gowans, A. (1973). Popular arts and historic artifacts: New principles for studying history in art. *Journal of Popular Culture*, *7* (2), 466–483.
Green, P. & Walzer, M. (Eds.) (1969). *The political imagination in literature*. New York: The Free Press.
Greenwood, D. J. (1977). Culture by the pound: An anthropological perspective on tourism as cultural commoditization. In V. L. Smith (Ed.), *Hosts and guests: The anthropology of tourism* (pp. 129–138). Philadelphia: University of Pennsylvania Press.
Griffin, J. B. (1956). The study of early cultures. In H. L. Shapiro (Ed.), *Man, culture, and society* (pp. 22–48). Oxford: Oxford University Press.
Gritzner, C. F. (1978). Country music: A reflection of popular culture. *Journal of Popular Culture*, *11* (4), 857–864.
Grolnick, S. A. & Lengyel, A. (1978). Etruscan burial symbols and the transitional process. In S. A. Grolnick & L. Barkin (Eds.), *Between reality and fantasy: Transitional objects and phenomena* (pp. 381–410). New York: J. Aronson.
Guthrie, A. (composer) (1967). *The motorcycle song* [song]. ASCAP.
Hamm, C. (1975). The acculturation of musical styles: Popular music, U.S.A. In C. Hamm, B. Nettl, & R. Byrnside (Eds.), *Contemporary music and music cultures* (pp. 35–70)Englewood Cliffs, NJ: Prentice-Hall.
Hanks, K. & Parry, J. A. (1983). *Wake up your creative genius*. Los Altos, CA: William Kauffmann.
Hansen, W. B. & Altman, I. (1976, December). Decorating personal places: A descriptive analysis. *Environment and Behavior*, *8*, 491–504.
Harvey Publications (publisher) (1960–1984). *Richie Rich* [comic]. New York: Harvey Publications.
Heisley, D. D. & Levy, S. J. (1985)." Familiar interlude: Autodriving in Consumer Analysis," paper presented at 1985 Association for Consumer Research Annual Conference, Las Vegas, Nevada.
Highwater, J. (1981). *The primal mind: Vision and reality in indian America*. New York: New American Library.
Hodgson, B. (1981). Singapore: Mini-size superstate. *National Geographic*, *159*, 541–561.

Holbein, H. (painter) (1533). *The Ambassadors* [painting]. London: National Gallery.

Holbrook, M. B. & Hirschman, E. C. (1982). Consumer fantasies, feelings, and fun: The experiential aspects of consumption. *Journal of Consumer Research*, *9*, 132–140.

Holbrook, M. B. & Zirlin, R. B. (1985). Artistic creation, artworks, and esthetic appreciation: Some philosophical contributions to nonprofit marketing. In R. W. Belk (Ed.), *Advances in Nonprofit Marketing: Vol. 1* (pp. 1–54). Greenwich, CT: JAI Press.

Holtz, J. A. (1975). The 'low-riders': Portrait of a youth subculture. *Youth and Society*, *6* (4), 495–512.

Hospers, J. (1946). *Meaning and truth in the arts*. Chapel Hill: University of North Carolina Press.

Hyde, L. (1983). *The gift: Imagination and the erotic life of property*. New York: Random House.

Inge, M. T. (1979). Introduction: The comics as culture. *Journal of Popular Culture*, *12* (4), 631–639.

Isaacs, S. (1935). Property and possessiveness. *British Journal of Medical Psychology*, *15*, 69–78.

Isenberg, M. T. (1973). A relationship of constrained anxiety: Historians and film. *History Teacher*, *6* (4), 553–568.

Isenberg, M. T. (1975). The mirror of democracy: Reflections of the war films of World War I, 1917–1919. *Journal of Popular Culture*, *9* (4), 878–885.

Isenberg, M. T. (1976). The historian and the myth of the 'objective reality': A critique of film reality. *Teaching History: A Journal of Methods*, *1* (1), 6–14.

James, H. (1881). *Portrait of a lady*. Boston: Houghton, Osgood and Co.

James, W. (1890). *The principles of psychology, vol. 1*. New York: Henry Holt and Company.

Janssen, H. (painter) (1650). *Interior with family* [painting]. Vienna: Liechtenstein Collection.

Jennings, W. (1980). Images of children in American film. *Indiana Social Studies Quarterly*, *33* (2), 85–92.

Jessup, B. (1965). On fictive expressions of cognitive meaning. *Journal of Aesthetics and Art Criticism*, *23* , 481–486.

Johnson, M. (1949). *Art and scientific thought: Historical studies towards a modern revision of their antagonism*. New York: Columbia University Press.

Joplin, J. & McClure, M. (composers) (1971). *Mercedes Benz* [song]. ASCAP.

Kassarjian, H. H. (1983). Social values and the Sunday comics: A content analysis. In R. P. Bagozzi & A. M. Tybout (Eds.), *Advances in Consumer Research: Vol. 10* (pp. 434–438). Ann Arbor: Association for Consumer Research.

Kelly, R. F. (1982, May 10). Museums as status symbols: A cynic's view of the museum-public interface. Paper presented at the Annual Meeting of the Canadian Ethnology Society.

Kelley, R. F. (in press). Museums as status symbols II: Attaining a state of having been. In R. W. Belk (Ed.), *Advances in nonprofit marketing: Vol. 2*. Greenwich, CT: JAI Press.

Kephart, W. M. (1950). Status after death. *American Sociological Review*, *15* , 635–643.

King, J. O. (1983). *The iron of melancholy: Structures of spiritual conversion in America from the Puritan conscience to Victorian neurosis*. Middletown, CT: Wesleyan University Press.

Klein, H. A. (1978). Pieter Bruegel the Elder as a guide to 16th century technology. *Scientific American*, *238* (3), 134–140.

Kliman, B. W. (1978). The biscuit eater: Racial stereotypes, 1939–1972. *Phylon*, *39* (1), 87–96.

Krauss, D. A. (1981a). The uses of still photography in counseling and therapy: Development of a training model. *Photo Therapy Quarterly*, *2*, 12–13.

Krauss, D. A. (1981b, August). On photography: Uses in psychotherapy. Paper presented at the Annual Convention of the American Psychological Association. Los Angeles, CA.

Krauss, D. A. (1982). Photography, imaging, and visually referent language in therapy: Illuminating the metaphor. *Camera Lucida*, *5*, 1–12.

Krieger, M. H. (1979). Truth and pictures: 'Fetishes,' 'goodness,' and 'clarity'. In J. Wagner (Ed.), *Images of information: Still photography in the social sciences* (pp. 249–257). Beverly Hills: Sage Publications.

Kron, J. (1983). *Home-psych: The social psychology of home and decor*. New York: Clarkson N. Potter.

Langer, S. K. (1963). *Philosophy in a new key: A study in the symbolism of reason, rite, and art* (3rd ed.). Cambridge, MA: Harvard University Press.

Lears, T. J. J. (1983). From salvation to self-realization: Advertising and the therapeutic roots of the consumer culture, 1880–1930. In R. W. Fox & T. J. J. Lears (Eds.), *The culture of consumption: Critical essays in American history* (pp. 3–38). New York: Pantheon Books.

Lee, R. B. (1979). *The Kung San: Men, women, and work in a foraging society*. Cambridge: Cambridge University Press.

Leob, D. J. (1973). The gamut from a to b: The image of the black in pre-1915 movies. *Political Science Quarterly*, *88* (1), 53–70.

Lesy, M. (1976). Snapshots: Psychological documents, frozen dreams. *Afterimage*, *4*, 12–13.

London, E. (Ed.) (1960). *The world of law, volume 1, the law in literature*. New York: Simon and Schuster.

Longhi, P. (painter) (c. 1750). *Masked women in Venice* [painting]. Milan: Ziolo.

Loy, J. M. (1977). The present as past: Assessing the value of Julien Bryan's films as historical evidence. *Latin American Research Review*, *12* (3), 103–128.

Luciano, D. (1982, September). Nostalgia, mice and ducks. *Comics Journal*, *75*, 20–28.

McAllister, L. (1984, Summer). The brittle mastery of Donald Duck. *The Barks Collector*, *25/26*, 12–23.

MacCannell, D. (1976). *The tourist: A new theory of the leisure class*. New York: Shocken Books.

McCracken, G. (1985). Clio in the marketplace: Theoretical and methodological issues in the history of consumption. In C. T. Tiong & J. N. Sheth (Eds.), *Historical perspective in consumer research: National and international perspectives* (pp. 151–154). Singapore: Association for Consumer Research.

McCracken, G. (in press). From graven images. *International Journal of Comparative Sociology*.

McGuire, W. J. (1973, June). The yin and yang of progress in social psychology: Seven koan. *Journal of Personality and Social Psychology*, *26*, 446–456.

McKendrick, N., Brewer, J. & Plumb, J. H. (1982). *The Birth of a consumer society: The commercialization of eighteenth century England*. London: Europa Publications.

Martin, B. (1979). The sacralization of disorder: Symbolism in rock music. *Sociological Analysis*, *40* (2), 87–124.

Mauss, M. (1967). *The gift: Forms and functions of exchange in archaic societies*. New York: W. W. Norton.

Meer, J. (1984, August). Pet theories. *Psychology Today, 18*, 60–67.

Meyer, R. H. & Subbiondo, J. L. (1972). *Borrowed time: Literature on man and his environment*. Belmont, CA: Wadsworth Publishing.

Meyerhoff, H. (1951). *Time in literature*. Berkeley: University of California Press.

Merriam, S. B. (1983). *Themes of adulthood through literature*. New York: Teachers College Press.

Milgram, S. (1976). The image-freezing machine. *Society* (November-December) 7–12.

Milgram, S. (1977a). The image-freezing machine. *Psychology Today*, (10 January), 50–54.

Milgram, S. (1977b). *The individual in a social world: Essays and experiments*. Reading, MA: Addison Wesley.

Mischel, W., Coates, B. & Raskoff, A. (1968). Effects of success and failure on self-gratification. *Journal of Personality and Social Psychology, 10*, 381–390.

Mitroff, I. I. & Kilmann, R. H. (1978). *Methodological approaches to social science*. San Francisco: Jossey-Bass Publishers.

Mohrmann, G. P. & Scott, E. (1976). Popular music and World War II: The rhetoric of continuation. *Quarterly Journal of Speech, 62* (2), 145–156.

Mooney, H. F. (1968). Popular music since the 1920s: The significance of shifting tastes. *American Quarterly, 20* (1), 67–85.

Moore, B. S., Clyburn, A. & Underwood, B. (1976). The role of affect in delay of gratification. *Child Development, 47*, 273–276.

Mukerji, C. (1978). Artwork: Collection and contemporary culture. *American Journal of Sociology, 84*, 348–365.

Mukerji, C (1983). *From graven images: Patterns of modern materialism*. New York: Columbia University Press.

Munson, J. M. & Spivey, W. A. (1981). Product and brand-user stereotypes among social classes. *Journal of Advertising Research, 21* (4), 37–48.

Musello, C. (1979). Family photography. In J. Wagner (Ed.), *Images of information: Still photography in the social sciences* (pp. 101–118). Beverly Hills: Sage Publications.

Neihardt, J. G. (1974). *Black Elk speaks*. London: Sphere Books.

O'Connor, J. E. (1973). Historians and film: Some problems and prospects. *History Teacher, 6* (4), 543–552.

von Oech, R. (1983). *A whack on the side of the head: Unlock your mind for innovation*. New York: Warner Books.

O'Guinn, T. C., Faber, R. J. & Marshall, R. (1985). Popular film and television as consumer acculturation agents: America 1900 to present. In C. T. Tan & J. N. Sheth (Eds.), *Historical perspective in consumer research: National and international perspectives* (pp. 297–301). Singapore: Association for Consumer Research.

O'Guinn, T. C., Lee, W.-N. & Faber, R. J. (in press). Acculturation: The impact of divergent paths on buyer behavior. In R. J. Lutz (Ed.), *Advances in consumer research*, Vol. 13. Provo, UT: Association for Consumer Research.

O'Reilly, L., Rucker, M., Hughes, R., Gorang, M. and Hand, S. (1984). The relationship of psychological and situational variables to usage of a second order marketing system. *Journal of the Academy of Marketing Science, 12* (3), 53–76.

Owens, B. (1973). *Suburbia*. San Francisco: Straight Arrow Books.

Patchen, K. (1941). *The journal of Albion moonlight*. New York: New Directions.

Patchen, K. (1967). *Hallelujah anyway*. New York: New Directions.

Paymans, H. (1976). Propagandistic aspects of modern comic-books. *Gazette*, *22* (4), 219–229.

Pecheau, L. (painter) (1776). *Marchese Rocapadali* [painting]. Turin: private collection.

Perebinossoff, P. (1974). What does a kiss mean? The love comic formula and the creation of the ideal teen-age girl. *Journal of Popular Culture*, *8* (4), 825–835.

Peter, J. P. & Olson, J. C. (1983). Is science marketing? *Journal of Marketing*, *47* (4), 111–125.

Peters, M. & Mergen, B. (1977). 'Doing the rest': The uses of photographs in American studies. *American Quarterly*, *29* (3), 280–303.

Pfeiffer, J. (1982). *The creative explosion: An inquiry into the origins of art and religion*. New York: Harper & Row.

Pine, V. R. & Phillips, D. L. (1970). The cost of dying: A sociological analysis of funeral expenditures. *Social Problems*, *17*, 405–417.

Pino, F. (1973). Chicano poetry: A popular manifesto. *Journal of Popular Culture*, *6* (4), 718–730.

Plato (1974). *The Republic* (Trans. D. Lee) (2nd ed.). Hammondsworth, England: Penguin Books.

Powers, R. G. (1980). Myth, ritual and the comic strip g-man. In. R. B. Browne (Ed.), *Rituals and Ceremonies in Popular Culture* (pp. 296–315). Bowling Green, OH: Bowling Green University Popular Press.

Praz, M. (1964). *An illustrated history of furnishing from the renaissance to the 20th century*. New York: George Brazdler.

Praz, M. (1971). *Conversation pieces: A survey of the informal group portrait in Europe and America*. University Park: The Pennsylvania State University Press.

R. W. (monogramist) (c. 1650). *Dutch interior of the 17th century* [painting]. Rome: formerly art market.

Rabkin, L. Y. (1966). *Psychopathology and literature*. San Francisco: Chandler Publishing Company.

Reagon, B. (1974). World War II reflected in black music: 'Uncle Sam called me'. *Southern Exposure*, *1* (3/4), 169–184.

Reiner, C. (director) (1979). *The jerk* [film]. Los Angeles: Universal.

Riesman, D. (1950). Listening to popular music. *American Quarterly*, *2*, 359–371.

Rogers, N. (producer) (1984). *Living in the material world* [video]. Nile Rogers Productions, Inc.

Rollins, P. C. (1974). Film and American studies: Questions, activities, guides. *American Quarterly*, *26* (3), 245–265.

Rook, D. (1985). "Consumers' video archives and household rituals," paper presented at Association for Consumer Research Annual Conference, Las Vegas, Nevada.

Ross, S. D. (1969). *Literature and philosophy*. New York: Meredith Corporation.

Rowlett, R. M. & Schneider, M. J. (1974). The material expression of Neanderthal child care. In M. Richardson (Ed.), *The human mirror: Material and spacial images of man* (pp. 41–58). Baton Rouge: Louisiana University Press.

Ruesch, J. & Kees, W. (1959). *Nonverbal communication: Notes on the visual perception of human relations*. Berkeley: University of California Press.

Ryder, G. A. (1976). Black women in song: Some socio-cultural images. *Negro History Bulletin*, *39* (5), 601–603.

Sanders, C. R. (1974). Icons of the alternate culture: The themes and functions of underground comix. *Journal of Popular Culture*, *8* (4), 836–852.

Schecter, H. (1977). Deep meaning comix: The archetypal world of R. Crumb. *San Jose Studies*, *3* (3), 836–852.

Schoeck, H. (1966). *Envy: A theory of social behavior* (M. Glennyard & B. Ross, Trans.). New York: Harcourt, Brace and World.

Scitovsky, T. (1976). *The joyless economy: An inquiry into human satisfaction*. New York: Oxford University Press.

Seale, W. (1981). *The tasteful interlude: American interiors through the camera's eye, 1860–1917* (2nd ed.). Nashville: American Association for State and Local History.

Sennett, R. (1980). *Authority*. New York: Alfred Knopf.

Shain, R. E. (1974). Hollywood's cold war. *Journal of Popular Film, 3* (4), 334–350.

Sharpless, F. P. (1976). *Symbol and myth in modern literature*. Rochelle Park, NJ: Hayden Book Company.

Shepherd, J., Virden, P., Vulliamy, G. & Wishart, T. (1977). *Whose music? A sociology of musical languages*. London: Latimer.

Sobchack, V. C. (1979). The grapes of wrath (1940): Thematic emphasis through visual style. *American Quarterly, 31* (5), 596–615.

Sontag, S. (1973). *On photography*. New York: Farrar, Straus, and Giroux.

Spradley, J. P. & McConough, G. E. (Eds.) (1973). *Anthropology through literature*. Boston: Little, Brown and Company.

Staats, G. R. (1979). Sexual imagery in blues music: A basis for black stereotypes. *Journal of Jazz Studies, 5* (2), 40–60.

Stein, B. (1985, June 13). The machine makes this man. *Wall Street Journal*, p. 30.

Steinbeck, J. (1939). *Grapes of wrath*. New York: Viking Press.

Stoll, E. E. (1933). *Art and artifice in Shakespeare*. Cambridge: Cambridge University Press.

Stone, H. S., Jr. (1966). Youths and motorcycles. In. B. Kepes (Ed.), *Man made object*. Los Angeles: Studio Vista Publishers.

Stone, M. (1979). Heav'n rescued land: American hymns and American destiny. *Journal of Popular Culture, 10* (1), 133–141.

Streicher, H. W. (1974). The girls in the cartoons. *Journal of Communication, 24* (2), 125–129.

Summer, E. (1981, Spring). Of ducks and men. *Panels, 2*, 3–15.

Titon, J. T. (1977). Thematic pattern in downhome blues lyrics: The evidence on commercial phonograph records since World War II. *Journal of American Folklore, 90* (357), 316–330.

Trautman, J. & Pollard, C. (1975). *Literature and medicine*. Philadelphia: Society for Health and Human Values.

Travuchis, N. & Goode, W. J. (1975). *The family through literature*. New York: McGraw-Hill Book Company.

Tuan, Y.-F. (1982). *Segmented worlds and self: Group life and individual consciousness*. Minneapolis: University of Minnesota Press.

Underwood, B., Moore, B. S. & Rosenhan, D. L. (1973). Affect and self-gratification. *Developmental Psychology, 8*, 209–214.

Uys, J. (director) (1980). *The gods must be crazy* [film]. Johannesburg: independent film.

Valenti, P. L. (1979). The cultural hero in the World War II fantasy film. *Journal of Popular Film and Television, 7* (3), 310–321.

Wagner, J. (1979). Photography and social science progress. In J. Wagner (Ed.), *Images of information: Still photography in the social sciences* (pp. 283–295). Beverly Hills: Sage Publications.

Wainwright III, L. (composer) (1973). *A. M. world* [song]. Snowden Music.

Wallendorf, M. (1984, October 12). *Social stratification, object attachment, and con-*

sumer life pattern. Paper presented at 1984 Conference of the Association for Consumer Research, Washington, D.C.

Walsh, D. (1969). *Literature and knowledge*. Middletown, CT: Wesleyan University Press.

Webster, J. (poet) (1613). A Monumental Column [poem]. In F. L. Lucas (Ed.), *The Complete Works of John Webster* (1937). New York: Oxford University Press.

Weiland, J. H. (1955, Fall). The adolescent and the automobile. *Chicago Review, 9*, 61–64.

Welles, O. (director) (1941). *Citizen Kane* [film]. RKO Pan.

Wepman, D., Newman, R. B. & Binderman, M. (1974). Toasts: The black urban folk poetry. *Journal of American Folklore, 87* (345), 208–224.

Whetmore, E. J. (1979). *Mediamerica: Form, content, and consequence of mass communication*. Belmont, CA: Wadsworth Publishing Company.

Williams, R. (1981). *Dream worlds: Mass consumption in late nineteenth century France*. Berkeley: University of California Press.

Wilson, B. & Usher, G. (composers) (1962). *409* [song]. Sea of Tunes Publishing Company.

Zoffany, J. (artist) (c. 1800). *Family group* [painting]. New York: Wildenstein Galleries.

Zoffany, J. (artist) (1790). *Charles Towneley and his friends in his library* [painting]. Burnley, Lancashire: Towneley Hall Gallery and Museum.

Zynda, T. H. (1979). The Hollywood version: Movie portrayals of the press. *Journalism History, 6* (1), 16–25.

2
Implications From the "Old" and the "New" Physics for Studying Buyer Behavior

MICHAEL J. RYAN

Introduction

Western science has traditionally emphasized the importance of subjecting theory to empirical scrutiny. My central thesis is that the field of consumer behavior has become preoccupied with empirical issues resulting in a lack of effort devoted to the development of theory that is needed to explain phenomena. First, I will argue that the field is preoccupied with empiricism and that this is unscientific whether one subscribes to the old science based on logical positivism and falsificationism or the newer philosophies of science. Second, I will attribute this preoccupation to the predominate influence in consumer behavior of empirically driven social psychological and marketing approaches to knowledge. Third, consumer behavior's present approaches to knowledge will be juxtaposed with the goals of the "old" and the "new" science. Fourth, the ideas expressed in this essay are illustrated by applying them to the well-known debate as to whether *affect* precedes or follows *cognition* in cognitive response models. My objective is to show that more attention must be given to conceptual analysis if we are to prevent empirical deadlocks that inhibit the expansion of our knowledge.

Assuming that the *Journal of Consumer Research* (*JCR*) contains the best work that buyer behavior has to offer, the contents of the first ten years of the *JCR* provides an orientation to the field. Of the 374 articles that appeared in *JCR*, 70% were empirical tests and 47% of these studies employed the experimental method. Fourteen percent of the studies focused on methdological issues centering about empirical matters such as operationalization (e.g., Smead, Wilcox, & Wilkes, 1981), model estimation procedures (e.g., Fornell, 1983), and the validity of experimental data (Calder, Phillips, & Tybout, 1982a, 1982b, 1983; Lynch, 1982, 1983; McGrath & Brinberg, 1983). The remaining studies (17%) did not contain primary data and consisted mainly of literature reviews (e.g., Sirgy, 1982), and conceptual models (e.g., Bagozzi & Van Loo, 1978). The empirical preoccupation inherent in most studies does, of course, emulate traditional or "old" science (cf. Kaplan, 1964, pp. 34–42) in the accepted tradition of the Vienna Circle. As Hume, commonly viewed as the father of modern empiricism, put it:

If we take in hand any volume of divinity or school of metaphysics, for instance, let us ask *Does it contain any abstract reasoning concerning quantity or number?* No. *Does it contain any experimental reasoning concerning matter of fact and existence?* No. Commit it then to the flames; for it can contain nothing but sophistry and illusion. (quoted in Passmore, 1961, p. 1)

Setting aside the call for abstractions for a moment, Hume began the notion that only verifiable, that is, empirically linked terms, are scientifically meaningful. This notion led to a dilemma: If theoretical terms are strictly defined in terms of observations, they cannot function explanatorily. However, if they are not defined observationally, then how did they have empirical support? Attempts to solve the problem by doing away with abstractions were not satisfactory since a science that restricts itself to directly observed entities and relations automatically loses predictive power. The science would tend, even when deductively formulated, to be merely descriptive. Hempel (1958) resolved this problem in his deductive-nomological model acknowledging that theoretical terms have meaning beyond their relation to observables through their connections to other terms in the theory. Thus, concepts depend on a theoretical network for their meaning.

JCR researchers are emulating highly respected disciplines, with many members who claim rigid adherence to traditional scientific methods, interpreting them as empiricism. As they have done, we can decry the deficiency in conceptual analysis and lack of theoretical frameworks (cf. Ferber, 1979; Jacoby, 1978; Kollat, Engel, & Blackwell, 1970; Sheth, 1967) and then sidestep the issue by compartmentalizing empirical and conceptual issues. This view of science holds that there is an empirical reality "out there" that exists independent of theories (notwithstanding ever-present contaminations that we must endeavor to control). Thus, detailed conceptual analysis is not needed, for the "truth" will come out as an empirical matter. This type of thinking will, of course, lead to even less conceptual development.

This leads to the suggestion that both business world and academic world consumer psychologists can have a common agenda item—if not a common agenda. This item, number one on our agenda, should be to enhance the reliability and validity of our basic measures of consumer behavior. This is a call for methodological studies. (Schnee, 1985)

I believe that a lack of original conceptualization or mere reliance on basic discipline theoretical networks weakens our potential for contributing to an understanding of society through its consumptive aspects. Hopefully, this argument will become palatable as it unfolds. Suffice it to say, at this point, that our exemplars are exemplary but they are based, on an idealized view of science that never existed (Laudan, 1977). McGrath and Brinberg (1983), for example, congratulate all members (Calder, Phillips, & Tybout, 1982a, 1982b, 1983; Lynch, 1982, 1983; McGrath and Brinberg, 1983) of the exchange on validity issues for adhering to falsificationism. Many important scientific theories would have been rejected in their infancy had their proponents been strict falsificationists. Newton's gravitational theory was falsified in its early years by observations of the moon's orbit, Bohr's theory of the atom was inconsistent with observations of matter stability, and Maxwell cited falsification evidence in his original work on the kinetic theory of gases. Hence, falsificationism was discarded by philosophers of science over 20 years ago (cf. Suppe, 1977) as it is incompatible with the historical progression of science. Scientists have proceeded as though theories cannot be conclusively proven false anymore than they can be confirmed. There are good reasons why this is so, such as the lack of an observational base that is independent of the theory being tested. In fact, due to the complexity of test situations, one is never certain if a failure is due to the theory or the method (cf. Chalmers, 1976, Chapter 6). This point was acknowledged by Popper (1968) in his original work, a fact usually overlooked by his overly zealous critics and followers. Once sensory perceptions replace infallible observations and are incorporated into the epistemology underlying the research process, a veritable Pandora's Box is opened that eventually undermines some of the basic tenets of the traditional view of science. Before moving to these issues, however, I would like to explain my earlier assertion that we are emulating the traditional view of science. Unfortunately, as implied in the falsification discussion above, disciplines that practice the traditional view may either have outdated views of science or consumer behavior theorists may not have noticed some subtle shifts. The *JCR* 10-year summary index (Langston, 1984) is quite unusual for an academic discipline in two ways. First, it lists basic topics such as attitudes and attribution theory and applied topics such as advertising and consumer credit. Whereas the *JCR* policy board is interdisciplinary, the majority of basic topics are recognizable as the subject matter of cognitive social psychology. Second, the applied topics generally fit into the category of marketing, a discipline that has been characterized as more of a technology than a science (Nord & Peter, 1980; O'Shaughnessy & Ryan, 1979; Sweeney, 1972). In short, *JCR* research consists primarily of tests of social psychological theories and marketing applications. A stream of research has yet to emerge that can be recognized uniquely as consumer behavior. In addition, editorial board members and authors reside primarily in the academic discipline of marketing. These issues have important implications for consumer behavior's potential as a basic discipline. I will address implications from the influence of psychology first and then turn to implications from marketing.

Psychology as a Traditional Science

There is wide belief that the only serious psychological theories date from the 19th century (Marx & Hillix, 1973; Murphy & Kovach, 1972). A mechanistic view of psychology as a science resulted from 17th century arguments in which Descartes, Leibniz, Spinoza, Mendelssohn, Newton, Hobbs, and Locke were the principal debaters. This was the approach taken in the late 1800s by Wundt who is generally regarded as the founder of scientific psychology. Wundt and his colleagues gathered a large following for their atomistic approach although they encountered strong criticism from Wertheimer, Goldstein, and James.

James refused to accept Descartes' duality believing that mind and body are interdependent. He emphasized a personal and continuous view of consciousness. James, however, did not take a strong advocacy position, a necessary condition for advancing scientific views (cf. Peter & Olson, 1983). Attention then turned to Watson's behaviorism. Watson was a strong advocate of a purely objective view of psychology that could be raised to the status of a natural science. He believed that by doing away with consciousness, psychological experiments could be subjected to the criteria used in physics. Two of these criteria, which will be dealt with later, are that phenomena are: (a) Independent of subject and observer, and (b) can be separated into meaningful parts (Zukav, 1979).

Thus, the compelling holistic views held by the well-known Gestalt school as well as the emerging views of lesser-known cognitive psychologists such as Otto Selz, who wrote in the 1920s, and which were not compatible with "science," were swept aside. Isen and Hastorf (1982) report that Selz believed that basic cognitive units are whole sets of relationships, trains of thought, or schemata, rather than atomistic particles or sensations. Such views, of course, were not compatible with the reductionistic methodologies employed by classical physicists.

> From the earliest days of the experimental pioneers, man's stipulation that psychology be adequate to science outweighed his commitment that it be adequate to man. (Koch, 1959, Vol. 3, p. 783)

As the above quote suggests, psychologists have themselves been critical of what the physicist Capra (1982) refers to as "Newtonian Psychology." These criticisms range from blind ideology (e.g., Heather, 1976) to concerned pleas for integration of noncognitive aspects (cf. Isen & Hastorf, 1982) to implications from the new philosophy of science (e.g., Gergen, 1985; Howard, 1985; Manicas & Secord, 1983). Implications for marketing from the new philosophy are also available elsewhere (Anderson, 1983). In addition, some of the holistic ideas are reemerging in recent psychological thought (e.g., Iran-Nejad & Ortony, 1984; Neisser, 1976). It is beyond the scope of this essay to detail these matters. Rather, the brief treatment above is meant to show how psychology came to embrace the methods of classical physics and, by emulating those social psychologists who are empirically driven, how consumer behavior researchers have implicitly embraced the same tenets. My attention now turns to a second major influence on consumer behavior.

The Influence of Marketing

Marketing has also been concerned with achieving scientific status (cf. Anderson, 1983; O'Shaughnessy & Ryan, 1979) and has developed almost as scientology. While marketing scholars have attempted to emulate the natural sciences, they have also been influenced by practical issues, as marketing practice was firmly entrenched long before it became an academic subject in 1902. Its academic origins are in applied economics, primarily agricultural economics; it grew to what it is today in professional business schools (Bartels, 1976). As a consequence marketing researchers have traditionally sought precision in prediction and control, and there is some confusion regarding the nature of basic or academic research (cf. O'Shaughnessy & Ryan, 1979). The scheme put forth in Table 2.1 will be used to sort these issues.

All research is to some extent applied but the breadth of application varies widely. In basic research, the inquirer is concerned primarily with understanding the world. The results are concepts or theories, or simply sets of relationships offered as new knowledge for the purpose of organizing and categorizing. The emphasis is on abstraction with the goal of explaining large sets of behavior. Two of the more well-known consumer behavior efforts in this regard are the Howard and Sheth (1969) and Webster and Wind (1972) models. They have served the field well in terms of orienting it and organizing its various aspects with concepts such as "evoked set." Less eclectic approaches have also served a similar function (e.g., Ratchford, 1975). Basic research, whether organizing the entire field or various topical issues, is frequently subjected to empirical tests. These tests, however, deal with variables as phenomena that are several levels of abstraction removed from the concepts. For example, "brand loyalty" may be considered, at a very abstract level, to organize terms such as "search," "intention," "repeat buying," and so forth, each of which is also an abstraction and must be reduced to successively lower levels of abstraction in order to be operationally defined. The empirical test is conducted to test the organizing capability of the nomological network, not to obtain accurate predictions in everyday affairs.

Applied research, on the other hand, is focused on the solution of practical problems. Hence, the researcher is motivated more by the ability to predict and control than by the need for general understanding. The applied researcher does incorporate general understanding as a way of grounding empirical findings which, while foreseeable and practical, are sought for use in a wide variety of specific situations. Thus, basic and applied research have the common goal of seeking abstractions, the major distinction being the relative emphasis on under-

TABLE 2.1. Research according to purpose.

Type	Abstraction: Status	Abstraction: Degree	Precision in Prediction and Control
Basic Research	Producer of Abstractions	high	low
Applied Research	Producer of Abstractions	↑	↓
Service Research	User of Abstraction	↑	↓
Action Research	User of Abstraction	low	high

standing and prediction. The review of Banks and Hart (1977) concerning promotional methods as well as Howard and Hulbert's (1973) review of advertising practices contain examples of applied research.

Both applied and basic research entail prediction, the former putting more emphasis on practical matters, the latter using it as a testing tool. The general level of understanding sought in basic research conflicts with the needs of applied researchers who seek precision in predicting and controlling. Thus, attempts to simultaneously fulfill the aims of both types of research is not possible.

Service research is done to solve a particular problem with which the researcher is faced or is trying to solve for someone else. Frequently, the initiation of service research, unlike basic and applied research, is not undertaken by the researcher but rather by a practitioner facing a problem or seeking an opportunity. Abstractions are used to generate alternative solutions or to give confidence to predictions, but the research is not concerned with producing generalizations. This type of research uses applied and basic research as a way of grounding predictions. It does not contribute to new understanding. A retailer, for example, who understands "why" people patronize the store is in a better position to predict future patronage than one who merely extrapolates past events since the impact of future events that have not yet been experienced can be considered. Service research is also known as grounded technology as contrasted to science that produces generalizations.

Action research seeks a solution to a particular problem without understanding why or how it came about. Thus, prediction is accomplished by extrapolating of past experiences and control is sought through trial. Such approaches may be appropriate when the problem or opportunity is immediate and the alternative actions few in number. Abstractions, however, are not explicitly utilized as the research deals solely with phenomena as both inputs and outputs. Thus, for example, one may increase advertising in one of two similar cities and, after observing sales volume, predict the impact of similar increases in similar cities. Hypothetically, one could carry out the study in ways that would assure concomitant variation, temporal ordering, and lack of spuriousness. The variables involved could also be modeled mathematically. These procedures would not produce understanding, however, without abstractions.

Neither service or action research produce generalizations. Yet they have been highly valued due to marketing's practical orientation. In the quest for status, they have sometimes been put forth as "science," usually on the basis of method or predictive ability (cf. O'Shaughnessy & Ryan, 1979).

To this point, this essay has argued that consumer behavior needs more conceptual development. My position on conceptualization is not radical, as the issues I have dealt with to this point, especially weak falsification and openness of conceptual meaning, are acceptable to most neo-positivists. In fact there is even a book in our field dealing with many of these issues (Zaltman, Pinson, & Angelmar, 1973). I simply feel that our heritage has led us to place undue emphasis on empiricism and too little emphasis on the need for concepts to achieve explanation. Belk (1984) argues that our preoccupation with empirical matters has caused a fundamental problem in that we do not know how to develop theory. At any rate, theories, whether viewed according to the "old" or "new" science cannot be developed without concepts.

Goals of the "Old" Science

Scientific endeavors have traditionally sought networks of concepts in which each concept accounts for a number of phenomena. Its objective, the explanation of the largest number of phenomena with the fewest number of concepts, is gained by overlaying networks of variables at more abstract levels (see Ryan & O'Shaughnessy, 1980). The illustration shown in Figure 2.1 captures this notion quite well. At the top are concepts that have no existence in the empirical world. Each concept is itself a mental process by which theoreticians account for concepts at lower levels of abstraction. For example, the concept cognitive dissonance may be useful in accounting for "anger," "frustration," and "complaint intentions." What is important to note is that by their very nature concepts have no direct connection to the observable world. They are general analogies useful for explaining "as if" they existed and their validity is judged by their usefulness.

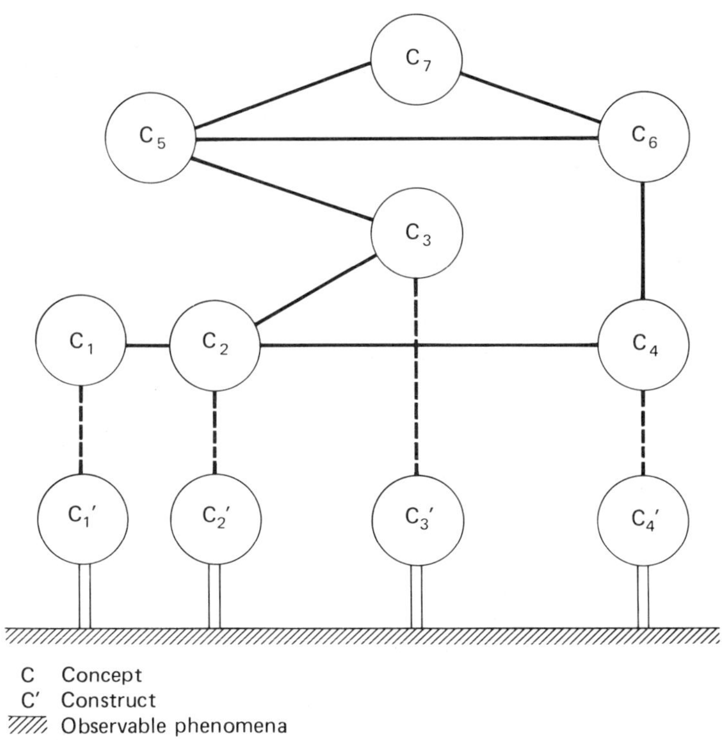

FIGURE 2.1. Relationships among abstract and empirical terms.

If, for example, the "consolidation theory of memory" is replaced with a "depth of processing" theory that does not contain "short term memory" this would imply that the new theory accounts for phenomena in a way more useful for the purpose at hand than did the old theory. The *existence* of "short term memory" is not an issue since it only exists in the theorists mind, it will not be found in observable phenomena.

A concept depends upon theory not observable phenomena for its meaning as it has only systemic meaning (Kaplan, 1964). For example, cognitive dissonance derives its meaning from its relationships (the solid lines in Figure 2.1) with other concepts contained in balance theory. Furthermore, meanings change depending on theoretical orientation. Thus, for example, the meaning of attitude depends on whether one subscribes to single component or tripartite attitude theory. A conception of attitude from a functional theory would change, for example, to enable it to fit into an instrumental theory because its network of associations would differ across the two theories.

Constructs are inventions whereby we link concepts to the empirical world. They contain both systemic and observational meaning and are linked to concepts through laws or propositions (the dashed line in Figure 2.1) and to phenomena through rules of correspondence (the solid parallel lines in Figure 2.1). Thus, "sensory input," "short term memory," and "long term memory" may be viewed as constructs having systemic meaning within "consolidation memory" and observational meaning through rules of correspondence linking them to appropriate phenomena. Whether a term is a concept or construct will, of course, depend on the theory that contains it. For example, attitude is viewed as both a concept and construct in the Howard and Sheth (1969) *Theory of Buyer Behavior.*

Phenomena refer to things recognizable by one or more of the five senses. By "an appropriate phenomenon" is meant something that falls within the domain of the construct (Nunnally, 1967). A specific type of recall, for example, may evidence a phenomenon only explainable by "long term memory" or a particular written statement may indicate "dissatisfaction." "Long term memory" and "dissatisfaction" depend on theoretical structure for their meaning and as a consequence any phenomena they represent will have different interpretations depending on the chosen theory.

Operational definitions state how certain characteristics of the phenomena are quantified. For example, "strength" may be a characteristic that we may quantify through use of a probability scale, or "duration" and "detail" may be characteristics that are also susceptible to paper and pencil testing. All three of these characteristics may be linked to the construct "intentions" with rules of correspondence. The important point here is that we never directly measure a construct no matter how low its level of abstraction. We can only quantify certain characteristics that we attribute to it. We may, for example, measure the width, height, light reflecting property, and so forth of a table. These characteristics or attributes, taken separately or together, do not, however, exhaustively define the abstraction. In the present example, "table" is an arbitrary category since the same characteristics could just as well refer to "cube" or "box." In order to know which concept is appropriate, one must know the theoretical structure being imposed on the characteristics by the theorist. The selected theory, will, of course, depend on the purpose at hand. In the same way, a galvanic skin response measure could be accounted for by a number of different abstractions such as sexual arousal, anger, frustration, and so forth.

An example of the problems that arise when induction is attempted from sensations without theory is provided for pupillometrics. Reviewers of this literature report that, among other things, pupil dilation-contraction may be accounted for by affect, sexual arousal, discrimination of auditory pitch, cognitive processing, task difficulty, and memory loading (e.g., Hess, 1972; Watson & Gatchel, 1979). Watson and Gatchel conclude there is doubt as to which psychological processes underlie pupil response. Yet, Hansen (1981), writing in the *Journal of Consumer Research*, reports that what is being measured is most frequently believed to be involvement, activity, or engagement in the issue. Without a conceptual explanation this interpretation of selected empirical findings is simply misleading. In fact, Hess (1972) cites a number of empirical studies to conclude that pupillometrics is valuable because it reflects *many* different types of nervous system function and mirrors ongoing neurological activity in *all* parts of the brain. He does not address the more interesting question of how this general level of neurological activity can be usefully organized by different mental constructs.

Given the empirical bias we have followed, it is not surprising that our foray into physiology has been conceptually naive. We simply have not recognized the differences in the psychologist's and the physiologist's theoretical systems (the Cs and their connections in Figure 2.1). For example, a tree sways back and forth in the breeze and a corresponding pattern of electrical impulses are detected in the brain. When the physiologist talks about electrical impulses as a representation of tree movement he is not referring to this representation as a mental construct. As Jacobson (1973) notes, "In electrophysiology, of course, we record signalization, not meaning" (p. 4). And ". . . when a physiologist speaks about mental activity to the experienced psychologist, he is talking in a foreign language" (p. 5). To the physiologist, then, a mental representation would consist of coordinated neural activity shifting and changing in an orderly position as the tree sways (Thatcher & John, 1977, p. 135). The internal representation does not, of course, resemble a tree. On the other hand, the behavioral theoretician would view the internal representation as the ideal type "tree" that, of course, does resemble a particular swaying tree, and is a concept useful for organizing and interpreting the world. For an interesting exchange regarding these issues, the reader is referred to Kroeber-Riel (1979, 1980) and Ryan (1980).

Consumer researchers do not have to cross disciplines, as in the above psychology-physiology examples, to become mired in empirical confusion. The focus of the current information overload debate, for example, is on measurement and data analysis. Malhotra (1984), for example, in his reflections on this debate lists the theoretical applications areas as: Conjoint Analysis, Questionnaire Design, Sense Modality of Questions, and Data Collection Methods. Each of these issues deals with operational matters. No one has yet to specify a conceptual system to account for the bewildering array of empirical results. Without a conceptual analysis, arguments about measures and data meaning will continue to be futile.

Implications From the "New" Science

Having argued in the tradition of classical Western science that we are conceptually deficient, my attention now turns to a brief consideration of the two tenets from classical physics mentioned earlier (separation of phenomena from observer and from each other). More detailed treatments, written at the layperson's level, will be found in Talbot (1980), Capra (1976), and Zukav's (1979) works.

In 1803 Young found that light has the property of a wave, and in 1905 Einstein found it to have the properties of a particle. No one has since been able to disprove either conclusion. This duality has been accepted and marks the end of the "either-or" way of looking at the world, at least for the "new" physics. How do the physicists explain this seemingly paradoxical situation? They believe we make light either a wave or a particle depending on how we choose to observe it. That is, by observing or measuring something we change its nature. The observer actualizes some possibilities and negates others. Wheeler, writing on the physicist's conception of nature, puts it as follows:

> Nothing is more important about the quantum principle than this, that it destroys the concept of the world as "sitting out there" with the observer safely separated from it by a 20 centimeter lab of plate glass. Even to observe so miniscule an object as an electron, he must shatter the glass. He must reach in. He must install his chosen measuring equipment. It is up to him to decide whether he shall measure position or momentum. To install the equipment to measure the one prevents and excludes his installing the equipment to measure the other. Moreover, the measurement changes the state of the electron. The universe will never afterwards be the same. To describe what has happened, one has to cross out the old word "observer" and put in its place the new word "participator." In some strange sense the universe is a participating universe. (John A. Wheeler as quoted by Talbot, 1980, p. 21)

My position is that we have neglected the conceptual dimension of theory that, according to the prevailing neo-positivistic view, is independent of reality. *Now we find the physicists have abandoned this viewpoint and believe instead that "reality" is determined by how they operationalize the theory.* The implication here is that the conceptual development of a theory becomes even more important. This is an understatement. If we continue to emulate the physicists model of science we must incorporate this change and view the observer and the observed as causally related and at the same time recognize that the theory tells the observer where to look and, therefore, largely defines reality and determines what will be found. Thus, phenomena and observer are inseparable.

The second issue has to do with the nature of subatomic particles. They act "organically" in that they are sensitive to their environment and to each other.

Individual particle activity cannot be predicted with certainty and "information" appears to get around the system instantaneously. The basic parts are not really parts but events that persist only momentarily and then only as transactions with other parts. Thus, that which physicists formerly viewed as isolated material particles now appear as do abstractions in that they are definable and observable only through systemic interaction. The philosopher/physicist David Bohm puts it as follows:

> One is led to a new notion of unbroken wholeness which denies the classical idea of analyzability of the world into separately and independently existing parts . . . We have reversed the usual classical notion that the independent "elementary parts" of the world are the fundamental reality, and that the various systems are merely particular contingent forms and arrangement of these parts. Rather, we say that inseparable quantum interconnectedness of the whole universe is the fundamental reality and that relatively independently behaving parts are merely particular and contingent forms within this whole. (Bohm as quoted by Capra, 1982, p. 124)

Upon reflection, the systemic view seems commonsensical as it reflects everyday language use. For example, the words cook and roast have only latent meaning until placed within a sentence structure. Thus "*cook* the *roast*" has an entirely different meaning than "*roast* the *cook*" as simply reordering these words actualizes some meanings and negates others. As this example illustrates, we have now come full circle in that the meaning is not the mere transaction among the parts, it is the transaction among the parts and the observer.

There is an important implication here for consumer behavior theory beyond the obvious need to consider a system as the basic unit. It is not only the observer, here considered in regard to both his perceptions and tools of observation, but the subject of the observed, the actor, here meant to be active in a literal sense, that imparts meaning. In addition to a *consumption object*, such as a good, service, or idea, and a way to cognitively represent its elements (e.g., Ratchford, 1975; Ryan & Bonfield, 1975), and a *context* within which to view behavior before, during, and after consumption (e.g., Belk, 1974, 1975), buyer behavior must have an *actor*, here viewed as an active processor of information in the pursuit of goals. The notion of *context* is reinforced and given added meaning from the new physics whereas the new notion of *actor* springs from it. The new notion of actor does not mean merely that we need to resurrect the idea of individual differences. It means we need to stop viewing the individual as an isolated passive phenomenon subject to environmental changes. We should view the consumer as an interrelated component that actively impacts in addition to being impacted upon by the consumption system.

These notions appear commonsensical, yet they are not obvious to many in the field. Consider, for example, the notion of "low involvement products" where the emphasis is usually, as the term implies, on products, not context or actor. It seems the degree of involvement would always entail and might possibly be predominated by context, actor, or their interaction with product. Tuna or cookies, commonly considered low involving products (cf. Lastovicka, 1979), may shift to high involvement for a socially sensitive consumer with household guests. It seems the most rudimentary consumption system must represent actor as well as situation and object. We should view product involvement the same way Robertson (1971) has taught us to view product innovation, through the user's eyes.

While I would maintain that the illustrative examples used to this point in the paper are well reasoned, I have offered little detailed evidence that this is so. Consequently, attention now turns to a more detailed application, a systemic view of affect, cognition, and purchasing intention.

Affect, Cognition, and Purchasing Intention

The role of affect in consumer behavior is controversial as there is disagreement as to whether it precedes or follows cognition. Over two decades of research have not resolved this issue as researchers continue to mount evidence supporting the view they favor and find fault with evidence congenial with the view they do not favor. An exemplar in this regard is a recent paper by Fred Van Raaij (1984) in which he cites evidence supporting his view that affect is primary. In a comment contained in the same paper, Brian Sternthal finds fault with the evidence cited by Van Raaij and cites additional evidence that supports the view that affect follows cognition. Both Van Raaij and Sternthal agree that these empirical anomalies may be resolved by employing physiological measures in future studies. Louis Stern, in a foreword to the paper, sums up the situation with the view that recent research has shed important light on the issue, but that the evidence is inconclusive, and more research is needed. These views embrace Newtonian epistemology. More specifically, they are based on the view that there is an "either/or" answer awaiting discovery, a "truth" that our present empirical methods have merely been unable to discover. Consequently, the answers may be found with new empirical methods. The reader will, of course, recognize that the scenario described above typifies many areas of consumer research.

At any rate, the current state of affairs regarding the affect-cognition argument is represented by the diagram in Figure 2.2 in which everything depends on everything thereby yielding a model with no apparent utility. A view that is consistent with the "new" physics suggests that the observer-observed continuum will ensure that this diagram will remain the same after the addition of 20 or so more years of empirical evidence. That is, researchers will continue to find evidence supporting their position and fault evidence supporting the opposite position. The same conclusion can be obtained by merely extrapolating from the present literature. In short, adding 20 more years of empirical data based on new measurement procedures will lead to the same conclusions Stern draws from the considerable amount of presently available evidence. An alternative, and potentially more fruitful approach, is to accept the evidence as adequate for indicating that the answer to "which comes first" is a resounding "yes" and then proceed with an examination of the different approaches researchers have taken in discovering and justifying their respective positions.

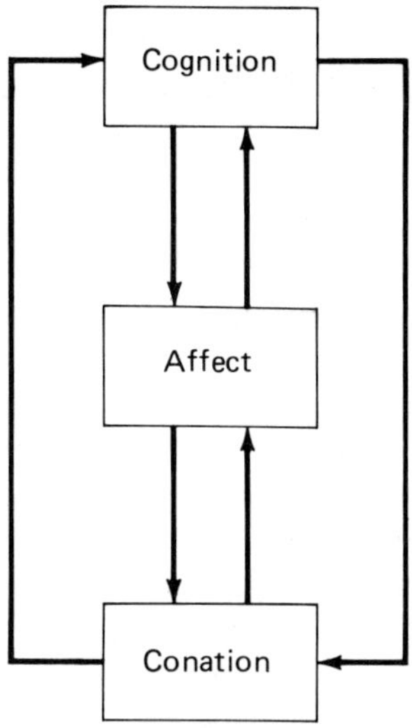

FIGURE 2.2. Summary of various cognitive response models.

Affect is a variable that has a long history in the social psychology literature. There is no commonly agreed upon definition and it is frequently interchanged with words such as evaluation, attitude, emotion, feeling, and sentiment. There is, however, general consensus, reflected in textbook approaches (e.g., Krech, Crutchfield, & Ballachey, 1962; Friedman, Sears, & Carlsmith, 1981), that affect entails the "feeling" or "emotion," the "overall evaluation" or "like" or "dislike" toward an object. It is the emotional part of an attitude that is thought to be motivational. Interestingly, Allport (1935), in his classic review, reported that a preparation or readiness for response was the one common element in a group of widely diverse attitude definitions. More currently, Cooper and Croyle (1984) note that researchers are returning to the notion of affect as it reflects motivation.

Since affect is a concept, it eludes definition and only has systemic meaning. Thus, it is appropriate for the purpose at hand to examine how affect has been used as a motivator in systems dealing with conation. As will be shown below, it has been used in systems based on actor, situation, and object—systems that have developed independently of each other. When these three approaches are combined into one rudimentary system, the paradox of "yes" as the answer to the question "which comes first, affect or cognition?" disappears.

Traditional Cognitive Approaches

The most common consumer research approach to affect is based on object. This approach is predominately based on the work of Fishbein (1963) and Rosenberg (1956) and follows the information processing scheme shown in Figure 2.3. In this model overall evaluation or affect is based on the Osgood, Suci, and Tannenbaum (1957) tradition (Fishbein & Raven, 1962) and is similar to the "affective"

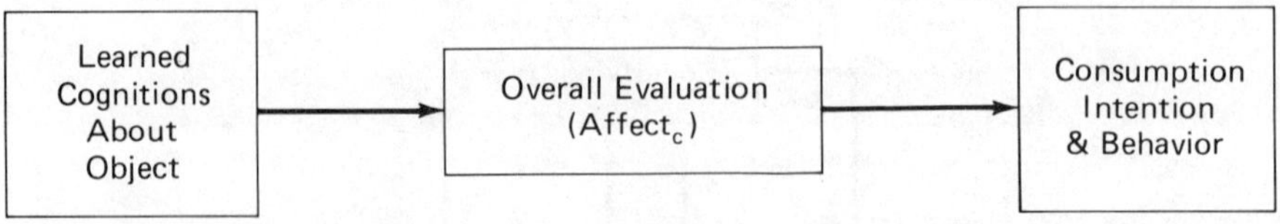

FIGURE 2.3. Multi-attribute approaches to affect and intentions.

component found in the tripartite attitude school of thought (Fishbein & Ajzen, 1975, Chapter 8), except that they posit a causal ordering [cognition → affect → conation (intention)]. Affect is viewed in the Gestalt tradition as a composite primarily arising from cognitions of object characteristics.

A large body of research suggests that consumer cognition and affect can be used to understand purchase behavior (see reviews by Ryan & Bonfield, 1975; Farley, Lehmann, & Ryan, 1981). The bulk of this research is based on the work of Fishbein and Ajzen (cf. Fishbein & Ajzen, 1975; Ajzen & Fishbein, 1977). The four main tenants of their approach is that (a) "behavioral intention" mediates the attitude-behavior link; (b) group or referent influences, referred to as the "social norm," also influence "behavioral intention"; (c) all variables must be measured at the same level of specificity; and (d) "other variables" only influence "intention" through their impact on "attitudes" or "social norms." The first three of these issues have been investigated in the consumer research literature, and results and discussion will be found elsewhere (Ryan & Bonfield, 1975; Ryan, 1982). Surprisingly, the fourth issue, which flies in the face of psychologists' (e.g., Fazio & Zanna, 1981; Abelson, 1982) generally held view that variables such as experience, emotion, context, and so forth have complex roles in predicting and understanding behavior, has, with few exceptions (e.g., Yalch, 1980), not been challenged or investigated. This is especially surprising since the construal shown in Figure 2.3 is considered inappropriate for many consumer behaviors (cf. Wright, 1975). Consequently, it seems appropriate to explore noncognitively formed variables that may impact intention directly or through the mediational effects of cognitively based affect.

Affect Without Cognition

A second approach, based on the individual (cf. Zajonc, 1980; Zajonc & Markus, 1982), conceptualizes affect as a concept independent of cognition. The approach argues, in the Freudian tradition, that ordinary perceptual recognition is often at the chance level in which case behavior is driven by unconscious processes. This view corresponds with the widely held opinion that purchasing behavior is a stochastic process (cf. Bass, 1974; Morrison, 1966). When not at the chance level, prior cognitions may have been abstracted to the extent that their components are no longer accessible. This finding has been frequently reported (e.g., Anderson & Hubert, 1963). The major distinction between Zajonc's and Fishbein and Ajzen's conceptualization is that the latter arises from cognitions about objects whereas the former arises from states within the individual, which are independent of objects.

Given the context within which it occurs, Zajonc's notion of affect does not appear to be a replacement for the affect as shown in Figure 2.3. It is different. Ajzen and Fishbein's (1980) model accounts for behaviors that are both reasoned and volitional. Zajonc, on the other hand, deals with nonreasoned behaviors. Purchasing encompasses both of these decision making aspects and both aspects may be present in the same behavior. According to Howard's (1977) well-known typology, the former involves extensive problem solving (EPS) whereas the latter involves routinized response behavior (RRB). Thus, a more general model, in that it would account for the presence of both types of decisions, is shown in Figure 2.4. EPS purchases would be primarily influenced by Affect_C, RRB purchases would be influenced primarily by Affect_A, and all purchases would be influenced to some relative extent by either. The third category of Howard's typology, limited problem solving (LPS), suggests a more balanced impact from Affect_C and Affect_A.

Affect Impacting Cognitions

There is a third view of affect, based on situation, that entails both enduring and transient impacts on conation. Cooper and Croyle (1984) cite considerable evidence suggesting that existing Affect has a complex relationship with cognitive processes such as perception, encoding, and recall. Similar recognition exists in the marketing literature where it is called the "halo effect" (Beckwith & Lehmann, 1973). It is thought that initial or prior feelings direct cognitive processes in ways that ensure consistency with those feelings. Consistent with this view,

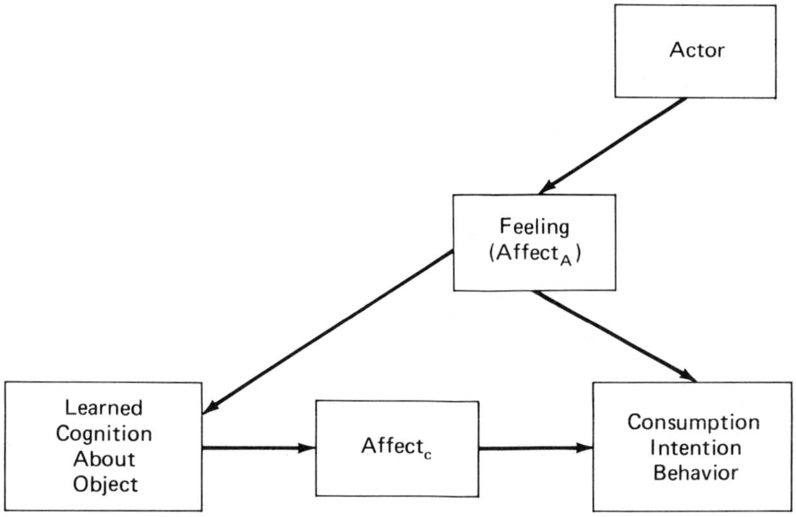

FIGURE 2.4. Affect distinguished by individual and object source.

Lingle and Ostrom (1981) summarized research evidence suggesting that attitude toward a person determines organization and later recall of trait descriptors. Fazio, Powell, and Herr (1983) found that a new stimulus was evaluated consistent with prior attitude toward an object. Thus, the model in Figure 2.4 must also account for the impact of Affect_A on Cognition.

Affect Arising From Situation

The discussion to this point has dealt with Affect as it arises from two sources, the Actor, or active individual, and Cognition, which involves learning about aspects of the consumption object. Situation, composed of contextual or transient factors, provides a third source of Affect. Petty, Ostrom, and Brook (1981) argue that favorable thoughts resulting from the decision situation should cause favorable attitude changes. In this regard, Isen (1984) has induced positive affect in multiple experiments. Her results suggest that positive affect increases the ability to discover relationships and the type of decision rule involved. Ryan and Holbrook (1985) found that inducing negative affect reduced the amount of information and increased the amount of time used in a purchase decision. Thus Affect_S is proposed to arise from the situation within which the decision takes place in addition to arising from Actor and Cognition.

A final issue deals with whether Affect_S can bypass Cognition and directly impact Intention in the same way as Affect_A operates. Abelson's (1981) notion of "scripts" supports this bypass. In short, scripted behavior is dictated by the norms of the situation regardless of individual differences or cognitive variation. The views expressed so far are shown in Figure 2.5.

The addition of Affect_S is consistent with consumer research evidence suggesting that "situations" cause the same product or brand to be considered quite

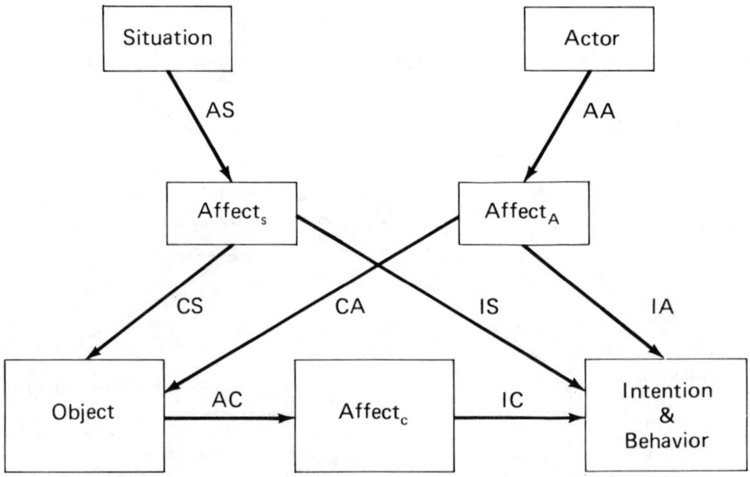

FIGURE 2.5. A systemic view of affect.

differently (Belk, 1975; Dickson, 1982). For example, Belk (1974) found that nearly one half of the explained variance in his studies on meat and snack preferences was due to situational main effects and their interactions. The evidenced furnished by Isen (1984) and her asssociates is also impressive as it spans many years and types of inductions. It also entails very mild Affect inductions, a level that seems appropriate for many consumption situations.

Discussion of the Three-Source Affect Model

The proposed model is rather intuitive, as introspection will reveal how important "feeling" is in making life's major decisions and most product-purchase decisions. Jokes abound concerning decision theorists who abandoned their rational models when they did not conform to a gut reaction when making personal decisions. Thus, Affect seems a likely influence that may take many forms. Rather than simply debate whether Affect precedes, follows, or is independent of cognitions, it seems more useful to view it as having systemically different meanings. These different views will, of course, lead to different operational models and attendant testing methods which, if viewed outside an organizing conceptual system that at its most rudimentary level contains Actor, Context, and Cognition, will continue to yield apparently conflicting empirical results.

The Fishbein and Ajzen (1975) framework is generally considered a major influence in supporting the notion that attitudes do cause behaviors. A good deal of current work attempts to specify when this relationship holds. However, Ajzen and Fishbein's work is usually positioned as primarily methodological in nature (e.g., Cooper & Croyle, 1984) and criticized for oversimplifying the complex roles of other variables (cf. Fazio & Zanna, 1981). For example, Abelson (1982) believes that the focus on measurement issues does not lead to an understanding of the dynamics of attitude and behavior. While these criticisms are valid given the objectives of those making them, they fail to recognize the model's potential for expansion to encompass and organize their viewpoints. Fishbein, on the other hand, does not seem to want to accommodate the other approaches. The real problem, of course, is that researchers are not reinforced for integrating different approaches.

The relationships shown in Figure 2.3 are widely accepted (Fishbein & Ajzen, 1975; Ajzen & Fishbein, 1980; Ryan & Bonfield, 1975; Farley et al., 1981). Thus, this portion of the model which is incorporated in Figure 2.5 may serve as a platform from which to begin integration and elaboration. In addition, cognitive structure is represented as a set of beliefs and evaluations that are assumed to combine in a linear multiplicative fashion. This representation may also serve as a starting point. Consumer researchers routinely test for cognitive structure dimensionality (e.g., Ryan, 1982; Shimp & Kavas, 1974). Lutz (1975) has found the components to be interrelated, and Bagozzi (1984) has suggested a number of alternative ways in which these cognitions may be organized. Thus, the Fishbein and Ajzen (1975) model has heuristic potential in that it can serve as a springboard for testing the various roles proposed for Affect in explaining Purchase Intentions.

The acceptance of cognitively driven models may be due to their familiarity to the well-known advertising effect models (cf. Robertson, 1971; Lavidge & Steiner, 1961). It is interesting to note, however, that the advertising industry, which routinely tests responses, has largely abandoned cognitive approaches to influence in favor of emotionally based appeals because they believe most consumer products are low involving (Resnik & Stern, 1977; Tom, Calvert, Goolkatsian, & Zumsteg, 1984). In reviewing this area, Lastovicka (1979) states that exposure increases familiarity which increases preferences for such products. This view parallels Zajonc's thinking and is consistent with Chaiken's (1980) finding that in high-consequence conditions, that is, conditions likely to be involving, attitudes were determined primarily by issue-relevant arguments whereas they were determined primarily by source likeability in the low-consequence condition. Perhaps academic researchers would do well to shift some effort toward developing emotionally driven models. The rich tradition of Affect research, the framework provided by the well-known multi-attribute model, and the scheme suggested here for organizing them and recognizing their relationships provides a basis for doing so.

The new physics has provided three ideas crucial to the model development presented above. First, consideration of the answer "yes" to the question of whether affect precedes or follows cognition is precluded by the "either or" way of viewing the world. By doing away with this view, new physics allows us to be more open to more alternatives. Second, new physics has shown that elements only exist in interaction with other parts of the system. This idea led to the view that the three systems in which affect has been viewed do not make much sense unless they are integrated. Third, new physics recognizes that elements act as though they have direction and purpose, that the interaction in the system is not one way or necessary toward the element under observation. This notion leads to an active consumer rather than to the traditional "passive receptor" view. This point, which has not so far been well developed in this essay, is related to the issue of observer-observed continuum, an issue that has not yet been incorporated into the affect model. Consequently, my attention now turns to both issues.

It has been suggested that the scientist wondering what to do with the green slime he has concocted might do well to wonder if the green slime faces the same dilemma. This situation does not appear as unlikely when the object of inquiry is the consumer to whom we would, of course, attribute consciousness. The answer, then, is that the consumer is as much an observer as the scientist, an observer with cognitive aims that impact the situation and the objective. In short, the consumer creates reality from the situation and object and becomes a participant in the same manner that the observer becomes a participant.

Whereas the consumer is captured in Figure 2.5 as Actor, the model does not account for the observer-observed continuum as it relates to the scientist. Laudan (1984) notes that the very idea of methodology emanates from the aims and goals of the researcher. I argued earlier that methods, as shown in the new physics, may inadvertently dictate results. This does happen in consumer research. For example, Belk (1974) used a within-person experimental design to show that when the same person is presented with different situations and other things are constant, situations do account for considerable variance. Using a between-subject design, Lutz and Kakkar (1975) explained considerably less variance. In a similar view, Fishbein model researchers have seldom dealt with the effects of similar-appearing items designed to tap different constructs that are spatially proximate in the questionnaire. Yet, this likely source of method variance, if present, would guarantee high correlations. My earlier arguments were that the consumer researchers' cognitive aims of acting as traditional scientists and solving practical problems has led to an undue emphasis on empirical methods. The observer-participant issues, however, goes beyond choice of method for it not only may dictate the method but also the conceptual viewpoint. My attention now turns to incorporating both of these issues into the affect model.

Figure 2.6 shows templates that represent different observer orientations toward the same system. A researcher interested in business management may focus on situation and object as they are, in view of their transiency, apt to be more manipulatable than the enduring characteristics of the actor thereby becoming the most efficient means to effect intention and behavior. A researcher preoccupied with consumer welfare may focus on the actor's impact on the system and may even consider affect rather than intention and behavior as the key outcome variable. Each of these views constitute different cognitive aims that would redirect the conceptual view as well as influence the methodology. Thus, for example, Cohen, Fishbein, and Ahtola (1972) point out that tests of multi-attribute models have not been faithful to social-psychological theory and Bass (1972) argues that the theory does not answer key managerial questions.

Tucker (1974) has stated that marketing researchers view consumers as a fisherman views fish rather than as a marine biologist views them. This statement, if taken in a pejorative sense, represents either/or thinking. Since both fishermen and marine biologists play a useful role in society, it seems both views have merit. They merely serve different cognitive aims. In drawing the analogy of fisherman to marketing and marine biologist to consumer science, it seems there is room for both views. Certainly both disciplines, marketing and consumer science, have contributed to society.

If one accepts the notion of "rudimentary system" underlying the affect model, then it is obvious the different cognitive aims will lead to the omission of elements deemed essential by others. Yet, consumer and affect are both vague concepts that are given meaning only by the system constructed by the theorist. To say that a true affect system exists to be discovered is to commit the sin of reification. When meanings from different systems are complimentary, their merger will lead to richer and more complete theories. To recognize such opportunities we must, as Bristor (1985) points out, first make implicit differences in cognitive aims explicit. Ryan and Holbrook (1982), for example, attempted to address the concerns of both management and social psychology theorists in sorting out some of the multi-attribute issues.

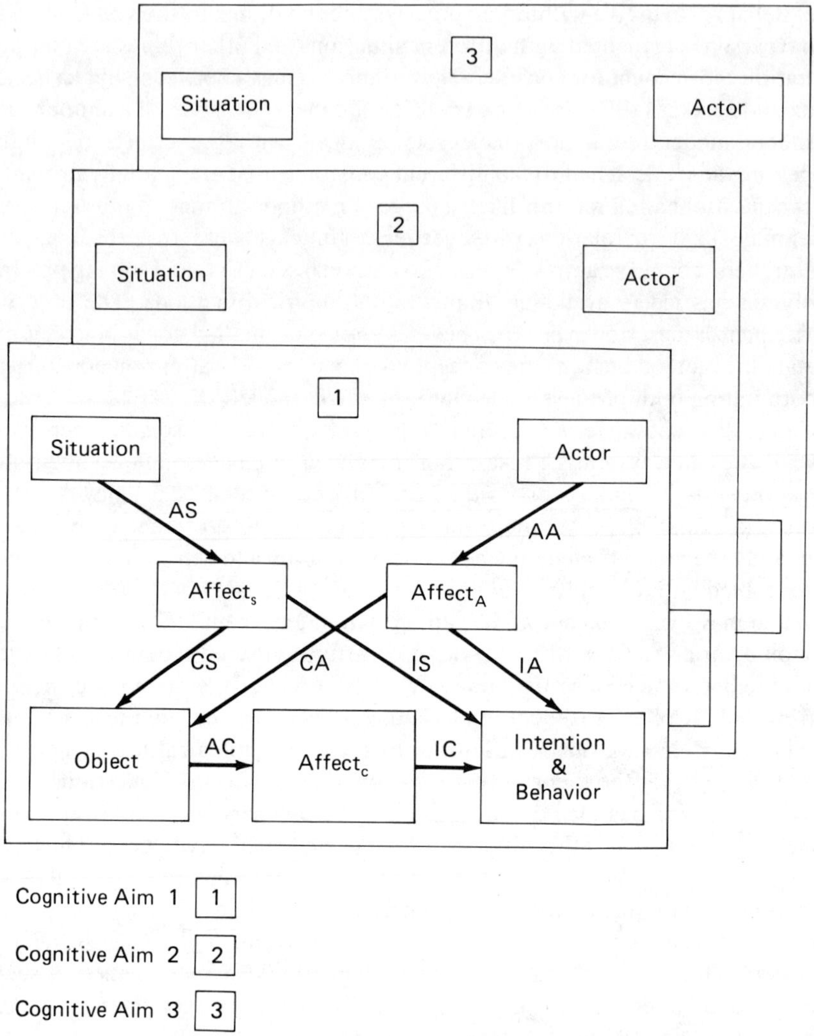

FIGURE 2.6. View of affect according to cognitive aims of the researcher.

Conclusion

I have argued that we are becoming compartmentalized and that this hinders theoretical development. If we resist this trend, however, and emphasize our interdisciplinary heritage, we have the potential for making important contributions to the basic behavioral disciplines. The newer epistemologies recognize that breakthroughs come from questioning and merging paradigms that may not be as incommensurate as they seem at first sight. For example, Watson and Crick combined chemistry and biology to discover the structure of DNA, one of the major accomplishments of our century. In carrying out interdisciplinary research, Watson and Crick actually defied their mentors. In contrast, the disciplines formally represented in buyer behavior, anthropology, communications, economics, home economics, marketing, management science, psychology, social psychology, public opinion research, sociology, and statistics and on the *JCR* editorial board encourage interdisciplinary research. Thus, we should capitalize more on our opportunity to integrate and leave more of the important work that requires compartmentalization to the individual disciplines whose members are apt to be ostracized if they cross disciplinary boundaries.

Whereas the influence of marketing has fostered empiricism, the discipline has three characteristics that suggest its future influence may foster acceptance of the newer epistemologies. First, due to the nature of marketing, members of the discipline are sensitive to change and new developments as attested to by two books (Hunt, 1983; Zaltman, LeMasters, & Heffring, 1982) and two conference proceedings (Anderson & Ryan, 1984; Bush & Hunt, 1982) devoted to philosophical issues. Second, marketing has and continues to be open to borrowings from every discipline imaginable—even astronomy. Thus, its members are open to new ideas. Third, a cornerstone of marketing-management thinking is the marketing concept that is based on the presupposition that the consumer creates his or her own reality. To hold this view one must accept the notion of observer-observed interdependence. If you are still having trouble accepting this idea please read Malhotra's (1984) reinterpretation of Jacoby's (1984) reinterpretation of Malhotra's reinterpretation of Jacoby's interpretation of his (Jacoby's) original data. This example provides striking evidence that data only speaks through the differing perceptions of the observer. At any rate, the traditional impact of marketing may change in nature.

Whether the reader agrees or not with the conceptual system or the substantive issues involved in the preceding Affect exposition is not the main issue. What is important is the recognition that empirical deadlocks can be broken by placing concepts within a system and analyzing their meaning as they relate to other concepts. The recognition that concepts have systemic meaning is compatible with the neo-positivitistic approaches, which are based on physical science methods, that predominate most modern behavioral science disciplines.

There have been debates from time to time as to whether the subject of human behavior can be adequately addressed using methods developed in the physical sciences to examine "inert" matter. Recent discoveries in physics and the resulting blurred distinctions in the two types of subject matter render these debates obsolete. We should take our epistemological cues directly from physics, including the "new physics," and not wait for mainstream psychology and social psychology to change their practices before we do. Whereas the adoption of some of the newer epistemologies may radically change the way we conduct research, the example in this paper suggests that this need not be so. It is certainly possible to deduce schemes amenable to laboratory experimentation from the Affect conceptualization presented above. The level of integration was also not radical as the three approaches that were combined are all well within the domain of cognitive social psychology. In fact, the notion of integrating person and situation approaches has been applied to market segmentation by Dickson (1982). Lutz and Kakkar (1975) have also suggested that situational differences will become much more meaningful if combined with individual differences although neither holds much promise when considered separately. My point is that we can avoid empirical confusion by not losing sight of the conceptual system from which phenomena sprang. In this regard it may be necessary, as Manicas and Secord (1983) suggest, to explicitly state which parts of the rudimentary conceptual system have been excluded due to methodological limitations or the cognitive aims of the researcher. A more integrated systemic approach may help us shift away from what Olson (1981) calls the "small" problems toward the "large" problems. A focus on problems would lead to more theories about consumer behavior per se, of which we have too few, compared to the numerous theories from other disciplines that have been tested in a consumer context. At the least, the adoption of the new methodologies will lead to richer concepts and theories, a goal that most of us share.

Acknowledgments. The author is indebted to David Brinberg, Julia Bristor, Alice Isen, Richard Lutz, Paul Peter, and Gerald Zaltman for their insightful comments on an earlier draft. This research was funded by a faculty summer grant from the School of Business Administration, University of Michigan.

References

Abelson, R. P. (1981). The psychological status of the script concept. *American Psychologist, 2*, 715–729.

Abelson, R. P. (1982). Three modes of attitude-behavior consistency. In M. P. Zanna, E. T. Higgins, & C. P. Hermann (Eds.), *Consistency in Social Behavior: The Ontario Symposium: Vol. 2*. Hillsdale, NJ: Erlbaum.

Allport, G. W. (1935). Attitudes. In C. Murchinson (Ed.), *Handbook of Social Psychology*. Worcester, MA: Clark University Press.

Ajzen, I. & Fishbein, M. (1977). Attitude-behavior relations: A theoretical analysis and review of empirical research. *Psychological Bulletin, 84*, 888–918.

Ajzen, I. & Fishbein, M. (1980). *Understanding attitudes and predicting social behavior*. Englewood Cliffs, NJ: Prentice-Hall.

Anderson, N. H. & Hubert, S. (1963). Effects of concomitant verbal recall on order effects in personality impression formation. *Journal of Verbal Learning and Verbal Behavior, 2*, 379–391.

Anderson, P. F. (1983). Marketing, scientific progress, and scientific method. *Journal of Marketing, 47*, 18–31.

Anderson, P. F. & Ryan, M. J. (Eds.) (1984). *Scientific method in marketing: Winter educator's conference*. Chicago: American Marketing Association.

Bagozzi, R. P. (1980). *Causal models in marketing*. New York: Wiley.

Bagozzi, R. P. (in press). Expectancy-value attitude models: An analysis of critical theoretical issues. *International Journal of Research in Marketing*.

Bagozzi, R. P. & VanLoo, M. F. (1978). Fertility as consumption: Theories from the behavioral sciences. *Journal of Consumer Research, 4*, 199–228.

Banks, S. & Hart, E. W. (1977). Advertising and promotional methods. In R. Ferber (Ed.), *Selected aspects of consumer behavior.* Washington, DC: U.S. Government Printing Office.

Bartels, R. (1976). *The history of marketing thought.* Columbus: Grid.

Bass, F. M. (1972). Fishbein and brand preference: A reply. *Journal of Marketing Research, 9,* 461.

Bass, F. (1974). The theory of stochastic preference and brand switching. *Journal of Marketing Research, 11,* 1–20.

Beckwith, N. E. & Lehmann, D. R. (1973). The importance of halo effects in multi-attribute models. *Journal of Marketing Research, 10,* 141–145.

Belk, R. W. (1984) Against thinking. In P. F. Anderson & M. J. Ryan (Eds.), *Scientific method in marketing.* Chicago: American Marketing Association.

Belk, R. W. (1974). An exploratory assessment of situational effects in buyer behavior. *Journal of Marketing Research, 11,* 13–15.

Belk, R. (1975). Situational variables and consumer behavior. *Journal of Consumer Research, 2,* 157–14.

Bristor, J. M. (1985). Consumer behavior from a contemporary philosophy of science perspective: An organizational framework. *Advances in consumer research: Vol. 12.* Provo, UT: The Association of Consumer Research.

Bush, R. F. & Hunt, S. D. (Eds.) (1982). *Marketing theory: Philosophy of science perspectives.* Chicago: American Marketing Association.

Calder, B. J., Phillips, L. W., & Tybout, A. M. (1982a). Designing research for application. *Journal of Consumer Research, 8,* 197–207.

Calder, B. J., Phillips, L. W., Tybout, A. M. (1982b). The concept of external validity. *Journal of Consumer Research, 9,* 240–244.

Calder, B. J., Phillips, L. W., & Tybout, A. M. (1983). Beyond external validity. *Journal of Consumer Research, 10,* 112–114.

Capra, F. (1976). *The tao of physics.* New York: Bantam.

Capra, F. (1982). *The turning point: Science, society and the rising culture.* New York: Simon and Schuster.

Chaiken, S. (1980). Heuristic versus systematic information processing and the use of source versus message cues in persuasion. *Journal of Personality and Social Psychology, 39,* 752–766.

Cohen, J. B., Fishbein, M., & Ahtola, O. T. (1972). The nature and uses of expectancy—value models in consumer attitude research. *Journal of Marketing Research, 9,* 456–460.

Cooper, J. & Croyle, R. T. (1984). Attitudes and attitude change. *Annual Review of Psychology, 35,* 395–442.

Dickson, P. R. (1982). Person-situation: Segmentation's missing link. *Journal of Marketing, 46* (4), 56–64.

Farley, J. U., Lehmann, D. R.; & Ryan, M. J. (1981). Generalizing from 'imperfect' replication. *Journal of Business, 54,* 597–610.

Fazio, R. H., Powell, M. C., & Herr, P. M. (1983). Toward a process model of the attitude-behavior relation: Accessing one's attitude upon mere observation of the attitude object. *Journal of Personality and Social-Psychology, 44,* 724–435.

Fazio, R. H. & Zanna, M. P. (1981). Direct experience and attitude-behavior consistency. *Advances in Experimental Social Psychology, 14,* 11–20.

Ferber, R. (1979). How not to write a prize-winning article. *Journal of Consumer Research, 5,* 302–305.

Fishbein, M. (1963) An investigation of the relationships between beliefs about an object and the attitude toward that object. *Human Relations*, *1*, 233–234.

Fishbein, M. & Raven, B. H. (1962). The ab scales: An operational definition of belief and attitude. *Human Relations*, *15*, 35–44.

Fishbein, M. & Ajzen, I. (1975). *Belief, attitude, intention, and behavior: An introduction to theory and research*. Reading, MA: Addison-Wesley.

Fornell, C. (1983). Issues in the application of covariance structure analysis: A comment. *Journal of Consumer Research*, *9*, 443–448.

Friedman, J. L., Sears, D. O., & Carlsmith, J. M. (1981). *Social psychology.* Englewood Cliffs, NJ: Prentice-Hall.

Gergen, K. V. (1981). The social constructionist movement is modern psychology. *American Psychologist*, *40*, 266–275.

Hansen, F. (1981). Hemispherical lateralization: Implications for understanding consumer behavior. *Journal of Consumer Research*, *8*, 23–36.

Heather, N. (1976). *Radical perspectives in psychology.* London: Muthen.

Hempel, C. G. (1958). The theoretician's dilemma. A study in the logic of theory construction. In *Minnesota Studies in the Philosophy of Science: Vol. 2*. Minneapolis: University of Minnesota Press.

Hess, E. H. (1972). Pupillometrics: A method of studying mental emotional, and sensory processes. In N. S. Greenfield & R. A. Sternback (Eds.), *Handbook of psychophysiology.* New York: Holt, Rinehart, and Winston.

Howard, G. S. (1985, March). The role of values in the science of psychology. *American Psychologist*, 255–265.

Howard, J. A. (1977). *Consumer behavior: An application of theory.* New York: McGraw-Hill.

Howard, J. A. & Sheth, J. N. (1969). *The theory of buyer behavior.* New York: Wiley.

Howard, J. A. & Hulbert, J. M. (1973). *Advertising and the public interest*. Chicago: Crain Communications.

Hunt, S. D. (1983). *Marketing theory.* Homewood, IL: Irwin.

Iran-Nejad, A. & Ortony, A. (1984). A biofunctional model of distributed mental content, mental structures, awareness, and attention. *The Journal of Mind and Behavior, 5*, 171–210.

Isen, A. M. (1984). The influence of positive affect on decision making and cognitive organization. In T. C. Kinnear (Ed.), *Advances in Consumer Research: Vol. 11*. Provo, UT: Association for Consumer Research.

Isen, A. M. & Hastorf, A. H. (1982). Some perspectives on cognitive social psychology. In A. H. Hastorf & A. M. Isen (Eds.), *Cognitive Social Psychology.* New York: Elsevier.

Jacobson, E. (1973). Electrophysiology of mental activities and introduction to the psychological process of thinking. In F. G. McGuigan & R. A. Schoonover (Eds.), *The Psychophysiology of Thinking*. New York: Academic Press.

Jacoby, J. (1978). Consumer research: A state of the art review. *Journal of Marketing*, *42*, 87–96.

Jacoby, J. (1984). Perspectives on information overload. *Journal of Consumer Research*, *10*, 432–435.

Kaplan, A. (1964). *The conduct of inquiry.* San Francisco: Chandler.

Koch, S. (1959). *Psychology: A study of a science: Vol. 3.* New York: McGraw-Hill.

Kollat, D. T., Engel, J. R., & Blackwell, R. D. (1970). Current problems in consumer behavior research. *Journal of Marketing Research*, *7*, 327–332.

Krech, D., Crutchfield, R. S., & Ballachey, E. L. (1962). *Individual and society: A textbook of social psychology.* New York: McGraw-Hill.

Kroeber-Riel, W. (1979). Activation research: Psychobiological approaches in consumer research. *Journal of Consumer Research*, *5*, 240–250.

Kroeber-Riel, W. (1980). Rejoinder. *Journal of Consumer Research*, *7*, 96–98.

Langston, A. L. (1984). *Ten year summaries and index of the journal of consumer research*. Los Angeles: Association for Consumer Research.

Lastovicka, J. L. (1979). Are attitude models appropriate for mass t.v. advertising. In J. Eighnery (Ed.), *Attitude research under the sun*. Chicago: American Marketing Association.

Laudan, L. (1977). *Progress and its problems*. Berkeley: University of California Press.

Laudan, L. (1984). Reconstructing methodology. In P. F. Anderson & M. J. Ryan (Eds.), *Scientific method in marketing*. Chicago: American Marketing Association.

Lavidge, R. & Steiner, G. A. (1961). A model for predictive measurements of advertising effectiveness. *Journal of Marketing*, *25*, 59–62.

Lingle, J. H. & Ostrom, T. M. (1981). Principles of memory and cognition in attitude formation. In R. E. Petty, T. M. Ostrom, & T. C. Brock (Eds.), *Cognitive Responses in Persuasion*. Hillsdale, NJ: Erlbaum.

Lutz, R. J. (1975). First-order and second-order cognitive effects in attitude change. *Communication Research*, *2*, 289–299.

Lutz, R. J. & Kakkar, P. (1975). The psychological situation as a determinant of consumer behavior. In *Advances in Consumer Research: Vol. 2*. Chicago: The Association for Consumer Research.

Lynch, Jr., J. G. (1982). On the external validity of experiments in consumer research. *Journal of Consumer Research*, *10*, 436–440.

Lynch, Jr., J. G. (1983). The role of external validity in theroretical research. *Journal of Consumer Research*, *10*, 109–111.

Malhotra, N. K. (1984). Reflections on the information overload paradigm in consumer decision making. *Journal of Consumer Research*, *10*, 436–440.

Manicas, P. T. & Secord, P. F. (1983, April). Implications for psychology of the new philosophy of science. *American Psychologist*, 399–413.

Marx, M. H. & Hillix, W. A. (1972). *Systems and theories in psychology* (2nd ed.). New York: McGraw-Hill.

McGrath, J. E. & Brinberg, D. (1983). External validity and the research process: A comment on the Calder/Lynch dialogue. *Journal of Consumer Research*, *10*, 115–124.

Murphy, G. & Kovach, J. K. (1972). *Historical introduction to modern psychology* (3rd ed.). New York: Harcourt, Brace, Jovanovich.

Morrison, D. (1966). Testing brand switching models. *Journal of Marketing Research*, *3*, 289–291.

Neisser, U. (1976). *Cognition and reality.* San Francisco: W. H. Freeman.

Nord, W. R. & Peter, J. P. (1980). A behavior modification perspective on marketing. *Journal of Marketing*, *44* (2), 36–47.

Nunnally, J. C. (1967). *Psychometric theory.* New York: McGraw-Hill.

Olson, J. C. (1981). Towards a science of consumer behavior. In A. Mitchell (Ed.), *Advances in consumer research: Vol. 9.* Ann Arbor: The Association for Consumer Research.

O'Shaughnessy, J. & Ryan, M. J. (1979). Marketing, science, and technology. In O. C. Ferrell, S. W. Brown, & C. W. Lamb, Jr. (Eds.), *Conceptual and Theoretical Developments in Marketing*. Chicago: American Marketing Association.

Osgood, C. E., Suci, G. J., & Tannenbaum, P. H. (1957). *The measurement of meaning*. Champaign-Urbana: University of Illinois.

Passmore, J. (1961). *Philosophical reasoning*. New York: Basic Books.

Peter, J. P. & Olson, J. C. (1983). Is science marketing? *Journal of Marketing*, *47*, 111–125.

Petty, R. E., Ostrom, T. M., & Brock, T. C. (1981). Historical foundations of the cognitive response approach to attitudes and persuasion. In R. E. Petty, T. M. Ostrom, & T. C. Brock (Eds.), *Cognitive Responses in Persuasion*. Hillsdale, NJ: Erlbaum.

Popper, K. R. (1968). *The logic of scientific discovery*. London: Hutchinson.

Ratchford, B. T. (1975). The new economic theory of consumer behavior: An interpretive essay. *Journal of Consumer Research*, *2*, 65–75.

Resnick, A. & Stern, B. L. (1977). An analysis of information content in television advertising. *Journal of Marketing*, *41*, 50–53.

Robertson, T. S. (1971). *Innovative behavior and communication*. New York: Holt, Rinehart, and Winston.

Rosenberg, M. J. (1956). Cognitive structure and attitudinal effect. *Journal of Abnormal and Social Psychology*, *53*, 37–372.

Ryan, M. J. (1980). Psychobiology and consumer research: A problem of construct validity. *Journal of Consumer Research*, *9*, 92–96.

Ryan, M. J. (1982). Behavioral intention formation: The interdependency of attitudinal and social influence variables. *Journal of Consumer Research*, *9*, 263–277.

Ryan, M. J. & Bonfield, E. H. (1975). The Fishbein extended model and consumer behavior. *Journal of Consumer Research*, *1*, 118–13.

Ryan, M. J. & Holbrook, M. B. (1982). Importance, elicitation order, and expectancy x value. *Journal of Business Research*, *10* (3), 309–317.

Ryan, M. J. & Holbrook, M. B. (1985). *The impact of decision stress on information use and self-evaluations*. Unpublished paper, Graduate School of Business Administration, University of Michigan.

Schnee, R. (1985). External affairs. *The Communicator*, *20* (1).

Sheth, J. N. (1967). A review of buyer behavior. *Management Science*, *13*, B718–B756.

Shimp, T. A., & Kavas, A. (1984). The theory of reasoned action applied to coupon usage. *Journal of Consumer Research*, *11*, 75–809.

Sirgy, M. J. (1982). Self-concept in consumer behavior: A critical review. *Journal of Consumer Research*, *9*, 287–300.

Smead, R. J., Wilcox, J. B., & Wilkes, R. E. (1981). How valid are product descriptions and protocols in choice experiments? *Journal of Consumer Research*, *8*, 37–42.

Suppe, F. (1977). *The structure of scientific theories, Sev. Edition*. Urbana, IL: University of Illinois Press.

Sweeney, D. J. (1972). Marketing: Management technology or social process? *Journal of Marketing*, *36* (4), 3–10.

Talbot, M. (1980). *Mysticism and the new physics*. New York: Bantam.

Thatcher, R. W. & John, E. R. (1977). *Foundations of cognitive processes*. Hillsdale, NJ: Lawrence Erlbaum.

Tom, G., Calvert, S., Goolkatsian, R., & Zumsteg, A. (1984). An analysis of information content in television advertising: An update. *Current Issues and Research in Advertising*, *1*, 159.

Torgerson, W. S. (1958). *Theory and methods of scaling*. New York: Wiley.

Tucker, W. T. (1974). Future directions in marketing theory. *Journal of Marketing*, *38* (2), 30–35.

Van Raaij, W. F. (1984). *Affective and cognitive reactions to advertising* (Report No. 84–111). Cambridge, MA: Marketing Science Institute.

Watson, P. J. & Gatchel, R. J. (1979). Autonomic measures of advertising. *Journal of Advertising Research*, *19*, 15–26.

Webster, Jr., F. E. & Wind, Y. (1972). *Organizational buying behavior.* Englewood Cliffs, NJ: Prentice-Hall.

Wright, P. (1975). Consumer choice strategies: Simplifying vs. optimizing. *Journal of Marketing Research*, *12*, 0–7.

Yalch, R. F. (1980, September). *Improving behavior predictions using nonattitudinal predictions: Effects of alternative behavioral measures and moderators*. Paper presented at the 88th Annual Convention of the American Psychological Association, Montreal, Canada.

Zajonc, R. B. (1980). Feeling and thinking: Preferences need no inferences. *American Psychologist*, *35*, 151–175.

Zajonc, R. B. & Markus, H. (1982). Affective and cognitive factors in preferences. *Journal of Consumer Research*, *9*, 123–131.

Zaltman, G., Pinson, C. R. A., & Angelmar, R. (1973). *Metatheory and consumer research*. New York: Holt, Rinehart, and Winston.

Zaltman, G., LeMasters, K., & Heffring, M. (1982). *Theory construction in marketing*. New York: Wiley.

Zukav, G. (1979). *The dancing Wu Li masters*. New York: William Morrow.

Part II Analytic Strategies

3
An Idiothetic Analysis of Behavioral Decision Making

James Jaccard and Gregory Wood

The need to develop methods for studying individuals has been evident for nearly fifty years. The vast majority of research in the social sciences has focused on aggregate level analyses, in which inferences are drawn about groups of individuals, considered as a whole. As Allport (1937) noted, the understanding of behavior at the aggregate level does not necessarily yield understanding of behavior at the individual (idiographic) level. When nomothetic (aggregate-based) principles are applied to individuals, there frequently exists considerable error. Because of such limitations, Allport suggested the creation of methodologies that would allow the social scientist to study the behavior of *individuals*.

Allport's call for the development of idiographic methods was greeted with skepticism. At the time, logical positivism and behaviorism were the dominant paradigms within the social sciences, and both approaches viewed the primary aim of science as the development of universal laws. Because of this, many critics felt that idiographic explanations of behavior were outside the realm of science. This skepticism was fueled by Allport's linking of idiographic approaches to disciplines such as history and literature, with the suggestion that methods for collecting data in these domains (e.g., analysis of letters, subjective biographical reports) be used in developing an idiographic science of human behavior. Allport's approach was criticized because of (a) the inability of the researcher to develop generalizable results, (b) difficulties with using single-subject experimental designs, and (c) a lack of adequate methods for conducting idiographic research (for a review of these criticisms, see Runyan, 1983). Despite these criticisms, Allport's motivation for suggesting new methodologies remained: Explanations of behavior based on aggregate or nomothetic methods of analysis fell short of explaining why a given individual performed behavior X in response to stimulus Y in context Z.

Since 1937, the terms "idiographic" and "nomothetic" have taken on a wide variety of meanings in the scientific literature. This proved so confusing that in 1962, Allport clarified his goals for the study of individual behavior in personality and labeled methodologies developed toward this end as "morphogenic." However, this new methodological description did not receive wide acceptance, and the terms "idiographic" and "nomothetic" are still used in a multitude of

TABLE 3.1. Characterizations of idiographic psychology.

Investigator	Definition
Allport (1937)	The identification of individualized traits and attitudes
Baldwin (1942)	
Broverman (1962)	The ipsative ordering of responses within the individual
Alfert (1967)	
Allport (1961)	The patterning or organization of variables within the single case
Cattell (1966)	
Holt (1962)	A branch of science that denies the existence of general laws and rejects automistic approaches to the study of human behavior
Chassen (1967)	The correlation of variables within the single case
Shapiro (1966)	
Bem and Allen (1974)	The identification of attitudes in the individual which do not exhibit cross-dimension consistency
Bromely (1977)	The causal relations of variables within the single case

ways in the current literature. Table 3.1 contains a list of some of the definitions of idiographic research. Clearly, the term "idiographic" invites controversy because of the multiple meanings attached to it. In the present chapter, we will follow the suggestion of Lamiell (1981) and label the methodologies discussed in this chapter as idiothetic, a blending of the terms "idiographic" and "nomothetic." In the spirit of Allport, we recognize that idiothetic methods should help us to understand and to predict the behavior of individuals. The researcher should be capable of demonstrating the reliability and validity of findings derived from these methods. Further, these methods should not rely on group norms or other nomothetic information in their analysis of the individual. We do not deny (or minimize) the important contribution of nomothetic procedures to the social sciences and the analysis of consumer behavior. Ideally, information collected and analyzed at the individual level should be capable of later analysis at the nomothetic (aggregate) level. In the sections that follow, we will discuss some of the limitations of nomothetic procedures in constructing theories about the individual consumer. We will then outline an idiothetic approach to consumer decision making which we have found to be useful in numerous applied settings.

Limitations of Nomothetic Treatment of Data

Consider the following experimental design in a study of consumer attitudes: A researcher is interested in whether social class is related to attitudes toward a given product and whether this attitude is differentially influenced by perceptions of the cost of the product in upper-class as opposed to lower-class individuals. The researcher begins by developing a set of questions that will measure attitudes toward the product in two groups, one consisting of upper-class individuals and the other consisting of lower-class individuals. He/she does this by consulting Osgood's tables of adjective descriptors (Osgood, Suci, & Tannenbaum, 1957) that load on an evaluative factor via the semantic-differential technique (e.g., good-bad, beautiful-ugly, clean-dirty, tasteful-distasteful). Each individual rates the product on the scales, and an overall attitude score is derived by summing the responses across items. In addition, the product is rated on an inexpensive-expensive dimension. The mean attitude scores are contrasted in the two groups by means of a t test, and a statistically significant difference is observed, with lower-class individuals revealing a higher (more positive) mean score. A correlation between the attitude score and the inexpensive-expensive rating is calculated for each group, separately. For lower-class individuals, there is a moderate negative correlation between the two variables, whereas for upper-class individuals, there is a moderate positive correlation between the variables. The difference in correlations is tested by means of the appropriate statistical test, and is found to be statistically significant. The investigator concludes that social class is related to attitudes toward the product, such that lower-class individuals evaluate the product more positively than upper-class individuals. In addition, the researcher concludes that the data support the proposition that perceptions of expense affect the attitudes differentially in the two groups. Upper-class individuals' attitudes are favorably influenced by cost, whereas lower-class individuals' attitudes are unfavorably influenced by cost.

Comparison of Mean Scores. A number of assumptions are required to compare mean scores to assess the relationship between social class and attitudes. First, one must assume that the rating scales are valid for both groups of individuals. To the extent that validity coefficients are low in magnitude in either group, the conclusions are called into question. Assuming valid measures (in a traditional psychometric sense), a second issue arises in the comparison of the mean scores. When an individual is asked to make a judgment about an object on a dimension, he/she must first make the judgment cognitively and then translate that judgment onto the rating scale provided by the investigator. Two individuals might make the same cognitive judgment, but differ in their observed ratings, if they translate that judgment differently onto the rating scale. At issue is whether group differences reflect differences in the true underlying attitude or whether they reflect differences in the way individuals in the groups use and experience the rating scale. Research in psychophysics (e.g., Wegner, 1982; Upshaw, 1962) suggests that the problem of response translation may be more serious than applied researchers realize.

How might an individual translate a judgment onto a numerical rating scale? One strategy suggested by psychophysicists is that the individual will position the center of the scale to correspond to the average subjective value of the stimuli he/she expects to judge. In this case, individuals who expect to evaluate stimuli with generally high values will make lower ratings than individuals who expect to rate stimuli with generally low values on the dimension in question. A second strategy, suggested by Parducci (1965), is that the individual will position the scale so that the two most extreme categories correspond to the most extreme values he/she would assign to stimuli of the type being studied. Having done this, the individual equates the intermediate categories with a range of judgments between these extremes. Parducci discusses several situations in which this strategy would produce different ratings for two individuals, even though their cognitive judgment is the same. In fact, Parducci has used such an interpretation as an alternative explanation for several "established" psychological phenomena. Although other plausible strategies could be elaborated, the point is that observed mean differences may reflect systematic differences in the response translation process. The assumption that all individuals use the rating scales in the same fashion, with similar experiences in mind, is required (or one must assume that the differences cancel or are irrelevant to the question at hand.)[1]

In the above example, suppose the product being rated was a certain type of appliance. One might reasonably assume that upper-class individuals have had experiences with, on the average, better appliances than lower-class individuals. If individuals use the first strategy identified above for response translation, then one would predict a lower mean attitude score for upper-class individuals as opposed to lower-class individuals. This was, in fact, observed.

Analysis of Correlations. The same issues discussed above apply with equal vigor to the analysis of correlations. First, one must assume that the scales are equally valid indicators within groups. Otherwise, differences in observed correlations may be an artifact of differential validity. Second, one must assume that all individuals within a group (but not necessarily between groups) use the response scale in the same fashion and with the same experiences as a referent. For example, consider the negative correlation between attitudes and perceived expense for the lower-class individuals. Suppose individuals with more positive attitudes have tended to encounter more expensive appliances in their experiences. If all individuals within this group adopt the first response translation strategy mentioned above, then individuals with more positive attitudes would tend to rate the appliance as being less expensive than individuals with more negative attitudes (even though true differences in expense judgments might be minimal). This would yield the observed negative correlation where possibly none exists (see Figure 3.1).

These examples illustrate a frequently neglected requirement of nomothetic analyses in consumer research, namely, the assumption of a common-response language across individuals. Violations of the assumption can affect either mean scores or correlations. The issue is particularly germane to consumer research that uses rating scales.

Inferences About Individuals. If the measurement assumptions noted above are met, then the theorist may still be restricted to aggregate-level conclusions. To illustrate the problem in the case of correlation coefficients, consider the above

[1]Even if individual differences in the use of rating scales cancel so as not to affect the mean, the within group standard deviations will be inflated, thereby reducing the power of statistical tests.

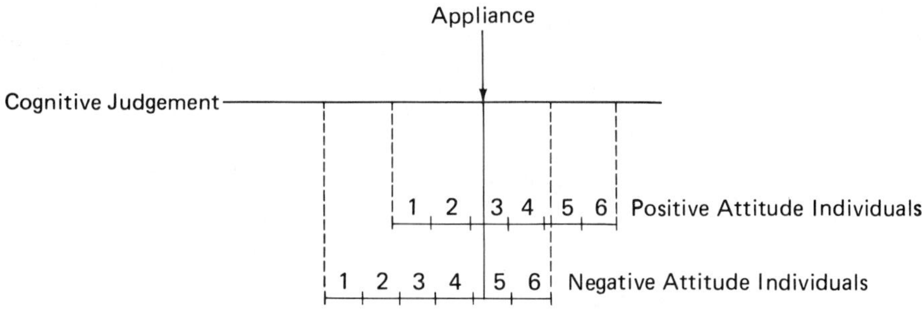

FIGURE 3.1. Dotted lines form endpoints of scale to judgment dimension and reflect the range of experience the individuals have had. The arrow represents actual cognitive judgement made (note: it is the same for both groups). Solid line downward indicates category that judgement would be translated into.

study, but assume that the observed correlations within social-class groups are not artifacts of response language. Suppose, also, that the investigator did not measure social class. For all individuals considered together, the correlation between perceived expense and attitude would probably be near zero (assuming common mean centroids), since the investigator has mixed two groups, one exhibiting a positive correlation and the other a negative correlation. The implication would be that a change in perceived expense would not result in a change in attitude. On an aggregate level, this would be true. Shifting perceived expense downward would cause the lower-class individuals to revise their attitude upward and the upper-class individuals to revise their attitude downward. The net change in attitude would be minimal. But at the individual level, considerable change would occur, contrary to what one might infer from the correlation coefficient. In this instance, the correlation coefficient would only have been descriptive of individuals if all individuals "weighted" expense in the same way (sign and magnitude) in forming an attitude toward the product. This phenomenon (a version of the classic Simpson's paradox) has obvious implications for popular regression-based approaches of intention and attitude formation in the consumer literature (e.g., models such as Fishbein, Sheth).

A second example of potentially misleading aggregate analysis for correlations is illustrated using market segments in Figure 3.2. In this example, the focus is on market segments versus the total market. There are three market segments (S1, S2, and S3), each of which exhibits a strong negative correlation between variables X and Y. If a correlation is computed ignoring segments, a strong positive correlation between X and Y results. One might infer from the across-segment analysis that positive changes in X will yield positive changes in Y, when exactly the opposite would occur, as revealed by the within-segment analyses.

Inferences about individuals may also be problematic in the comparison of group means. This can be illustrated from an example in the family area.

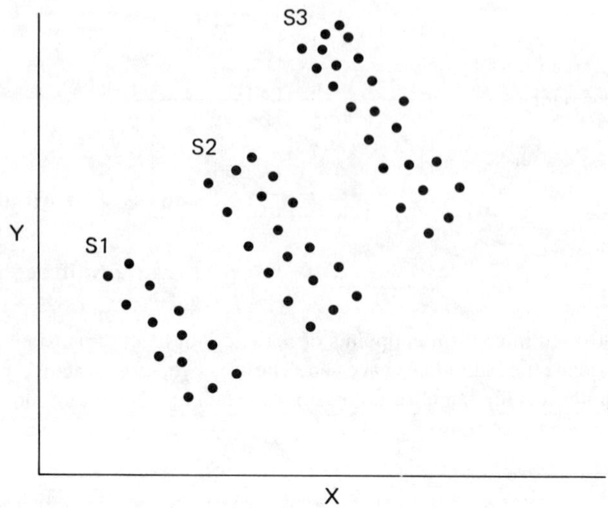

FIGURE 3.2.

Researchers have asked newlyweds the number of children they intend to have in their completed family and then contrasted the expected mean number with the mean number of children the couples actually have. The correspondence is remarkably close, indicating that at the aggregate level, little change has occurred. At the individual level, however, expectations prove to be a poor match with actual behavior. Some couples have fewer children than expected, while others have more children than expected. The "overs" cancel the "unders" and the aggregate-level means are quite similar. Simple examination of the means, in this case, does not permit accurate statements about the individual level. This process probably characterizes several marketing phenomena, such as the strong correspondence observed between actual prices of products and the average (calculated across individuals) perceived prices of those products (Louviere & Meyer, 1981).

A second example of misleading aggregation for mean scores is illustrated in Table 3.2.[2] There are four distinct segments of a market, the members of which were asked to rate each of three brands (A, B, and C) on a 10 point, "strongly dislike" (1) to "strongly like" (10) scale. Assume that each segment is homogeneous in its ratings and that individuals purchase the brand that they like the most. In this case, brand B would have a zero market share, yet if ratings are averaged across segments, brand B is the most liked. Mean score analysis would lead to the conclusion that preferences are unrelated to purchase behavior, when, in fact, a

[2]We would like to thank John Lynch for suggesting this example.

TABLE 3.2. Market segments for like-dislike ratings for three brands of a product.

	Brand		
Segment 1	10*	9	1
Segment 2	9*	7	3
Segment 3	1	7	8*
Segment 4	2	9	10*
Mean Scores	5.5	8.0	5.5

*Most preferred brand.

marketing strategy that changed preferences might have considerable impact on purchase behavior.

A final example of potentially misleading aggregate analyses focuses on proportions (again, in the form of Simpson's paradox). Consider two segments of a market in the analysis of brand switching, as illustrated in Table 3.3. For each segment considered separately, purchases at time 2 are independent of those at time 1. If the data for the segments are pooled, however, the brand switching matrix suggests a first-order process.[2] This paradox is discussed in a consumer context by Massey, Montgomery, and Morrison (1970).

In sum, inferences about individuals from group level data can encounter problems with respect to reliability, validity, response language used in interpreting scales, and within-group variability. The above comments should not be taken to imply that means, proportions, and correlations in traditional consumer studies, when calculated on the aggregate level, will always be misleading about individual cases. However, they *can* be misleading and must be interpreted carefully when making inferences about individual behavior.

An Idiothetic Approach to Behavioral Decision Making

In this section, we will describe the use of an idiothetic approach to consumer decision making. The approach can be applied to either a single individual, or to groups of individuals via some form of aggregation. The intent is to outline briefly idiothetic methods that may be well-suited to the analysis of choice behavior and which minimize the problems noted above.

Preliminary Considerations

Types of Decisions. Behavioral decisions can be classified into three types. *Impulsive* decisions are those which are determined by impulsive or emotional reactions, without reflection. *Routine* decisions concern familiar situations in which decisions are made with little reflection and in accordance with habits, customs, or moral/social rules. *Thoughtful* decisions are made after giving

TABLE 3.3. Within-segment versus across-segment analysis of brand switching.

Segment 1		Brand Choice at Time 2: Brand A	Brand B
Brand Choice at Time 1	Brand A	.64	.16
	Brand B	.16	.04

Segment 2		Brand Choice at Time 2: Brand A	Brand B
Brand Choice at Time 1	Brand A	.04	.16
	Brand B	.16	.64

Aggregate		Brand Choice at Time 2: Brand A	Brand B
Brand Choice at Time 1	Brand A	.34	.16
	Brand B	.16	.34

Note: Assume equal N in the two segments.

thought to such factors as the problem situation, the alternative courses of action available, and the probable consequences of each course of action.

When making a decision in a familiar situation, the individual typically accepts the suggestion of impulse, habit, custom or rule, without serious reflection. Most behavioral decisions in everyday life are of this character. However, when the decision is perceived as being important or when impulse, habit, or custom are questioned, then the individual will reflect on the matter, considering one or more alternative courses of action.

The present framework is concerned with thoughtful behavioral decisions, as described above. One can further distinguish between two types of decision-making modes: active and passive. Active decision making refers to those points in time when the individual is actively reflecting on the problem or situation of interest (e.g., choosing a method of birth control). Passive decision making refers to the case where the decision is governed by conclusions reached at some point in time earlier, as a result of active decision making. Of primary interest in the present framework are those factors that an individual considers when making a decision during the active decision-making state. These factors are of obvious theoretical interest when passive decision making is in effect, because passive decisions reflect conclusions drawn during active decision making.

Activities in Behavioral Decision Making. There are at least eight types of activities that an individual can engage in during active decision making. First, is problem recognition, where an individual determines that a problem state exists and that a decision must be considered. Second, is goal identification, where the individual specifies, a priori, the purpose of the decision; that is, the ideal outcome of the decision. Third, is option generation/identification, in which the individual thinks of potential alternative solutions to the problem at hand. Fourth, is information search, in which the individual seeks information, either about what additional options might be available or about properties of one or more of the options under consideration. Fifth, is the assessment of option information, in which the individual considers the information he or she has about different decision options. The term "information" is used in a general sense and refers to any consequence or concept subjectively associated with a given decision option. It is similar to the concept of "belief" in the attitude literature.

In considering the information about the options, the individual forms a preference structure. Specifically, the individual forms an attitude toward performing each option. Given p decision options, the preference structure is the set of p attitudes. Consistent with Fishbein (1972) and most contemporary attitude theories, an attitude is defined as a general feeling of favorableness or unfavorableness with respect to the attitude object (in this case, the decision option). Sixth, is the choice process, where one of the decision options is chosen for purposes of future behavioral enactment. The choice will be some function of the individual's preference structure. Seventh, is behavioral translation, where the individual translates the decision into overt behavior. Eighth and finally, is post-decision evaluation, whereby the individual reflects on the decision after the option has been enacted and evaluates the decision process in light of the outcomes that have resulted.

Not all of the above activities will necessarily be performed by the individual. Nor must they be performed in the sequence described. Each activity forms the basis of our theory of the relationship between beliefs, attitudes, behavioral decisions, and behavior. Unfortunately, space limitations do not permit consideration of each activity in this chapter. Our primary focus will be on characterizing the information that an individual possesses about a set of decision options, and how this information is integrated to form a preference structure and a choice.

Rating Scales. The methods to be described use rating scales, and some comments are in order about their format. Judgments are made on either unipolar or bipolar scales. The scales combine a numerical and verbal format. For example, the attitude toward choosing a given decision option is measured on a 21-point unfavorable-favorable scale in response to the probe "How favorable or unfavorable do you feel about choosing this ______." The numbers on the scale range from -10 to $+10$ in single-unit increments, with zero being labeled as the neutral point. The following labels appear below the numbers indicated: -9 = extremely unfavorable, -6 = quite unfavorable, -3 = slightly unfavorable, 0 = neutral, 3 = slightly favorable, 6 = quite favorable, 9 = extremely favorable. Individuals are told that the larger the number they circle on the scale, the more favorable their attitude is toward choosing the option. They are told to first orient their response in terms of the words beneath the scale, and then to make finer discriminations as necessary with the numbers above those words. The adjectives "extremely, quite, and slightly" were chosen because of research in psychophysics (e.g., Cliff, 1959; Messick, 1957), which has shown that these qualifiers tend to produce equal interval judgments. The use of 21 numbers ensures that the individual can make fine distinctions, whereas the verbal anchors beneath the numbers ensure that the individual is not "overwhelmed" by the number of discriminations available. Further, the numbers are useful because individuals tend to think of numbers in a ratio sense (e.g., 8 is twice as much as 4).

The following two procedures are also routinely performed to increase the quality of the measurement procedures. First, individuals are given several practice tasks with the scale, to eliminate warm-up effects and to familiarize the individual with the scale. Our pilot research has shown that practice items can greatly increase the reliability of the measures. Second, individuals are told or shown the range of stimuli that they will judge (e.g., "here is a list of options you will be rating"). This allows the individual to set appropriate anchors in using the scale.

The methods to be described do not assume that any two individuals use a scale in the same fashion. The measures of interest are derived within individuals such that this assumption is unnecessary. The proposed aggregate level analyses will also circumvent the requirement of common across-subject response translation. The primary assumptions are that a given individual will interpret a scale in the same fashion when rating different stimuli (e.g., the individual will interpret the unfavorable-favorable scale in the same fashion when rating each of the decision options) and that the ratings will have approximately interval (linear) level properties. The format and practices described above help to ensure this (see Anderson, 1981).

Overview. In the remainder of this chapter, we will discuss three major facets of our decision framework. First, we will discuss procedures for analyzing the ways that individuals perceive different options. The central concept in this section is that of a perceptual structure matrix. Second, we will develop the importance of the preference structure in understanding the choice process. And finally, we will describe a method for linking perceptual structure analysis to preference structure analysis. The approach is designed to isolate how individuals combine perceptions to form brand and product preferences.

Analysis of Perceptual Structures

Considerable effort has been expended by consumer researchers in developing procedures for analyzing product perceptions (e.g., Green, Rao, & DeSarbo, 1978; Johnson, 1971; Hauser & Koppelman, 1979). In general, these approaches are limited because they either make strong measurement assumptions about a common response language across individuals, or they assume a common perceptual space across individuals. The present approach makes neither of these assumptions.

A perceptual structure is characterized in the present methodology as an mXp matrix of p options and m informational dimensions along which each option is evaluated (see Table 3.4). For example, the options might be different brands within a product class that an individual is considering purchasing (e.g., Bayer

TABLE 3.4. Perceptual structure matrix.

	Option 1	Option 2	Option 3	....	Option p
Dimension 1	R_{11}	R_{12}	R_{13}	....	R_{1p}
Dimension 2	R_{21}	R_{22}	R_{23}	....	R_{2p}
Dimension 3	R_{31}	R_{32}	R_{33}	....	R_{3p}
.	.	.	.	....	.
.	.	.	.	....	.
.	.	.	.	....	.
.	.	.	.	....	.
Dimension m	R_{m1}	R_{m2}	R_{m3}	....	R_{mp}

aspirin, Excedrin, Tylenol, etc.) and the informational dimensions (or properties) might be factors such as cost and effectiveness. The content of the options and dimensions are elicited from individuals by asking them (1) to name all of the options they can think of (e.g., name all of the over-the-counter headache remedies you can think of), and (2) to name all of the factors they would consider when evaluating the options. The individuals are next asked to rank order the dimensions in terms of their importance in evaluating options and to rate each dimension on a 21-point importance scale (ranging from 0 to 100 with adverbs "not at all, slightly, quite, and extremely" appropriately spaced). Finally, the individuals are asked to rate each option on each dimension in terms of its "standing" on that dimension (e.g., is it "good" in terms of cost, is it "neutral," or is it "bad" in terms of cost). These ratings use a special format that is central to later procedures and analyses. The individuals are told to assign a letter rating such that an A means the option is good on the dimension, a B means the option is neutral on the dimension, and a C means the option is bad on the dimension. The individuals can make finer distinctions if they desire by assigning a plus or a minus to a letter (e.g., A+, B−). This yields a nine point scale, scored from 1 (C−) to 9 (A+). These ratings are the cell entries (R_{ij}) in the perceptual structure matrix. All of the analyses to be discussed are applied to an individual's R scores.

Analysis of Option Similarity. Consumer researchers are frequently interested in determining which brands (options) of a product class are perceived as similar to each other and which brands are perceived as different. The perceptual structure matrix can be analyzed to determine similarities between options. This requires calculating an option dissimilarity matrix consisting of Euclidean distance scores. Given p options, the matrix will be a symmetric $p \times p$ matrix. The dissimilarity between any two options, i and j, is defined as

$$d_{ij} = 1/m \sum_{k=1}^{m} (R_{ki} - R_{kj})^2 \tag{1}$$

where d_{ij} is the dissimilarity between options i and j, R_{ki} is the rating of option i on dimension k, R_{kj} is the rating of option j on dimension k, and m is the number of dimensions. The matrix of dissimilarity measures can then be subjected to cluster analysis or multidimensional scaling (see Pruzansky, Tversky, & Carroll, 1982, for a discussion of empirical criteria that permit choosing between cluster analysis and multidimensional scaling) to determine clusters of options that have similar profiles across dimensions. From a marketing standpoint, the cluster analysis would identify, for any given brand, which other brands are perceived as similar to it across dimensions. On a more general level, research may reveal interesting individual differences in both the number and content of clusters in different applied domains. For example, holding the number of options and dimensions constant across individuals, we have observed differences in the number of clusters that emerge for perceptions of banks. Some individuals tend to see most banks as being alike (yielding a single cluster), whereas other individuals perceive multiple clusters. The number and type of clusters are related to individual-difference variables (e.g., income), which provide a context within which perspectives on the market can be gained.

Analysis of Dimension Similarity. A second concern of consumer researchers has been the isolation of similarities and differences between product attributes (dimensions). For example, a researcher might want to know if perceptions of quality across different brands are related to perceptions of cost. The perceptual structure matrix can also be analyzed to determine similarities among dimensions. This requires calculating a dimension dissimilarity matrix consisting of Euclidean distance scores. Given m dimensions, the matrix will be a symmetric m×m matrix. The dissimilarity between any two dimensions, *i* and *j*, is defined as

$$d_{ij} = 1/p \sum_{k=1}^{m} (R_{iq} - R_{jq})^2 \tag{2}$$

where d_{ij} is the dissimilarity between dimensions i and j, R_{iq} is the rating of dimension i on option q, R_{jq} is the rating of dimension j on option q, and p is the number of options. The matrix of dissimilarity measures can be subjected to cluster analysis to determine clusters of dimensions that have similar profiles across options. The cluster analysis would identify dimensions that appear to be related to each other. Our research has suggested that changing a perception of an option on a given dimension may also affect the perception of that option on the other dimensions within the same cluster as the target dimension. Thus, the proposed analysis can aid in the identification of impact effects (Fishbein & Ajzen, 1975) of a change strategy. In addition, research may reveal interesting individual differences in the number and content of dimension clusters, again providing perspectives on the nature of the market of interest.

Decomposition of Dissimilarity Scores. Three or more options may be dissimilar, but for quite different reasons. It will often be instructive to explore specific features of the data that contribute to option (or dimension) dissimilarity. We have found the following approach to be useful. The distance score between any two options can be conceptualized as a function of three components: (1) elevation, (2) scatter, and (3) shape. *Elevation* refers to the mean difference between options

TABLE 3.5. Example of elevation and scatter.

	Difference in elevation		Difference in scatter	
	Option 1	Option 2	Option 3	Option 4
Dimension 1	3	5	3	2
Dimension 2	4	6	4	3
Dimension 3	6	8	4	4
Dimension 4	5	7	4	5
Dimension 5	1	3	5	6

collapsing across dimensions. Table 3.5 illustrates two options that differ in elevation. Note that the options have identical patterning of scores across dimensions, with the only difference being that option 2 is consistently rated 2 units higher than option 1. In this case, the nonzero distance score is due to differences in elevation. *Scatter* refers to the standard deviation of ratings for a given option across dimensions. Table 3.5 presents two options that differ in scatter. In this case, the nonzero distance score is due, in part, to differences in the standard deviations of the option ratings. *Shape* refers to the correlation between ratings for two options across dimensions, and focuses on common patterning of ratings across dimensions. The correlation between options 1 and 2 in Table 3.5 is 1.00, indicating an identical "shape" (patterning) of ratings.

The distance score in Equation 1 can be expressed in terms of these components as follows:

$$d_{ij} = (M_i - M_j)^2 + (s_i - s_j)^2 + 2\, s_i\, s_j\, (1 - r) \tag{3}$$

where M = the mean rating for a given option across dimensions, s = the standard deviation for a given option across dimensions, and r = the correlation between ratings across dimensions for the two options in question. The first component of the right hand side of Equation 3 reflects elevation, the second component reflects scatter, and the third reflects a scatter by shape interaction. The relative contributions of these three components to any given distance score can be computed as follows:

$$C_e = (M_i - M_j)^2 / d_{ij} \tag{4}$$

$$C_{sh} = (s_i - s_j)^2 / d_{ij} \tag{5}$$

$$C_{\mathrm{sh.sc}} = (2\, s_i\, s_j\, (1 - r)) / d_{ij} \tag{6}$$

where C_e is the contribution of elevation, C_{sh} is the contribution of scatter, and $C_{\mathrm{sh.sc}}$ is the contribution of the shape by scatter interaction. The three contribution indices will sum to one, and when multiplied by 100 can be interpreted as percents.

We have found it useful to calculate a matrix of C_e scores, with cells corresponding to those of the original matrix of dissimilarity scores. The contribution of elevation to any given dissimilarity score is then readily available. In addition, summary statistics in the form of the lowest C_e score, the highest C_e

score, the average C_e score, and the standard deviation of C_e scores help to provide perspectives on the impact of elevation on option similarity/dissimilarity. Similar matrices can be computed for the C_{sh} scores and the $C_{\text{sh.sc}}$ scores for either option or dimension similarity analysis.

The cluster analysis of option and dimension dissimilarity matrices can also be performed so as to distinguish the three components. One strategy would be to first cluster options (or dimensions) on the basis of shape. This would require standardizing scores for each option relative to the mean and standard deviation (across dimensions) for that option, and then calculating the distance score using Equation 1 with these standard scores. The standardization of scores has the effect of removing the effects of both elevation and scatter from the data, and the resultant distance score will only reflect the influence of shape. At a second stage, one would perform a cluster analysis on options *within* each of the resultant clusters, where a new set of distance scores are defined to reflect only scatter. This involves substituting deviation scores for the raw scores in the application of Equation 1. A deviation score is the relevant raw score minus the mean rating for the option across dimensions. Finally, at a third stage, options in each of these subgroups would be cluster analyzed using distance scores that reflect only the influence of elevation. For example, the distance between options A and B can be indexed as the squared difference of the respective mean ratings of the two options across dimensions. This approach is consistent with Morrison's (1976) treatment of profile analysis of independent groups via the Hotelling T^2 statistic.

The theoretical and applied implications of dissimilarity score decomposition will depend on the research area. As an example, several researchers (e.g., Holbrook & Huber, 1979; Huber & Holbrook, 1979; Kaffrey, Jacobs, & Zedeck, 1979) have suggested that perceptual distortions, called "halo effects," can bias respondent ratings and create "artificial" correlations between options. The assumption is that the overall evaluation of the option distorts the ratings in the direction of the evaluation, thereby increasing the correspondence between ratings for products which share common evaluations. Halo effects have been treated as artifacts, despite the fact that they represent a valid psychological process which is of interest in its own right. Nevertheless, the researcher may be interested in examining the correspondence between ratings of two options, with halo effects removed from the data (Dillon, Mulani, & Frederick, 1984). Halo effects in the dissimilarity scores defined by Equation 1 would manifest themselves in the elevation component. Thus, the C_e index would reflect the relative contribution of halo effects (as well as other response biases and true mean differences between options) to the similarity/dissimilarity of any two options. One can formally remove the elevation component from the cluster analysis using the three-stage strategy discussed above (see Dillon, Mulani, & Frederick, 1984 for an alternative approach).

Cluster Differences. Once clusters of options have been identified for an individual, it is useful to document attribute dimensions that distinguish the clusters. We will illustrate the issues involved in isolating the differences at the individual level, using cost as an example.

At the simplest level, one would first calculate the mean cost rating across options for each cluster. If brands 1, 2, and 3 define a cluster, then the mean cost rating across brands would be based on $n=3$. The mean differences between clusters would then be examined informally, identifying relatively "large" and "small" differences.[3] This approach is reasonable, but ignores measurement error. One solution is as follows. The perceptual structure matrix ratings are obtained at three (or more) points in time, using a test-retest reliability design. The mean cost rating of a given option across the three sessions is an estimate of the "true" score for that option (Cronbach, Gleser, Nanda, & Rajaratnam, 1974).[4] The variability of ratings across sessions is an estimate of random measurement error. If replicates are the ratings in each session, contrast coefficients can be defined that formally compare one set of grouped options to another set of grouped options by means of an F test (see Kirk, 1968, p. 70). In this case the mean square between reflects the size of the difference in the true scores between the clusters, and the mean square within reflects measurement error. The traditional F test applies if session differences reflect only random error.

There are two limitations to this approach. First, if the number of options is small, the test may lack statistical power. This can be offset by increasing the number of test-retest sessions. Second, when a large number of contrasts is made across many attribute dimensions, the probability of a Type I error increases. Despite these limitations, the approach explicitly takes into consideration measurement error and is desirable to the alternative of ignoring measurement error. The researcher will have increased confidence in a between cluster mean difference, if it is substantially larger than what one would expect on the basis of random error.

Relative Score Matrix. The perceptual structure matrix can be transformed to a relative score matrix to provide further insights into option-dimension perceptions. The relative score matrix involves calculating a mean rating for each dimension across options and a standard deviation for ratings within dimensions and across options (see Table 3.6). The scores within a row are then standardized relative to this mean and standard deviation. The mean score for a given row indicates the tendency for the individual to view options, on the average, as positive (large scores) or negative (low scores). The standard deviation reflects variability in options across the dimension. A small standard deviation would indicate that options tend to be perceived as being the same on the dimension. Finally, the within-cell standard scores indicate how "unique" an option is on the dimension (relative to the mean and standard deviation). We have found the relative score matrix to be useful in selecting perceptions to change via educational/advertising efforts. For example, if a dimension has a small standard deviation, then it is

---

[3]Formal definitions of what constitutes a "large" or "small" difference, as with any statistical comparison, is a function of substantive criteria within the domain of interest.

[4]These estimated true scores would be used in defining the dissimilarity scores in the original cluster analysis.

TABLE 3.6. Relative score matrix.

	Option 1	Option 2	Option 3	....	Option *p*	Mean *sd*
Dimension 1	Z_{11}	Z_{12}	Z_{13}	....	Z_{1p}	
Dimension 2	Z_{21}	Z_{22}	Z_{23}	....	Z_{2p}	
Dimension 3	Z_{31}	Z_{32}	Z_{33}	....	Z_{3p}	
.	.	.	.	....	.	
.	.	.	.	....	.	
.	.	.	.	....	.	
.	.	.	.	....	.	
Dimension *m*	Z_{m1}	Z_{m2}	Z_{m3}	....	Z_{mp}	

easier for a change effort to make a given option "stand out from the rest" relative to a dimension with a large standard deviation. Similarly, the mean scores can signal potential problems with "floor" and "ceiling" effects.

In sum, the perceptual structure matrix for an individual can be analyzed to reveal clusters of options that are perceived as similar or different across dimensions. It is possible to identify these clusters, controlling for the effects of either elevation, shape, or scatter. The analysis will reveal to the marketer which competing brands are perceived as similar or distinct from his/her brand. Once clusters are identified, it is possible to isolate attribute dimensions that contribute most to option dissimilarity. Finally, the relative score matrix indicates those attribute dimensions along which brands are perceived by the individual to exhibit little variability or considerable variability. The matrix also indicates the "uniqueness" of a brand, given this variability. Analyses of dimension similarity can also be undertaken, to identify potential impact effects of an advertising/education campaign.

Some Qualifications. The results of an option similarity analysis depend upon the dimensions on which the options are rated. The choice of options and dimensions to include define the conceptual domain across which similarity is defined. The idiothetic approach uses options and dimensions that are generated by the individual, and hence, they are both salient and meaningful to the individual (nomothetic applications are discussed shortly). This circumvents several problems frequently attributed to derived distance scores. For example, Dillon, Frederick, and Tangpanichee (1984) note that if one attribute with high variance across brands is asked repeatedly in several different forms (e.g., individuals rate cars on miles per gallon, repair costs, power, etc., all of which reflect an "economy" dimension), the attribute may dominate the perceptual structure merely as a function of item redundancy. In the idiothetic approach, the multiple attributes are generated by the individual and thus probably constitute meaningful psychological distinctions for that individual.

Dissimilarity scores in Equation 1 reflect differences in options across dimensions without regard to the subjective importance of the dimensions. Weights can be introduced to amplify differences on dimensions that are subjectively more important to the individual. This involves defining weights using the importance ratings (ranging from 0 to 100 scale) discussed earlier. One possibility is to calculate a proportional weight, where the importance rating for a given dimension is divided by the sum of the importance ratings across dimensions. The importance weight, *w*, for dimension *k* would then be included in Equation 1, weighting the difference between *R*s by the appropriate *w*. An alternative weighting scheme would use normalized weights (Tatsuoka, 1971). At present, the advantages of including a weighting parameter in cluster analyses is unclear (see Aldenderfer & Blashfield, 1984).[5]

Nomothetic Perspectives. All of the above analyses can be conducted at the level of the single individual. Individually derived indices may then be aggregated for purposes of group comparisons. For example, it would be possible to compare two or more groups on the mean number of option clusters, the mean number of dimension clusters, the mean contributions of shape, elevation or scatter to a given distance score, the mean standard deviation for a given dimension from a relative perceptual structure, the mean z score (see Table 3.5) for a given option/dimension from a relative perceptual structure, the nature of judgmental schemes, and the content of cluster categories (see Jaccard & Wan, in press). None of these comparisons would require the measurement assumptions detailed at the outset of this chapter.

In our research, where we have studied decision making at the aggregate level, we have found one deviation from a purely idiothetic approach to be useful. This deviation involves measuring the perceptual structure matrix for a common set of options and dimensions that are imposed on the individual by the investigator. This facilitates aggregate level analyses in which a specific set of options or dimensions are of interest. There are two potential limitations to this practice. First, we may exclude an option/dimension from those presented which the individual would otherwise consider. Second, we might include options/dimensions that the individual would not normally consider. To minimize these possibilities, we typically conduct a pretest in which we ask a representative sample of respondents to list relevant options and dimensions. A content analysis of items elicited determines the list of options/dimensions used (with a criterion that at least 10% of the sample must mention the option/dimension for it to be included). In addition, when the list of options/dimensions is presented, we include an "other: please specify" category, so that the individual can write in an option/dimension if an important one has been omitted. Finally, introduction of

[5]In the analysis of dimension (or option) similarity, it is possible for two dimensions to be highly correlated (in a Pearson sense), yet fall into different clusters, even with minor differences in elevation and scatter. This occurs when the dimensions are negatively correlated across options. The consequences of negative correlations between dimensions depend on the purposes of the analysis. If one is interested in what dimensions "covary" in either a positive or negative fashion, then the cluster analysis of Euclidean distance scores will fail to group positively correlated dimensions with negatively correlated dimensions. In such cases, analytic techniques other than cluster analysis are necessary.

the importance weights into the dissimilarity indices can further reduce the possibility of including irrelevant dimensions. Although none of these practices guarantee the integrity of the individual, we have found them to be effective in research applications where our focus is aggregate-level descriptions.

If the researcher is willing to make the assumption that individuals use rating scales with the same response language, then the cluster analytic strategy noted above can be augmented with a useful nomothetic strategy that permits clustering of individuals as well as options and dimensions. Consider a study with 50 subjects, each of whom responded to the same 8 (dimensions) × 10 (options) matrix of stimuli. For any given pair of subjects, A and B, a dissimilarity score can be calculated by subtracting the rating of subject A from the rating of subject B for a given cell of the matrix, and then summing the squared differences across all cells. A 50 × 50 matrix of dissimilarity scores can be formed for all possible pairs of subjects. A cluster analysis of the matrix would identify clusters of individuals who tend to rate the options in a similar fashion across the dimensions. The three-step procedure discussed above could also be applied to control for elevation, shape, or scatter in the identification of subjects' clusters (e.g., to eliminate respondent differences in scale origin). Mean rating scores for the 8 × 10 dimension-by-option matrix can be computed for each cluster of subjects, and the resulting matrices subjected to the analyses discussed above.[6] The subgroups can then be compared on the measures detailed earlier, as well as on relevant market segmentation variables.

Preference Structures

This section focuses on the nature of preference structures. An individual's preference structure refers to his or her attitude toward each of the decision options. The preference structure is a key concept in our theoretical framework, because a person's choice is conceptualized as being, in large part, a function of the preference structure. As discussed later, the preference structure is linked to the individual's perceptual structure matrix (i.e., the way he or she construes the options on the informational dimension).

Preference Structure Analysis. An attitude is conceptualized in very restricted terms in our framework. It refers to the extent to which an individual feels favorable or unfavorable toward enacting a given behavioral option. A preference structure is measured by asking the individual to rate each decision option on a −10 to +10 unfavorable-favorable scale. Consistent with subjective-expected-utility (SEU) theory, it can be argued that an individual will choose to perform that option toward which the most positive attitude is held (exceptions to this principle will be discussed shortly). Thus, the attitude measures are analogous to global measures of SEU, without requiring the measurement of specific probabilities and utilities (see Jaccard, 1981). On a conceptual level, preference structure

[6]For the analysis of attribute dimension that distinguish clusters, one would use traditional multivariate analyses instead of those presented earlier.

analysis represents a theory of the relationship between attitudes and behavior. It is quite distinct from traditional, nomothetic-based consumer models that attempt to explain discrepancies between attitudes and behaviors. We will elaborate these differences and then consider the applied implications of preference structure analysis.

Theoretical Implications. Several theorists have attempted to explain attitude-behavior discrepancies by suggesting that variables other than attitudes may influence behavioral decisions (or behavioral intentions, as they are called in most theories). These theories are typically stated in the form of a multiple regression equation such that

$$\mathrm{BI} = w_1 X_1 + w_2 X_2 + \ldots + w_n X_n \tag{7}$$

where BI = the intention to perform the behavior; X_1 through X_n = the relevant predictor variables, of which the attitude toward performing the behavior is X_1; and w_1 through w_n = empirically determined regression weights which are said to reflect the importance of the respective variable in determining BI. According to these models, discrepancies between traditional measures of attitude and behavior occur because (a) the traditional attitude measured is usually not specific to the behavioral criterion (i.e., it is an attitude toward an object and not an attitude toward a behavior), (b) there may be other factors (e.g., normative beliefs) determining the behavior such that attitude is irrelevant, and (c) attitude may only determine intentions to perform a behavior and thus, should be predictive of the action only to the extent that these intentions are highly related to the behavioral criterion. The approach of the present chapter is consistent with point a (since the preference structure consists of a set of attitudes towards behaviors) and point c. However, several differences can be highlighted with regard to point b and Equation 7.

First, the preference structure approach differs from the regression approach in terms of an emphasis on behavioral predictability from a within-subject versus between-subject perspective. This difference may best be illustrated by considering only the first component of Equation 7 (i.e., we will assume that weights 2 through *n* are zero). The regression model would involve measuring different people's attitudes toward performing a behavior (e.g., using brand A) and correlating these measures with a behavioral criterion (e.g., use of brand A). It is assumed that the more favorable the attitude, the more likely it is the behavior will be performed. Table 3.7 presents a hypothetical example of three individuals

TABLE 3.7. Preference structures.

Individual	Brand A	Brand B
1	6	9
2	4	8
3	2	−5

and their attitudes towards brand A. According to the regression model, individual 1 should be most likely to use A, followed by individuals 2 and 3, respectively. In contrast, the preference structure approach suggests that behavioral prediction requires knowledge of the distribution of attitudes across decision options. If a person possesses a positive attitude toward b_1, and an even more positive attitude toward b_2, it is unlikely he will perform b_1 even though he has a positive attitude toward it. In Table 3.7, the preference structure approach would predict that individual 3 will use brand A, whereas individuals 1 and 2 will use brand B (given that the most positive attitude dictates the choice). In the regression model, it is assumed that the more positive the attitude *relative to other people's attitudes*, the more likely it is the individual will perform the behavior. By contrast, in the preference structure approach, it is assumed that the more positive the attitude *relative to the person's attitude toward other decision options*, the more likely it is the person will perform the behavior.

A second difference in the two approaches concerns the specification of factors other than attitudes that are relevant to behavioral prediction. A number of social scientists (e.g., Wicker, 1969; Triandis, 1977) have argued that a person's attitude toward an act is only one of a number of variables that influence behavior or behavioral intent. Several models have been proposed which investigate such additional factors as attitude toward the situation (Rokeach & Kliejunas, 1972), morals (Triandis, 1977), and normative beliefs (Fishbein, 1972). In the preference structure approach, the "additional variables" are attitudes toward performing the other decision options. Most regression based models do not focus on different decision options. Thus, the approaches differ in where they direct the theorist to look for other variables that can account for attitude-behavior discrepancies.

A third difference between the two approaches concerns the way in which the "other variables" are used within the theoretical network. In the regression model, the predictor variables are given weights representing the importance of the variable in determining intention. Generally, these weights are estimated via multiple regression procedures. The weighted predictor variables are summed to yield an index of predicted behavior. In the preference structure approach, no such weighting parameters are employed nor is there a summative relation among the weighted predictors. Rather, the attitudes toward performing each of the decision options are compared with one another and the option toward which the most positive attitude is held represents the predicted behavior.

One might be tempted to extend regression models of behavioral intention to include decision options, thus resulting in a more "complete" model of decision behavior. Such an approach was suggested by Ajzen and Fishbein (1969, 1980). In the context of Fishbein's model, this involves measuring Aact (attitude towards the behavior) and SN (subjective norm) toward each option and regressing an intention measure for each option onto the appropriate Aact and SN. The combination of Aact and SN would then be dictated by the results of the various regression equations.

There are three problems with this approach relative to the present one. First, the preference structure approach is idiothetic and allows prediction of an individual's behavior knowing only that individual's attitudes toward the decision options. The regression approach, in contrast, is not idiothetic. It requires that a group of individuals be studied so that least squares estimates of the weights (w_1 and w_2) can be obtained for any given option. This approach requires that all individuals within the group be homogeneous in terms of how they weight Aact and SN for a given option and also requires some rather stringent measurement assumptions (e.g., all individuals interpret the rating scales in the same way). Thus, deriving accurate estimates of how to weight the multiple predictors is problematic from the standpoint of psychological explanation (see Gordon, 1968, for additional issues in this respect). These assumptions are not requisite in the preference structure approach, because no weighting parameters are involved. Second, if behavioral predictions are based on Aact and SN, the regression approach requires that the standard errors of estimate be low and homogeneous across all options. If the regression analysis yielded a poor goodness-of-fit for just one option, the entire analysis could be jeopardized. Third, there is no empirical evidence to indicate that normative factors, when used in the context of the preference structure approach, will yield increased behavioral prediction over and above Aact. Initial research efforts therefore might best employ the more parsimonious perspective of focusing on just the attitude construct. This practice would be consistent with the literature on decision making and makes the assumption that the influence of other variables on behavioral decisions is mediated by attitudinal variables. Empirical support for the preference-structure approach relative to regression models is presented in Jaccard (1981) and Jaccard and Becker (1985).

Preference structure analysis can also be contrasted with other formal choice models proposed in the consumer literature. Space limitations do not permit detailed comparison, however, four general observations can be made. First, the importance of measuring attitudes (or some related concept) toward alternative brands has been widely recognized in consumer research (as opposed to psychological theories of behavioral intention which have tended to focus on the analysis of a single option). However, many applications (e.g., Wilkie & Pessimer, 1973) use cross-sectional, regression-based strategies for relating the attitude indices to brand choice. Such strategies are subject to the limitations discussed above and contrast with the preference structure approach which uses a purely idiothetic method for generating predicted choice.

Second, the majority of applications in the consumer area have focused on attitudes toward "objects" as opposed to attitudes toward "behaviors" (Ajzen & Fishbein, 1977). Thus, the attitude toward the brand per se (e.g., a Rolls Royce) is measured as opposed to the attitude toward actually *purchasing* (i.e., choosing) the brand. Research in psychology has demonstrated the superior predictive power of attitudes toward behaviors (e.g., Jaccard, King, & Pomazal, 1977; Ajzen & Fishbein, 1977). The preference structure approach uses attitudes toward behaviors.

Third, the preference structure approach conceptualizes attitude as the extent to which the individual feels favorable or unfavorable toward choosing the option in question. Measures of attitude follow directly from the attitude scaling literature, in which the attitude is measured on an unfavorable-favorable rating scale (Jaccard, Weber & Lundmark, 1975). Many applications in the consumer area estimate attitude by use of compositional methods, in which perceptions about individual attributes of an option are combined (frequently using a variant of expected-utility theory) to yield an index of attitude. These approaches are generally inferior to the present measurement strategy, because they (a) make strong measurement assumptions (e.g., the presence of ratio level properties), (b) assume that all relevant attributes and no irrelevant attributes have been included in the analysis, (c) vary in the conceptualization of what the relevant attribute-level measures should be (e.g., measures might include indices of certainty, probability, evaluation, importance, salience, relevance) and/or (d) impose a combinatorial rule on the individual attribute measures which may not be valid. The resulting measures may not reflect the relevant attitude, as conceptualized in the preference structure approach.

Fourth, the preference structure approach states that an individual will choose to perform that option toward which the most positive attitude is held (however, see exceptions discussed later). Several models of choice functions have been suggested in the consumer literature (e.g., Louviere & Woodworth, 1983; Currim, 1981; Batsell & Lodish, 1981; Reibstein, 1978), the most popular being a form of the Luce multinomial logistic function. The model states that the probability of choosing an option A from a set of options can be expressed as the (natural log) evaluation of option A divided by the sum of the (natural log) evaluations of all options considered. This function has primarily been evaluated for aggregate level phenomena, as opposed to individual choice functions. Batsell and Lodish (1981) evaluated the model at the individual level for repeat purchase decisions over time. Psychological research on the model at the individual level has found it to be unsatisfactory (e.g., Becker, DeGroot, & Marschak, 1963; Tversky, 1972).[7] In its present form, the choice function of the preference structure approach is crude, but has proven to be effective. Future research is needed to better quantify and conceptualize preference structure choice functions.

Applied Implications. Preference structure analysis has numerous applied implications. Consider the case where a consumer psychologist is attempting to influence an individual to perform one of four behavioral options (purchase product A from the class A, B, C, D). The attitude toward each of the options can be measured. Depending on the distribution of the attitudes, different influence strategies would be dictated. For example, it may be found that the attitudes toward options C and D are quite low and, hence, these options can be ignored. Three strategies are then possible: (a) Make the attitude toward A more positive, (b) make the attitude toward B more negative, or (c) some combination of the

[7]Most consumer applications have also estimated utilities associated with product attributes, based on choice data. This procedure is not recommended, because utilities are best estimated from evaluative judgments, as discussed later. Our research has shown that using choice data to estimate utilities can be misleading.

above. The attitude scores will, in part, dictate the strategy used. For example, if the attitude toward option B is highly positive, the psychologist would be ill-advised to make the attitude toward alternative A more positive. There would probably be a "ceiling effect" and the only effective strategy would be to lower the attitude toward alternative B in conjunction with raising the attitude toward A. In contrast, if the attitude toward B was moderately positive, with the attitude toward A being slightly less positive, then any of the three strategies could be effective.

If one wanted to *strengthen* the decision to perform A (i.e., make the decision resistant to change), then this would involve maximizing the discrepancy between option A and option B. This could be accomplished by using any of the three influence strategies outlined above.

The preference structure approach also has implications for the selection of target populations. If the psychologist is trying to increase the number of individuals who perform A, then those individuals most likely to change their behavior will be those whose attitudes towards options A and B are roughly equal (i.e., those who are only slightly more positive toward B than A). In contrast, individuals who have much more positive attitudes toward B than A should be relatively difficult to influence because the discrepancy between attitudes is large. Initial change efforts therefore might be focused on the former group. The strategies used to induce change could differ for one group as opposed to the other. (Parenthetically, the size of the discrepancy between the two most positively viewed options should also be related to the stability of behavior over time: The larger the discrepancy, the more likely it is the behavior will be stable.)

The above comments are theoretical approximations, at best, and are made in the spirit of suggesting potential applied implications of preference structure analysis. More precise statements will be possible as research on the choice function is forthcoming.

Error Theory for Preference Structure Analysis. The comparison of attitudes across options for a single individual should address the problem of measurement error. Consumer research which has used individual choice functions to predict choice behavior has ignored the problem of unreliability of measures. In our research, we typically obtain ratings of attitudes on three separate occasions, and use the mean attitude score as an index of the "true" score. Differences between mean scores for any two options are then evaluated relative to an index of the average unreliability across options. This is accomplished using a one way analysis of variance model, in which the different options define the levels of the analysis, and replicates are the ratings in each session. Tukey-based (Kirk, 1968, p. 70) critical differences are defined for pairwise comparisons of options to isolate attitude differences that can not be attributed to measurement error. This strategy is similar to the error theory of functional measurement (Anderson, 1981, 1982). The major assumption is that within-cell variation reflects only random measurement error. The approach becomes problematic if the number of options is small, because the statistical tests may lack power. This can be offset by increasing the number of repeated assessments.

Nonoptimizing Decision Rules. Thus far, our statement of preference structure analysis assumes an optimizing choice process: The individual chooses that option towards which the most positive attitude is held. Although this will generally be the case, there are instances where behavior will not correspond to the most positive option. One such case can occur when the behavior is not volitional and is controlled by other people or events. In this instance, individuals may be unable to enact the option that they are most positive toward.

Our research on choice of banks has revealed a second moderating variable on the use of an optimizing rule. When individuals first move to a community, they choose the bank toward which they feel most positive. Over time, they might acquire information about a competing bank which leads them to be more positive toward that bank relative to their own bank. However, their behavior does not change because of the costs (both economic, social, and psychological) of switching from one bank to another. This suggests that the costs of switching options relative to the benefits to be gained will be an important mediator of attitude-behavior consistency from an optimizing perspective.

Nomothetic Analyses. Nomothetic (mean) level analyses, requiring minimal assumptions about a common response language, can be conducted on preference structures, if the mean comparisons are between two or more decision options (i.e., between "repeated measures" means). The necessary assumption is one of an approximately common scale unit across individuals (the origin being irrelevant). This assumption will probably be met if the measurement practices discussed earlier are effected. Subgroup comparisons can also be made without recourse to common origin assumptions, if the focus is on group differences in the differences between means (e.g., the difference in mean attitude scores between options A and B for upper-class individuals as compared with the difference between mean attitude scores for options A and B for lower-class individuals).

Perceptions Underlying Preference Structures

This section integrates the previous material on perceptual structures and preference structures. We present an idiothetic methodology for studying the relationship between these classes of variables, and then extend the analysis to nomothetic perspectives. The focus is on isolating the impact of different perceptions on the attitudes comprising the preference structure, and estimating how individuals "trade off" or "integrate" perceived positive and negative characteristics of an option in forming an attitude.

The assessment of perceptual impact and integration processes is problematic, because verbal reports of these phenomena are of questionable validity. Research has shown that individuals have difficulty in accurately characterizing these complex mental processes (McGuire, 1976). For example, individuals tend to overestimate the amount of information they consider and to report using more complex integration processes than appears to be the case (Wiggins, 1972; see also Nisbett & Wilson, 1977). The present approach uses an indirect assessment procedure which does not require individuals to report complex mental processes. The strategy is to describe to individuals a set of hypothetical options. The options are rated in terms of how favorable or unfavorable the individual would feel about choosing each one. The options are defined so that the pattern of ratings provided by the individual will allow one to *infer* the impact of perceptions and plausible integration strategies that might be operative.

Functional Measurement. The methodology used in our framework is similar to the popular conjoint methods used in consumer research, but relies more heavily on Anderson's (1980, 1981) functional measurement approach. Functional measurement has been the foundation of numerous studies of social judgment. A major gap, however, has been the failure to link the approach to the study of existing attitudes and behaviors. Typically, the information integration process is studied with hypothetical stimuli in a laboratory context. Although this approach describes how people process information in hypothetical situations, it is not sufficient to understand attitudes and behavior that occur outside of hypothetical contexts. There exists a substantial literature showing that responses to hypothetical situations may not be predictive of real life behavior. Further, because the focus of functional measurement is on social judgment, its ability to help us understand social *behavior* rests on framing the approach within the context of a theory of social behavior. This section confronts both of these issues.

Functional Measurement and Preference Structures. Functional measurement has been used in psychology to study evaluative judgments that are quite similar to those comprising a preference structure. Most of this research has been in the impression formation area in which like-dislike judgments of hypothetical individuals are analyzed. In another vein, Shanteau (1974; Shanteau & Nagey, 1976) has used functional measurement to analyze dating preferences in college students and for the analysis of choice of risky alternatives in a gambling situation. Although functional measurement has never been applied to an attitude toward a behavior per se, a straightforward extension would involve application of the approach to the analysis of preference structures. By focusing functional measurement on attitudes toward behavioral options, the approach is grounded within a broader framework that links social judgment to social behavior. Thus, a three-link network is posited: (a) A person's behavior is influenced by his or her decision to perform that behavior, (b) a person's decision to perform a behavior is influenced by his or her preference structure, and (c) the attitudinal judgments comprising the preference structure are influenced by perceptions about the behavioral alternatives, which can be assessed by means of functional measurement analysis.

One approach to conceptualizing the trade-off process of individuals has been Anderson's (1981) information integration theory. Integration theory states that an attitude towards a behavioral alternative is a function of information that the individual has with respect to that alternative. One common variant of integration theory suggests that the individual integrates information by means of an averaging process. Thus, the positive and negative features of an option are psychologically "tallied" (with the positive features offsetting the negative features) and the attitude formed accordingly. An averaging model can be represented mathematically as follows:

$$A_P = \sum_{i=1}^{N} w_i \, s_i / \sum_{i=1}^{N} w_i \tag{8}$$

where A = the attitude toward behavior "p," s = the scale value of the ith piece of information, w = a weighting coefficient reflecting the importance of the ith piece of information, and N = the number of pieces of information. Functional measurement permits a test of the viability of Equation 8 as well as other integration strategies that the individual might employ.

The present approach will be illustrated with an idiothetic analysis of an individual's choice of banks. Although functional measurement requires that individuals respond to hypothetical banks, a procedure will be outlined that directly evaluates the applicability of these responses to existing banks. Numerous issues arise when attempting to apply functional measurement in this context. We will now consider these problems and possible solutions to them.

Specification of Amount and Type of Information. Functional measurement usually involves factorially manipulating different types of information (e.g., interest rate, check charges) and then obtaining measures of attitude toward each of the resulting hypothetical stimuli. For example, eight hypothetical banks can be described as a result of a 2 × 2 × 2 factorial design manipulating interest rate, check charges, and number of money machines. Attitudes towards each of the eight banks would then be obtained. Our preliminary research suggests at least eleven types of informational dimensions may underly a given attitude. These are (a) interest rate, (b) check charges and fees, (c) location, (d) number of money machines, (e) number of services, (f) penalties, (g) efficiency and quality of service, (h) reputation, (i) bank hours, (j) minimum amounts of money required for an active account, and (k) FDIC insurance. Obviously, it is not feasible to orthogonally manipulate all eleven informational dimensions. Using two levels per factor would yield 2,048 stimuli, a prohibitively large number. The number of stimuli can be dramatically reduced by assuming an additive integration rule and using a fractional factorial design. However, this is unsatisfactory because the nature of the integration rule must be assumed and not empirically tested. In addition, individuals would be forced to simultaneously consider eleven distinct items of information for a given bank, a task which could prove to be confusing and difficult. (We will discuss fractional factorial designs in more detail, shortly.)

One solution to the above problem is to manipulate only a small number of informational dimensions. In the present approach, three dimensions are manipulated with three levels per factor. The dimensions can differ for each individual studied and are selected by presenting to the individual a list of the eleven types of information. The individual rank orders the dimensions from most important to least important, and the three highest-ranked dimensions are used to construct the 27 (3 × 3 × 3) hypothetical banks. Each individual responds to the same stimuli in the sense that the three most subjectively important dimensions to them were manipulated, although the actual content of the dimensions might differ between individuals.

Consumer research which has used full factorial designs (in the context of conjoint measurement) generally has not provided psychological or practical justification for the choice of dimensions to manipulate. This is problematic because dimensions selected arbitrarily may have little external validity for understanding preferences. In contrast, the selection of dimensions to manipulate in the present approach is psychologically guided. It is based on individually generated dimensions that are subjectively important to the individual.

Manipulation of Information. Given that one has identified the dimensions to be manipulated, the selection of the values that will be used to manipulate a dimension is of primary importance. For example, if "number of money machines" is being manipulated with two levels, one could choose the values 10 versus 20, or 5 versus 15, or 10 versus 15, and so on. The selection of a particular set of values potentially can influence the outcome of the study, both in terms of the integration rule used by the subject and estimates of $w_i \, s_i$. To the extent that the values are selected arbitrarily, the results of the analysis will also be arbitrary.

There are two perspectives one can assume on the above problem. First, one can select a set of values that are of theoretical interest in their own right. The number of money machines might be manipulated using the levels "10" versus "20" because these two values are of theoretical interest. The resulting analyses would then yield $w_i \, s_i$ estimates of the two values and also indicate how the particular information was integrated with the other information used in the study.

This approach generally will be of limited utility in applied contexts. It is rare that one is interested in two or three specific values that characterize a dimension, such as 10 versus 20. When forming an evaluative judgment about a behavioral option, people probably translate specific values into two or three general subjective categories on the dimension of interest. A bank that has only two money machines might be translated into the category "relatively bad" on this dimension and an attitude formed accordingly. Each category will have a range of values associated with it. For example, any bank having between zero and five money machines might be viewed as being "relatively bad" in terms of their "standing" on the dimension of money machines. Based upon research in information processing and psycholinguistics, people probably categorize options into three general-purpose categories. Using past experience and perceptions of all other options, an individual will use a subjective "good on the dimension" category, a subjective "neutral" category, and a subjective "bad on the dimension" category. Each general-purpose category has a range of values associated with it, and finer distinctions can be made within categories (e.g., extremely good vs. quite good).

The present methodology manipulates informational dimensions in terms of the three subjective categories discussed above. A given hypothetical bank is assigned a "grade" or a letter rating of A, B, or C on a dimension, where B is described as neutral on that dimension, A as good, and C as bad. Note that this is the same scale used to assess the "standing" of existing options in the analysis of perceptual structures. For the sake of exposition, assume that an additive integration rule holds as described by Equation 1. Because both w_i and s_i are free to vary, differences in marginal means for a main effect will reflect differences in w_i and s_i for the corresponding dimension. The means will estimate the weighted-scale values associated with the above average (A), average (B), and below average (C) categories used by the subject. The weighted-scale values probably reflect a central tendency of the range of values associated with a given category, weighted by the psychological importance of that category.

Consumer research that has manipulated informational dimensions (in the context of conjoint measurement) typically provides no psychological or practical justification for the chosen levels of manipulation. The usual practice is to manipulate specific values of the stimulus dimension, such as five versus ten money machines. These values are selected either arbitrarily from the wide range of values possible, or are based on the experimenter's guess about the relevant range of values for the group of individuals being studied (see Green & Srinivasan, 1978). In contrast, the present approach does not manipulate specific values of the dimensions, but rather manipulates more meaningful psychological translations of the values in terms of three general purpose categories.

Validation of Approach. Consumer research that has used decompositional strategies such as conjoint or functional measurement rarely test the external validity of inferences made from the analysis of responses to the hypothetical stimuli. This is problematic because a substantial literature in social psychology suggests that responses in hypothetical situations may have little generalization to responses in nonhypothetical situations. The present methodology includes an external validation criterion which can be illustrated with our bank study. An attitude toward banking at each of seven banks in the Albany area was measured on a 21-point unfavorable-favorable scale. The attitude measures represent the *observed* preference structure. Each bank was also rated using the A, B, C grading system on the eleven dimensions identified above. Twenty-seven hypothetical banks were then described (in accord with a $3 \times 3 \times 3$ factorial design) and an attitude toward using each bank was obtained on the 21-point unfavorable-favorable scale. This task was performed three times, in separate sessions, for purposes of reliability analysis. The responses were subjected to traditional information integration analysis, and the estimated integration rule and $w_i\, s_i$ values isolated. The resulting math model was then used in conjunction with the letter ratings of the real banks to generate a predicted preference structure (computational details are discussed later). To the extent that the approach suggested is valid, the predicted and observed preference structures will be comparable. To the extent that any one aspect of the approach is inappropriate or invalid, the fit between the predicted and observed preference structure will be adversely affected. For example, if using only the three most highly ranked informational dimensions in defining the hypothetical banks is inappropriate (because individuals actually use

TABLE 3.8. Main effect means for analysis of variance.

Location	A = 8.34	B = .33	C = −2.00
Service charges	A = 7.00	B = .17	C = − .50
Interest Rate	A = 3.65	B = 3.45	C = − .43

more than three dimensions), then the ability to predict the existing preference structure from the resulting model will be decreased accordingly.

Single-Subject Analysis. Data for the individual in question was analyzed by means of a 3 × 3 × 3 analysis of variance, where the dependent measure was the attitude ratings of the hypothetical banks. Replicates were the ratings obtained at each of the three sessions. Only the main effects achieved statistical significance. The following eta squares (proportion of explained variance) were observed; the most important dimension (location) = .50, the second most important dimension (service charges and fees) = .30, and the third most important dimension (interest rate) = .08. These results suggest an additive integration rule in which the strengths and weaknesses of a bank are psychologically tallied to form an attitude toward using it. In contrast, the data are inconsistent with integration rules that would suggest the operation of interaction effects (e.g., differential weight averaging rules, noncompensatory rules; see Jaccard & Becker, 1985). The total amount of explained variance for the additive model was .88, indicating a good level of model fit.

Table 3.8 presents the mean scores for each of the main effects. For a given dimension, the differences between means reflect interval-level differences in the weighted-scale values for the three general-purpose categories. For example, for location, the difference between "good" and "neutral" is 8.34 − .33 = 8.01. The effect of a perception changing from "good" to "neutral" on this dimension is to decrease the attitude by approximately eight scale points (on a 21-point scale).

In order to validate the integration analysis, a predicted attitude toward each existing bank was computed using the A-B-C ratings assigned to that bank on each of the three dimensions. These A-B-C ratings were used to determine the cell in the 3×3×3 factorial design that the given bank was perceived as being in. The predicted attitude score was obtained by summing the grand mean and the relevant treatment effects for each of the statistically significant effects in the analysis of variance on hypothetical banks.[8] The seven observed attitudes (one

[8]Predicted scores were further modified to take into account "+" "−" distinctions the individual used in rating existing banks. For example, if the individual assigned a bank a B+, then the treatment effect for the B category was increased by 1/3 the difference between means of the A and B categories. This procedure assumes the individual uses the pluses and minuses in a fashion that approximates equal intervals. A similar approach has been used by Pekelman and Sen (1979) and Green, Carroll, and Goldberg (1981) in the context of conjoint measurement.

toward each of the existing banks) were correlated with the seven predicted attitudes. The correlation was .94, indicating a strong correspondence between predicted and observed scores.

Change Implications. The present approach has several strengths for studying efforts to change attitudes and behavior. The analysis of responses to the factorially defined stimuli can suggest, a priori, the effects that changing a perception will have on attitudes. For example, if a behavioral option was rated as "bad" (a C rating) on an important dimension, a change strategy might be to alter this perception and raise it to "neutral" (a B rating). The results of the analysis of variance on the attitudes toward the hypothetical options could then be used to predict the amount of attitude change that should result. Specifically, a predicted attitude would be computed based upon the cell in the factorial design in which the option is located, as illustrated above. A predicted attitude score based upon the new cell representing the alternative as a result of the C to B change would also be calculated. The difference between the two predicted scores would indicate the amount of attitude change that should result. Such analyses can guide the researcher in selecting the most effective change strategy to use because this will identify informational changes that will have maximum impact on the preference structure. We have observed empirical support for the above change analysis in the context of a laboratory study on the use of over-the-counter headache remedies.

An important issue in the planning of change strategies is to anticipate *impact effects* of a message. Fishbein and Ajzen (1975) define impact effects as changes in perceptions that were not directly targeted in the message. For example, a message might be designed to influence the perception of a product on "cost" and unwittingly produce a change in perceptions of "cost" and "quality" (because the two dimensions may be perceived by the individual as being related). The problem is to anticipate such impact effects and counteract them when designing a message to induce attitude change. One perspective is offered by the analysis of perceptual structures (discussed earlier) in which a cluster analysis is performed on distance scores between dimensions. Dimensions that cluster together are candidates for impact effects in that a change in a dimension within a cluster may produce changes in the other dimensions associated with it (but not in dimensions grouped in different clusters). We are currently conducting research to explore the ability of our framework to predict, a priori, impact effects.

Another issue within our framework is the mapping of specific stimulus values onto the three general-purpose categories used in the functional measurement analysis. For example, if the price of brand A is \$5 this might correspond to a judgment of "good" on the dimension of cost. A price of \$10 might correspond to a judgment of "bad" on the dimension of cost. Psychophysical procedures (Wegner, 1982) can be used to map specific stimulus values onto the three general-purpose categories and gradations within them. Once the relevant judgmental scheme has been isolated, the scheme can be used in conjunction with the functional measurement analysis to make a priori predictions of the effects of specific stimulus changes (e.g., a change from \$5 to \$10) on attitudes. (See footnote 5 for the use of "pluses" and "minuses" in the functional measurement analysis.)

Finally, the framework we propose can provide insights into why certain messages fail to impact on behavior. There are at least four factors that should be examined when analyzing message failure. First, the message may not have influenced the perception it was designed to change. Second, the message may influence the relevant perception, but also may produce impact effects which offset this influence. Third, the message may influence the relevant perception (with no impact effects) and, in turn, also influence the attitude toward the option in question. However, the amount of attitude change that occurs may not be sufficient to make the option the most positively evaluated one in the preference structure. In this case, choice behavior would remain unchanged. Fourth, the message might induce sufficient change in the attitude to influence choice, but the choice may not be translated into behavior (see Jaccard, 1975, for a discussion of factors that influence the relationship between decisions and behavior).

Comparison With Alternative Approaches. The use of functional measurement methodology in our framework for studying the relationship between perceptions and attitudes is distinct from other popular approaches in the consumer literature. This section briefly contrasts the integration theory/functional measurement approach with expectancy-value models typified by Fishbein (1963) and conjoint measurement models.

Fishbein (1972) argues that an attitude toward a behavioral option is a summative function of subjective probability (*b*) and evaluation (*e*) products for each relevant belief (attribute or consequence). In most applications, a measure of the subjective likelihood of consequence "*i*" is obtained on a -3 to $+3$ unlikely-likely scale, as is a measure of the evaluation of the consequence on a -3 to $+3$ bad-good scale. A $b \times e$ product is computed for each consequence and then summed to yield an index of Aact.

In the integration theory/functional measurement approach, $w_i\ s_i$ products take on an analogous role to the $b_i\ e_i$ products. However, the w parameter reflects an importance weight and not a subjective probability. Belief strength (subjective probability) can be reflected in the present approach in two ways. First, differences in belief strength may be reflected in the subjective judgment of the alternative as being good, neutral, or bad on a given dimension. Ultimately, this impacts on the scale value. Second, differences in belief strength may impact on the importance of the information, w, independent of its impact on s.

In Fishbein's approach, the values of the $b_i\ e_i$ products are calculated from the multiplication of rating scales, an algebraic manipulation which assumes approximately ratio level measures. In integration theory, the values of the $w_i\ s_i$ products are inferred from an analysis of variance on attitudinal responses to hypothetical stimuli. Fishbein's approach may thus be characterized as a compositional model, because the individual *b* and *e* are used to "compose" an attitude measure. Functional measurement may be characterized as a decompositional approach, because the overall attitude responses are "decomposed" into estimates of w_i s_i (however, see Anderson, 1981, p. 76).

Fishbein's approach assumes a summative model for the b_i e_i products. Functional measurement assumes no single encompassing integration rule, but provides a means for testing the integration possibilities. The isolation of the integration rule can prove elusive. For example, it may be the case that several different integration rules could account for an observed pattern of means. Multiple experimental designs might be required to isolate the most viable integration rule (see Lynch, 1985 and Anderson, 1981 for further discussion of the "uniqueness" issue and methods for resolving it).

Other differences between the approaches could be highlighted. Interested readers are referred to Anderson (1981, 1982), Jaccard (1981), Lynch (1985), and Fishbein and Ajzen (1975). Future research should reveal the relative merits of the respective approaches as more applications are forthcoming in the consumer literature.

Conjoint measurement approaches (e.g., Green & Srinivasan, 1978; Green, Carroll, & Goldberg, 1981) are closely related to functional measurement. Two major distinctions are noted here. First, functional measurement has a formal error theory, in which unreliability of measures is explicitly taken into consideration when evaluating the integration rule and the impact of information on attitudes. The structure of the error theory is defined by the analysis of variance model, in which replicates in the factorial design are assumed to reflect measurement error. The mean-square error is an index of the average squared unreliability in the cells of the factorial design, and all effects are evaluated relative to this error. By contrast, conjoint measurement has no formal error theory (however, see Falmagne, 1976).

Second, the functional measurement approach requires that the dependent measure approximate interval level (i.e., linear) properties (Anderson, 1981, p. 6). If the measurement practices discussed earlier are followed, this will probably hold for the attitudinal judgments comprising the preference structure. In contrast, conjoint measurement only requires ordinal level measures of the dependent variable to isolate the integration function (Krantz & Tversky, 1971). The consequence of the weaker measurement assumption, however, is that the conjoint model is more limited in the number of integration rules it can test (Messier & Emery, 1980).[9]

Most consumer applications of conjoint measurement impose an additive integration rule on all individuals, and then focus efforts on isolating the impact of different pieces of information on attitude (in the form of utilities). If the integration rule is not additive, then the estimation procedures used can be subject to considerable error. For a further discussion of the differences between conjoint and functional measurement, see Lynch (1985).

---

[9]Functional measurement can allow for monotone transformation and still provide a valid error theory, based on the replicates method. (See Anderson, 1982).

Although we have conceptualized previous examples in terms of Anderson's information integration theory, functional measurement is not restricted to evaluating algebraic models of the type characterizing Anderson's approach. The methodology can be used to evaluate the applicability of a wide class of integration rules, both compensatory and noncompensatory in nature, and which have no reliance on the concept of "cognitive algebra." This includes models that assume processing of information on either a within-dimension or across-dimension basis (see Jaccard & Becker, 1985, for an illustration).

Qualitative Variables. The present approach incorporates qualitative variables into the analysis of integration processes, using a conceptualization which is distinct from most consumer applications (e.g., conjoint measurement). If a qualitative variable involves up to four levels, the convention has been to include all levels in the description of the hypothetical options. However, when the number of levels is large, the number of hypothetical options to be rated can become unwieldy. Usually the investigator resorts to selecting an arbitrary subset of levels to include or uses an external criterion to eliminate levels (e.g., those that are not cost effective in the market).

In the present approach, qualitative variables with any number of levels can be incorporated, using the same A-B-C rating scheme applied to quantitative variables. If the informational dimension is "type of radio," then a hypothetical car might be described as having an "A" on this dimension (i.e., the car is "good" in terms of the type of radio it has). The question of what type of radios are perceived as "good" or "bad" is a separate issue that can be addressed outside the context of analysis of the integration process (see earlier section on change implications). Note that this conceptualization also permits the inclusion of qualitative variables in the analysis of perceptual structures.

Methods of Presenting Hypothetical Options. Methods for presenting hypothetical options have been diverse in the consumer literature. Presentation formats have included verbal and paragraph descriptions, pictorial representations, and numerical descriptions. Research has suggested that the results one obtains may differ as a function of method of presentation (Cattin & Wittnik, 1982). The present method for describing options in terms of letter ratings on dimensions (note: we typically include verbal descriptions with the letter ratings) has not been formally compared with other formats. However, if the approach is suspect, then one would expect a poor fit betwen the observed and predicted preference structures in the external validation of model analysis. To date, the observed levels of fit have been quite good (see Jaccard & Becker, 1985). Future research might compare different presentation formats using the external validation method as a criterion for choosing between formats.

Fractional Factorial Designs and Related Approaches. A problem faced by most decompositional approaches, such as the present one, is to limit the number of hypothetical options that an individual must rate. The current paper advocates a procedure that restricts analysis to the three most important informational dimensions (conceivably, four or five could be manipulated, if judgments are spread over multiple sessions). This approach has the advantage of providing the most insights on the integration process, but suffers from the fact that only a limited number of information dimensions can be investigated. Fractional factorial designs have been popular in the consumer literature, in which one prespecifies one or more integration rules that will be evaluated, and then selects a smaller set of hypothetical options that will permit evaluation of those rules. For example, Green, Carroll, and Carmone (1978) specify designs that can assess the impact of all main effects and selected interactions, yet still retain multiple (e.g., 7 or 8) informational dimensions. These procedures are appropriate for the present approach, given that one can specify a priori the set of viable integration rules an individual might use. If the set excludes the true integration rule employed by the individual, then inferences are subject to error.

Lynch (1985) and others (e.g., Lerman & Louviere, 1978) have suggested an approach in which pilot studies are conducted to isolate potentially relevant integration rules. Fractional factorial designs are then used in the main investigation so as to permit testing of the viable rules suggested by the pretests. This approach is reasonable, given that the pilot studies accurately identify all viable integration rules for individuals in the main investigation.

Space limitations do not permit a discussion of other approaches to the problem of defining hypothetical options. Interested readers are referred to Green and Srinivasan (1978); Johnson (1974); Pekelman and Sen (1979); Lerman and Louviere (1978); Green (1974); Green, Carroll, and Carmone (1978); Louviere (1984); and Lynch (1984).

A related issue for fractional factorial designs is that individuals can find the presentation of large numbers of information dimensions confusing and complicated. This can be alleviated, in part, by the use of nested designs, with the corresponding trade-off of decreasing the number of integration rules that can be tested. Alternatively, a strategy of selecting only the n most important dimensions can be used.

Factorial Versus Representative Designs. The definition of hypothetical options using factorial designs has been criticized, because options which have no basis in reality may be presented to the individual to rate (e.g., a birth control method that is 99% effective and which has no side effects). This criticism is minimized with the proposed A-B-C scheme, although it is still possible to define nonmeaningful hypothetical options. In such instances, the nonmeaningful options can be omitted, without necessarily disrupting the estimation of the integration rule or the estimation of the impact of information on attitude. The consequences of omitting the nonmeaningful option will depend on the nature of the research question.

Evaluation of Methodological Practices. Controversy sometimes arises about the choice of methodological practices in presenting hypothetical stimuli to individuals. For example, is it better to use three or five informational dimensions in defining the stimuli? Is it better to manipulate a dimension with three or four levels? What is the best presentation format? And so on. The external validation procedure described here (see also Jaccard & Becker, 1985) provides a criterion against which different practices can be evaluated. The procedure which yields the best fit between observed and predicted preference structures will usually be the preferred practice.

Lack of Information and Psychological Imputations. When evaluating a set of options, an individual will sometimes have incomplete information about selected options. For example, when evaluating a set of banks, the individual may have no idea what the interest rate is at banks he/she is less familiar with. Of psychological interest is how individuals deal with "missing data" (other than obtaining the information from the environment). We have been investigating five distinct processes. First, the individual could impute the "average" value of all other banks on the dimension of interest, and form an attitude accordingly. Second, the individual could simply ignore the dimension when evaluating the option for which there is missing information. Third, the individual could "downgrade" the option on the dimension, equating no information with a "bad" standing. Fourth, the individual might "downgrade" the option entirely, and eliminate it from consideration (thus forming a very negative attitude toward it). Finally, the individual might infer the missing value based on other options which are related to the option in question or other dimensions which are related to the dimension in question. Our preliminary research suggests that individuals tend to impute an average value and form attitudes accordingly.

When rating existing options, we instruct individuals to "guess where they are not sure." This encourages them to impute a value on whatever basis they prefer, and is probably representative of what they would do in everyday life (i.e., we have found little support for the process of "downgrading" the option entirely). Given this procedure, application of our framework is straightforward for the case of "missing data."

Survey Research. One drawback to functional measurement methodology has been the difficulty in applying the approach in large scale survey situations. Fishbein and Ajzen's theory of reasoned action is relatively conducive to such applications, and has been used accordingly. The procedures developed here, could be readily adapted for use in survey situations. Respondents would first rank order a list of informational dimensions in terms of their importance. The A-B-C rating system would be explained for each dimension, together with the 21 point attitude scale. Each of the 27 hypothetical cases would then be described and rated. We have found it useful to write each case on a 3×5 card and to have respondents rate each card, in turn. The task could be completed at the beginning of the interview and if feasible, again at the end. Two replications permit analyses at the idiothetic level. With only one replication, approximate tests of statistical significance might still be possible, if one assumes a negligible three way interaction and forms an error term accordingly. Such an approach, however, will lack power due to the limited degrees of freedom in the error term. An alternative would be to conduct the analysis using one replicate per cell (hence, no error term would result) and set an eta square (e.g., 5% explained variance) as a criterion for "significance."

Nomothetic Analysis. The above analysis of the relationship between perceptual structures and preference structures focused on the single individual. It is possible to use the approach at the nomothetic level to characterize groups of individuals, although some complications arise. The major problem focuses on the fact that the *content* of the dimensions manipulated in the analysis of hypothetical options may differ across individuals. This would occur if there is within group variability in the ranking of the three most important dimensions. If this variability is minimal, then content is, for all intent and purposes, constant across individuals and nomothetic analyses are straightforward. When within group variability in the ranking of the top three dimensions is large, an alternative strategy can be used. This strategy would involve imposing the same three dimensions on all individuals. The dimensions can be selected either because they are of interest in their own right or on the basis of an empirical criterion (e.g., the three dimensions with the highest modal rank). The imposition of dimensions on individuals will have the effect of decreasing the fit between observed and predicted preference structures and will bias the investigator toward missing the perceptions underlying an attitude. However, it does permit an analysis of the effects of specific dimensions on attitudes toward behavioral options. An alternative strategy for dealing with this issue is discussed in Jaccard and Wan (in press).

Given a common set of dimensions across individuals, group level analysis of variance can be performed in the $3 \times 3 \times 3$ design. One can also include grouping factors in the analysis (e.g., males vs. females). Minimal assumptions (common scale unit) of uniform response language are in effect, as long as the focus is on differences between "repeated measure" means or on how differences between means are different in the various subgroups (e.g., for males, the difference between a "good" and "neutral" rating on the dimension of price is 4.12 units, whereas the corresponding difference for females is only 1.3 units).

A nomothetic issue that has arisen in our research is that of identifying groups of individuals with similar integration rules and informational effects. One approach is to use cluster analysis, in which individuals are grouped empirically. This involves the following: For a given individual, calculate the mean score for each cell of the factorial design. Subtract the grand mean from each score, to eliminate effects of the origin. Form a distance score between individuals A and B, by subtracting the score in a given cell for individual A from the corresponding cell for individual B, and summing the squared differences of all cells. This is repeated for all possible pairs of individuals, and the resulting NXN matrix of dissimilarity scores is then subjected to cluster analysis, using the methods discussed earlier. This approach requires the assumption of a common scale unit. The resulting clusters of individuals can then be subjected to functional measurement analysis. An alternative approach would be to retain the effects of the grand mean, thereby discriminating individuals with distinct origins.

Concluding Remarks

This chapter has identified some of the problems inherent with nomothetic analyses of psychological data. An idiothetic framework for the study of decision making was developed. We do not believe that the framework is without limitations, nor do we believe that it is applicable to all decision areas. However, we have found it to be useful in several applied settings and believe it is a reasonable first step toward the development of an idiothetic methodology in this domain. The logic of the approach can be adapted to other areas, and our hope is to stimulate the development of methods that can truly bridge the sizeable gap between idiographic and nomothetic approaches.

References

Ajzen, I., & Fishbein, M. (1969). The prediction of behavioral intentions in a choice situation. *Journal of Experimental Social Psychology, 5*, 400–416.

Ajzen, I., & Fishbein, M. (1977). Attitude-behavior relations: A theoretical analysis and review of empirical research. *Psychological Bulletin, 84*, 888–918.

Ajzen, I., & Fishbein, M. (1980). *Understanding social behavior.* Englewood Cliffs: Prentice-Hall.

Aldenderfer, M., & Blashfield, R. (1984). *Cluster analysis.* Beverly Hills: Sage.

Alfert, E. (1967). An idiographic analysis of personality differences between reactors to a vicariously experienced threat and reactors to a direct threat. *Journal of Experimental Research in Personality, 2*, 200–207.

Allport, G. (1937). *Personality: A psychological interpretation.* New York: Holt, Rinehart and Winston.

Allport, G. (1961). *Pattern and growth in personality.* New York: Holt, Rinehart and Winston.

Anderson, N. (1981). *Foundations of information integration theory.* New York: Academic Press.

Anderson, N. (1982). *Methods of information integration theory.* New York: Academic Press.

Baldwin, B. (1942). Personal structure analysis: A statistical method for investigation of the single personality. *Journal of Abnormal and Social Psychology, 37*, 163–183.

Batsell, R., & Lodish, L. (1981). A model and measurement methodology for predicting individual consumer choice. *Journal of Marketing Research, 18*, 1–12.

Becker, G., DeGroot, H., & Marschak, J. (1963). An experimental study of some stochastic models for wagers. *Behavioral Science, 3*, 199–202.

Bem, D., & Allen, A. (1974). On predicting some of the people some of the time: The search for cross-situational consistencies in behavior. *Psychological Review, 81*, 506–520.

Broverman, D. (1962). Normative and ipsative measurement in psychology. *Psychological Review, 69*, 295–305.

Bromely, D. (1977). *Personality description in ordinary language.* New York: Bancroft Books.

Cattell, R. (1966). *Handbook of multivariate experimental psychology.* Chicago: Rand McNally.

Cattin, P., & Wittnik, D. (1982). Commercial use of conjoint analysis: A survey. *Journal of Marketing*, *46*, 44–53.

Chassen, J. (1967). *Research design in clinical psychology and psychiatry.* New York: Irvington.

Cliff, N. (1959). Adverbs as multipliers. *Psychological Review*, *66*, 27–44.

Cronbach, L., Gleser, G., Nanda, H., & Rajaratnam, N. (1974). *The dependability of behavioral measurements*. New York: Wiley.

Currim, I. (1981). Using segmentation approaches for better prediction and understanding from consumer mode choice models. *Journal of Marketing Research*, *18*, 301–309.

Dillon, W., Frederick, D., & Tangpanichee, V. (1984). *Decision issues in building perceptual product spaces with multiattribute rating data*. Unpublished manuscript, Baruch College, Department of Marketing.

Dillon, W., Mulani, N., & Frederick, D. (1984). Removing perceptual distortions in product space analysis. *Journal of Marketing Research*, *21*, 184–193.

Emery, D., & Barron, F. (1980). Axiomatic and numerical conjoint measurement: An evaluation of diagnostic efficacy. *Psychometrika*, *44*, 195–210.

Falmagne, J. (1976). Random conjoint measurement and loudness summation. *Psychological Review*, *83*, 65–79.

Fishbein, M. (1963). An investigation of the relationships between belief about an object and the attitude toward the object. *Human Relations*, *16*, 233–240.

Fishbein, M. (1972). Towards an understanding of family planning behaviors. *Journal of Applied Social Psychology*, *2*, 216–227.

Fishbein, M., & Ajzen, I. (1975). *Belief, attitude, intention, and behavior: An introduction to theory and research*. Reading, MA: Addison-Wesley.

Gordon, R. (1968). Issues in multiple regression. *American Journal of Sociology*, *73*, 592–616.

Green, P. (1974). On design of choice experiments involving multifactor alternatives. *Journal of Consumer Research*, *1*, 61–68.

Green, P., Carroll, D., & Carmone, F. (1978). Some new types of fractional factorial designs for marketing experiments. In J. Seth (Ed.), *Research in Marketing: Vol. I.* Greenwich, CT: JAI Press.

Green, P., Carroll, D., & Goldberg, S. (1981). A general approach to product design optimization via conjoint analysis. *Journal of Marketing*, *45*, 17–37.

Green, P., Rao, V., & DeSarbo, W. (1978). Incorporating group-level similarity judgements in conjoint analysis. *Journal of Consumer Research*, *5*, 187–193.

Green, P., & Srinivasan, V. (1978). Conjoint analysis in consumer research: Issues and outlook. *Journal of Consumer Research*, *5*, 103–123.

Hauser, J., & Koppelman, F. (1979). Alternative perceptual mapping techniques: Relative accuracy and usefulness. *Journal of Marketing Research*, *16*, 495–506.

Holbrook, M., & Huber, J. (1979). Separating perceptual dimensions from affective overtones: An application to consumer aesthetics. *Journal of Consumer Research*, *15*, 272–283.

Holt, R. (1962). Individuality and generalization in the psychology of personality. *Journal of Personality*, *30*, 377–404.

Howe, E. (1962). Probabilistic adverbial quantifications of adjectives. *Journal of Verbal Learning and Verbal Behavior*, *1*, 225–242.

Huber, J., & Holbrook, M. (1979). Using attribute ratings for product positioning: Some distinctions among compositional approaches. *Journal of Marketing Research*, *16*, 507–516.

Jaccard, J. (1975). A theoretical analysis of selected factors important to health education strategies. *Health Education Monographs*, *3*, 152–166.

Jaccard, J. (1981). Attitudes and behavior: Implications of attitudes towards behavioral alternatives. *Journal of Experimental Social Psychology*, *25*, 41–78.

Jaccard, J., & Becker, M. (1985). Attitudes and behavior: An information integration perspective. *Journal of Experimental Social Psychology*, *33*, 201–215.

Jaccard, J., King, G., & Pomazal, R. (1977). Attitudes and behavior: An analysis of specificity of attitudinal predictors. *Human Relations*, *30*, 817–824.

Jaccard, J., & Wan, C. (in press) Cross-cultural analysis of behavioral decision making. *Journal of Cross-Cultural Psychology.*

Jaccard, J., Weber, J., & Lundmark, J. (1975). A multitrait-multimethod analysis of four attitude assessment procedures. *Journal of Experimental Social Psychology*, *11*, 149–154.

Johnson, R. (1971). Market segmentation: A strategic management tool. *Journal of Marketing Research*, *8*, 13–18.

Johnson, R. (1974). Trade off analysis of consumer values. *Journal of Marketing Research*, *11*, 121–127.

Kafrey, D., Jacobs, R., & Zedeck, S. (1979). Discriminability in multidimensional performance evaluations. *Applied Psychological Measurement*, *3*, 187–192.

Kirk, R. (1968). *Experimental design procedures for the behavioral sciences*. Belmont, CA: Wadsworth.

Krantz, D., & Tversky, A. (1971). Conjoint measurement analysis of composition rules in psychology. *Psychological Review*, *78*, 151–169.

Lamiell, J. (1981). Toward an idiothetic psychology of personality. *American Psychologist*, *38*, 276–289.

Lerman, S., & Louviere, J. (1978). Using functional measurement to identify the form of utility functions in travel demand models. *Transportation Research Record*, *78*, 673–676.

Louviere, J. (1983). Integrating conjoint and functional measurement with discrete choice theory: An experimental design approach. In R. Bagozzi, & A. Tybout (Eds.), *Advances in consumer research: Vol. 10*. Ann Arbor, MI: Association for Consumer Research.

Louviere, J., & Meyer, R. (1981). A composite attitude-behavior model of traveler decision making. *Transportation Research*, *15b*, 411–420.

Louviere, J., & Woodworth, G. (1983). Design and analysis of simulated consumer choice or allocation experiments: An approach based on aggregate data. *Journal of Marketing Research*, *20*, 350–367.

Lynch, J. (1984). *Adventures in paramorphic modeling: Models of consumer processing negative information*. Working Paper No. 39. Gainesville: University of Florida, Center for Consumer Research.

Lynch, J. (1985). Uniqueness issues in the decompositional modeling of multiattribute overall evaluations: An information integration perspective. *Journal of Marketing Research*, *22*, 1–19.

Massey, W., Montgomery, D., & Morrison, D. (1970). *Stochastic models of buying behavior*. Cambridge, MA: MIT Press.

McGuire, W. (1976). Some internal psychological factors influencing consumer choice. *Journal of Consumer Research*, *2*, 302–319.

Messick, S. (1957). Metric properties of the semantic differential. *Educational and Psychological Measurement*, *17*, 200–206.

Messier, W., & Emery, D. (1980). Commercial use of conjoint analysis: A survey. *Journal of Marketing*, *46*, 44–53.

Nisbett, R., & Wilson, T. (1977). Telling more than we can know: Verbal reports on mental processes. *Psychological Review*, *84*, 231–259.

Osgood, C., Suci, G., & Tannenbaum, P. (1957). *The measurement of meaning*. Urbana, IL: University of Illinois Press.

Parducci, A. (1965). Category judgement: A range frequency model. *Psychological Review*, *66*, 27–44.

Pekelman, D., & Sen, S. (1979). Measurement and estimation of conjoint utility functions. *Journal of Consumer Research*, *5*, 263–271.

Pruzansky, S., Tversky, A., & Carroll, J. (1982). Spacial versus tree representations of proximity data. *Psychometrika*, *47*, 3–27.

Reibstein, D. (1978). The prediction of individual probabilities of brand choice. *Journal of Consumer Research*, *5*, 163–168.

Rokeach, M., & Kliejunas, P. (1972). Behavior as a function of attitude-toward-object and attitude-toward-situation. *Journal of Personality and Social Psychology*, *22*, 194–201.

Runyan, W. (1983). Idiographic goals and methods in the study of lives. *Journal of Personality*, *51*, 413–437.

Shanteau, S. (1974). Component processes in risk decision making. *Journal of Experimental Psychology*, *103*, 680–691.

Shanteau, J., & Nagey, G. (1976). Decisions made about other people: A human judgement analysis of dating choice. In J. Carroll and J. Payne (Eds.), *Cognition and social behavior*. Potomac, MD: Erlbaum.

Shapiro, M. (1966). The single case in clinical psychological research. *Journal of General Psychology*, *74*, 3–23.

Tatsuoka, M. (1971). *Multivariate analysis: Techniques for educational and psychological research*. New York: John Wiley & Sons.

Triandis, H. (1977). *Interpersonal behavior*. Monterey, CA: Brooks/Cole Publishing.

Tversky, A. (1972). Elimination by aspects: A theory of choice. *Psychological Review*, *79*, 281–299.

Upshaw, H. (1962). Own attitude as an anchor in equal-appearing intervals. *Journal of Abnormal and Social Psychology*, *64*, 85–96.

Wegner, B. (1982). *Social attitudes and psychophysical measurement*. Hillsdale, NJ: Lawrence Erlbaum.

Wicker, A. (1969). Attitudes vs. actions: The relationship of verbal and overt behavioral responses to attitude objects. *Journal of Social Issues*, *25*, 41–78.

Wiggins, J. (1972). *Personality and prediction: Principles of personality assessment*. Reading, MA: Addison-Wesley.

Wilkie, W., & Pessimer, E. (1973). Issues in marketing use of multiattribute attitude models. *Journal of Marketing Research*, *10*, 428–441.

4
Building Consumer Behavior Models With LISREL: Issues in Applications

WILLIAM R. DILLON

Confirmatory factor analysis and structural equation modeling with unobservable variables have recently become prominent tools in the investigation and expression of behavioral- and social-science theory. The increased use of this more sophisticated methodology can, in large measure, be traced to the recognition that many variables of frequent interest cannot be observed directly. The recognition of unobservable latent variables has proven to be a source of fascination as well as consternation in consumer research because of the demands and challenges this poses for both measurement and theory. The role of measurement is to find rules of correspondence that relate latent variables to manifest indicators of latent constructs. However, it is sometimes difficult to know whether a given set of latent variables adequately represents the observable variables. The problem is that there is generally no operational method for directly measuring latent constructs. Latent variables are hypothetical constructs invented by a researcher in order to better understand the phenomena under investigation. The role of theory is to specify the relations among the latent constructs. A model then expresses measurement and theory in mathematical form and provides a means of optimally estimating the parameters of the model and determining the goodness-of-fit of the model to sample data on the manifest indicators.

Over 20 years ago, Jöreskog (1970) published a seminal paper that outlined a general framework for relating latent and manifest variables. In that paper Jöreskog developed a maximum likelihood (ML) estimation procedure for the analysis of covariance structures, which subsumes confirmatory factor analysis and linear structural equation models as special cases. In 1973, Jöreskog formulated a model for systems of structural equations, which he called LISREL, and provided the first LISREL computer program (Jöreskog & van Thillo, 1973). Today, LISREL is in its sixth commercial version (Jöreskog & Sörbom, 1982). The newest version, LISREL VI, offers several different options for parameter estimation (including maximum likelihood estimation and generalized least squares), generates automatic starting values for parameter estimates, and provides improved diagnostics.

Although the LISREL model is very flexible, it is nevertheless a special model in the general covariance structure analysis context. We should also add that there have been other contributors and other models in the literature. For example, the Bentler and Weeks (1980) model and program ESQ (Bentler, 1983) and the McDonald (1978) model and program COSAN (McDonald, 1980) stand as important, pioneering contributions. These models and programs are, in general, more flexible than the LISREL model in terms of the kinds of covariance structure models and constraints that can be handled, but are less accessible and require a sophisticated user.

In the past decade, consumer research evolving from Jöreskog's work has begun to flourish. In this time span the LISREL model has been used for parameter estimation in nearly every application of structural modeling in consumer and marketing research investigations. Specific applications of the LISREL model to substantive problems in experimental and correlational field studies cover such topics as consumer satisfaction, attitude organization, attitude-behavior relationships, involvement, and interorganizational analysis. A diverse yet representative set of applications can be found in the November 1982 special issue on causal modeling of the *Journal of Marketing Research*.

There is no doubt that the LISREL model and its many variants have greatly enhanced our ability to analyze correlational data. The ability to specify and restrict parameter values to be consistent with a prehypothesized covariance structure, based upon substantive theory, known experimental conditions, or an accumulated body of knowledge, has made all of us feel more comfortable as legitimate social scientists. The ability to "confront theory with data" is the most attractive feature of the LISREL model, and one that is central to evaluating cause and effect relationships. However, as potentially powerful as this method is, there are nevertheless problems in application and subtle nuisances that must be recognized if LISREL models are to provide meaningful results.

Admittedly the objectives of this chapter are audacious. The chapter is oriented to have a didactic function, with particular emphasis on our present accumulated knowledge of the problems and pitfalls involved in the application of the LISREL model and its many variants. The first major section of this chapter contains an introduction to the LISREL model. The second major section presents applications with illustrations of validity assessment, the use of inequality constraints, and the analysis of multitrait multimethod data. The third major section focuses on issues and problems which occur frequently in applications, including Heywood cases and the phenomenon of interpretational confounding.

The LISREL Model

In this section we present an introduction to the LISREL model and the LISREL VI computer program. The discussion is succinct since technical details can be found elsewhere (cf. Jöreskog & Sörbom, 1978, 1982). Readers familiar with the LISREL VI model can skip this section without loss of continuity. Those wanting an introductory treatment should consult Long (1983a, 1983b).

Representing Causal Systems[1]

Path diagrams are useful for displaying graphically the pattern of causal relationships among sets of observable and unobservable variables. In a causal model certain variables are singled out as causes and other variables as effects. Variables that cause other variables and whose variability is assumed to be determined by other causes outside the causal model are called *exogenous*. Since the relationship between exogenous variables is not under consideration in the model, no attempts are made at explaining their intercorrelations. On the other hand, variables whose variation is explained by exogenous variables or other variables in the system are called *endogenous*.

Several conventions are followed in drawing path diagrams. Observable exogenous variables are denoted by X's; observable endogenous variables are denoted by Y's. All observable variables are represented by squares; all unobservable variables are represented by circles. Unobservable exogenous variables are denoted by ξ (xi); unobservable endogenous variables are denoted by η (eta). The effects of endogenous on endogenous variables are denoted by β (beta) coefficients; the effects of exogenous variables on endogenous variables are denoted by γ (gamma) coefficients. The correlations between unobservable exogenous variables are denoted by ϕ (phi). The error term for each equation relating a set of exogenous and endogenous explanatory variables to an endogenous criterion variable is denoted by ζ (zeta). The regression coefficient relating each observable variable to its unobservable counterpart is denoted by λ (lambda). Errors in the measurement of exogenous variables are denoted by δ (delta); errors in the measurement of endogenous variables are denoted by ϵ (epsilon). The correlation between exogenous variables is depicted by curved lines with arrowheads at both ends. This signifies that one variable is not being conceived as a cause of the other variable. Paths, in the form of unidirectional arrows, are drawn from the variables taken as causes (exogenous, independent) to the variables taken as effects (endogenous, dependent).

Consider, as an example, the causal system shown in Figure 4.1. The model consists of three latent exogenous variables (ξ_1, ξ_2, and ξ_3) and two latent endogenous variables (η_1 and η_2). According to the model, ξ_1 is measured by two indicators(X_1 and X_2), ξ_2 is measured by two indicators (X_3 and X_4), and ξ_3 is measured by a single indicator (X_5). It is further assumed that η_1 is measured by a single indicator (Y_1), and η_2 is measured by two indicators (Y_2 and Y_3).

The model depicted in the figure states that ξ_1 affects η_2 directly, and η_1 indirectly via η_2. ξ_2 and ξ_3 affect η_1 directly, and η_2 indirectly via η_1. According to the model, η_1 has a direct effect on η_2, and η_2 has a direct effect on η_1. Models that postulate reciprocal causation between endogenous variables are called *nonrecursive* models. Note that there is no requirement that $\beta_1=\beta_2$. Models that postulate unidirectional, one-way causal flows—which means that, at a given

[1]This section follows the discussion found in Dillon and Goldstein (1984, Chapter 12).

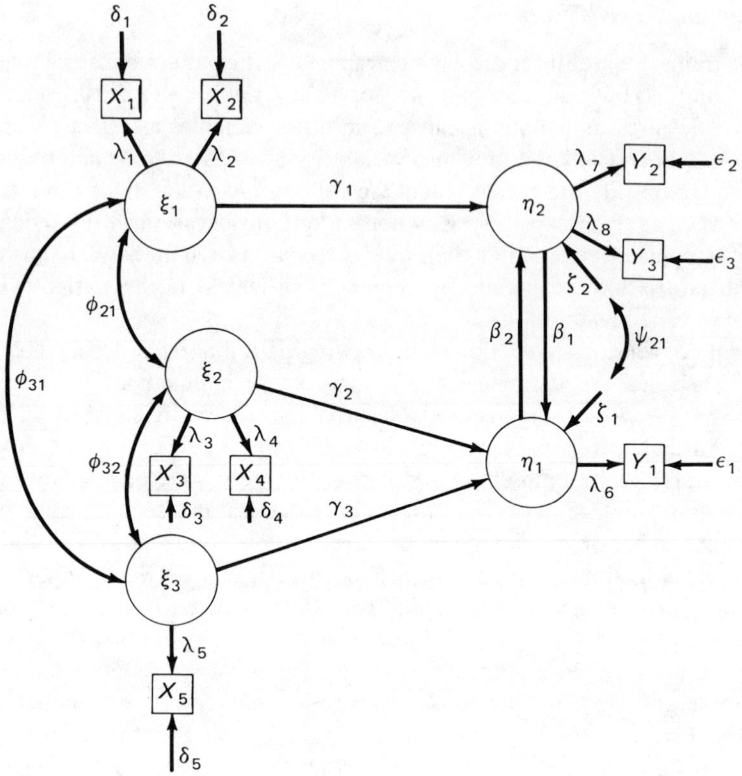

FIGURE 4.1.

point in time, a variable is not permitted to be both a cause and an effect of another variable—are called *recursive* models. If we had hypothesized that η_1 directly affects η_2, but not vice versa, then the model shown in Figure 4.1 would be a recursive one; that is, β_1 would be set to zero.

The model shown in the figure corresponds to the following system of structural equations:

$$\eta_1 = \beta_1\eta_2 + \gamma_2\xi_2 + \gamma_3\xi_3 + \zeta_1 \tag{1}$$

$$\eta_2 = \beta_2\eta_1 + \gamma_1\xi_1 + \zeta_2 \tag{2}$$

where ζ_1 and ζ_2 are *residuals*, that is, errors in equations. Note that in the figure ψ_{21} (psi) gives the correlation between the residuals ζ_1 and ζ_2.

Structural and Measurement Components

The LISREL model, as implemented in the LISREL VI program, considers random vectors $\eta'=(\eta_1,\eta_2,\ldots,\eta_m)$ and $\xi'=(\xi_1,\xi_2,\ldots,\xi_h)$ of latent dependent (endogenous) and latent independent (exogenous) variables, respectively, and the following system of linear structural relations

$$\eta = \alpha + \beta\eta + \Gamma\xi + \zeta \tag{3}$$

In model (3), $\alpha(m \times 1)$ is a vector of (mean) intercept coefficients, $\beta(m \times m)$ and $\Gamma(m \times n)$ are coefficient matrices, whose elements give the direct causal effects of η variables on other η variables (the β matrix) and the direct causal effects of ξ variables on η variables (the Γ matrix), and $\zeta' = (\zeta_1, \zeta_2, \ldots, \zeta_m)$ is a random vector of residuals (i.e., errors in equations), where $E(\zeta) = 0$.

For those readers who are still using LISREL IV note that there is a new definition of β in model (3). The matrix β now has zeros in the diagonal and contains the direct effects of each η on other η's. The β matrix in LISREL IV, β_{IV}, is related to the β matrix in LISREL VI by

$$\beta_{IV} = \mathbf{I} - \beta_{VI} \,.$$

The obvious advantage of this new definition is that the path comes out with the correct signs and therefore corresponds exactly to the direct paths from one η to another—no algebraic change in sign is needed. It is assumed that ζ is uncorrelated with ξ and that $\mathbf{I}$-β is nonsingular. Equation 3 is often referred to as the structural equation component of the LISREL model.

The vectors η and ξ of latent endogenous and exogenous variables are not observed. What is observed instead are the vectors $\mathbf{y}' = (y_1, y_2, \ldots, y_p)$ and $\mathbf{x}' = (x_1, x_2, \ldots, x_q)$ whose elements are the readings on the manifest endogenous and exogenous variables, respectively. The relations between the endogenous latent and manifest variables and the exogenous latent and manifest variables are such that

$$\mathbf{y} = \mathbf{V}_y + \Lambda_y\eta + \epsilon \tag{4}$$

and

$$\mathbf{x} = \mathbf{V}_x + \Lambda_x\xi + \delta \tag{5}$$

where ϵ and δ are vectors of errors of measurement in $\mathbf{y}$ and $\mathbf{x}$, respectively; $\Lambda_y(p \times m)$ and $\Lambda_x(q \times n)$ are regression weights of $\mathbf{y}$ on η and of $\mathbf{x}$ on ξ, respectively; $\mathbf{V}_y$ and $\mathbf{V}_x$ are (mean) location parameters. Under suitable conditions these regression weights can be interpreted as *loadings*. The errors of measurement, ϵ and δ, are assumed to be uncorrelated with η, ξ and ζ; however, they may be correlated among themselves. Equations 4 and 5 are commonly referred to as the measurement component of the LISREL model.

Because in a single sample there is little interest in location parameters of the latent variables or in intercept terms of the equations, we will hereafter assume that all variables, both latent and manifest, are measured in deviations from their means.[2] Thus $E(\alpha) = E(\mathbf{V}_y) = E(\mathbf{V}_x) = \mathbf{0}$, and the structural and measurement equations become

$$\eta = \beta\eta + \Gamma\xi + \zeta \tag{6}$$

[2]Actually, in a single population, all mean parameters α, V_y, and V_x will not, in general, be identified unless further conditions are imposed (for more details see Sörbom, 1981).

and

$$\begin{aligned}\mathbf{y} &= \Lambda_y \eta + \epsilon \\ \mathbf{x} &= \Lambda_x \xi + \delta\end{aligned} \tag{7}$$

Letting the covariance matrices of ξ and ζ be denoted by $\phi(n \times n)$ and $\Psi(m \times m)$, respectively, and the covariance matrices of ϵ and δ be denoted by Θ where

$$\Theta = \begin{pmatrix} \Theta_\epsilon & \\ & \Theta_\delta \end{pmatrix}$$

We can express the covariance matrix $\Sigma[(p+q)\times(p+q)]$ of the manifest variables $\mathbf{z}=(\mathbf{y}', \mathbf{x}')'$ in terms of the elements of Λ_y, Λ_x, β, Γ, Φ, Ψ, and Λ as follows:

$$\Sigma = \left(\begin{array}{c|c} \Lambda_y(\mathbf{I}-\beta)^{-1}(\Gamma\Phi\Gamma'+\Psi)(\mathbf{I}-\beta')^{-1}\Lambda_y'+\Theta_\epsilon & \Lambda_y(\mathbf{I}-\beta)^{-1}\Gamma\Phi\Lambda'_x \\ \hline \Lambda_x\Phi\Gamma'(\mathbf{I}-\beta')^{-1}\Lambda_y' & \Lambda_x\Phi\Lambda_x'+\Theta_\delta \end{array}\right) \tag{8}$$

In substantive investigations the LISREL model requires that the researcher specify the elements of the matrices described above according to whether they contain:

1. Fixed parameters that have been assigned given values such as zero or one.
2. Constrained parameters that are unknown, but equal to one or more other parameters.
3. Free parameters that are unknown and left unconstrained (Jöreskog & Sörbom, 1982, p. I.8).

The LISREL VI computer program does not require that start values for the elements of all the matrices be supplied, as did earlier versions. Automatic starting values are provided in LISREL VI by using instrumental variables methods and least-squares methods developed by Hägglund (1982). Technical details on these methods as applied to LISREL models can be found in Jöreskog and Sörbom (1982). In addition to the constraints described above it is also possible to impose inequality constraints on structural parameter coefficients (Rindskopf, 1984). In one of the application sections that follow we discuss and illustrate how the various types of constraints can be imposed.

The LISREL model provides a very general and flexible system for testing causal hypotheses. The LISREL VI computer program can handle a variety of submodels as special cases in a simple manner. For example, consider the following possibilities:

1. No **y**- and η-variables. By specifying no endogenous manifest **y**-variables and no endogenous latent η-variables the basic model becomes

$$\mathbf{x} = \Lambda_x \xi + \delta \tag{9}$$

   which is, of course, the classic factor–analytic model.
2. No **x**- and ξ-variables. By specifying no exogenous **x**-variables and no exogenous latent ξ-variables we have the factor-analytic model defined by

$$\mathbf{y} = \Lambda_y \eta + \epsilon$$
$$\eta = \beta\eta + \zeta \tag{10}$$

where the elements in β give the relations among the factors which can be used in fitting various simplex models (cf. Jöreskog, 1977; Sörbom, 1975, 1981).

3. No **x**-variables and $\beta = \mathbf{0}$. By specifying no exogenous manifest variables and $\beta = \mathbf{0}$ the basic model becomes

$$\eta = \Gamma\xi + \zeta$$
$$\mathbf{y} = \Lambda_y \eta + \epsilon \tag{11}$$

which is a second-order factor analysis model. We will discuss and illustrate higher-order factor analysis models in later sections.

Estimation

The objective of the LISREL model is to reproduce the observed covariance matrix as closely as possible and to determine the goodness-of-fit of the model to sample data on the observed variables. The basic input to a LISREL analysis is either the observed covariance or correlation matrix. With correlational input the standard errors of the parameter estimates are likely to be affected (see, Lawley & Maxwell, 1971). In longitudinal investigations the researcher may not wish to use correlational input if the variance of the manifest indicators is different across the various time periods. The LISREL VI computer program offers three options with respect to parameter estimation: (1) initial estimates (IE), (2) unweighted least-squares estimates (ULS), and (3) maximum likelihood estimates (ML). The IE, which also serves as starting values, are based on a noniterative ad hoc procedure. Because the estimation procedure is noniterative, IE requires small amounts of CPU time. As we indicated, further details on the IE procedure can be found in Jöreskog and Sörbom (1982). The ULS estimates are based on an iterative procedure which minimizes the following fitting function

$$\mathrm{F} = 1/2\ \mathrm{tr}[(\mathbf{S} - \Sigma)^2] \tag{12}$$

where Σ is the covariance matrix implied by the model and $\mathbf{S}$ is the sample covariance matrix, by successively improving the parameter estimates starting with the IE. The ULS estimation procedure does not require that distributional assumptions be in place. The ML estimates are also based on an iterative procedure which minimizes the following fitting function

$$F = \log|\Sigma| + \mathrm{tr}(\mathbf{S}\Sigma^{-1}) - \log|\mathbf{S}| - (p+q), \tag{13}$$

where Σ is the covariance matrix implied by the model and $\mathbf{S}$ is the sample covariance matrix, by successively improving the parameter estimates starting with the IE. The ML estimation procedure is based on the assumption that the observed variables have a multinormal distribution (Jöreskog, 1967). If multinormality is in place, then the ML estimates are optimal in the sense of being most precise in large samples. We will discuss the consequences of using the ML fitting function when the observed variables deviate from normality in a later section.

All three methods of estimation give consistent estimates which means that if the model is correct estimates are close to parameter values in large samples (Jöreskog & Sörbom, 1982). It is important to note, however, that several local minima of the fitting function can be obtained. Because the LISREL VI computer program does not constrain variances to be positive or correlations to be less than unity, and so forth, improper solutions, that is, parameter estimates outside the admissible parameter space, are also possible. The only constraint imposed in LISREL VI is that the fitted matrix, $\hat{\Sigma}$, reproduced by the model is positive definite (Jöreskog & Sörbom, 1982). Improper solutions and related issues in applications will be discussed in later sections.

Hypothesis Testing

Hypothesis testing can be carried out using "critical ratios" and an approximate χ^2-test statistic. The ratio of the parameter estimate to its standard error (ML estimates only) indicates whether individual parameter estimates are statistically different from zero.

The LISREL VI computer program reports standardized parameter effects. Note, however, that the standardized parameter effects reported are a bit different from conventionally calculated ones. To convert the LISREL standardized parameter estimates to a more conventional form we simply need to apply the following relationship:

$$\lambda^S_{x_i} = \frac{\lambda^S_{x_i}(\text{LISREL})}{\sqrt{\text{var}(X_i)}}$$

$$\lambda^S_{y_i} = \frac{\lambda^S_{y_i}(\text{LISREL})}{\sqrt{\text{var}(X_i)}}$$

where $\lambda^S_{x_i}$ and $\lambda^S_{y_i}$ are the conventional standardized effects, and $\lambda^S_{x_i}$ (LISREL) and $\lambda^S_{y_i}$ (LISREL) are the standardized effects reported by LISREL VI. As we indicated, standard errors in LISREL are strictly valid only when the covariance matrix is analyzed. These ratios are commonly referred to as "critical ratios."

The χ^2-test statistic compares the goodness-of-fit between the covariance matrix for the observed data (**S**) and covariance matrix ($\hat{\Sigma}$) derived from a theoretically specified model. The null hypothesis (H_o) is that the observed covariance matrix (**S**) corresponds to the covariance matrix derived from the theoretical specification $\hat{\Sigma}$. The alternative hypothesis (H_1) is that the observed covariance matrix is any arbitrary matrix whose eigenvalues are all nonzero. The χ^2-test statistic is equal to $N-1$ times the minimum value of the fitting function for the specified model and under multinormality and large sample sizes it is distributed as a chi-square random variable with degrees-of-freedom given by $[(p+q)(p+q+1)/2]-Z$, where Z is the total number of independent parameters estimated for the specified model. The probability level of the χ^2-test statistic is the probability of having a χ^2 value larger than the value actually obtained given that the model is correct. As discussed by Fornell (1983), the overall χ^2 test in LISREL (and, in general, covariance structure analysis) reverses the traditional role of hypotheses in statistical theory. In other words, in the LISREL model if the null hypothesis is rejected, then one's research hypothesis must be rejected. However, the power of this test is not known. Low power in the context of the LISREL model has serious implications since it means that one's model may find support when in fact it is incorrect. Thus, in terms of significance levels, setting p at .10, for example, does not constitute strong support for the research hypothesis.

These are also sample size considerations. Large samples are needed in order to provide a sufficiently valid statistical test; however, with large samples it is almost certainly assured that nearly any $\hat{\Sigma}$ will be rejected as different from S, because the χ^2 statistic is a direct function of the sample size. With small samples, statistically significant differences between Σ and $\mathbf{S}$ are unlikely; however, unlike most conventional statistical tests, a statistically nonsignificant χ^2 means that the test fails to reject the null hypothesis that the proposed model provides a plausible representation of $\mathbf{S}$. Thus, with large samples, there is a bias against proposed models, whereas with small samples there is a bias for them.

The χ^2-test statistic described above can also be used to compare alternative competing models. Let $\chi^2{}_{M_A}$ be the χ^2 value associated with Model A and $\chi^2{}_{M_B}$ be the χ^2 value associated with Model B, where the latter model is a nested version of the former one; that is, Model B is hierarchically related to Model A in that it contains all of the same structural relations as in Model A plus at least one unique constraint. A difference in χ^2-test statistic, denoted by χ^2_d, can be computed by taking

$$\chi^2_d = \chi^2_{M_A} - \chi^2_{M_B} \tag{14}$$

where χ^2_d is itself distributed as a chi-square random variable with degrees of freedom found by subtraction, $\text{d.f.}_d = \text{d.f.}_{M_A} - \text{d.f.}_{M_B}$. If the probability value associated with χ^2_d for two competing models is greater than some specified critical level, then the additional terms included in Model B are nonsignificant and the more parsimonious model (Model A) is just as good. Such χ^2_d tests are an improvement over the overall testing strategy since they reduce the problem of sample size and eliminate the problem of the reversal of the research hypothesis. It is important to note, however, that the χ^2_d test is strictly appropriate only when one of the models being compared (i.e., the less restricted one) adequately fits the data. This is frequently overlooked in substantive applications (cf. Bagozzi, 1978, 1980).

Bentler and Bonett (1980) have proposed the use of a χ^2_d-test statistic in the context of a null model that is different from the traditional one. The traditional model states *the covariance matrix implied by the proposed model does not differ from the sample covariance matrix*. The new null model is an incremental fit hypothesis, which states: *The covariance matrix implied by the proposed model is closer to the sample covariance matrix than is the covariance matrix implied by a null model of complete independence in which no epistemic or structural relations are specified*. Letting χ_o^2 denote the χ^2 value associated with the null model that specifies r structural relations then $\chi_d^2=\chi_o^2-\chi_r^2$ with $\text{d.f.}_d=\text{d.f.}_o-\text{d.f.}_r$ gives the relevant model comparison test.

Goodness-of-Fit

Because the assumptions underlying the χ^2test statistic (multinormality and large sample sizes) are seldom met in practice, the general thinking today is to view the χ^2 measure as a goodness (or badness)-of-fit index rather than as a formal test statistic. For example, Jöreskog and Sörbom (1982, pp. I.40) suggest three heuristic goodness-of-fit indices. The first measure is GFI, the goodness-of-fit index, defined by

$$\text{GFI} = 1 - \frac{\text{tr}(\hat{\Sigma}^{-1}\mathbf{S}-\mathbf{I})^2}{\text{tr}(\hat{\Sigma}^{-1}\mathbf{S})^2} \quad \text{for ML} \tag{15a}$$

and

$$\text{GFI} = 1 - \frac{\text{tr}(\mathbf{S}-\Sigma)^2}{\text{tr}(\mathbf{S}^2)} \quad \text{for ULS.} \tag{15b}$$

The second measure is AFGI, the goodness-of-fit index adjusted for degrees of freedom, defined by

$$\text{AGFI} = 1 - [k(k+1)/2d](1-\text{GFI}) \tag{16}$$

where $k=p+q$ and d denotes degrees of freedom for the specified model. Jöreskog and Sörbom (1982) give the following as properties of GFI and AGFI: (1) Both should be between zero and one (although negative values are theoretically possible), (2) both indicate the relative amount of variance and covariance explained by the specified model, (3) both are independent of sample size, and (4) both are relatively robust to violation of multinormality (although their sampling distributions are at present unknown). Finally, the third measure is RMR, the root mean square residual, defined by

$$\text{RMR} = [2 \sum_{i=1}^{k} \sum_{j=1}^{k} (s_{ij}-\hat{\sigma}_{ij})^2/k(k+1)]^{1/2} \tag{17}$$

where s_{ij} and $\hat{\sigma}_{ij}$ are the elements of $\mathbf{S}$ and $\hat{\Sigma}$, respectively. This goodness-of-fit index gives a measure of the average magnitude of the residuals.

Bentler and Bonett (1980) have also proposed the use of heuristic goodness-of-fit indices. They suggest the index RHO (ϱ):

$$\varrho = \frac{Q_o - Q_r}{Q_o - 1} \tag{18}$$

where

$$Q_o = \chi_o^2/\text{d.f.}_o$$

and

$$Q_r = \chi_r^2/\text{d.f.}_r$$

The index ϱ gives the increment in fit obtained by using r structural relations rather than none, as implied by the null model of independence.

Other Program Diagnostics

The LISREL VI program gives other program diagnostics which can prove helpful in evaluating LISREL models. For example, large standard errors or parameter estimates that are highly correlated are signals that the model is nearly nonidentified and that some parameters cannot be determined from the sample data (Jöreskog & Sörbom, 1982). The program also gives (a) squared multiple correlations for each observed variable separately, (b) squared multiple correlations for each structural equation, and (c) coefficients of determination for all structural equations jointly. Computational details can be found in Jöreskog and Sörbom (1982).

Other important diagnostic features of the LISREL VI program relate to normalized residuals, first-order derivatives and modification indices. The overall measure described in previous sections provide no diagnostic information since if a poor fitting model is obtained, there is no indication of what is wrong with the model or which part of the model needs adjustment. In contrast, the normalized residuals and modification indices are particularly useful in suggesting which parameter restrictions should be freed up so as to improve model fit. Interest centers on residuals larger than two in absolute magnitude since residuals of this size are indicative of specification error. The modification indices are derived from the derivatives of the fitting function with respect to the fixed and constrained parameters. Jöreskog and Sörbom (1982, pp. I.42) explain that the modification indices give the expected decrease in χ^2 if a single constraint is relaxed and all estimated parameters are held fixed at their estimated value. Therefore, these indices can be judged on the basis of a χ^2 distribution with one degree of freedom. The fixed parameter with the largest modification index is the one which when relaxed will improve fit maximally, that is, produce the largest decrease in the χ^2-test statistic. Through Jöreskog's residuals and modification indices can prove quite useful in identifying models with improved fits, they should not be used without regard for the substantive interpretation of the parameters freed up and the relationship of the revised model to one's original hypothesized model.

Applications

The LISREL model and its many variants have been used to address many substantive questions in consumer research. The three sections to follow present selected applications of the LISREL technology. The first application deals with the use of LISREL in validity assessment and specifically on how it can be used to assess convergent, discriminant and nomological validity in the context of an attitude-behavior relationship investigation. The second application demonstrates how inequality constraints and phantom variables can be used judiciously to test consumer behavior relationships, again in the context of an attitude-behavior relationship investigation. Finally, the last application considers the issue of construct validity of attitude but this time in the context of a multitrait-multimethod (MTMM) design. The discussion will be brief. The intent is not to provide an exhaustive description of LISREL uses, but to acquaint the reader with some standard as well as novel applications and with the fact that the LISREL model makes it possible to address interesting consumer research questions that would be otherwise difficult to handle with other methods.

Application 1: Validity Assessment and the Attitude-Behavior Relationship[3]

The LISREL model has been used frequently to investigate the convergent and discriminant validity of attitude and the predictive/nomological validity of attitude-behavior relationships. In this section we demonstrate how these types of validity analyses have been undertaken in the context of a study reported by Bagozzi and Burnkrant (1979)—hereafter referred to as B & B—which reanalyzed data originally reported by Fishbein and Ajzen (1974). The data relate to attitude-behavior relationships concerning religion. Table 4.1 summarizes the observed correlations between the attitude and behavioral criterion measures. Attitude measures were collected on five traditional scales. The first measure was a (single item) Guilford self-rating scale. The second measure used a semantic differential format consisting of five evaluative bipolar scales. The sum across all five semantic differential scales was taken as an index of attitude toward religiosity scales constructing using the techniques of summated ratings (Likert, 1932), scalogram analysis (Guttman, 1944), and equal-appearing intervals (Thurstone & Chave, 1929), respectively. Two types of behavioral responses were collected: self-reported behaviors and behavioral intentions. Sixty-two subjects were asked to check which of 100 behaviors they had performed (self-reported behaviors—SRB), while the remaining 63 subjects constituting the sample were asked to check which of 100 behaviors they would perform (behavioral intentions—BI). Each set of behavioral responses was used to form five behavioral criteria: a single-act behavioral criterion measure, a multiple-act behavioral criterion measure, and three scaled multiple-act behavioral criterion measures meeting the requirements of the Likert, Guttman, and Thurstone scaling procedures.

Convergent and Discriminant Validity

Convergent validity has been investigated with the LISREL model by the fit of rival confirmatory factor-analytic models. Specifically, in the context of Fishbein

---

[3]Parts of the following discussion and analysis are taken from Dillon and Kumar (1985).

TABLE 4.1. Correlations of verbal attitude scales, single-act and multiple-act behavioral criteria, and behavioral scales from Fishbein and Ajzen (1974)[a]

Variable	1	2	3	4	5	6	7	8	9	10
1. Self-report	—	.800	.519	.652	.584	.137	.640	.451	.582	.701
2. Semantic differential	.765[b]	—	.644	.762	.685	.149	.714	.591	.688	.727
3. Guttman	.688	.773	—	.790	.744	.121	.608	.531	.647	.570
4. Likert	.743	.837	.878	—	.785	.142	.684	.660	.656	.611
5. Thurstone	.672	.666	.818	.786	—	.131	.628	.575	.624	.542
6. Single-act criterion[c]	.162	.178	.176	.202	.170	—	—	.143	.178	.156
7. Multiple-act criterion[d]	.604	.658	.656	.749	.648	—	—	.699	.898	.789
8. Guttman behavior	.444	.517	.501	.563	.483	.189	.750	—	.776	.631
9. Likert behavior	.594	.640	.656	.727	.649	.229	.915	.851	—	.792
10. Thurstone behavior	.545	.566	.663	.677	.628	.202	.797	.553	.793	—

[a] Above diagonal for respondents indicating self-reported behaviors ($n = 62$); below diagonal for respondents indicating behavioral intentions ($n = 63$).
[b] $r_{.05} = .250$; $r_{.01} = .325$.
[c] Mean correlation with 100 behaviors or intentions.
[d] Sum over 100 behaviors or intentions.
Note. From M. Fishbein & T. Ajzen (1974). Attitudes towards objects as predictors of single and multiple behavioral criteria, *81*, 59–74.

and Ajzen's (1974) data, we can investigate the fit of two competing models which are shown in Figure 4.2. The rival hypotheses correspond to (a) a single factor, unidimensional model in which the nonerror variance in traits is captured by one underlying attitude construct (A), and (b) a two-factor, multidimensional model which posits that the attitude construct is reflected by an affective compo-

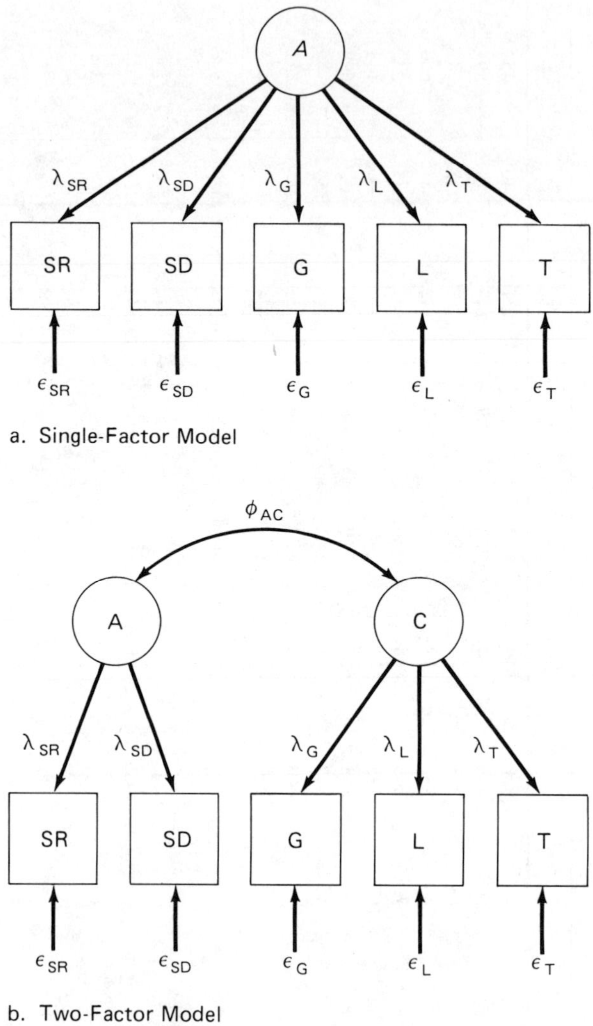

A = Single component attitude construct
A = Affective attitude component
C = Cognitive attitude component
SR = Guilford self-rating
SD = Semantic differential
G = Guttman
L = Likert
T = Thurstone scales

The remaining symbols represent parameters to be estimated and are defined in the text.

FIGURE 4.2.

nent (A) and a cognitive or belief component (C). In the latter model the two components of attitude are conceptualized to be independent, although they can be related empirically as indicated by the ϕ_{AC} parameter.

Considering the SRB and BI samples separately, it appears that the convergent validity of the single-factor model (Figure 4.2, Panel a) can be rejected in both samples: $\chi^2(5) = 23.91, p < .01$, GFI = .862, AGFI = .587—SRB sample and $\chi^2(5) = 13.98, p < .02$, GFI = .919, AGFI = .758—BI sample; whereas for the two-factor two-component model (Figure 4.2, Panel b) the results are more encouraging: $\chi^2(4) = 2.30, p \simeq .68$, GFI = .986, AGFI = .946—SRB sample and $\chi^2(4) = 7.65, p \simeq .08$, GFI = .949, AGFI = .807—BI sample.

To investigate the relatively poor fit of the single-factor model, the normalized residuals were examined. In both samples, the largest (absolute value) residuals corresponded to the self-rating and semantic differential items, which indicates that these items share variation that is not adequately captured by a single-factor model. As we argue later, there are many alternative models, in addition to a two-factor affective/cognitive model, that can capture this covariation.

In evaluating constructs, discriminant validity is also important. Discriminant validity is the degree to which measures of distinct constructs differ. In the two-factor two-component model this means that measures of the affective attitude construct should share little common variance (in a relative sense) with the measures of the cognitive attitude construct; too high a covariation casts doubts on the uniqueness of the measures and/or the constructs. In the present case, we can assess the degree of discriminant validity of the two-factor two-component model by examining the magnitude of the ϕ_{AC} parameter estimate, which links the affective and cognitive components. Specifically, the correlation between the two components of attitude should be "meaningfully" less than unity; if this correlation is close to unity, it would suggest that there is no meaningful distinction between these constructs. In the SRB sample $\hat{\phi}_{AC} = .82$, and in the BI sample $\hat{\phi}_{AC} = .93$. Thus the evidence suggests that it may be difficult to distinguish between these two constructs in a meaningful way.

Predictive/Nomological Validity

The validity of the attitude construct can also be judged by its ability to predict behavioral criteria. Consider Figure 4.3 which shows a path-like model. This model, which was considered by B & B (1979, p. 926), hypothesizes that the two-factor, affective/cognitive model of attitude can predict scaled multiple behavioral criteria. The fit of this model was satisfactory ($\chi^2(10) = 13.11, p \simeq .22$, GFI = .942, AGFI = .852). In essence, the predictive validity of the hypothesized model rests on the statistical significance of the $\gamma_{B \cdot A}$ and $\gamma_{B \cdot C}$ structural parameters. And thus to test the predictive validity of this model presumes that the individual effects of the affective and cognitive constructs can be separated and tested independently through the $\gamma_{B \cdot A}$ and $\gamma_{B \cdot C}$ parameters. But herein lies the problem.

The ability to make statements concerning the relative effects of predictor variables in a multiple regression analysis rests, in general, on the variables being uncorrelated. In the presence of correlated predictor variables (a) the model

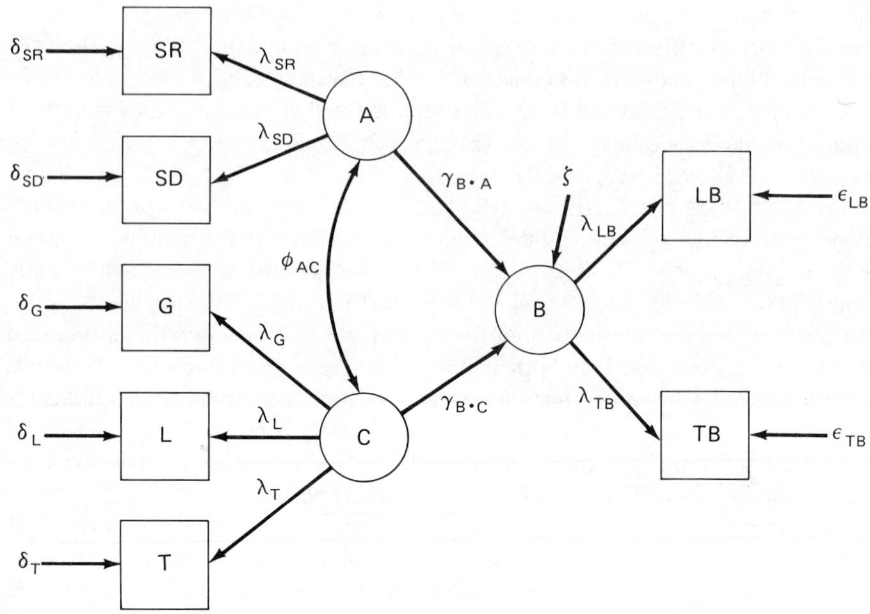

A = Affective component of attitude
C = Cognitive component of attitude
SR = Guilford self-rating
SD = Semantic differential
G = Guttman
L = Likert
T = Thurstone
B = Scaled behavior construct
LB = Likert-scaled behavior
TB = Thurstone-scaled behavior

The remaining symbols represent parameters to be estimated and are defined in the text

FIGURE 4.3.

coefficients may have the wrong signs, (b) regression coefficients may change drastically as a result of minor changes in the data due to, for example, omitting one or two observations or even changing the number of significant digits for measuring variables, and (c) the usual significance tests may lead to conflicting conclusions (Belsley, Kuh, & Welsch, 1980). The consequences of correlated predictors can obviously affect theory validation and even the predictive capability of the model (Belsley, 1981). In the case of unobservable variables the situation is much the same—multicollinearity is likely to pose difficulties for both theory testing and forecasting with structural equation models (cf. Jagpal, 1982).

Given the substantial correlation between the affective and cognitive components, we suspected that the $\gamma_{B \cdot A}$ and $\gamma_{B \cdot C}$ parameter estimates would be extremely unstable. To further investigate the instability of the structural parameters, several alternative model specifications were run. The models described below were fit to the SRB sample, the BI sample, and the "combined sample." By combined sample we mean that the models were fit simultaneously with all parameters specified to be invariant across the two samples. Four types of models were examined: Model 1 was consistent with the specification tested by B & B as shown in Figure 4.3; Model 2 imposed an additional restriction on the baseline model of Figure 4.3, namely that the structural parameter linking the affective component to the behavioral construct is zero (i.e., $\gamma_{B \cdot C} = 0$); Model 3 imposed a different restriction on the baseline model of Figure 4.3, namely that the structural parameter linking the cognitive component to the behavioral construct is zero (i.e., $\gamma_{B \cdot C} = 0$); finally, Model 4 modified the baseline model of Figure 4.3 by postulating that the structural parameters linking each attitude component to the behavioral construct are equal (i.e., $\gamma_{B \cdot A} = \gamma_{B \cdot C}$).

Table 4.2 gives summary results on each of the models. The table reports on the goodness-of-fit of each model, the standardized structural parameter estimates ($\gamma^*_{B \cdot A}$ and $\gamma^*_{B \cdot C}$), the empirical correlation between the two attitude components ($\hat{\phi}_{AC}$), and the proportion of the behavioral construct's total variance not accounted for by the attitude construct, i.e., the residual variance associated with the behavioral construct (VC_B). The first point to note is that under the baseline model of Figure 4.3 the structural parameter estimates were, as expected, very unstable across the samples. The $\hat{\gamma}_{B \cdot A}$ standardized parameter estimates ranged from a statistically nonsignificant negative value of −.08 in the BI sample to a statistically significant positive value of .65 in the SRB sample; similarly, the $\hat{\gamma}^*_{B \cdot C}$ standardized parameter estimates ranged from a statistically nonsignificant positive value of .23 in the SRB sample to a statistically significant positive value of .90 in the BI sample. In the combined sample both parameter estimates were positive in value and statistically significant. Interestingly, the results for Models 2 and 3 support the contention that neither attitude component incrementally accounts for variance in the behavioral construct; in other words, assuming no effect for one of the latent factors does not adversely affect fit. The results reported for Model 4, on the other hand, support the hypothesis that the two attitude components predict the behavioral construct equally well. Note finally that in all cases the empirical correlation between the respective attitude components is substantial and that all four models do about equally well in terms of accounting for variance in the behavioral construct.

Application 2: Inequality Constraints

In certain settings the consumer researcher may wish to consider alternative parameterizations of the usual LISREL model in order to place inequality constraints on factor loadings, unique variances, and other structural model coefficients. In this section we demonstrate how such inequality constraints can be used judiciously.

TABLE 4.2. Predictive validity models investigating multicollinearity (*LISREL* estimates).

	Description	χ^2	df	p	ϕ_{AC}	$\gamma^*_{B\cdot A}$	$\gamma^*_{B\cdot C}$	$VC_{(B)}$
Model 1								
B & B model	SRB sample	13.11	11[a]	.28	.834	.651	.226[b]	.279
	BI sample	12.22	11	.34	.928	−.084[b]	.899	.325
	Simultaneous fit	39.98	39	.43	.878	.365	.481	.326
Model 2								
B & B model	SRB sample	22.16	12	.04	.851	0	.814	.337
$\gamma^*_{B\cdot A}$ restricted	BI sample	12.27	12	.42	927	0	.819	.329
to zero	Simultaneous fit	44.22	40	.30	.886	0	.816	.334
Model 3								
B & B model	SRB sample	14.07	12	.30	.848	.857	0	.266
$\gamma^*_{B\cdot C}$ restricted	BI sample	16.28	12	.18	.966	.817	0	.333
to zero	Simultaneous fit	45.78	40	.24	.907	831	0	.309
Model 4								
B & B model	SRB sample	14.10	12	.29	.829	.439	.439	.294
$\gamma^*_{B\cdot C}$ and $\gamma^*_{B\cdot A}$	BI sample	13.92	12	.31	.938	.411	.411	.345
restricted to	Simultaneous fit	40.09	40	.47	.879	.424	.424	.325
be equal								

[a] Degrees of freedom is 1 higher than reported by Bagozzi and Burnkrant (1979) because of restrictions imposed for identification purposes.
[b] Statistically nonsignificant (i.e., t-value < 2).

Ordered Inequalities of Error Variance

Rindskopf (1983) considers a situation in which the relative sizes of the error variances of a set of variables are in a hypothesized order. For example, suppose that in the case of our illustrative example, there is reason to believe that the error variance of the self-rating (SR) scale item will be greater than that of the semantic differential (SD) scale item. By using the ideas presented in the discussion of Rindskopf's method for handling negative error variances and, in addition, by using equality constraints on parameters we show how this can be done.

Figure 4.4 shows a diagrammatic representation of this model. Following Rindskopf's method we introduce a ξ for each of the observed and latent variables. Thus, the Λ matrix contains more than one type of effect. Notice, however, to ensure the proper ordering of error variance we have introduced an additional ξ^*_{SR} for the self-rating scale item. All of the ξ's, except for those representing the attitude components, are constrained to be pairwise orthogonal and, in addition, we set $\gamma_{SR} = \gamma_{SD}$. This results in a model in which the error term for the self-rating scale (SR) item is the sum of two terms, and since $\hat{\gamma}_{SR} = \hat{\gamma}_{SD}$ the total error variance (i.e., the sum of the two constituents) associated with this scale item must by necessity be equal to or greater than that of the semantic differential (SD) scale item.

The following gives advice on how this model can be implemented with the LISREL program. Specify:

$$\begin{array}{llll} \underline{\text{NX}} = 5 & & \underline{\text{TD}} = \text{ZERO} \\ \underline{\text{NK}} = 8 & & \underline{\text{PH}} = \text{SYMMETRIC, FREE} \\ \underline{\text{LX}} = \text{FULL, FREE} & & \end{array}$$

The Λ and Φ matrices assume, in the case of our illustrative example, the form

$$\Lambda = \begin{pmatrix} \lambda_{SR} & 0 & \gamma_{SR}(=\gamma_{SD}) & \gamma^*_{SR} & 0 & 0 & 0 & 0 \\ \lambda_{SD} & 0 & 0 & 0 & \gamma_{SD} & 0 & 0 & 0 \\ 0 & \lambda_G & 0 & 0 & 0 & \gamma_G & 0 & 0 \\ 0 & \lambda_L & 0 & 0 & 0 & 0 & \gamma_L & 0 \\ 0 & \lambda_T & 0 & 0 & 0 & 0 & 0 & \gamma_T \end{pmatrix}$$

$$\Phi = \begin{pmatrix} 1 & & & & & & & \\ \phi_{AC} & 1 & & & & & & \\ 0 & 0 & 1 & & & & & \\ 0 & 0 & 0 & 1 & & & & \\ 0 & 0 & 0 & 0 & 1 & & & \\ 0 & 0 & 0 & 0 & 0 & 1 & & \\ 0 & 0 & 0 & 0 & 0 & 0 & 1 & \\ 0 & 0 & 0 & 0 & 0 & 0 & 0 & 1 \end{pmatrix}$$

This model provided a more than adequate fit (e.g., $\chi^2(4)=2.3$, $p=.68$). With respect to the parameters of interest, we find

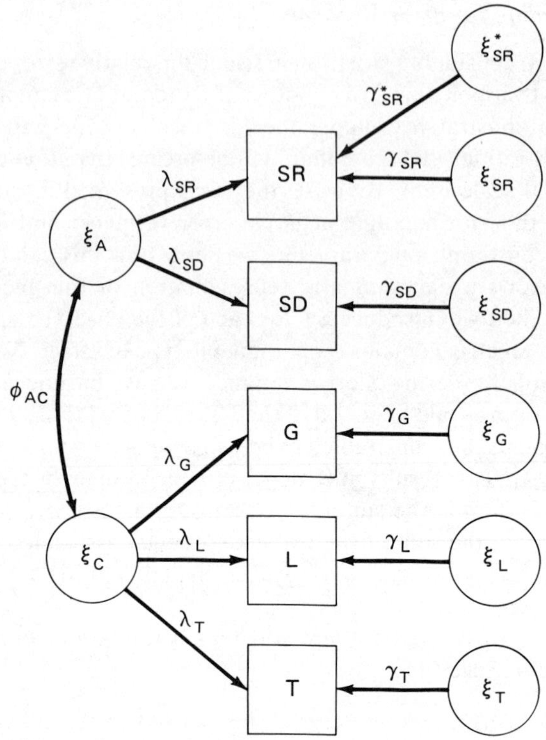

SR – Guilford self-rating; SD – Semantic Differential;
G – Guttman; L – Likert; T – Thurstone

The remaining symbols represent parameters to be estimated and are defined in the text

FIGURE 4.4.

$$\hat{\Theta}_{SR} = 2.3^2 + .52^2 = .325$$
$$\hat{\Theta}_{SD} = .053$$

so that $\hat{\Theta}_{SR} > \hat{\Theta}_{SD}$ as desired.

Phantom Variable Models

Rindskopf (1984) has recently introduced the notion of a "phantom variable" in order to place inequality constraints on structural model coefficients. Since such models may be of interest to consumer behavior and marketing researchers who use the LISREL model we now illustrate how this can be done.

Consider Figure 4.5 which shows a diagrammatic representation of a model which contains a phantom variable—$\eta*$ is introduced for the sole purpose of imposing the constraint that the effect of the cognitive component on behavior

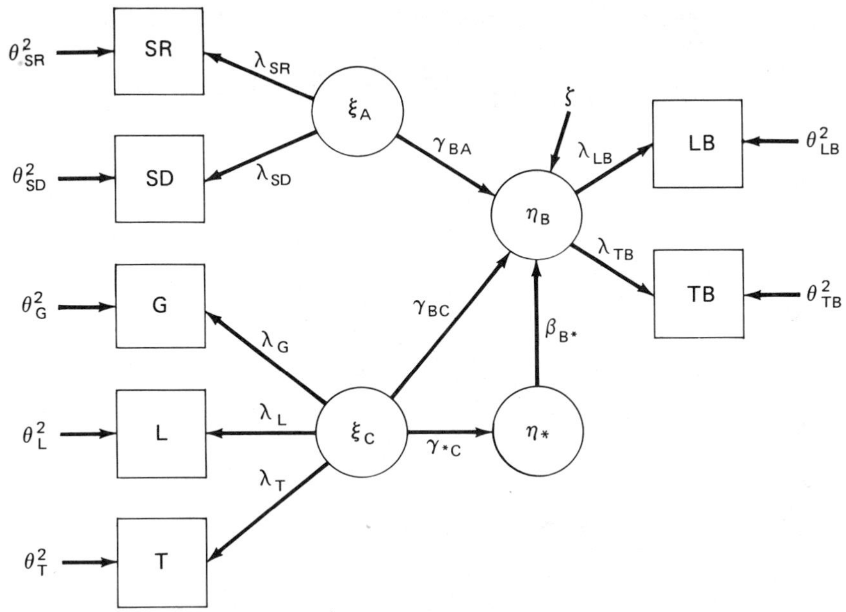

LB – Likert-scaled behavior; TB – Thurstone-scaled behavior; SR – Guilford self-rating; SD – Semantic Differential; G – Guttman; L – Likert; T – Thurstone

The remaining symbols represent parameters to be estimated and are defined in the text

FIGURE 4.5.

should be greater than that of the affective component. The structural equations are

$$\eta_B = \gamma_{BA}\xi_A + \gamma_{BC}\xi_C + \beta_{B*}\eta* + \zeta_B$$
$$\eta* = \gamma_{*C}\xi_C \tag{19}$$

However, by setting $\gamma_{BA}=\gamma_{BC}$ and $\gamma_{*C}=\beta_{B*}$ the relationship holds that

$$(\hat{\gamma}_{BC} + \hat{\gamma}_{*C}) \geq \hat{\gamma}_{BA}$$

which is the desired result. Table 4.3 displays the LISREL parameter specifications for this model.

To the extent that this model adequately fits the data and $\hat{\gamma}_{*C}(=\hat{\beta}_{B*})$ is large and statistically significant we can conclude that the cognitive component dominates the attitude-behavior relationship. Interestingly, for the Fishbein and Ajzen data this is clearly not the case since the parameter estimates for the γ_{*C} and β_{B*} coefficients are equal to zero, within rounding. This is consistent with the results reported by Dillon and Kumar (1985) in their reanalysis of Bagozzi and Burnkrant's (1979) findings.

TABLE 4.3. LISREL parameter specifications for phantom variable model.

```
MO  NY = 2   NE = 2   LY = FU,FR  TE = DI,FR  BE = FU,FR  PS = DI,FR
    NX = 5   NK = 2   LX = FU,FR  TD = DI,FR  GA = FU,FR  PH = SY,FR
PA  LY
*
0   0
1   0
PA  TE
*
1   1
PA  BE
*
0   1
0   0
PA  PS
*
1   0
PA  LX
*
0   0
1   0
0   0
0   1
0   1
PA  TD
*
1   1  1  1  1
PA  PH
*
1
1   1
PA  GA
*
1   1
0   1
EQ  BE(1,2)     GA(2,2)
EQ  GA(1,1)     GA(1,2)
```

Application 3: MTMM Data

Ostrom (1969) presented data on attitudes toward the church. Four verbal measures of *affect* (*A*)—expressions of liking or disliking, *cognitions* (*C*)—expressions or perceptions, concepts, and beliefs about the referent object, and *behavioral intentions* (*B*)—expressions of what the respondent says he or she would do in given situations, were independently constructed using the techniques of *Likert* (*L*) summated ratings, *Guttman* (*G*) scalogram analysis, *Thurstone* (*T*) equal-appearing intervals, and *Guilford* self-rating (*SR*). Seven indices of overt church-

TABLE 4.4. MTMM matrix of correlations from Ostrom (1969).*

		Thurstone *(T)*			Likert *(L)*			Guttman *(G)*			Self-rating *(SR)*		
		A	*B*	*C*	*A*	*B*	*C*	*A*	*B*	*C*	*A*	*B*	*C*
	A	—											
T	*B*	57	—										
	C	63	62	—									
	A	71	59	68	—								
L	*B*	67	67	71	79	—							
	C	69	62	72	79	81	—						
	A	54	39	49	58	51	56	—					
G	*B*	59	61	58	60	69	60	43	—				
	C	63	50	63	69	67	71	49	56	—			
	A	65	63	69	72	73	72	54	66	65	—		
SR	*B*	61	51	56	62	68	64	53	52	56	76	—	
	C	56	48	60	63	66	66	46	48	62	77	68	—

*The decimal point of each correlation has been omitted. $N = 189$, A = affective, B = behavioral, C = cognitive. *Note.* From Ostrom, T. (1969). The relationship between the affective, behavioral, and cognitive components of attitude. *Journal of Experimental Social Psychology, 5*, 12–30. Copyright © Academic Press, 1969. Reprinted with permission.

related behavior were collected. Thus there are three traits and four methods. Table 4.4 presents the 12×12 MTMM correlation matrix.

Confirmatory Factor Model for MTMM Data

The MTMM data of Table 4.4 can be decomposed in terms of the following three-trait four-method factor-analytic model

$$\mathbf{x}' = \Lambda^*\Gamma^* + \epsilon \tag{20}$$

where

$$\mathbf{x}' = (\mathrm{A_L}, \mathrm{A_G}, \mathrm{A_T}, \mathrm{A_{SR}}, \mathrm{C_L}, \mathrm{C_G}, \mathrm{C_T}, \mathrm{C_{SR}}, \mathrm{B_L}, \mathrm{B_G}, \mathrm{B_T}, \mathrm{B_{SR}})$$

$$\Lambda^{*\prime} = \begin{pmatrix} \lambda_1 & \lambda_5 & \lambda_9 & 0 & 0 & 0 & 0 & 0 & 0 & 0 & 0 & 0 \\ 0 & 0 & 0 & \lambda_2 & \lambda_6 & \lambda_{10} & 0 & 0 & 0 & 0 & 0 & 0 \\ 0 & 0 & 0 & 0 & 0 & 0 & \lambda_3 & \lambda_7 & \lambda_{11} & 0 & 0 & 0 \\ 0 & 0 & 0 & 0 & 0 & 0 & 0 & 0 & 0 & \lambda_4 & \lambda_8 & \lambda_{12} \\ \gamma_1 & 0 & 0 & \gamma_2 & 0 & 0 & \gamma_3 & 0 & 0 & \gamma_4 & 0 & 0 \\ 0 & \gamma_5 & 0 & 0 & \gamma_6 & 0 & 0 & \gamma_7 & 0 & 0 & \gamma_8 & 0 \\ 0 & 0 & \gamma_9 & 0 & 0 & \gamma_{10} & 0 & 0 & \gamma_{11} & 0 & 0 & \gamma_{12} \end{pmatrix}$$

$$\Gamma^{*\prime} = (\mathrm{A}, \mathrm{C}, \mathrm{B}, \mathrm{L}, \mathrm{G}, \mathrm{T}, \mathrm{SR})$$

$$\epsilon' = (\epsilon_1, \epsilon_2, \epsilon_3, \epsilon_4, \epsilon_5, \epsilon_6, \epsilon_7, \epsilon_8, \epsilon_9, \epsilon_{10}, \epsilon_{11}, \epsilon_{12})$$

In the basic model above $\mathbf{x}$ is the vector of 12 measurements, Δ^* is a column vector of 7 hypothesized factors (3 trait and 4 method), Λ^* is a (12×7) matrix of factor loadings relating measures to traits and methods, and ϵ is a column vector of 12 errors, each corresponding to one measure. With the assumptions that $E(\Gamma^*) = E(\epsilon) = 0$, $E(\Gamma^*\Gamma^{*\prime}) = \Phi$ and $E(\epsilon\epsilon') = \text{Diag}(\psi)$, the variance-covariance matrix of $\mathbf{x}$ may be expressed as

$$\Sigma = \Lambda^*\Phi\Lambda^{*\prime} + \Psi \tag{21}$$

where

$$\Phi = \begin{pmatrix} 1 & & & & & & \\ \phi_{AC} & 1 & & & & & \\ \phi_{AB} & \phi_{CB} & 1 & & & & \\ \phi_{AL} & \phi_{CL} & \phi_{BL} & 1 & & & \\ \phi_{AG} & \phi_{CL} & \phi_{BG} & \phi_{LG} & 1 & & \\ \phi_{AT} & \phi_{CG} & \phi_{BT} & \phi_{LT} & \phi_{GT} & 1 & \\ \phi_{ASR} & \phi_{CSR} & \phi_{BSR} & \phi_{LSR} & \phi_{GSR} & \phi_{TSR} & \end{pmatrix}$$

is the (7×7) matrix of between trait, between method, and trait-by-method correlations.

Use of Inequality Constraints in MTMM Analysis

Of particular importance in the analysis of MTMM data is the explicit partitioning of variance due to trait, method, and error since it provides insights as to why convergent and discriminant validity has or has not been attained. With the basic factor analytic model described above such an explicit partitioning of variance is easily accomplished. Assuming traits and methods to be uncorrelated, the λ_i^2 give the variances attributable to traits, the γ_j^2 give the variances attributable to methods, and the Ψ_i, $i = 1,2,\ldots,p$, give the error variances. Though the partitioning of variance is a useful feature of the basic factor-analytic model, the investigator may also wish to perform an explicit test of the hypothesis that trait variance exceeds method variance. We now discuss and illustrate how such a test can be performed using the basic factor-analytic model and the LISREL VI program.

To test the hypothesis that trait variance exceeds method variance we essentially need to impose inequality constraints that result in $\lambda_i^2 > \gamma_j^2$. As we discussed and illustrated in the previous section, Rindskopf (1983, 1984) has discussed how inequality constraints can be imposed on unique variances and structural coefficients in covariance structure models implemented with the LISREL program. In the context of the MTMM design the approach taken in the imposition of inequality constraints is a bit different, though, in spirit at least, consistent with Rindskopf's approach. In the case of the three-trait, four-method matrix under study here, the approach to imposing inequality constraints will be to partition the trait variance into two components, where one variance component is restricted, by use of an equality constraint, to equal the variance due to methods. To accomplish this we simply need to add three extra trait factors and impose the appropriate set of restrictions across trait and method factor loadings. The augmented factor loading matrix is of the order (12×10) with elements

$$\Lambda^* = \begin{pmatrix}
\lambda_1 & 0 & 0 & \gamma_1 & 0 & 0 & 0 & \lambda_{13} & 0 & 0 \\
\lambda_4 & \cdot & \cdot & 0 & \gamma_4 & \cdot & \cdot & \lambda_{14} & \cdot & \cdot \\
\lambda_7 & \cdot & \cdot & \cdot & 0 & \gamma_7 & \cdot & \lambda_{15} & \cdot & \cdot \\
\lambda_{10} & \cdot & \cdot & \cdot & \cdot & 0 & \gamma_{10} & \lambda_{16} & \cdot & \cdot \\
0 & \lambda_2 & \cdot & \gamma_2 & \cdot & \cdot & 0 & 0 & \lambda_{17} & \cdot \\
\cdot & \lambda_5 & \cdot & 0 & \gamma_5 & \cdot & \cdot & \cdot & \lambda_{18} & \cdot \\
\cdot & \lambda_8 & \cdot & \cdot & 0 & \gamma_8 & \cdot & \cdot & \lambda_{19} & \cdot \\
\cdot & \lambda_{11} & \cdot & \cdot & \cdot & 0 & \lambda_{11} & \cdot & \lambda_{20} & \cdot \\
\cdot & 0 & \lambda_3 & \gamma_3 & \cdot & \cdot & 0 & \cdot & 0 & \lambda_{21} \\
\cdot & \cdot & \lambda_6 & 0 & \gamma_6 & \cdot & \cdot & \cdot & \cdot & \lambda_{22} \\
\cdot & \cdot & \lambda_9 & \cdot & 0 & \gamma_9 & \cdot & \cdot & \cdot & \lambda_{23} \\
0 & 0 & \lambda_{12} & 0 & 0 & 0 & \gamma_{12} & 0 & 0 & \lambda_{24}
\end{pmatrix}$$

where we set

$$\begin{array}{lll}
\lambda_1 = \gamma_1 & \lambda_2 = \gamma_2 & \lambda_3 = \gamma_3 \\
\lambda_4 = \gamma_4 & \lambda_5 = \gamma_5 & \lambda_6 = \gamma_6 \\
\lambda_7 = \gamma_7 & \lambda_8 = \gamma_8 & \lambda_9 = \gamma_9 \\
\lambda_{10} = \gamma_{10} & \lambda_{11} = \gamma_{11} & \lambda_{12} = \gamma_{12}
\end{array}$$

Note that because of the equality constraints imposed, the variance due to traits must by necessity be (equal to) or greater than the variance due to methods. For example, consider the A_L observed variable and assume, without loss of generality, $E(A^2) = E(C^2) = E(B^2) = 1$. The trait variance is given by $(\lambda_1^2 + \lambda_{13}^2)$, the method variance is given by γ_1^2, but since $\lambda_1 = \gamma_1$ it holds that $(\gamma_1^2 + \gamma_{13}^2) \geq \gamma_1^2$. Similar relationships hold for each of the other observed variables.

Some interesting relationships follow from this specification. First, if it happens that the (true) trait and method variances are equal, then λ_{13} through λ_{24}, the free trait factor loadings, should evaluate to zero. Second, to the extent that the free trait factor loadings, λ_{13} through λ_{24}, are large and statistically significant, that is, twice their standard errors, then we can conclude that (true) trait variance exceeds (true) method variance. Third, to the extent that (true) method variance exceeds (true) trait variance then the augmented factor-analytic model which constrains trait variances to be greater than method variances will not adequately fit the data from a statistical point of view. Fourth, in the experience of these authors, use of the augmented factor-analytic approach often leads to more interpretable solutions. Finally, though the temptation will be to compare the χ^2 goodness-of-fit of the augmented factor analytic model against the χ^2 goodness-of-fit of the standard factor-analytic model with a difference in χ^2-test statistic this will not be possible since the type of inequality constraints imposed does not use degrees of freedom. In other words, both model specifications have the same degrees of freedom and the usual practice of computing the difference in χ^2-test statistic will not work for the obvious reason that the degrees of freedom associated with this test statistic is zero. However, we can evaluate the overall fit of the augmented factor analytic model and compare it to the standard factor model specification on the bases of various fit indices (Bentler & Bonett, 1980) or compare each competing specification against a common baseline model of which each is a nested version.

Table 4.5 presents summary results for the model that posits (true) trait variance exceeds (true) method variance. Note first that the imposition of these additional restrictions did not adversely affect the fit of the model; indeed, approximately the same χ^2 -test statistic was obtained. Second, most of the trait factor loadings that were free had estimates that were twice their respective standard errors which indicates that (true) trait variance is statistically greater than (true) method variance. Finally, though not specifically shown in the table, the method factor correlations were, for the most part, substantially lower and thus compared to the baseline factor analytic model, this solution was slightly more interpretable.

Issues and Caveats in Applications

Like all multivariate techniques, the LISREL model can be misused. For instance, the χ^2 likelihood ratio test statistic assumes that: (a) all variables have multivariate normal distributions, hence only linear, additive models are permissible; (b) all observations are independent; and (c) all data are complete (i.e., no missing data). Collectively these assumptions will be rarely satisfied in practice. There are other issues and caveats that must be understood if the LISREL model is to be used intelligently and honestly. Recently, Fornell (1983) and Fornell and Larcker (1981a,b) have provided excellent, informative discussions of several of

TABLE 4.5. Partitioning of variance due to trait, method and error components for the model with inequality constraints.

	Trait	Method	Error
Thurstone			
Affect	.556	.074	.370
Behavior	.428	.203	.369
Cognition	.561	.102	.337
Likert			
Affect	.699	.079	.222
Behavior	.673	.171	.156
Cognition	.729	.083	.188
Guttman			
Affect	.410	.019	.571
Behavior	.524	.347	.129
Cognition	.612	.042	.346
Self-Rating			
Affect	.714	.230	.056
Behavior	.546	.095	.359
Cognition	.585	.083	.332

$\chi^2 = 39.58$, df $= 36$, $p = .321$.

the issues involved in the application of covariance structure models. In the remaining sections we discuss and illustrate three problematic application issues plaguing LISREL analysis.

Issue 1: Do We Really Believe Our Models?

Methods of confirmatory factor analysis have greatly enhanced our ability to analyze correlational data and to seemingly "confront theory with data." However, as those of us who have used confirmatory factor analysis know all too well, rarely does the initial confrontation between theory, in the form of a hypothesized model, and the data yield the results that we would like. All too often, the initial hypothesized model is not accepted because of a highly significant chi-square, unimpressive fit indices, and/or the presence of estimates that simply do not make sense either from a statistical or substantive point of view.

In cases of poor fit, the natural tendency is to attempt to find out why the model does not fit. This can be accomplished in LISREL VI by copiously inspecting the modification indices and the normalized residuals, along with any other ad hoceries that the researcher has come to rely on.[4] Eventually, the tenacious researcher can usually identify some combination of changes in the initial hypothesized model which produces a new *posthypothesized* model that adequately fits the data from a statistical criterion or satisfies the GFI and AGFI goodness-of-fit indices. Though our theories are not so well-defined as to stand up to data without modification, the temptation when one writes up the study is to ignore the combination of judgment and purpose that went into the specification process and to treat the final posthypothesized model as if it were the only model considered and the one the researcher always believed in.

The danger in all of this is the possibility of forgetting the basic principles of scientific inference. Recently, Cliff (1983) has provided an excellent discussion of some cautions concerning the application of causal modeling methods. In the course of the discussion, four basic principles that underlie the scientific method but which are likely to be violated when using modern, computerized modeling methods are highlighted. The principles that are particularly vulnerable to abuse are as follows: (a) Data do not confirm a model, they only fail to disconfirm it; and its corollary that when the data do not disconfirm a model, there are many other models that are not disconfirmed either; (b) *post hoc* does not imply *propter hoc*; (c) naming something does not imply that we understand it or that we have named it correctly; and, finally, (d) *ex post facto* explanations are untrustworthy. Of these four basic principles, the first and the last appear to be routinely forgotten in consumer behavior research applications.

---

[4]Leamer (1978) presents an interesting discussion of specification searches. He uses the term "specimetrics" to describe the process by which a researcher is led to choose one specification of the model rather than another.

First with respect to the principle that data do not confirm a model, they only disconfirm it, let us reexamine Bagozzi and Burnkrant's (1979) conclusions concerning the dimensionality of attitude which was the subject of the first application. Recall, B & B could not disconfirm the convergent validity of the two-factor, two-component attitude model, but disconfirmed the single-factor, one-component attitude model. The implication in the work of B & B is that rejection of the single-factor, one-component attitude models leads to *one* plausible alternative hypothesis, namely that the underlying theoretical construct is characterized by a two-component affective/cognitive model. However, as we discussed earlier, one reason why the single factor, one-component attitude model does not fit the covariance structure of the five attitude measures is because of the relatively high covariation between the Guilford self-rating and semantic differential scales. In essence, this covariation cannot be accounted for by a single latent factor that is shared with the other indicators. There are, however, several ways of allowing the residual covariance between these two scales to enter into the model. Figure 4.6 presents four alternative plausible hypotheses, all of which are algebraically indistinguishable. First, B & B's two-factor, affective/cognitive model will do it (Figure 4.6a). Second, a model that allows the residuals associated with those two indicators to covary will do it (Figure 4.6b). Third, a model that allows these indicators to load on a methods factor will do it (Figure 4.6c). And fourth, an extended second-order model that represents the

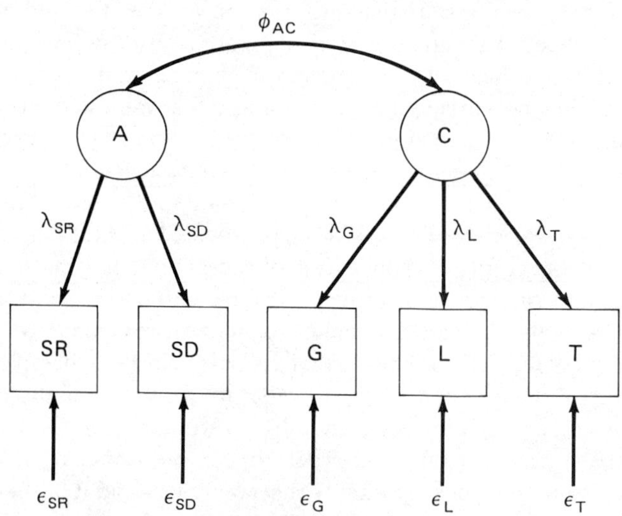

A = Single component attitude construct
A = Affective attitude component
C = Cognitive attitude component
SR = Guilford self-rating
SD = Semantic differential
MF = Method factor
G = Guttman
L = Likert
T = Thurstone scales

The remaining symbols represent parameters to be estimated and are defined in the text

FIGURE 4.6a.

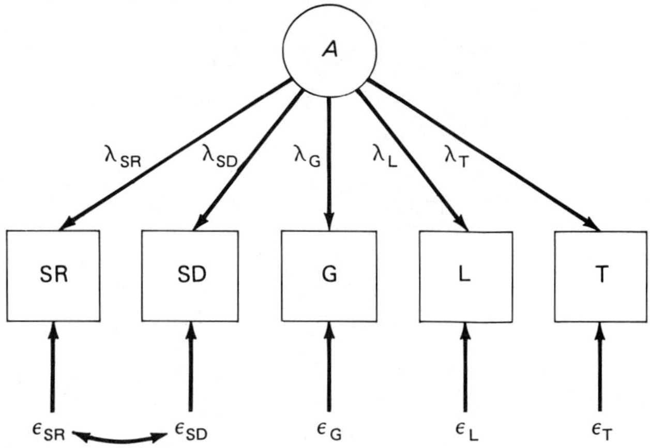

FIGURE 4.6b.

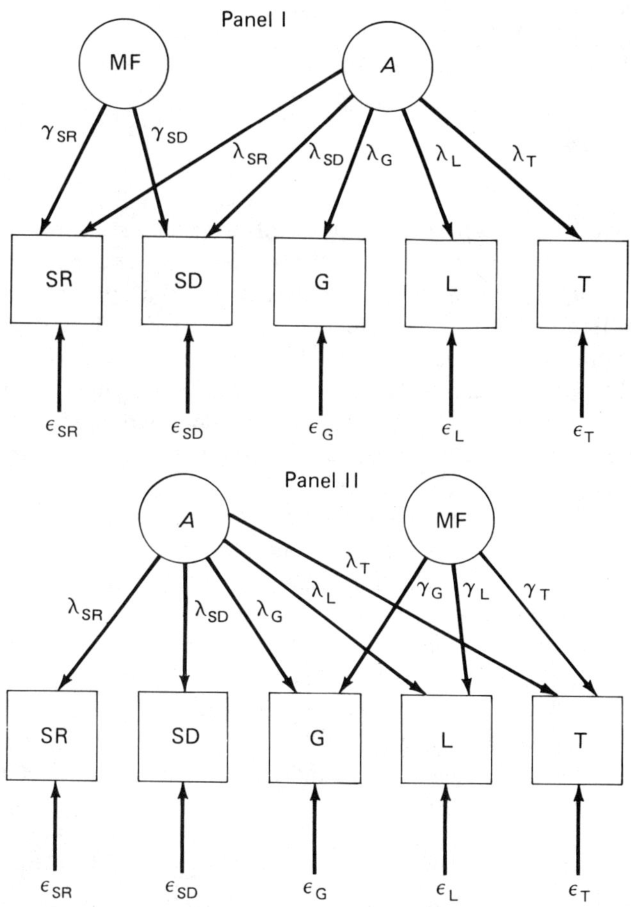

FIGURE 4.6c.

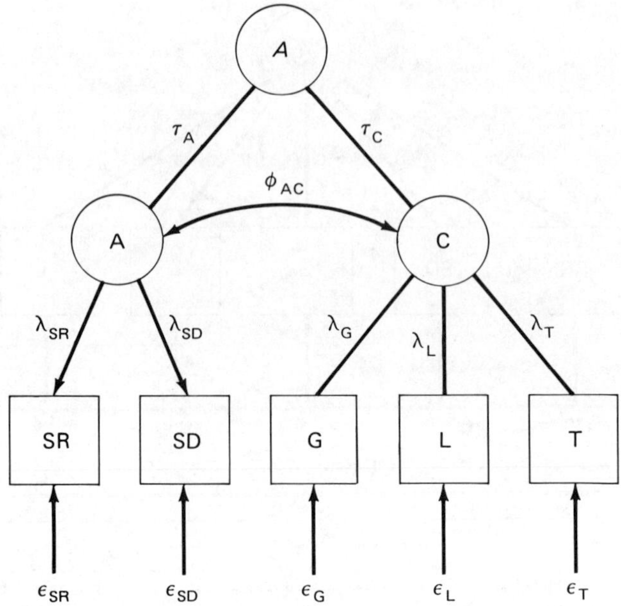

FIGURE 4.6d.

unidimensional attitude construct in terms of two subdimensions will also do it (Figure 4.6d). The point is that all of these models do exactly the same thing: They all account for the residual covariance between the Guilford self-rating and semantic differential indicators which is left unaccounted for by the single-factor, one-component model, and thus provide identical fits to the data. Thus there is nothing in the attitude data alone that can be used to argue that B & B's conclusion of a two-factor, affective/cognitive model is wrong—but there is nothing wrong with the other conceptualizations either. These models are all consistent with the data.

With respect to the principle that *ex post facto* explanations are untrustworthy it is important to realize that *ex post facto* analyses are not in a strict sense confirmatory since in estimating the final specification (posthypothesized model) information obtained from the prior specifications (prehypothesized model) is utilized and thus the (same) data are used more than once. As we stated in the beginning of this section, it is not uncommon to find that the prehypothesized model and one's data do not conform. Having the model rejected by data will generally lead one to question why the model failed. In this regard the normalized residuals, first order derivatives, and modification indices seemingly hold great promise. However, blind use of such heuristic devices can lead to posthypothesized models which are quite different in a substantive sense from the initial hypothesized model. If the final model is one that was originally conceived of, then not all is lost; however, if it is not, then we can use the perjorative content of the word "fishing" to describe this process which, by its very nature, invalidates the traditional models of statistical inference. A case in point is the use of correlated measurement models. In many applications correlated error models are employed in a post hoc manner to obtain an acceptable fit of the model to data (Bagozzi, 1983; Fornell, 1983). As we discussed above, if the factors specified in a prehypothesized model do not account for the observed covariation between a given pair of indicators, then improvements in fit can always be obtained by adding a correlated error term. Bagozzi (1983), Fornell (1983), and Gerbing and Anderson (1984) have all discussed the use of correlated error models. From these discussions it is clear that correlated measurement error models should not be employed unless there is strong theoretical and methodological reasons. The post hoc use of a correlated measurement model will undoubtedly improve fit, but it accomplishes this at the expense of substantive meaning since the indicator covariation is attributed to an *unknown* common source; in other words, with post hoc correlated measurement models, the correspondence between the latent construct and its empirically defined factor lacks clear substantive interpretation.

Issue 2: Empirical Identification

The concept of empirical identification (Kenny, 1979) can be used to understand why improper solutions (and such related problems as factor loadings and factor correlations outside the permissible range and large variances of parameter estimates) may occur. Empirical identification is intimately related to the concept of identification. As noted by Koopmans (1949), in establishing the identifiability of a model one often imposes certain seemingly innocuous assumptions which may not be true. When these assumptions are fallacious, the model is not identified and thus, in a strict sense, one cannot say that the model is identified, but only that it may be identified if certain conditions are in place.[5] The conditions that we refer to generally take the form of requiring that certain parameters not be zero, or that parameters not equal one. Thus, whenever factor loadings are close to zero, factor correlations close to one, and factor correlations close to zero there can potentially be a problem.[6]

Examples of empirical underidentification can be found in Kenny (1979), McDonald and Krane (1977, 1979), and Rindskopf (1984). A simple yet insightful example of how empirical underidentification can cause a number of problems can be seen in the following model specification:

---

[5]This line of reasoning is also implicit in the work of Koopmans and Reiersol (1950), Reiersol (1950), and Anderson and Rubin (1956).

[6]In discussing these problems, Rindskopf (1984) offers the following guidelines: Factor loadings less than .1 in absolute value should be considered small, while one smaller than .20 in absolute value should be considered suspect; a correlation greater than .95 should be considered close to one, while one greater than .90 should be considered suspect; similar remarks apply to correlations that are within .05 to .10 of zero.

$$\Lambda = \begin{pmatrix} \lambda_G \\ \lambda_L \\ \lambda_T \end{pmatrix} \qquad \Psi = \text{Diag}(\Psi_G, \Psi_L, \Psi_T)$$

$$\Sigma = \Lambda\Lambda' + \Psi$$

This model tests for convergent validity of the "cognitive" component of attitude defined by the Guttman (G), Likert (L), and Thurstone (T) scale items. In general, a three-variable, one-factor model is thought to be exactly identified. However, as Kenny (1979) and McDonald and Krane (1979) have shown, if one of the factor loadings is zero, the model is not identified. If one of the factor loadings is close to zero, some parameter estimates will have large standard errors. The problem is more insidious than we might think since the variable whose standard error has been adversely affected is not the one with the small factor loadings. Instead the factor loading standard errors and the error variances for the other variables are the parameter estimates that will be affected. This can be seen by examining the following relationships:

$$\lambda_G^2 = \frac{\text{Cov}(G, L)\,\text{Cov}(G, T)}{\lambda_L\,\lambda_T}$$

$$\lambda_L^2 = \frac{\text{Cov}(G, L)\,\text{Cov}(L, T)}{\lambda_L\,\lambda_T}$$

$$\lambda_T^2 = \frac{\text{Cov}(T, G)\,\text{Cov}(L, T)}{\lambda_L\,\lambda_T}$$

Note that if one of the factor loadings is close to zero, this means that in the covariance matrix of the observed variables two covariances will be almost zero; hence, in practice we will generally have strong indication from the covariance matrix as to which factor loading is close to zero. However, because of the covariance structure, the standard error for the factor loading close to zero will not be large. As the above relationships show, this is not the case for the other two factor loadings. For example, if we arbitrarily take $\lambda_T \approx 0$, then since terms involving this parameter appear in the denominator of the formulas for the other factor loadings shown above, a value for λ_T close to zero means that the estimates of λ_G and λ_L will be very unstable with correspondingly large standard errors. As a by-product of this, the error variances for these variables will also have large standard errors and it could happen that estimates of error variances for some of them are negative. It is also obvious that as $\lambda_T \rightarrow 0$, that any values for λ_G and λ_L that reproduce the observed correlation are possible, regardless of whether the estimates fall within the permissible range. In other words, it is only the product of $\lambda_G\lambda_L$ that is well-determined and hence either λ_G or λ_L can be greater than one, accompanied by a negative error variance. This appears to be the most common type of Heywood case.

Consider next the following model representation:

$$\Lambda = \begin{matrix} \lambda_{SR} & 0 \\ \lambda_{SD} & 0 \\ 0 & \lambda_G \\ 0 & \lambda_L \\ 0 & \lambda_T \end{matrix} \qquad \Phi = \begin{matrix} 1 & \\ \phi_{AC} & 1 \end{matrix}$$

$$\Psi = \text{Diag}(\Psi_{SR}, \Psi_{SD}, \Psi_G, \Psi_L, \Psi_T)$$

$$\Sigma = \Lambda\Phi\Lambda' + \Psi$$

The model is consistent with the two-component, affective/cognitive conceptualization of the attitude construct: The self-rating (SR) and semantic differential (SD) scale items load only on the affective component (A), whereas the Gutmann (G), Likert (L), and Thurstone (T) scale items load only on the cognitive component (C).

This example is interesting in that it illustrates a situation that runs contrary to what is actually expected. Usually, to make a model identified we add restrictions, however under certain conditions we must remove rather than add restrictions. To see this we simply have to note that if ϕ_{AC} is set to zero (i.e., the attitude components are presumed to be uncorrelated), the model shown above is not identified since under this condition the model is equivalent to two one-factor models where one component has only two indicators and thus is not identified. If we had actually fit this model, LISREL would correctly indicate that there is an identification problem corresponding to the unique variance estimate of either the self-rating (SR) or the semantic differential (SD) scale items. Freeing up the ϕ_{AC} parameter may not help and, in fact, may cause the problem to go unnoticed if $\phi_{AC} \approx 0$ (instead of exactly zero). In such cases the standard errors of many parameter estimates will be large and it is quite likely that negative variance estimates will occur. Once again the problem is insidious in that the variable that seemingly produces the irregularities is actually not the offending culprit.

The problem can become more acute as the complexity of the model increases. In the next example we consider the structural equation model shown in Figure 4.7. The model corresponds to a second-order factor model in which the affective and cognitive components act as subdimensions of the attitude construct which itself is hypothesized to influence the behavioral construct defined in terms of self-reported behaviors scaled according to Likert (LB) and Thurstone (TB) procedues. The structural equations corresponding to this model are

$$\eta_B = \gamma_B \xi_A + \zeta_B$$

$$\eta_A = \gamma_A \xi_A + \zeta_A$$

$$\eta_C = \gamma_C \xi_A + \zeta_C$$

where

$$\text{Var}(\eta_B) = \gamma_B^2 \text{Var}(\xi_A) + \Psi_B$$

$$\text{Var}(\eta_A) = \gamma_A^2 \text{Var}(\xi_A) + \Psi_A$$

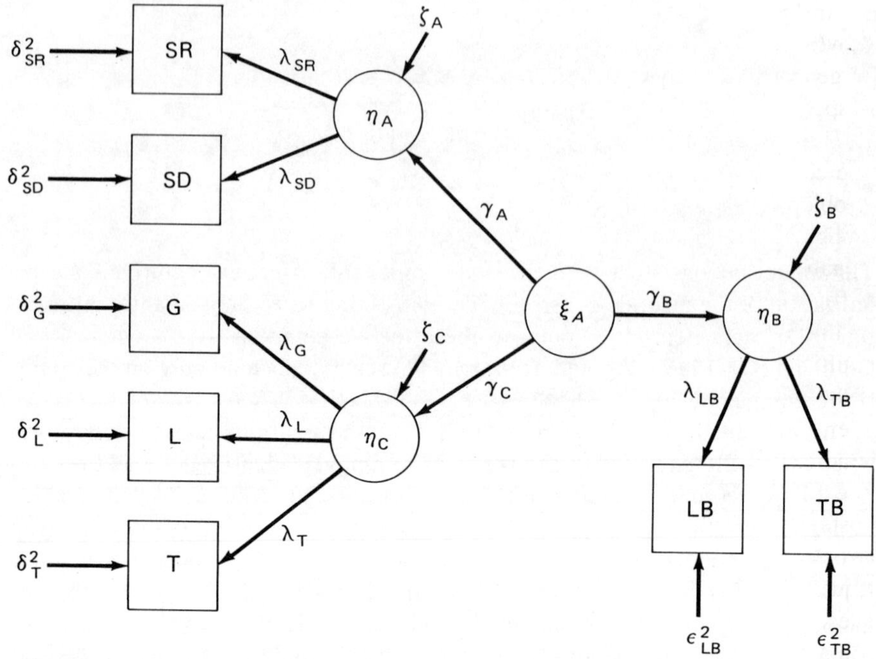

A—Single component attitude construct; A—Affective attitude component;
C—Cognitive attitude component; B—Behavioral component;
LB – Likert-scaled behavior; TB – Thurstone-scaled behavior; SR – Guilford self-rating;
SD – Semantic Differential; G – Guttman; L – Likert; T – Thurstone
The remaining symbols represent parameters to be estimated and are defined in the text

FIGURE 4.7.

$$\mathrm{Var}(\eta_C) = \gamma_C^2\,\mathrm{Var}(\xi_A) + \Psi_C$$
$$\mathrm{Cov}(\eta_B\eta_A) = \gamma_B\gamma_A\,\mathrm{Var}(\xi_A)$$
$$\mathrm{Cov}(\eta_B\eta_C) = \lambda_B\gamma_C\,\mathrm{Var}(\xi_A)$$
$$\mathrm{Cov}(\eta_A\eta_C) = \gamma_A\lambda_C\,\mathrm{Var}\,(\xi_A)$$

and Ψ_B, Ψ_A, and Ψ_C are the variances of ζ_B, ζ_A, and ζ_C, respectively. For identification purposes, we would typically set γ_A=1. Under this condition we find that

$$\gamma_C = \frac{\mathrm{Cov}(\eta_B\eta_C)}{\mathrm{Cov}(\eta_B\eta_A)}$$

$$\mathrm{Var}(\xi_A) = \mathrm{Cov}(\eta_A\eta_C)\,\frac{\mathrm{Cov}(\eta_B\eta_A)}{\mathrm{Cov}(\eta_B\eta_C)}$$

$$\gamma_B = \frac{\mathrm{Cov}(\eta_B\eta_C)}{\mathrm{Cov}(\eta_B\eta_A)}$$

so that Ψ_B, Ψ_A, and Ψ_C are uniquely determined. However, if $\gamma_B \approx 0$ then $\mathrm{Cov}(\eta_B \eta_A)$ and $\mathrm{Cov}(\eta_B \eta_C)$ are near zero and the standard error for γ_C will be large and certain of the unique and residual variances (i.e., Ψ_A, Ψ_C and $\mathrm{Var}(\xi_A)$, respectively) can be negative, so again a whole range of symptoms can result.

The discussion to this point has been concerned with the population values of the covariances and structural model coefficients. Obviously, the potential for problems is greatly increased when sample values are considered; for example, a slight change from a population value may cause a variance estimate to become negative. In addition, by no means are these the only sources that can cause difficulties. There are other potential sources of the same problems: Violations of linearity, additivity and normality, model misspecification, correlated errors, multicollinearity and overfitting are all potentially troublesome (cf. Rindskopf, 1984). It is unfortunate that there are many situations in which certain kinds of identification problems may slip by unnoticed. As we indicated when factor loadings and standardized structural model coefficients are exactly zero or one, the LISREL VI program will usually detect the problem. However, in other instances the LISREL VI program may not detect empirical identification problems because the maximum likelihood estimation procedure uses implicit equation systems. In such cases, as one may easily verify with numerical examples, the program will return without comment one of the infinitely many available solutions. Here is where the problems begin.

Issue 3: Offending Estimates

A difficulty common to all methods of finding maximum likelihood estimates is that the likelihood function may not have any true maximum within the region for which all the unique variances are positive. The terminal solutions obtained using computer programs such as LISREL VI (Jöreskog & Sörbom, 1982) and its relatives may well represent a local maximum of the likelihood function rather than the global maximum. An immediate distinction that should be made is between improper solutions and Heywood cases. Heywood cases, apparently first coined by Harman (1971, p. 117), refer to maximum likelihood solutions in which negative error variances are obtained. Improper solutions, on the other hand, refer to cases where the maximum likelihood solution is at a boundary minima and zero (or very small) error variance estimates are obtained. Thus, a Heywood case will necessarily yield an improper solution, but not every improper solution is a Heywood case. In terms of the common sense expectations that error variances should always be positive and present to some degree in our observed measures, both results are clearly unacceptable.

Unfortunately, these so-called improper solutions are frequently found (cf. Jöreskog, 1967); in fact, according to Lee (1980), "it is well known that in practice about one-third of the data yield one or more nonpositive estimates of the unique variances" (p. 313). Because Heywood cases represent a very common series of problems in factor analysis and structural equation models, it is important to examine why such irregularities may occur.

Conceptual Explanations

Until recently, there have been few attempts to explain why improper solutions occur. One common explanation of improper solutions is that the common factor model does not fit the empirical data. Though lack of fit can cause improper solutions, it is not the only cause. For example, in the context of exploratory factor analysis Driel (1978) identified and empirically explicated three major causes of improper solutions: (a) Sampling fluctuations, in combination with a population value close to the boundary of an interpretable region (e.g., a negative error variance estimate when the true value approaches zero due to fluctuations in sampling); (b) the inappropriate fitting of the common factor model to empirical data (e.g., the patterns of signs and magnitudes of the elements of the correlation matrix are not consistent with a single factor model); and (c) the indefiniteness of the model (e.g., when a factor contains a number of small loadings, admitting alternative solutions, none of which is unique and some of which may be uninterpretable). In order to analyze improper solutions Driel adopted a nonclassical approach to the common factor model which removes the constraint of positive definiteness in the matrices containing the parameters (i.e., $\Lambda\Lambda'$ and Ψ).

Depending on the results of the nonclassical approach Driel recommends either modifying the solutions so that it is interpretable in the case of sampling fluctuations, possibly by setting certain parameter estimates to zero which would result in a mixed factor-components model, or altering the data matrix by adding or deleting offending variables in prescribed ways. Both of these resolutions are considered in later sections.

Heywood Cases: Possible Solutions

Until recently, few options existed for dealing with negative variance estimates and related irregularities. This section discusses three approaches for handling Heywood cases and comments on the ease or difficulty of implementing each.

Setting Error Variance Estimates to Zero. Several researchers (cf. Jöreskog, 1967; Lawley & Maxwell, 1971) have suggested a simple, practical approach to handling negative error variance estimates: When negative error variance estimates occur simply fix them at zero. Though this approach which requires fixing error variance estimates at zero can be handled by the LISREL VI program, it suffers from a number of well-known drawbacks. First, and perhaps most serious, maximum likelihood theory has not been proven to be valid at boundary minima. Second, as discussed by Bentler (1976), setting negative error variances to zero results in a mixed factor-component model. The problem with mixed factor-component models is that the parameter estimates obtained by maximum likelihood methods are, in a strict sense, nonunique when viewed as nonrestricted estimates. In more technical terms, the estimation, in such instances, forces the analog Hessian to be positive definite and thus is inherently incapable of evaluating whether the solution is actually nonunique (Bentler, 1976). Third, setting negative variance estimates to zero can cause offending estimates to appear in other parameters.

Reparameterization of the Model. Recently, several researchers have developed different conceptualizations of linear structural models than that of Jöreskog's LISREL model (cf. Bentler, 1976; Bentler & Weeks, 1980; Lee, 1980; Lee & Tsui, 1982; McDonald, 1980). These alternative conceptualizations allow the user to impose rather general types of inequality and equality constraints on model parameters. In theory, at least, the nature of the constraints permitted are such that all error variance estimates must be strictly positive. Unfortunately these methods are not currently available to the typical user of structural equation models nor, in general, can they be implemented with the LISREL VI computer program. An exception is Bentler's (1976) structural factor analysis model. As we demonstrate below, the LISREL model, in certain instances, can be viewed as a restricted version of this model and thus implemented with the LISREL VI computer program.

The usual form of the common factor model is

$$\mathbf{x} = \Lambda \mathrm{f} + \mathbf{e} \tag{22}$$

where

$$\mathrm{E}(\mathbf{x}) = \mathrm{E}(\mathbf{f}) = \mathrm{E}(\mathbf{e}) = 0 \qquad \mathrm{E}(\mathbf{ef}') = 0 \tag{23}$$

Under regular conditions the factoring of the covariance matrix is of the form:

$$\Sigma = \Lambda\Phi\Lambda' + \Psi \tag{24}$$

In contrast, Bentler's (1976) structural factor analysis model is

$$\mathbf{x} = \mu + \boldsymbol{Z}\mathbf{A}\boldsymbol{f} + \boldsymbol{ZL} \tag{25}$$

with $\mathbf{x}$, μ and $\boldsymbol{L}$ of order $(p\times l)$, $\boldsymbol{Z}(p\times p)$, $\mathbf{A}(p\times r)$, and $\boldsymbol{f}(r\times l)$,where $\boldsymbol{Z}$ is taken to be diagonal and

$$\mathrm{E}(\boldsymbol{L}) = E(\boldsymbol{f}) = \mathrm{E}(\boldsymbol{Lf}') = 0$$

$$\mathrm{E}(\boldsymbol{LL}') = \mathbf{I}$$

and

$$\mathrm{E}(\boldsymbol{ff}') = \mathbf{M}. \tag{26}$$

The covariance matrix of $\mathbf{x}$ has the structural form

$$\Sigma = \boldsymbol{Z}(\mathbf{AMA}' + \mathbf{I})\boldsymbol{Z}. \tag{27}$$

The structure shown in Equation 27 has several interesting features. First, because of the assumptions specified in Equation 26, the structural form of the covariance matrix shown in Equation 27 cannot reduce to a principal components model of the form $\Sigma = \Lambda\Lambda'$. Second, the structural form of the covariance matrix shown in Equation 27 can, however, reduce to form the structural covariance matrix shown in Equation 24, specifically if $\Lambda = \mathbf{ZA}$, $\Phi = \mathbf{M}$, and $\Psi = \mathbf{Z}^2$. Interestingly, $\mathbf{Z}$ cannot be taken as null, because of the positive variances in Σ; in addition, even if some elements in $\mathbf{Z}$ are negative, all error variances must be strictly positive since $\Psi = \mathbf{Z}^2 > \mathbf{0}$.

To understand how to implement Bentler's structural factor analysis model consider once again the oblique two-component factor-analytic model originally shown in Figure 4.2, panel b. In Figure 4.8 we show an alternative representation of this model which is consistent with Bentler's. In this figure there are two ξ's and five η's, where the x's are mapped directly onto the η's. Thus, the structural equation is

$$\eta = \beta\eta + \Gamma\xi + \zeta. \tag{28}$$

Under standard assumptions, squaring both sides of Equation 28 yields

$$\mathbf{B}\eta\eta'\mathbf{B}' = \Gamma\xi\xi'\Gamma' + \zeta\zeta', \tag{29}$$

where, for notational convenience, $\mathbf{B} = (\mathbf{I} - \beta)$. After premultiplication (postmultiplication) by $\mathbf{B}^{-1}(\mathbf{B}^{-1\prime})$ and taking expectations note the following:

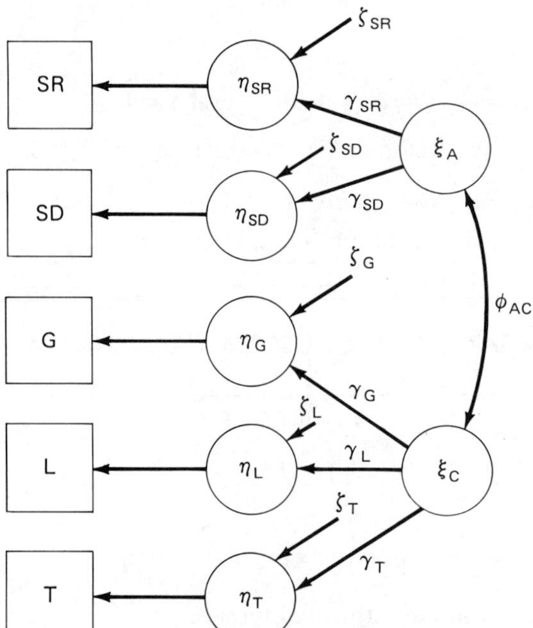

A–Affective attitude component; C–Cognitive attitude component;
SR – Guilford self-rating; SD – Semantic Differential;
G–Guttman; L– Likert; T– Thurstone

The remaining symbols represent parameters to be estimated and are defined in the text

FIGURE 4.8.

$$E(\eta\eta') = \mathbf{B}^{-1}(\Gamma E(\xi\xi')\Gamma')\mathbf{B}^{-1\prime} + \mathbf{B}^{-1}E(\zeta\zeta')\mathbf{B}^{-1\prime}$$
$$\Sigma = \mathbf{B}^{-1}(\Gamma\Phi\Gamma')\mathbf{B}^{-1\prime} + \mathbf{B}^{-1}\mathbf{I}\mathbf{B}^{-1\prime}. \tag{30}$$

Thus, in relation to Equation 27 we see that $\mathbf{B}^{-1}$ plays the role of $\mathbf{Z},\Gamma$ the role of $\mathbf{A}$, and $\Phi = \mathbf{M}$. Interestingly, in relation to Equation 30, $\Lambda = \mathbf{B}^{-1}\Gamma$ and $\Psi = \mathbf{B}^{-1}\mathbf{B}^{-1\prime}$ so that unique variances must be strictly positive. To implement this model with the LISREL VI computer program specify the following:

NY = 5	NX = 0
NE = 5	NK = 2
LY = IDENTITY	GA = FULL, FREE
TE = ZERO	PH = SYMMETRIC, FREE
BE = DIAGONAL, FREE	PS = DIAGONAL, FIXED

Placing Constraints on the Unique Variances. Recently, Rindskopf (1983) has demonstrated a method for preventing Heywood cases. His method utilizes the parameterization presented by Bentler and Weeks (1980) and combines a suggestion made by Bentler (1976) with a class of models proposed by Werts, Linn, and Jöreskog (1971) in which the unique variances were viewed as factors with the same nominal status as other latent variables to allow errors to be correlated.

In the usual parameterization of structural models with LISREL the *coefficients* for residuals and unique variances are usually fixed at one, whereas their variances are considered free and thus need to be estimated. As we have discussed, the conventional model there is no requirement that the error variances be positive. Using the Bentler and Weeks parameterization, however, Rindskopf (1983) demonstrates a simple solution to this problem: Fix the *variance* of the residual or unique variance at one and estimate the coefficient. According to Rindskopf, "regardless of whether the coefficient is positive or negative, the square of the coefficient will be positive, so the variance will be positive" (1983, p. 75).[7] How this can be implemented with the LISREL VI computer program is demonstrated below.

To implement Rindskopf's method we simply need to introduce as many ξ's as there are independent variables and common factors, whether observed or latent, whether they represent unique or residual variables or not. In the case of our illustrative model, two of the ξ's are reserved for the latent factors, whereas each of the remaining five ξ's correspond to one of the unique factors. Thus, the factor loadings matrix has as many rows as there are observed independent variables and as many columns as there are latent factors varibles in the model. We see, therefore, that the matrix contains more than one type of effect: It contains the loadings that map the observed variables onto their latent counterparts as well as the effects of the unique variables, where the squares of these unique variable effects give the error variance estimates. To fix the variance of the unique

[7]It should be noted that Rindskopf's method does not use degrees of freedom. These restrictions represent *inequality constraints* which in general do not reduce the dimensionality of the parameter space (cf. Rindskopf, 1983).

variables at one we need to simply set the relevant elements in Φ to 1.0. Note that Φ also contains more than one type of effect: It contains the variances and covariances of the common factors as well as the unique variances.

Figure 4.9 shows a diagrammatic representation for Rindskopf's method in the context of the oblique two component factor-analytic model originally shown in Figure 4.2, panel b. To distinguish the various effects we have used γ's for the unique variance effects. In terms of the LISREL computer program we need to specify the following:

$$\underline{\text{NX}} = 5 \qquad \underline{\text{TD}} = \text{ZERO}$$
$$\underline{\text{NK}} = 7 \qquad \underline{\text{PH}} = \text{SYMMETRIC, FIXED}$$

where

$$\underset{(5\times7)}{\Lambda} = \begin{pmatrix} \lambda_{X1} & 0 & \gamma_1 & 0 & 0 & 0 & 0 \\ \lambda_{X2} & 0 & 0 & \gamma_2 & 0 & 0 & 0 \\ 0 & \lambda_3 & 0 & 0 & \gamma_3 & 0 & 0 \\ 0 & \lambda_4 & 0 & 0 & 0 & \gamma_4 & 0 \\ 0 & \lambda_5 & 0 & 0 & 0 & 0 & \gamma_5 \end{pmatrix}$$

$$\underset{(7\times7)}{\Phi} = \begin{pmatrix} 1 & & & & & & \\ \phi_{21} & 1 & & & & & \\ 0 & 0 & 1 & & & & \\ 0 & 0 & 0 & 1 & & & \\ 0 & 0 & 0 & 0 & 1 & & \\ 0 & 0 & 0 & 0 & 0 & 1 & \\ 0 & 0 & 0 & 0 & 0 & 0 & 1 \end{pmatrix}$$

Discussion

The differences among the various forms of the models discussed above can be clearly seen in terms of three different versions of the factor analysis model. The conventional form of the model is

$$\Sigma = \Lambda\Phi\Lambda' + \Psi.$$

Heywood cases are possible under this formulation. In the event of Heywood cases we can drop the offending variable from the analysis. In most instances, this will not result in a satisfactory solution. Alternatively, another simple approach is to fit this form of the model but fix the offending (negative) error variance to zero. This results in a mixed factor analysis, principal component model with one more degree of freedom than the unrestricted model. As previously discussed, this approach has also been criticized. Two other forms of the model have been suggested. In one form of the model (Bentler, 1976) unique variances must be strictly positive:

$$\Sigma = \mathbf{Z}(\mathbf{AMA}' + \mathbf{I})\mathbf{Z}$$

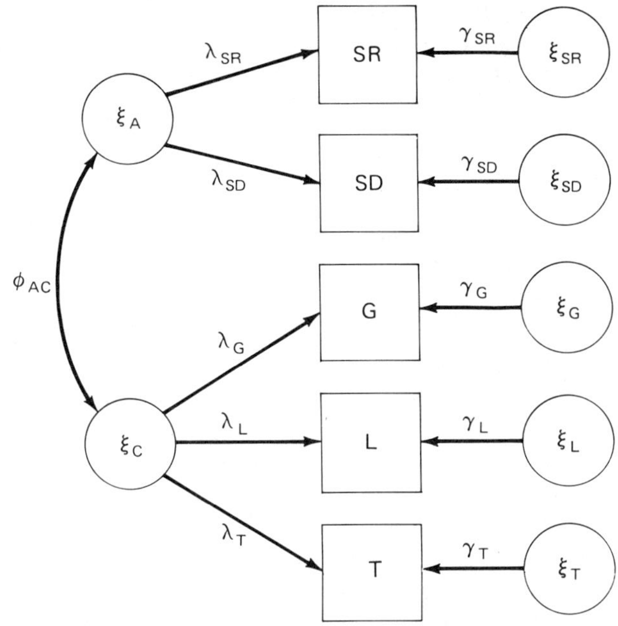

A—Affective attitude component; C—Cognitive attitude component; SR – Guilford self-rating; SD – Semantic Differential; G – Guttman; L – Likert; T – Thurstone

The remaining symbols represent parameters to be estimated and are defined in the text

FIGURE 4.9.

where **Z** is diagonal and Diag(**M**)=**I**. In the other form of the model (Rindskopf, 1983), negative error variances are not possible, though zero error variances are possible:

$$\Sigma = \Lambda\Phi\Lambda'$$

where both Λ and Φ contain more than one type of effect and usually Diag(Φ)=**I**. The usual form of the model can be viewed as restricted versions of these latter two forms, although the inequality constraints are never made directly (cf. Rindskopf, 1983).

On the surface, at least, the second and third forms of the model appear to offer great promise as potential methods for preventing negative error variance estimates. However, though these two approaches represent theoretically elegant ways for this problem, they have limited practical usefulness compared to the simpler approach in which the offending parameter estimate is fixed at zero. Consider first Bentler's formulation. In cases where the maximum likelihood solution produces a negative error variance estimate, attempts to restrict all of the error variance estimates to be strictly positive will generally cause identification problems to appear. In other words, there is a basic indeterminacy in the solution. Because the loadings and error variances are parameterized in terms of the product of other parameters, the effect estimates for the offending variable(s) can be made arbitrarily large; in other words, the individual effect estimates are underidentified, only the product is uniquely determined.

In the case of Rindskopf's (1983) method (the third form of the model) the results are more encouraging than with Bentler's parameterization, but in a practical sense they are no different from the simpler approach in which the offending estimate is set to zero. Though theoretically positive error variance estimates are possible (i.e., the offending variable's unique effect estimate in the Λ matrix could be negative, the square of which is positive), these authors know of no empirical applications in which a nonzero error variance estimate was produced by adopting this particular parameterization. This agrees with Rindskopf's experiences,[8] in which every application of this form of the model produced zero error variance estimates for all of the offending variables, and the simulation results recently reported by Dillon, Kumar, and Mulani (1986) and Gerbing and Anderson (1985). There is an intuitive explanation for this result. Consider the case where the global solution produces a negative error variance estimate. In constrained versions of the model the program is not "allowed" to enter that part of the parameter space for which the estimate is negative. Though we offer no formal mathematical proof, even after reparameterizing the model it is reasonable to expect that the second most "desirable" position (on the likelihood) will be the one at which the offending parameter estimates is zero. Thus, it is hard to conceive of situations where this constrained form of the model will yield parameter estimates for the offending variables that are other than zero.

There are two additional features of Rindskopf's method that deserve some further comment. First, as we indicated, this parameterization of the factor analysis model does not use degrees of freedom. Thus, the chi-square test of goodness-of-fit has the same degrees of freedom whether or not the constraints are made. In such cases, the usual practice of taking the differences of chi-square values between two nested models to test for the statistical significance of the restricted parameters will not work for the obvious reason that the degrees of freedom associated with the differences in chi-square test statistic is zero. Actually, Rindskopf's method produces a model which is not a nested version of the model without constraints. We can test a model with restrictions, and a model without restrictions; however, we cannot directly test the statistical validity of the restrictions (cf. Rindskopf, 1983). Second, we should note that (a) in the experience of these authors, Rindskopf's method will generally not produce offending estimates in other parameters, which typically does happen when we adopt the simpler approach in which the offending estimate is simply fixed at zero,[9] and (b) it

[8]Personal communication (1984, August).

[9]This property of Rindskopf's (1983) method warrants further investigation. In Gerbing and Anderson's (1985) simulations they did not find this to uniformly hold.

can be judiciously used in more complex models to ensure that negative error variances do not occur.

Recommendations

It seems reasonable to recommend the following approaches to "handling" improper solutions. If the confidence interval for the offending estimates covers positive values (i.e., $\hat{\Theta}_j + 2\sigma > 0$) and the magnitude of the corresponding estimated standard error is approximately the same as the other standard errors, the improper solution is probably due to sampling variation. In such cases the model should be refit with the offending estimate fixed at zero, or possibly some very small value.

There are two other possibilities. First, the confidence interval for the offending estimate may not cover zero (i.e., $\hat{\Theta}_j + 2\sigma < 0$). In this case the improper solution is probably due to the inability of any factor model to adequately fit the data. Second, the estimated standard error for the offending estimate may be extremely large, relative to the other estimated standard errors, leading to an elongated confidence interval that does cover positive values. In such cases the improper solution is probably due to indefiniteness of the model. Unfortunately, in these two latter cases very little can be done, since the heart of the problem is neither methodological nor statistical. Rather, problems arise because the models under consideration are ad hoc and atheoretical. When models are not guided by sound theory offending estimates can appear and any attempts to apply "after the fact" methodological solutions will rarely, if ever, provide satisfactory results. In short, theoretical difficulties rarely have ready-made methodological solutions.

Issue 4: Interpretational Confounding

In an innovative, pioneering and instructive paper Burt (1976) discusses the effects of what he calls *interpretational confounding* on causal model solutions. In the presence of interpretational confounding the empirical meaning ascribed to a construct is determined not from its observable indicators but from the indicators of other unobservable constructs. Interpretational confounding adversely affects one's ability to estimate the epistemic correlations linking the observed measures and their underlying unobservable constructs, with the end result that structural criteria, as opposed to epistemic criteria, emerge as the significant determinants of epistemic correlations. Thus, the problem lies not in the precision of the structural parameter estimates per se, but in their role in assigning empirical meaning to other unobservable constructs in the system. Burt (1976) indicates that interpretational confounding is likely to surface when (a) the indicants of the construct have low covariances among themselves and (b) the covariances of the indicants of the unobserved variable with the indicants of other unobserved variables in the model are widely different (p. 10).

The problem of interpretational confounding can be investigated by following the limited-information approach recommended by Burt (1976). Essentially, this

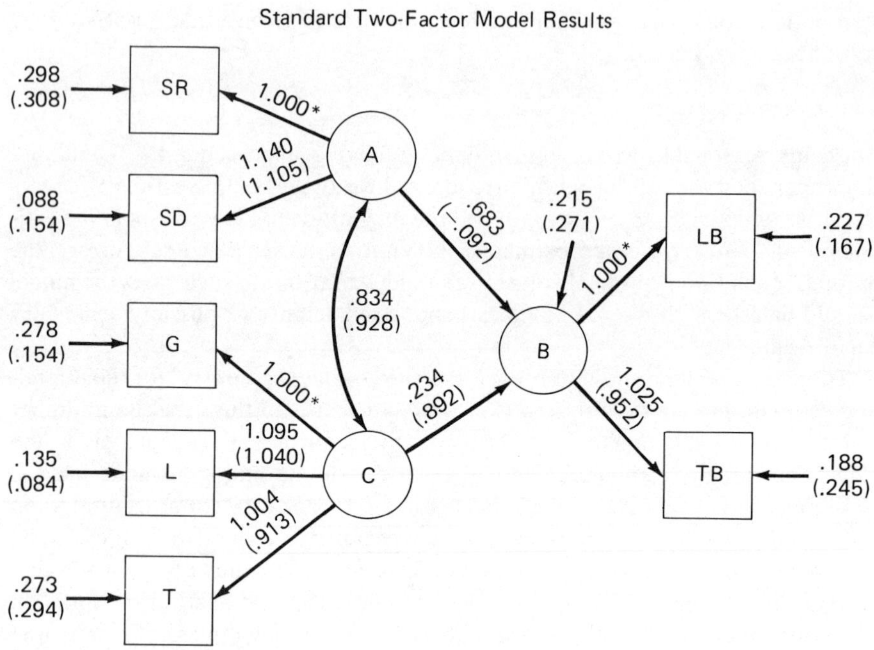

*Indicates parameters restricted for identification purposes.
Figures in parentheses are corresponding parameter estimates for the behavioral intentions sample.

A = Affective component of attitude
C = Cognitive component of attitude
SR = Guilford self-rating
SD = Semanitc differential
G = Guttman
L = Likert
T = Thurstone
B = Scaled behavior construct
LB = Likert-scaled behavior
TB = Thurstone-scaled behavior

FIGURE 4.10.

approach involves reestimating the epistemic correlations linking substantially distinct unobserved variables with their indicators as separate models. Using the Fishbein and Ajzen (1974) data once again, we first estimated the epistemic correlations linking each of the observable attitude measures to its respective unobservable affective or cognitive component in a manner consistent with Figure 4.2, panel b. This is equivalent to a "within-block" factor analysis. Next we examined the structural relationship between the attitude components and the behavioral criterion by fitting the model of Figure 4.3, except that the epistemic correlations linking the attitude measures to their respective affective or cognitive components were fixed to be equal to the values obtained from the previously undertaken within-block factor analysis. Figures 4.10 and 4.11 summarizes the

Within-Block Two-Factor Model

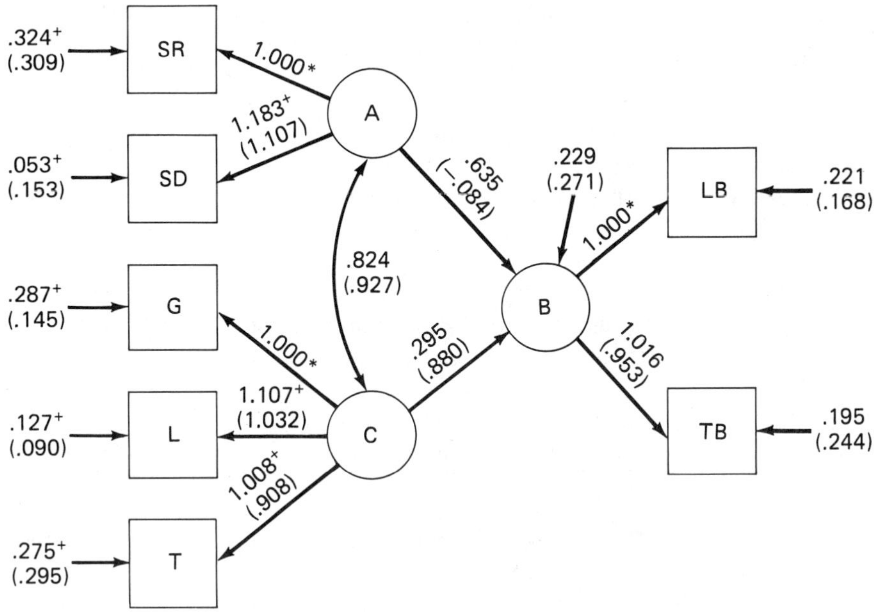

⁺Indicates parameters estimated together as a separate model and then restricted.

*Indicates parameters fixed for identification purposes.

Figures in parentheses indicate corresponding estimates for the behavioral intentions sample.

Estimates of the ϕ_{AC} parameter are standardized values.

A = Affective component of attitude	L = Likert
C = Cognitive component of attitude	T = Thurstone
SR = Guilford self-rating	B = Scaled behavior construct
SD = Semantic differential	LB = Likert-scaled behavior
G = Guttman	TB = Thurstone-scaled behavior

FIGURE 4.11.

results. Figure 4.10 shows the parameter estimates obtained under full-information maximum likelihood estimation, whereas Figure 4.11 shows the limited-information parameter estimates. From the figures it is apparent that there is not much difference between corresponding parameter estimates in the two models for either the self-reported behaviors or behavioral intention samples. Thus, the decision to use a full-information estimation procedure has little influence on the results, and, hence, interpretational confounding appears not to be a serious issue.

Concluding Remarks

In this chapter we have put forth two primary arguments. First, the LISREL model and its many variants provide unprecedented opportunities for consumer researchers to attack substantive problems that heretofore could not have been easily addressed. Second, because consumer research is serious business, the consumer behavior researcher has the responsibility to approach the analysis intelligently and honestly and consequently must be aware of the issues and caveats in applying LISREL models. The specific applications and issues in application we have discussed have simply touched the tip of the iceberg. More work needs to be done in order to understand the many nuances involved in fitting and evaluating LISREL models, especially with regard to the analysis of MTMM data and the causes and evaluation of interpretational confounding.

References

Anderson, T. W., & Rubin, H. (1956). Statistical inference in factor analysis. *Proceedings of the Third Berkeley Symposium on Mathematical Statistics and Probability, 5*, 111–150.

Bagozzi, R. P. (1978). The construct validity of the affective, behavioral and cognitive components of attitude by analysis of covariance structures. *Multivariate Behavioral Research, 13*, 9–31.

Bagozzi, R. P. (1980). *Causal models in marketing*. New York: John Wiley.

Bagozzi, R. P. (1983, March). Issues in the application of covariance structure analysis: A further comment. *Journal of Consumer Research, 9*, 449–450.

Bagozzi, R. P., & Burnkrant, R. E. (1979). Attitude organization and the attitude-behavior relationship. *Journal of Personality and Social Psychology, 37*, 913–929.

Belsley, D. A. (1981). *Collinearity and Forecasting* (Technical Report No. 27). Cambridge, MA: Sloan School of Management, MIT, Center for Computational Research in Economics and Management Science.

Belsley, D. A., Kuh, E., & Welsch, R. E. (1980). *Regression diagnostics: Identifying influential data and sources of collinearity*. New York: John Wiley.

Bentler, P. M. (1976). Multistructure statistical model applied to factor analysis. *Multivariate Behavioral Research, 11*, 3–25.

Bentler, P. M. (1983). *Theory and implementation of ESQ, structural equation program*. Los Angeles: BMDP Statistical Software.

Bentler, P. M., & Bonett, D. G. (1980). Significance tests and goodness-of-fit in the analysis of covariance structures. *Psychological Bulletin, 88*, 588–606.

Bentler, P. M., & Weeks, D. G. (1980). Linear structural equations with latent variables. *Psychometrika, 45*, 285–308.

Burt, R. S. (1976). Interpretational confounding of unobserved variables in structural equation models. *Sociological Methods and Research, 5*, 3–52.

Cliff, N. (1983). Some cautions concerning the application of causal modeling methods. *Multivariate Behavioral Research, 18*, 115–126.

Dillon, W. R., & Goldstein, M. (1984). *Multivariate analysis: Methods and applications*. New York: John Wiley.

Dillon, W. R., & Kumar, A. (1985). Attitude organization and the attitude-behavior relationship: A critique of Bagozzi and Burnkrant's reanalysis of Fishbein and Ajzen. *Journal of Personality and Social Psychology, 49*, 33–46.

Dillon, W. R., Kumar, A., & Mulani, N. (1986). Offending estimates in covariance structure analysis: Comments on the causes and solution to Heywood cases. *Psychological Bulletin*, forthcoming.

Driel, O. P. van (1978). On various causes of improper solutions in maximum likelihood factor analysis. *Psychometrika, 43*, 225–243.

Fishbein, M., & Ajzen, I. (1974). Attitudes towards objects as predictors of single and multiple behavioral criteria. *Psychological Review, 81*, 59–74.

Fornell, C. (1983). Issues in the application of covariance structure analysis: A comment. *Journal of Consumer Research, 9*, 443–448.

Fornell, C., & Larcker, D. F. (1981a, February). Evaluating structural equation models with unobservable variables and measurement error. *Journal of Marketing Research, 18*, 39–50.

Fornell, C., & Larcker, D. F. (1981b, August). Structural equation models with unobservable variables and measurement error: Algebra and statistics. *Journal of Marketing Research, 18*, 382–388.

Gerbing, D. W., & Anderson, J. C. (1984, June). On the meaning of within-factor correlated measurement errors. *Journal of Consumer Research, 11*, 572–580.

Gerbing, D. W., & Anderson, J. C. (1985). Improper solutions in the analysis of covariance structures: Their interpretability and a comparison of alternative respectifications. Working Paper, Baylor, TX: Baylor University.

Guttman, L. A. (1944). A basis for scaling qualitative data. *American Sociological Review, 9*, 139–150.

Hägglund, G. (1982). Factor analysis by instrumental variable methods. *Psychometrika, 47* (2), 209–222.

Harman, H. H. (1971). *Modern factor analysis*. Chicago: University of Chicago Press.

Jagpal, H. (1982, November). Multicollinearity in structural equation models with unobservable variables. *Journal of Marketing Research, 19*, 431–439.

Jöreskog, K. G. (1967, December). Some contributions to maximum likelihood factor analysis. *Psychometrika, 32*, 443–482.

Jöreskog, K. G. (1970). A general method for analysis of covariance structures. *Biometrika, 57*, 239–251.

Jöreskog, K. G. (1971). Statistical analysis of sets of congeneric tests. *Psychometrika, 36*, 109–133.

Jöreskog, K. G. (1977). Structural equation models in the social sciences: Specification, estimation, and testing. In P. R. Krishnaiah (Ed.), *Applications of Statistics* (pp. 265–287). Amsterdam: North-Holland.

Jöreskog, K. G. (1979). Simultaneous factor analysis in several populations. In K. G. Jöreskog, & D. Sörbom (Eds.), *Advances in factor analysis and structural equation models*. Cambridge, MA: Abt Books.

Jöreskog, K. G., & Sörbom, D. (1978). *LISREL: Analysis of linear structural relationships by the method of maximum likelihood*. Chicago: National Education Resources.

Jöreskog, K. G., & Sörbom, D. (1982). *LISREL VI: Analysis of linear structural relationships by maximum likelihood*. Morresville, IN: Scientific Software.

Jöreskog, K. G., & van Thillo, M. (1973). *LISREL: A general computer program for estimating a linear structural equation system involving multiple indicators of unmeasured variables*. Princeton, NJ: Educational Testing Service.

Kenny, D. A. (1979). *Correlation and causality*. New York: Wiley.

Koopmans, T. C. (1949). Identification problems in econometric model construction. *Econometrica, 17*, 125–143.

Koopmans, T. C., & Reiersol, O. (1950). The identification of structural characteristics. *Annuals of Mathematical Statistics*, *21*, 165–181.

Lawley, D. N., & Maxwell, A. E. (1971). *Factor analysis as a statistical method*. London: Butterworth.

Leamer, E. E. (1978). *Specification searches: Ad hoc inference with nonexperimental data*. New York: John Wiley.

Lee, S. Y. (1980). Estimation of covariance structure models with parameters subject to functional restraints. *Psychometrika*, *45*, 309–324.

Lee, S. Y., & Tsui, K. L. (1982). Covariance structure analysis in several populations. *Psychometrika*, *47*, 297–308.

Likert, R. A. (1932). A technique for the measurement of attitudes. *Archives of Psychology*, No. 140.

Long, J. S. (1983a). *Confirmatory factor analysis*. Menlo Park, CA: Sage Publications.

Long, J. S. (1983b). *Covariance structure models*. Menlo Park, CA: Sage Publications.

McDonald, R. P. (1978). A simple comprehensive model for the analysis of covariance structures. *British Journal of Mathematical and Statistical Psychology*, *31*, 59–72.

McDonald, R. P. (1980). A simple comprehensive model for the analysis of covariance structures: Some remarks on applications. *British Journal of Mathematical and Statistical Psychology*, *33*, 161–183.

McDonald, R. P., & Krane, W. R. (1977). A note on local identifiability and degrees of freedom in the asymptotic likelihood ratio test. *British Journal of Mathematical and Statistical Psychology*, *30*, 198–203.

McDonald, R. P., & Krane, W. R. (1979). A Monte Carlo study of local identifiability and degrees of freedom in the asymptotic likelihood ratio test. *British Journal of Mathematical and Statistical Psychology*, *32*, 121–132.

Ostrom, T. M. (1969). The relationship between the affective, behavioral and cognitive components of attitude. *Journal of Experimental Social Psychology*, *5*, 12–30.

Reiersol, O. (1950). On the identifiability of parameters in Thurstone's multiple factor analysis. *Psychometrika*, *15*, 121–149.

Rindskopf, D. (1983). Parameterizing inequality constraints on unique variances in linear structural models. *Psychometrika*, *48*, 73–83.

Rindskopf, D. (1984). Structural equation models: Empirical identification, Heywood cases, and related problems. *Sociological Methods and Research*, *13*, 109–119.

Rindskopf, D. (1984, August). Personal communication.

Rindskopf, D. (1984). Using phantom and imaginary latent variables to parameterize constraints in linear structural models. *Psychometrika*, *49*, 37–47.

Sörbom, D (1981). Structural equation models with structured means. In K. G. Jöreskog & H. Wold (Eds.), *Systems with indirect observation: Causality, structure, and prediction* (pp. 119–131). Amsterdam: North-Holland.

Thurstone, L. L., & Chave, E. J. (1929). *The measurement of attitude*. Chicago: University of Chicago Press.

Werts, C. E., Linn, R. L., & Jöreskog, K. G. (1971). Estimating the parameters of path models involving unmeasured variables. In H. M. Blalock, Jr. (Ed.), *Causal models in the social sciences* (pp. 214–229). Chicago: Aldine-Atherton.

5
Meta-Analysis: Techniques for the Quantitive Integration of Research Findings

DAVID BRINBERG and JAMES JACCARD

With the rapid growth of empirical findings in consumer behavior, there is a need to integrate research results into a coherent body of knowledge. In this chapter, we discuss an approach that can provide the researcher with tools to integrate a body of literature. The chapter is divided into three sections. In section one, we present a brief historical overview of the procedures used to integrate research findings. In section two, we describe a set of facets that can be used to partition a body of literature about some focal problem and which may provide the researcher with insights concerning that problem. In section three, we discuss the types of statistical procedures that can be used for the integration of research findings, and we present examples of the use of these procedures.

Integrating Research Findings: A Brief Historical Review

Statistical procedures for the integration of research findings have been available to social science researchers for over 50 years (cf. Pearson, 1933; Pearson, 1938; Wallis, 1942; Fisher, 1948; Jones & Fiske, 1953; Birnbaum, 1954; Mosteller & Bush, 1954; Adcock, 1960). Those procedures focused primarily on the development of transformations (e.g., natural log, z score transformation) and strategies for weighting individual studies and allow the researcher to combine or to compare the probability levels obtained from independent studies. Recent work on these statistical procedures (e.g., Rosenthal, 1978, 1982; Glass, McGaw, & Smith, 1981; Hunter, Schmidt, & Jackson, 1982; Hedges, 1982, 1983) has extended the work on transformations and has focused on the estimation of the nature and strength of a hypothesized relation. *Meta-analysis* has been the term developed to describe the use of these statistical procedures for the integration of a set of empirical findings across independent studies (Glass, McGaw, & Smith, 1981).

In recent years, meta-analytic procedures have been introduced to consumer researchers. Sawyer and Peter (1983) discuss issues associated with meta-analysis in their presentation of statistical significance testing. Substantive applications of meta-analysis have examined the relation between research design and response rates to questionnaires (Yu & Cooper, 1983); research design and the reliability of rating scales (Churchill & Peter, 1984); and advertising and sales (Assmus, Farley, & Lehmann, 1984). Several researchers have discussed the strengths and weaknesses of meta-analysis (Houston, Peter, & Sawyer, 1983; Monroe & Krishnan, 1983; Reilly & Conover, 1983), although these authors do not provide a discussion of the analytic procedures. In section three of this chapter, we focus on a detailed discussion of these procedures.

Limitations of Literature Reviews

Two types of reviews are discussed: (a) narrative reviews and (b) meta-analytic reviews. In our view, the primary feature that distinguishes narrative from meta-analytic reviews is that the latter uses precise and formal procedures whereas the former uses the reviewers' subjective judgments to address the following set of questions: (a) Is there a relationship between two (or more) variables? (e.g., consumer attitudes and purchase behavior) (b) What is the strength of this relationship? and (c) Under what conditions (e.g., subjects, behaviors, measures, and contexts) will the findings hold?

Narrative reviews can be characterized as an integration of findings by either itemizing each result or by some vote-counting technique (i.e., by tabulating the number of studies consistent with a particular hypothesis). Proponents of meta-analysis have described narrative reviews as limited in their potential for useful information. For instance, Axelson, Federline, and Brinberg (1985) conducted a meta-analysis on the relation between food attitudes and food-related behavior. In their review, nine studies were found that examined this relation. Seven of those nine studies had a nonsignificant correlation between attitude and behavior. Using a vote-counting procedure, these authors would have concluded that no relation exists between food attitudes and food-related behavior. Using meta-analytic procedures, however, these authors found a statistically significant (though small) relation between food attitude and food behavior. Thus, the meta-analytic procedures reduced the likelihood of these authors making a Type II error.

There are several limitations associated with the narrative approach. First, when the number of studies is large, the reviewer may have difficulty estimating (a) whether there is a relationship among the variables being examined and (b) the strength and nature of that relationship. Second, there are losses of information that may occur if information is integrated incorrectly (Light & Smith, 1971), (a) weak inferences; that is, the relation under study is stronger than the reviewer infers; (b) overlooked inferences; that is, the reviewer ignores systematic variation in the set of findings and (c) wrong inferences; that is, the reviewer integrates the set of findings in a manner that is inconsistent with the more accurate statistical integration. Third, reviewers may ignore the impact of statistical power when using just the level of significance in their integration of a set of findings (Cook & Leviton, 1980). A finding may not reach statistical significance because of a lack of power but still be consistent with the direction of the hypothesized relation. Ignoring that finding or treating it as nonsupport for the hypothesis may result in a misleading conclusion as illustrated above.

Several researchers have presented limitations that apply to both narrative and meta-analytic reviews, although the discussion by these authors focuses on meta-analytic techniques. Wilson and Rachman (1983) and Mintz (1983) have argued that bias can occur in the selection of studies both in terms of the specification of the sampling frame (e.g., only published studies or only those studies with quantified results) as well as in the specification of hypothesized relations. For instance, studies that examine the attitude-behavior relation may measure attitude several ways (e.g., semantic differential, set of belief statements). The reviewer needs to make a judgment concerning what studies are appropriate for inclusion in the literature review; that is, he/she needs to determine what studies will be treated as replicates (and thus, included in the review) and what studies will be treated as different (and thus, excluded from the review).

Another major source of controversy in conducting reviews is the integration of seemingly unrelated studies. For instance, Glass, McGaw, and Smith (1981) report a meta-analysis in which they combined a wide variety of psychotherapy treatments and a wide variety of illnesses. A single, overall effect size estimate concerning the effectiveness of psychotherapy was computed. That estimate, however, can be misleading because it may mask ineffective treatments. These authors point out that useful information concerning psychotherapy can be gained when the set of studies are partitioned into different groups and the scope and limits of treatments can be identified.

For most research, we assume those units we treat as a replication factor are homogeneous (e.g., subjects in a between-subject factorial design). The reviewer makes a similar assumption concerning the set of studies to be integrated because the studies are treated as the replication factor. Procedures (discussed in section three) are available to determine the uniformity of these studies and to test the viability of this assumption.

The impact of poor quality studies is another source of controversy when conducting literature reviews. Glass and Kliegl (1983) argue that *all* studies should be included in a review and that the quality of the study should be coded and correlated with outcome variables to determine their relation. If there is a nonsignificant correlation, the researcher might then conclude that study quality is unrelated to study outcome. Mintz (1983) and Wilson and Rachman (1983), however, argue that including poor studies provides no useful information because no accurate inferences may be made concerning their outcomes. Further, Mintz (1983) argues that coding the quality of the study assumes the researcher is able to develop a valid coding system. Mintz suggests that the reviewer not include all studies but make explicit his/her reasons for excluding any particular study from the review.

A final source of controversy concerns the treatment of studies as independent replicates of a hypothesized relation. If a single study includes more than one piece of information concerning the hypothesized relation and each piece of information is included separately in the review, the researcher is faced with the problem of biasing the integration of the set of studies by placing undue weight on findings from the same study and violating statistical assumptions of independence. Two approaches have been suggested to deal with this problem (Light & Pillemer, 1984). First, the researcher may develop a single statistic for that study. Second, the researcher can include each piece of information in the review but weigh the information in such a way that it receives the same overall weight as the findings from a single study. We do not recommend the use of the second approach because it violates the assumption of independence, although some techniques have been developed recently to adjust for nonindependent findings (Strube, 1985).

The Role of Meta-Analysis in the Conduct of Research

Our position is that meta-analytic procedures should be viewed as one strategy within a general research program for studying a focal problem. The primary advantages of the meta-analytic procedures are two-fold: (a) Statistical procedures are more precise than intuition in identifying the presence, strength, and nature of a hypothesized relation, and (b) these procedures can be used to identify the scope and limits of the hypothesized relation.

Several sources of controversy were raised concerning literature reviews which we would like to address. First, in our view, the researcher conducting a meta-analysis is faced with many of the same "subjective" choices as the narrative reviewer (e.g., specification of the sampling frame, the hypothesized relation, the quality of the study, factors that potentially interact with the study outcomes, the scope and limits of the findings). We view both procedures as subjective, although we acknowledge that the meta-analytic procedures may help the researcher to be more explicit in his/her assumptions and be more precise in the integration of probability levels and effect size estimates. Second, the issue concerning the integration of unrelated studies is a question concerning the conceptual clarity of the original hypotheses. A researcher may be interested in only combining studies that operationalize a concept similarly or may be interested in examining all studies that claim to examine the same concept (even if they are operationalized differently). There is no single approach that is correct because the selection of studies depends on the purposes of the reviewer. Each reviewer needs to choose and make explicit the criteria he/she has used to select a set of studies. Third, poor quality studies (i.e., those studies with design flaws or poor execution that result in confounded findings) should *not* be included in an integration of a set of findings because the outcome of those studies is unclear and will add uninterpretable variation in a review.[1] Fourth, to reduce the problems that occur when including multiple findings from a single study, we recommend that

---

[1]We have argued to exclude poor quality studies for two reasons: (a) Poor quality studies have confounded (i.e., ambiguous) outcomes; thus, no reasonable inference can be made concerning the relation between those studies and other "external" variables, and (b) if

only a single finding from any one study be included in a review. A conservative approach (in terms of Type I errors) is to select the weakest relationship, and a liberal approach is to select the strongest relationship (see Strube (1985) for an alternative approach).

The major source of information in any literature review is not in single summary statements concerning the relation but in identifying its scope and limits. Knowing the overall significance level and the overall effect size of a set of studies provides the reviewer with limited information. Only when the reviewer is able to fit it into some nomological network will he/she come to a deeper understanding of that relation.

In the following section, we discuss issues involved in increasing our understanding and confidence about some hypothesized relation. In doing so, we describe a framework that may be used to identify facets for examining the scope and limits of that relation.

Increasing Our Confidence and Understanding in a Research Finding

Brinberg and McGrath (1985) present two issues that influence the confidence a researcher may have *after* he/she has obtained an empirical finding: (a) Whether the results of a study can be replicated if the study were repeated, and (b) whether the researcher can identify the scope and limits of the finding if various features of a study were varied systematically. The importance of establishing the scope and limits of a finding in the acquisition of knowledge and establishing confidence in it has been discussed by several authors (e.g., McGrath & Brinberg, 1983; Wimsatt, 1981).

A portion of the Validity Network Schema developed by Brinberg and McGrath (1982, 1985) will be used to organize the facets to consider when assessing the scope and limits of an empirical relation. Brinberg and McGrath (1985) argue that all research involves three interrelated but analytically separate domains: methodological, substantive, and conceptual. We will focus on two levels in each of the three domains: elements and relations.

The methodological domain contains measures at an element level and design features at a relations level. The substantive domain contains states and actions of individuals at an element level and patterns of two or more states or actions of individuals at a relations level. The conceptual domain contains *attributes* of states or actions of individuals at an element level and relations among attributes at a relations level.

The advantage of using the validity network schema to discuss the facets involved when conducting a meta-analysis is that it provides a systematic analysis

---

the number of studies is sufficiently large to examine the difference between poor and good quality studies, then the researcher is likely to have a sufficient sample size to simply use the good quality studies to examine the hypothesized relation.

of the research process and an overall framework within which to integrate the findings for any given empirical relation. Partitioning the findings across these facets will provide the researcher with an estimate of the scope and limits of the empirical relation, thus, increasing his/her confidence and understanding in that relation. The set of facets also provide a secondary function: They may be used by the researcher to identify areas of research where there are insufficient studies. The subdivision of each of these facets are presented in a general form because each facet will vary as a function of the literature under review. Finally, the set of facets are discussed separately although combinations of facets from the three domains also may be used to partition the literature under review.

Facets in the Methodological Domain

As noted above, the two levels within this domain are measures and design features. Each of these levels can be further partitioned to provide useful information to the meta-analyst.

Element Level. Measures can be divided as a function of two general dimensions. One is the source of the information (respondent vs. observer vs. recorder in past) and the second is whether the respondent is aware he/she is providing the information in the context of an experiment (Runkel & McGrath, 1972). These two dimensions may be used to form a 3 $\times$ 2 table. Table 5.1 contains a description of the set of six techniques for obtaining empirical information.

A meta-analyst may use the categories found in Table 5.1 to partition the literature under review. For instance, in the area of involvement, researchers have proposed two distinct measures of the involvement concept: one based on a direct observation of some physiological response and a second based on a self-report measure (e.g., Krugman, 1965; Houston & Rothschild, 1978). The researcher can assess the scope and limits of the relation between involvement and choice by using the type of measure as a partition. This type of partition allows the researcher to determine the impact of measurement procedures on the empirical relation.

Each of the techniques described in Table 5.1 may be further divided. For instance, the category of self-report questionnaires may be divided into different scaling techniques (e.g., Thurstone, Semantic differential, Likert scaling). The category of observations may be divided into event-based versus time-based

TABLE 5.1. Facets for the elements of the methodological domain.

	Actor awareness of research	
Source	Aware	Not aware
Respondent	self-report	trace measures
Researcher	visible observer	hidden observer
Recorder in past	records of public behavior	archival records

observations. The specific subdivisions of these techniques and their use as partition variables will depend on the particular literature under review.

Relation Level. Different types of design features have been used to allow a researcher to assess the relations between the measures or manipulations in their study. These features typically vary across three facets: (a) the rule used to assign subjects to conditions (i.e., random assignment, nonrandom but known assignment rule, unknown assignment rule), (b) treatment of the "independent variable" (i.e., manipulated, observed, used as a matching variable or held constant), and (c) the number of times one respondent is observed (i.e., repeated measures vs. single observation).

Several strategies may be used to partition a body of literature as a function of the research design. Birnbaum (1982) has argued that a particular empirical finding may vary depending on whether the researcher uses a between- or a within-subject factorial design. For example, research in the area of choice set composition and Bayesian inferences (e.g., Ofir & Lynch, 1984; Payne, 1982) may be divided using the type of design (i.e., between- vs. within-subject factorial design) as a facet to partition the set of studies.

In addition to the repeated (or single) observation of a respondent, the treatment of the independent variable may serve as a partition variable. For instance, in studies which used the Fishbein theory of reasoned action, researchers have both observed (cf. Ajzen & Fishbein, 1980) and manipulated (e.g., Lutz, 1977; Miniard & Cohen, 1979) the independent variables. This type of partition variable can provide the researcher with the chance to gain insights into the impact of design factors on the relations among the variables in the model.

The element and relation levels can be viewed within the context of an embedding system (Brinberg & McGrath, 1985). The set of strategies used in research may be organized using two dimensions. One is the degree of obtrusiveness and the second is the degree of abstractness of that strategy. Runkel and McGrath (1972) describe eight strategies using these two dimensions. Figure 5.1 contains these strategies.

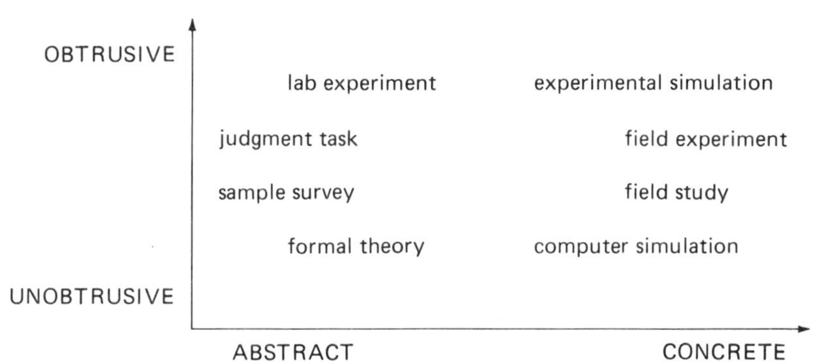

FIGURE 5.1. Facets for the strategies in the methodological domain.

The eight strategies may also be used by the meta-analyst to partition a set of studies. For instance, researchers examining advertising effectiveness have conducted studies using both laboratory and field settings (e.g., Gardner & Raj, 1983). Using the research strategy as a partition variable provides the reviewer with an assessment of the scope and limits of advertising effectiveness across research strategies.

Facets in the Substantive Domain Facets

As noted earlier, the two levels within this domain are states or actions of individuals and patterns among the states or actions of two or more individuals.

Element Level. Many aspects of the states or actions of individuals have been examined in the social sciences. Two broad groupings may be used to characterize the states of individuals. One is biographic/demographic characteristics of the individual (e.g., age, education, gender, income, race, religion). A second is psychological characteristics of the individual (e.g., beliefs, attitudes, values, motives, needs, personality traits, emotion).

Actions performed by individuals may also be grouped into two broad categories. One is interpersonal behaviors; that is, behaviors directed toward some individual. Three underlying dimensions of interpersonal behavior have been identified (Triandis, 1977): (a) intimacy-formality, (b) association-disassociation, and (c) super-subordination. A second broad category of actions may be characterized as task or choice behavior (e.g., donating blood, voting, having a child, changing careers, purchasing a product, completing an assignment).

These broad categories may be used by reviewers in many research areas to partition the set of studies. For instance, research using a subjective probability model (e.g., Jaccard & King, 1977) has assessed model fit for both college and noncollege respondents. A reviewer, integrating the research on this model, can determine the model's scope and limits across respondent type by partitioning the set of studies using this facet.

Relation Level. Relations are the patterns among two or more elements (i.e., states or actions of individuals within a context). For instance, a researcher reviewing the literature that examines one particular algebraic model (e.g., a differential weighted averaging model, Lynch, 1979) can determine the scope and limits of that model by partitioning the set of studies using the "content" of the judgment as the partition variable. If the findings from a particular model hold across the different "content" areas (e.g., birth control decisions, altruistic decisions) or the researcher can explain why the findings do not hold across the different content areas. his/her confidence in that model is increased.

Conceptual Domain Facets

Finally, as noted earlier, the two levels within this domain are *attributes* of the states or actions of individuals and relations among these attributes. These facets would not be useful to the meta-analyst because statistical procedures have not been developed to contrast the findings of two different sets of empirical relations. We present these facets because they can provide the reviewer with some general insights concerning the similarities and differences across two or more hypothesized relations.

Element Level. As researchers, we are interested in variables that *uniquely* and *adequately* account for some phenomenon. If alternative variables can account for a phenomenon, our confidence in any one set of explanatory variables decreases. When conducting a review, the researcher can increase his/her confidence in an empirical relation by determining whether the hypothesized set of variables are the necessary and sufficient set or whether an alternative set is better. For instance, various researchers (e.g., Zajonc, 1980; Brinberg, 1979) have questioned whether affect (i.e., emotion) is different than attitude and whether both (or just one) are needed to predict an individual's decision. These researchers and others (e.g., Dillon, 1986) have compared models which include either and both of these constructs in the prediction of behavior. This type of competitive theory testing is analogous to Platt's (1964) argument for strong inference. The reviewer summarizing the literature on models separating affect from attitude can determine the scope and limits of one model, relative to the other, by dividing the set of studies using the type of model as the partition variable.

Relation Level. Several categories of relations can be developed: (a) the causal relations (e.g., necessary and sufficient causes) among elements, (b) quantitative relations among elements (e.g., greater than, equal to, less than as well as linear, nonlinear, step-function), (c) logical relations among elements (e.g., intersection, union, exclusion from set theory; recursive, symmetric and asymmetric from math theory), and (d) relations that describe structural forms (e.g., parallel, serial, hierarchical, and circumplex).

The reviewer may gain additional knowledge about a hypothesized empirical relation by partitioning and contrasting studies that vary as a function of the form of the relation among the variables. For instance, research in the area of the attitude-behavior relationship may contrast a threshold function postulated by Campbell (1963) with a linear relation between the two variables. A reviewers' confidence in a linear form of the relation should increase if it is more accurate than some other form of the relation.

Summary of Methodological, Substantive, and Conceptual Facets

Table 5.2 contains a summary of the primary levels described in the preceding sections. Our presentation of these facets is meant to illustrate the basic areas a meta-analyst can consider to increase his/her confidence and understanding about an empirical relation. Few, if any, bodies of literature will have studies that vary across all the levels discussed within the conceptual, methodological, and substantive domains. If the studies under review are treated as homogeneous, however, the reviewer conducting a meta-analysis restricts the knowledge he/she is able to acquire.

TABLE 5.2. Summary of the levels and examples of facets within the conceptual, methodological, and substantive domains.

	Substantive	Methodological	Conceptual
Elements	states (e.g., demographic or psychological) actions (e.g., choices or interpersonal behaviors contexts (e.g., temporal, location, situation)	operations (i.e., measures and manipulations—see Table 1)	attributes of states and actions of entities within a context (e.g., affect, norms, static/dynamic variables)
Relation	relations among states for one entity (e.g., the relation between attitudes and beliefs) relations between states or actions for one entity (e.g., the relation between attitudes and choice) relations between actions of two or more entities (e.g., two individuals involved in an exchange)	comparison forms (e.g., factorial designs, regression designs)	relations among variables (e.g., logical, causal quantitative)

In addition to the domains derived from the Validity Network Schema, the researcher needs to consider characteristics of the study when conducting a meta-analysis.

Study Facets

Several researchers (e.g., Glass, McGaw, & Smith, 1981; Monroe & Krishnan, 1983) have developed systems to code the characteristics of studies. A detailed discussion of these coding schemes will not be presented although we will describe briefly the primary facets of these schemas. One facet deals with characteristics of the researcher (e.g., academic or industrial, rank, affiliation). A second facet deals with the source of the study (e.g., refereed journal, book chapter, dissertation thesis, unpublished manuscript). A third facet deals with the funding of the research (e.g., grant, contract, university). A fourth facet deals with the "quality" of the empirical finding. There is no single index concerning the quality of a study's finding. One aspect of quality is the reliability of the measures used in the study. A second aspect is the validity of the finding, i.e., the internal and construct validity associated with the finding. A detailed discussion of the potential set of validity issues and their corresponding threats is beyond the scope of this chapter. The interested reader, however, should see Cook and Campbell (1979), Runkel and McGrath (1972), or Brinberg and McGrath (1985).

Section Summary

In the second section of this chapter, we have presented a framework for partitioning a set of findings. That framework can be used by the meta-analyst as a systematic approach toward identifying potential sources of variation in a set of findings. The facets presented represent, collectively, the three basic components of a research study. No single body of literature is likely to contain sufficient variation on all the facets described in the substantive, methodological, and conceptual domains for the researcher to use each facet as a partition variable when conducting a meta-analysis. We have argued, however, that the researcher can gain insight into the phenomenon of interest by examining, systematically, variations in the findings across some set of facets.

Statistical techniques have been developed to estimate the impact of partition variables on the presence or absence of a hypothesized relation, across a set of independent studies, and on the strength and nature of that relation. A detailed, and somewhat formal presentation of these techniques is the topic of discussion for the remainder of this chapter.

Quantitative Procedures

This section describes statistical methods for analyzing multiple research studies. We begin by discussing methods for abstracting statistical information from research reports. We then consider the characteristics of effect size measures used in most meta-analyses. Finally, after describing the statistical focus of meta-analytic techniques, we consider approaches to the quantitative analysis of multiple studies.

Retrieving Statistical Information

Meta-analytic approaches involve the analysis of either p values or effect size estimates based on commonly reported statistics such as t, χ^2, F, and r. In the case of F and χ^2 statistics, meta-analytic techniques are only applicable to the case where df = 1 for the numerator of an F = test, or df = 1 for a chi-square test of independence.[2] Many investigations report the results of omnibus F tests in which more than two levels characterize the independent variable in question. Currently, meta-analytic techniques require that the test be converted to an analysis of differences between any given pair of means within the overall set, using a

[2]When the degrees of freedom are greater than one, the statistical foundations for the meta-analytic procedures described in this chapter do not apply.

t statistic. Similarly, a chi square analysis with df > 1 involves calculating a chi-square for any given 2 × 2 contingency table. Although the focus is on the case of df = 1, this is not problematic because most theoretical questions focus on specific comparisons within the omnibus test.

Investigations reporting contingency tables with df > 1 typically report the necessary frequency data to form a smaller 2 × 2 table for the purposes of conducting a chi square analysis with df = 1. In contrast, *F* tests with df > 1 usually report only the value of the overall *F*, the degrees of freedom, the sample sizes (*n*) for each group, and the group means. The relevant *t* for any comparison between two groups can be estimated as $t = (M_1 - M_2)/\text{SE}$ where

$$\text{SE} = \sqrt{(\text{MSW}/(n_1 + n_2))} \tag{1}$$

and M_1 is the mean for group 1, M_2 is the mean for group 2, n_1 = the number of subjects in group 1, n_2 = the number of subjects in group 2, and MSW is the mean square within for the *F* ratio. The statistic usually missing from research reports for purposes of estimating *t* is MSW. However, this can be calculated from the information typically provided. Let *g* be the number of groups, *G* be the grand mean, and SSB be the sum of squares between groups. *G* is calculated by summing the group means $M_1 + M_2 + \ldots + M_g$, and then dividing this sum by *g*. SSB is

$$\text{SSB} = \sum_{i=1}^{g} n\,(M_i - G)^2 \tag{2}$$

and

$$\text{MSW} = \frac{\text{SSB}/(g - 1)}{F} \tag{3}$$

In the cases where unequal *n* are present, the definition of terms in Equation 2 will depend upon whether an unweighted means or least-squares analysis of variance solution was used. For a least-squares solution, the grand mean is computed by weighting each group mean by its sample size (Hays, 1963, p. 209). For an unweighted means solution, the harmonic mean of *n* is substituted for *n* (Winer, 1971, p. 402), with the grand mean being computed in the same manner as the equal *n* case.

Measures of Effect Size

Numerous indices of effect size have been proposed in the social sciences. One of the more popular indices has focused on the proportion of explained variance in the dependent variable relative to the independent variable. Statistics such as *t*, *r*, *F* (where df = 1), and χ^2 (where df = 1) can be converted to measures reflecting the proportion of explained variance (EV) in a set of data as follows:

$$\text{EV} = r^2 \tag{4}$$

$$\text{EV} = \chi^2/N \tag{5}$$

$$\mathrm{EV} = F/(F + \mathrm{df\ within}) \tag{6}$$

$$\mathrm{EV} = t^2/(t^2 + \mathrm{df}) \tag{7}$$

Meta-analytic techniques typically use two indices of effect size. The approach advocated by Rosenthal (1983) uses an index, r_R, which is the square root of any of the EV measures. The second index is based upon Glass (1977) and Cohen (1977) and concerns the case of mean scores in two conditions. This index, called d, is defined as

$$d = (M_1 - M_2)/s \tag{8}$$

where s is a pooled standard deviation from the two conditions. Cohen (1977) suggests that a d of .2 represents a "weak" relationship, a d of .5 represents a "moderate" relationship, and a d of .8 represents a "strong" relationship (however, see Cohen, 1977, p. 24 for additional perspectives on this problem). d is mathematically related to r_R (e.g., d values of .2, .5, and .8 equal r values of .10, .25, and .37 respectively; see Cohen (1977) for the mathematical translation of d to r_R and vice versa).

In Equation 8, there is some controversy as to the optimal method for defining s in sample data. The value of σ in the population parameter $\delta = (\mu_1 - \mu_2)/\sigma$ is assumed to stem from populations with equal variances. It follows that the best estimate of σ will be based upon traditional formulas used in t tests. In cases where the two groups in question represent a treatment and control group, Glass, McGaw, and Smith (1981) recommend the use of the control group standard deviation as the estimate of σ. In contrast, Hunter, Schmidt, and Jackson (1982) advocate the traditional pooled estimate of σ. For most consumer applications, the pooled estimate of σ will be the most appropriate. Discussions in the sections that follow will therefore assume an s based upon a pooled standard deviation estimate. For further consideration of this issue, see Glass et al. (1981), Hunter et al. (1982), and Hedges (1981).

Few studies report the information necessary to compute d directly. However, it can be derived from the t statistic by $d = t\sqrt{(1/n_1 + 1/n_2)}$.

Statistical Focus of Meta-Analysis

Meta-analysis involves addressing one or more of the following four statistical questions: (a) Given k independent studies examining the relationship between an independent and dependent variable, what is the probability that the observed p values in the studies, considered as a whole, could result given that the null hypothesis of no relationship is true?; (b) Given k independent studies examining the relationship between an independent and dependent variable, what is the probability that the effect sizes observed in each study could have come from a common population (i.e., are the effect sizes truly different across studies, taking into consideration sampling error, or is homogeneity of effect sizes a viable hypothesis); (c) if the homogeneity of effect sizes is tenable, what is the estimate of the magnitude of the population effect size?; and (d) if homogeneity of effect sizes is not tenable, what factors can explain the sources of heterogeneity. Although other questions can be addressed through meta-analysis, the above constitute the major issues that consumer researchers will find of interest. We will address each question in turn.

Analyzing p Values

Methods for estimating the statistical significance of a relationship across independent studies as a function of p values have been reviewed by Rosenthal (1978) and his associates (Rosenthal & Rubin, 1979). The two most popular methods are the method of adding z's and the method of adding weighted z's (also called Stouffer's method). Table 5.3 presents five hypothetical studies that examined the relationship between an independent and dependent variable by means of a t test. Column 2 of the table presents the t values observed in each study and column 3 indicates the direction of the mean difference (+ means $M_1 > M_2$, − $M_1 < M_2$). Column 4 reports the df on which each t was based. Column 5 is the one-tailed p associated with each t reported in column 2. A one-tailed p is always used in this approach by virtue of statistical considerations. Most statistics texts do not provide tables that readily provide these p values. A FORTRAN program for computing the p associated with a t, r, F, or χ^2 statistic is presented in Veldman (1968, p. 222). Column 6 of Table 5.3 presents the z score equivalents of the p values in question. These are obtained from tables of the standard normal distribution.

The method of adding z's involves summing the scores in column 6 and dividing by the square root of k. This calculation yields a z of 2.39. The one-tailed p value associated with a z score of 2.39 is obtained from a table of the standard normal distribution and in this case, $p = .008$. For an alpha level of .05, the null hypothesis of no effect or no relationship would be rejected because $.008 < .05$. Note that if the vote counting procedure was applied to these studies, the result would be a failure to reject the null hypothesis.

The method of adding weighted z's is similar to the above, but each z in column 6 is weighted by the degrees of freedom. This approach gives greater weighting to studies with large N. The critical z uses columns 4 and 6 of Table 5.3 such that

$$z' = (\sum_{j=1}^{k} \mathrm{df}_j z_j) / \sqrt{(\sum_{j=1}^{k} \mathrm{df}^2)} \tag{9}$$

In this case $z' = 3.01$ with an associated p of .0013.[3] Again, the null hypothesis is rejected. Note that the method of adding unweighted z's is more conservative than the method of adding weighted z's. This results from the fact that studies with smaller N typically will observe larger p values, and these are weighted equally in the unweighted case.

[3]Hereafter, a summation sign will imply a sum across the k independent studies, beginning with $j = 1$.

TABLE 5.3. Numerical examples for analyzing p values.

Study	t	Direction of difference	df	One tail p value	z
A	1.19	+	40	.12	1.17
B	2.39	+	60	.01	2.33
C	.60	−	10	.72	−.58
D	1.52	+	30	.07	1.48
E	.98	+	20	.17	.95

When analysis focuses on p values associated with chi-square, p values are, by definition, two tailed. Column 5 of Table 5.3 must therefore be derived by dividing the p value in half. Also, for purposes of executing the weighted z method, the weights are the respective sample sizes (N) rather than df.

One problem with the above meta-analysis procedures is the potential bias introduced by editorial policies of journals. It is commonly believed that statistically nonsignificant results are less likely to be published, the result being a tendency to underestimate the true value of p. Rosenthal (1980) has referred to this as the "file drawer problem," because numerous unpublished studies with large p values may be tucked away in the researchers' file drawers. One method for addressing this issue is to calculate the number of studies that would have to exist whose mean z is zero such that the observed z' would become marginally nonsignificant at the .05 alpha level. This can be calculated by

$$\text{NS} = ((\Sigma\ z_j)^2/2.706) - k \tag{10}$$

where NS is the number of studies. As an example, Rosenthal estimated that approximately 3,444 studies with a mean z of zero would have to exist in file drawers for doubt to be cast on the existence of experimenter bias effects. In the current example, the number of such studies would be six.

The above approach assumes that all p values are generated from a common population. This assumption may not be correct in certain instances, in which case it is inappropriate to combine p values. If the individual p values in the studies are quite heterogeneous (holding constant df), then the assumption of a common population is questionable. The procedures outlined in the next section provide a mechanism for testing this assumption.

Analyzing Effect Size Indices

The analysis of effect size indices across studies typically involves a two-stage analysis. Given k independent investigations, the first stage is to determine if the population effect sizes across the k studies are equal. If the effect sizes are homogeneous, then the second stage focuses on estimating the size of the effect, based on the k investigations. If the effect sizes are heterogeneous, then the second stage focuses on isolating the sources of heterogeneity.

TABLE 5.4. Numerical example for analysis of homogeneity of d scores.

Study	n_1	n_2	t	d	$\tilde{d}$	V
A	30	30	.71	.183	.181	.06694
B	30	30	−2.04	− .527	−.520	.06893
C	280	290	−1.56	− .131	−.131	.00703
D	6	11	1.99	1.010	.959	.28462
E	44	40	.45	.098	.097	.04778
F	37	55	2.00	.425	.421	.04617

Stage 1: Testing Homogeneity of Effect Sizes

Many approaches have been suggested for testing homogeneity of effect sizes. We will focus discussion on the analysis of the *d* statistic and correlation coefficients, emphasizing approaches that, at present, seem to have the most desirable statistical properties.

Analysis of Mean Differences. Hedges (1981, 1982, 1983) has developed an approach that is applicable to the case of independent means. The technique uses the effect size measure *d*. Table 5.4 presents an example with six studies that examine the difference between two means on a common dependent measure. The *t* was converted to a *d* statistic by $d = t\sqrt{1/n_1 + 1/n_2}$. The first step involves translating each sample d to an unbiased estimate of δ by multiplying the *d* by $1 - (3/(4N - 9))$ (see Hedges & Olkin, 1985, p. 81). This has been done in column 5 of Table 5.4. Let $\tilde{d}_j$ be the unbiased estimate of δ in study "*j*." The intermediate statistic, *V*, is computed for each study such that

$$V_j = \frac{n_1 + n_2}{n_1 n_2} + \frac{\tilde{d}_j^2}{2(n_1 + n_2)} \tag{11}$$

Column 7 of Table 5.4 presents the corresponding *V*. Then,

$$\text{TS} = \Sigma \tilde{d}_j^2/V - \frac{(\Sigma \tilde{d}_j/V_j)^2}{\Sigma\ 1/V_j} \tag{12}$$

and for large samples, TS is approximately distributed as a chi square with $k - 1$ degrees of freedom. For the present example, TS = 14.12 − (80.22/217.79) = 13.75. The null hypothesis of homogeneous effect sizes is rejected.

Correlation Coefficient. Rosenthal (1983) has described an approach which can be used to test the homogeneity of a set of correlation coefficients. Table 5.5 presents an example with six studies that report the correlation between two variables. r is first converted to Fisher's *Z* using the transformation $Z = .50\ (\ln\ (1 + r) - \ln\ (1 - r))$, where $\ln$ = the natural logarithm. Most statistics texts provide tables for converting *r* to Z. The relevant *Z* appear in column 4 of Table 5.5. An average *Z* is computed as follows:

TABLE 5.5. Numerical example for the analysis of homogeneity of correlations.

Study	N	r	Z	(N-3) Z
A	50	.30	.310	14.57
B	60	.33	.343	19.55
C	40	.25	.255	9.44
D	50	.28	.288	13.54
E	60	.44	.472	26.90
F	40	.46	.497	18.39
				Σ 102.39

$$\bar{Z} = w_1 Z_1 + \ldots + w_k Z_k \tag{13}$$

where $w_j = (N_j - 3)/\Sigma(N_j - 3)$ and N_j = the sample size for study "j". TS is calculated by

$$TS = \Sigma(N_j - 3)(Z_j - \bar{Z})^2 \tag{14}$$

For the present data, $\bar{Z} = 102.39/282 = .363$ and TS = 2.19. TS is approximately distributed as a chi square with $k - 1$ degrees of freedom. For a chi square of $6-1 = 5$ degrees of freedom, the critical value of chi square for alpha = .05 is 11.07. Because 2.19 does not exceed this value, the null hypothesis of homogeneous correlations is not rejected.

Measurement Error. The above techniques do not take into account fallible measures. Hedges and Olkin (1985, pp. 136–137) propose a modification to their formulas to incorporate the effects of measurement error when good reliability estimates are available. The modification involves the use of equations 15 and 16.

$$TS = \sum_{j=1}^{k} \frac{[d_j - d_R\sqrt{r_{yy}}]^2}{V_j} \tag{15}$$

where

$$d_R = \sum_{j=1}^{k} \frac{d_j\sqrt{r_{yy}}}{V_j} \quad \sum_{j=1}^{k} \frac{r_{yy}}{V_j} \tag{16}$$

and r_{yy} = the reliability estimate for the dependent measure for study j, and all other terms are as previously defined. TS is distributed approximately as a chi square with k − 1 degrees of freedom.

For the analysis of correlations, the original r's are multiplied by $1/\sqrt{(r_{xx}\, r_{yy})}$. Equations 13 and 14 are then applied to the adjusted r, yielding an approximate χ^2, assuming reasonably high reliabilities.

The problem with the above approaches is that they assume accurate estimates of reliability are available. This is rarely the case in consumer research. The most frequently used reliability estimate, test-retest correlation is subject to considerable sampling error and, at best, represents a crude approximation to reliability. This creates a dilemma. On the one hand, the analyst can use the crude reliability estimate, with the knowledge that sampling error in the estimate could undermine the validity of the conclusions made from the analysis. On the other hand, the analyst can ignore the reliability adjustments, which is tantamount to assuming perfectly reliable measures.

We recommend a two step approach in which the test is performed first without the reliability adjustment and then with the reliability adjustment. The reliability estimates used should be a best-guess (based upon theory, past research, and present reliability data) of the *lower bound* of the reliability of the measures in question. If the results of both analyses lead to the same conclusion, then one has increased confidence in that conclusion. However, if the results of the analysis are discrepant, then any conclusions must be tentative.

Stage 2: The Case of Homogeneous Effect Sizes

If one is confident that homogeneous effect sizes exist, then it is reasonable to average the effect sizes in some manner to estimate the population effect size.

Mean Differences. Hedges has suggested several methods for estimating δ. We will describe the approach advocated in Hedges (1982). The estimate of δ, d', is calculated from

$$d' = \frac{(\Sigma \tilde{d}_j / V_j)}{\Sigma\ 1/V_j} \tag{17}$$

where all terms are as previously defined. Approximate 95% confidence intervals can be formed by first defining the constant $c = 1.96\sqrt{1/(\Sigma\ 1/V_j)}$ and then forming the lower limit by $d' - c$, and the upper limit by $d' + c$.

Correlation Coefficients. Several methods for estimating ϱ from a set of k correlation coefficients across k studies have been proposed (e.g., Viana, 1980; Rosenthal, 1982; Hedges and Olkin, 1985). Hedges and Olkin (1985) suggest the use of equation 13 for studies with large *N*. 95% confidence intervals then can be found by defining the constant $c = 1.96/\sqrt{TN - 3k}$, where TN = the sum of *N* across the k studies. The confidence intervals are defined as $\bar{Z} - c$ to $\bar{Z} + c$.

Measurement Error. Estimates calculated in the above techniques can be adjusted for measurement error using procedures discussed earlier. This involves calculating an adjusted d or an adjusted *r*, and applying the formulas to the adjusted values rather than the observed values.

Biased Estimates. The validity of all estimation procedures are subject to editorial policies of journals. To the extent that journals only accept articles reporting "large" effect sizes and reject articles reporting "weak" effect sizes (and which are methodologically sound), then estimates will be biased upward. This possibility should be considered when interpreting effect size estimates.

Recent perspectives on this problem, and methods for addressing it, are discussed in Hedges (1984) and Hedges and Olkin (1985).

Orwin (1983) has developed an analogy to Rosenthal's "file drawer" formula for measures of d. One can compute the number of studies ("fail-safe" n) whose mean d is zero that would have to exist in order to reduce the sample mean d to some specified value (e.g., .2 corresponding to a "weak" effect in Cohen's analysis, .5, a "medium" effect, or a .8, a "strong" effect). The estimated number of studies is defined by

$$\text{NS} = (k\,(\bar{d} - d_c))/d_c \tag{18}$$

where NS = the number of studies in the "file drawer," k = the number of studies on which the mean sample effect size is based, $\bar{d}$ = the absolute value of the unweighted mean of the observed d scores across the k studies, and d_c = the criterion value (e.g., .2, .5, .8).

There are several limitations to Equation 18. First d_c must always be greater than zero. At best, the investigator can compute the "fail-safe" n for some trivial criterion effect size (e.g., .01) but not for an effect size of zero. Second, the formula assumes that the k studies have equal N. If the N are not very discrepant, then Equation 18 should give a reasonable approximation to the "fail-safe" n. We therefore recommend Equation 18 be used cautiously and as a rough guideline.

A similar formula can be derived for correlation coefficients. The formula is

$$\text{NS} = (k\,(\bar{Z}_o - Z_c))/Z_c \tag{19}$$

where $\bar{Z}_o$ is the Fisher Z transform of the mean sample correlation across the k studies, Z_c is the Fisher Z transform of the criterion correlation value, and NS and k are as previously defined. Equation 19 has the same limitations as Equation 18.

Stage 3: The Case of Heterogeneous Effect Sizes

When the effect sizes are found to be heterogeneous, it is not appropriate to average them to estimate the relevant population parameter. Instead, additional analyses are required to determine which subsets of effect sizes are heterogeneous. This can be accomplished from either an exploratory perspective or a theory driven perspective. We will consider each, in turn.

Exploratory Analyses. Hedges and Olkin (1983) discuss exploratory procedures for the analysis of d and the correlation coefficient, r. One procedure is based on the Bonferonni multiple comparison procedure developed in analysis of variance. We will first consider the case of d.

The procedure begins by rank ordering effect sizes for the k studies from smallest (rank = 1) to largest (rank = k). This has been done in column 3 of Table 5.6, which presents d measures (column 4) for five studies. The d_j are first transformed to U statistics by $U_j = 2\,c_j\sqrt{n_j}$, where $c_j = \log\,(d + \sqrt{d + 8}) - 1.0536$ and $n = (1/k\,(\Sigma\sqrt{n_j}))^2$. n refers to the number of subjects per group in a given

TABLE 5.6. Numerical example for analysis of d measures based on Hedges and Olkin.

Study	n	Rank	d	U
G	30	1	−.587	−2.257
E	30	2	−.494	−1.907
F	30	3	−.235	− .910
A	30	4	−.079	− .307
D	30	5	−.058	− .220
C	30	6	.091	.350
E	30	7	.699	2.563

study, assuming equal n in the two groups (the case of unequal n will be considered shortly). Column 5 presents the U measure for each d. The absolute difference between the two effect sizes is tested against zero by comparing the absolute difference between corresponding U's with a critical value from Table 5.7. The critical value is determined by specifying the number of "steps," ns, between the effect sizes. ns will equal the larger of the two ranks minus the smaller of the two ranks plus one. For example, to compare effect sizes for study F and D, ns = 5 − 3 + 1 = 3. The absolute difference between U_F and U_D is .69 and the critical value (alpha = .05) is 3.68. Because .69 does not exceed 3.68, we fail to reject the hypothesis of homogeneous effect sizes for these studies. Using this approach, exploratory comparisons can be made with the possibility that post hoc analyses of differences in effect size will make substantive sense when study characteristics defining "similar" and "different" effect sizes are considered.

TABLE 5.7. Critical values for Hedges and Olkin technique.

	Alpha		
Number of steps	.10	.05	.01
2	2.33	2.77	3.64
3	3.30	3.68	4.42
4	3.83	4.17	4.85
5	4.18	4.50	5.15
6	4.44	4.75	5.38
7	4.65	4.95	5.55
8	4.83	5.11	5.71
9	4.97	5.25	5.82
10	5.10	5.37	5.94
11	5.21	5.48	6.04
12	5.31	5.57	6.16
13	5.40	5.66	6.20
14	5.48	5.74	6.27
15	5.55	5.80	6.34
20	5.86	6.10	6.59
50	6.72	6.93	7.38

For correlation coefficients, the r is transformed to U by first transforming the sample r to Fisher's Z and then multiplying the Z by $\sqrt{(N-3)}$, where $N = (1/k\,(\Sigma N_j - 3))^2$.

Both approaches formally assume roughly equal N across studies, although Hedges and Olkin suggest that unequal N will not drastically affect the outcome. Further, the analysis of d assumes that the two conditions within a study have equal n. In cases of unequal n within a study, a conservative approach is to define n by the smaller n of the two, a liberal approach is to define n by the larger n of the two, and a compromise is to define n as the mean n.

Theoretical Analysis. Hedges (1982) discusses a useful approach for analyzing heterogeneous d measures when the measures can be grouped into clusters a priori on the basis of theoretical concerns. For the data in Table 5.4, assume the first three studies were conducted with upper class individuals whereas the second three studies were conducted with working class individuals. Using Equation 12, the overall chi square, TS is calculated to test the null hypothesis of homogeneous effect sizes across all k studies. The total chi square is then decomposed into two components, one due to between group differences (as defined by social class) and the other due to within group differences. This procedure is analogous to the partitioning of variance in analysis of variance problems. The chi square for between-group differences is calculated as follows: Let p = the number of clusters (in this case $p = 2$, upper and working class), m_i = the number of studies in cluster i, $\tilde{d}_{ij}$ = the unbiased estimated effect size of study j in cluster i, V_{ij} = the V measure for study j in cluster i, and d_i' = the average d measure in cluster i (note: the mathematical definition of d_i' is given shortly). Then, the between groups chi square, TSB, is

$$\text{TSB} = \sum_{i=1}^{p}\sum_{j=1}^{m} \tilde{d}_i'^2 / V_{ij} - \frac{\left(\sum_{i=1}^{p}\sum_{j=1}^{m} \tilde{d}_{ij}' / V_{ij}\right)^2}{\left(\sum_{i=1}^{p}\sum_{j=1}^{m} 1/V_{ij}\right)} \tag{20}$$

where

$$d' = \frac{\sum_{j=1}^{m} \tilde{d}_{ij} / V_{ij}}{\sum_{j=1}^{m} 1/V_{ij}} \tag{21}$$

TSB is distributed approximately as a chi square with $p - 1$ degrees of freedom. For the data in Table 5.4, $d_1' = -.137$, $d_2' = .315$, and TSB = 7.43. The chi square for within group differences is TSW = TS − TSB = 13.75 − 7.43 = 6.32. TSW is approximately distributed as a chi square with $k - p$ degrees of freedom.

The critical value for TSB, alpha = .05, is 3.84. Because 7.43 exceeds 3.84, the null hypothesis of homogeneous population d is rejected. It is useful to calculate 95% confidence intervals for each d (see discussion of Equation 17). For upper class studies, these are −.286 to .012. For lower class studies, they are

$-.026$ to $.604$. Nonoverlapping confidence intervals indicate statistically significant differences.

The critical value for TSW, alpha = .05 is 9.49. Because 6.32 is less than 9.49, we fail to reject the null hypothesis of homogeneous effect sizes within clusters, indicating that the calculations of d for the clusters is meaningful. If TSW is statistically significant, then Equation 12 can be applied to each cluster separately to determine which group(s) has heterogeneous effect sizes.

The above procedures hold for the case of d measures. Analogous procedures are applicable to the case of correlation coefficients. Each correlation coefficient is converted to Fisher's Z. The total chi square, TS, is computed using Equation 14. The between group chi square involves calculating an average Z, $\overline{Z}$, for each cluster separately using Equation 13. Let N_i = the sum of the sample sizes across studies in cluster i, and $Z..$ = the average Z (using Equation 13) across all studies. Then

$$\text{TSB} = \sum_{i=1}^{p} (N_i - 3m)(\overline{Z}_i - Z..)^2 \tag{22}$$

and TSW = TS − TSB. TSB is approximately distributed as a chi square with $p-1$ degrees of freedom. TSW is approximately distributed as a chi square with $k-p$ degrees of freedom. Significance tests are applied, as above. Approximately 95% confidence intervals about each mean r can be calculated, as described earlier.

Continuous Variables. When one wishes to relate effect-size measures across studies to a continuous variable, the typical approach has been to correlate the k measures with the k values of the continuous measure and then to interpret this correlation in a descriptive sense. For example, if effect size is presumed to vary with the intelligence of respondents used in k studies, then the k effect size measures are correlated with the mean intelligence scores reported in each study. The resulting r is based on k observations and indexes the correlation between intelligence and effect size. Traditional tests of significance do not apply in this situation. More promising approaches for this type of analysis are currently being developed (see Hedges, 1983; Rosenthal & Rubin, 1983).

Summary and Conclusions

In this chapter, we have discussed two basic features in the use of meta-analytic techniques. First, we described a framework for organizing the many facets across which a set of studies may vary. In that presentation, we argued that the researcher can increase his/her understanding of some phenomenon by partitioning the set of findings into meaningful subgroups (e.g., studies that examine different behaviors, use different research strategies, or competitively test different models that examine the same phenomenon). Second, we discussed a set of statistical techniques that can be used for summarizing the findings across a set of independent studies. In that discussion, we described two basic summary statistics: a correlation coefficient between an independent and dependent variable and a d statistic (Glass, McGaw, & Smith, 1981). We also discussed the impact of unequal sample size and measurement error on those statistics. Researchers are currently examining the statistical properties of these meta-analytic techniques in great detail (e.g., Hedges, 1984).

In many areas of the social sciences, meta-analytic techniques are receiving increased use as a tool for the systematic integration of a body of literature. Our goal in this chapter was two-fold: (a) to make the reader aware of current statistical advances in meta-analytic techniques and (b) to describe how meta-analytic techniques can be used to increase a researcher's understanding about the many facets that can influence a set of findings. Our hope is that the reader will make greater use of these techniques in their own area of interest.

References

Adcock, C.J. (1960). A note on combining probabilities. *Psychometrica, 25*, 303–305.

Ajzen, I., & Fishbein, M. (1980). *Understanding attitudes and predicting social behavior.* Englewood Cliffs, NJ: Prentice-Hall.

Assmus, G., Farley, J. U., & Lehmann, D. R. (1984). How advertising affects sales: A meta-analysis of econometric results. *Journal of Marketing Research, 21*, 65–74.

Axelson, M. L., Federline, T. L., & Brinberg, D. (1985). Food- and nutrition-related knowledge, attitudes, and behavior—A meta-analysis. *Journal of Nutrition Education, 17*(2), 51–54.

Birnbaum, A. (1954). Combining independence tests of significance. *Journal of the American Statistical Association, 49*, 559–574.

Birnbaum, M. H. (1982). Controversies in psychological measurement. In B. Wegener (Ed.) *Social attitudes and psychophysical measurement.* Hillsdale, NJ: L. Erlbaum.

Brinberg, D. (1979). An examination of the determinants of intention and behavior: A comparison of two models. *Journal of Applied Social Psychology, 6*, 560–575.

Brinberg, D., & McGrath, J. E. (1982). A network of validity concepts within the research process. In D. Brinberg & L. Kidder (Eds.) *New directions for methodology of social and behavioral science: Forms of validity in research* (12). San Francisco, CA: Jossey-Bass.

Brinberg, D., & McGrath, J. E. (1985). *Validity and the research process.* Beverly Hills, CA: Sage Publications.

Campbell, D. T. (1963). Social attitudes and other acquired behavioral dispositions. In S. Koch (Ed.) *Psychology: A study of science: Vol. 9.* New York: McGraw-Hill.

Campbell, D. T., & Stanley, J. C. (1966). *Experimental and quasi-experimental designs for research.* Chicago: Rand-McNally.

Churchill, G. A., & Peter, J. P. (1984). Research design effects on the reliability of rating scales: A meta-analysis. *Journal of Marketing Research, 21*, 360–375.

Cohen, J. (1977). *Statistical power for the behavioral sciences.* New York: Academic Press.

Cook, T. D., & Campbell, D. T. (1979). *Design and analysis of quasi-experiments for field settings.* Chicago: Rand-McNally.

Cook, T. D., & Leviton, L. C. (1980). Reviewing the literature: A comparison of traditional methods with meta-analysis. *Journal of Personality, 48*, 449–472.

Dillon, W. R. (1986). Building consumer behavior models with LISREL: Issues in applications. In D. Brinberg & R. J. Lutz (Eds.) *Perspectives on methodology in consumer research* (pp. 175–245). Springer-Verlag, New York.

Fisher, K. A. (1948). Combining independent tests of significance. *American Statistician*, *2*, 30.

Gardner, M. P., & Raj, S. P. (1983). Responses to commercials in laboratory versus natural settings: A conceptual framework. In R. P. Bagozzi & A. M. Tybout (Eds.) *Advances in consumer research*, *10*, 142–146.

Glass, G. V. (1977). Integrating findings: The meta-analysis of research. In L. Schulman (Ed.) *Review of research in education*. Itasca, IL: Peacock.

Glass, G. V., & Kliegl, R. M. (1983). An apology for research integration in the study of psychotherapy. *Journal of Consulting and Clinical Psychology*, *51*, 28–41.

Glass, G. V., McGaw, B., & Smith, M. L. (1981). *Meta-analysis in social research*. Beverly Hills, CA: Sage Publications.

Hays, W. L. (1963). *Statistics for psychologists*. New York: Holt, Rinehart & Winston.

Hedges, L. V. (1981). Distribution theory for Glass's estimator of effect size and related estimates. *Journal of Educational Statistics*, *6*, 107–128.

Hedges, L. V. (1982). Estimation of effect size from a series of independent experiments. *Psychological Bulletin*, *92*, 490–499.

Hedges, L. V. (1983). A random effects model for effect sizes. *Psychological Bulletin*, *93*, 388–395.

Hedges, L. V. (1984). Estimation of effect size under non-random sampling: The effects of censoring studies yielding nonsignificant mean differences. *Journal of Educational Statistics*, *9*, 61–85.

Hedges, L. V., & Olkin, I. (1983). Clustering estimates of effect magnitude from independent studies. *Psychological Bulletin*, *93*, 563–573.

Hedges, L. V., & Olkin, I. (1985). *Statistical methods for meta-analysis*. New York: Academic Press.

Houston, M. J., & Rothschild, M. L. (1978). Conceptual and methodological perspectives on involvement. In S. Jain (Ed.) *Research frontiers in marketing: Dialogues and directions, 1978 Educators' proceedings*. Chicago: American Marketing Association.

Houston, M. J., Peter, J. P., & Sawyer, A. G. (1983). The role of meta-analysis in consumer research. In R. P. Bagozzi & A. M. Tybout (Eds.) *Advances in Consumer Research*, *10*, 497–502.

Hunter, J. E., Schmidt, F. L., & Jackson, G. B. (1982). *Meta-analysis: Cumulating research findings across studies*. Beverly Hills, CA: Sage Publications.

Jaccard, J., & Becker, M. A. (1985). Attitudes and behavior: An information integration perspective. *Journal of Experimental Social Psychology*, *21*, 440–465.

Jaccard, J., & King, G. W. (1977). A probabilistic model of the relationship between beliefs and behavioral intentions. *Human Communications Research*, *3*, 332–342.

Jones, L. V., & Fiske, D. W. (1953). Models for testing the significance of combined results. *Psychological Bulletin*, *50*, 375–382.

Judd, C. M., & Kenny, D. A. (1982). Research design and research validity. In D. Brinberg & L. Kidder (Eds.) *New Directions for Methodology of Social and Behavioral Science: Forms of Validity in Research*, (12). San Francisco: Jossey-Bass.

Krugman, H. E. (1965). The impact of television advertising: Learning without involvement. *Public Opinion Quarterly*, *29*, 349–356.

Light, R. J., & Smith, P. V. (1971). Accumulating evidence: Procedures for resolving contradictions among different studies. *Harvard Educational Review*, *41*, 429–471.

Light, R. J., & Pillemer, D. B. (1984). *Summing Up*. Cambridge, MS: Harvard University Press.

Lutz, R. J. (1977). An experimental investigation of causal relations among cognitions, affect and behavioral intentions. *Journal of Consumer Research, 3*, 197–208.

Lynch, J. G. (1979). Why additive models fail as descriptors of choice behavior. *Journal of Experimental Social Psychology, 15*, 397–417.

McGrath, J. E., & Brinberg, D. (1983). External validity and the research process: A third-party comment on the Calder/Lynch dialogue. *Journal of Consumer Research, 10* (1), 115–124.

Mintz, J. (1983). Integrating research evidence: A commentary on meta-analysis. *Journal of Consulting and Clinical Psychology, 51*, 71–75.

Monroe, K., & Krishnan, R. (1983). A procedure for integrating outcomes across studies. In R. P. Bagozzi & A. M. Tybout (Eds.) *Advances in Consumer Research, 10*, 503–508.

Mostellar, F. M., & Bush, R. R. (1954). Selected quantitative techniques. In G. Lindzey (Ed.) *Handbook of Social Psychology, Vol. 1: Theory and Method*. Reading, MA: Addison-Wesley.

Mullen, B., & Rosenthal, R. (1985). *BASIC meta-analysis*. Hillsdale, NJ: L. Erlbaum.

Ofir, C., & Lynch, J. G. (1984). Context effects on judgment under uncertainty. *Journal of Consumer Research, 11*(2), 668–679.

Olkin, I., & Pratt, J. (1958). Unbiased estimators of certain correlation coefficients. *Annals of Mathematical Statistics, 29*, 201–211.

Orwin, R. (1983). A fail-safe N for effect size in meta-analysis. *Journal of Educational Statistics, 8*, 157–159.

Payne, J. (1982). Contingent decision behavior. *Psychological Bulletin, 92*, 382–402.

Pearson, E. S. (1938). The probability integral transformation for testing goodness of fit and combining independent tests of significance. *Biometrika, 30*, 138–148.

Pearson, K. (1933). On a method of determining whether a sample of size *n* supposed to have been drawn from a parent population having a known probability integral has probably been drawn at random. *Biometrika, 25*, 379–410.

Platt, J. R. (1964). Strong inference. *Science, 146* (Whole No. 3642), 347–353.

Reilly, M. D., & Conover, J. N. (1983). Meta-analysis: Integrating results from consumer research studies. In R. P. Bagozzi & A. M. Tybout (Eds.) *Advances in Consumer Research, 10*, 509–513.

Rosenthal, R. (1978). Combining results of independent studies. *Psychological Bulletin, 85*, 185–193.

Rosenthal, R. (1980). The "file drawer problem" and tolerance for null results. *Psychological Bulletin, 86*, 638–641.

Rosenthal, R. (1982). Valid interpretation of quantitative research results. In D. Brinberg & L. Kidder (Eds.) *New Directions for Methodology of Social and Behavioral Science: Forms of Validity in Research* (12). San Francisco: Jossey-Bass.

Rosenthal, R. (1983). Assessing the statistical and social importance of the effects of psychotherapy. *Journal of Consulting and Clinical Psychology, 51*, 4–13.

Rosenthal, R., & Rubin, D. B. (1979). Comparing significance levels of independent studies. *Psychological Bulletin, 86*, 1165–1168.

Rosenthal, R., & Rubin, D. B. (1983). Ensemble-adjusted p values. *Psychological Bulletin, 94*, 540–541.

Runkel, P. J., & McGrath, J. E. (1972). *Research on Human Behavior: A systematic guide to method*. New York: Holt, Rinehart & Winston.

Sawyer, A. G., & Peter, J. P. (1983). The significance of statistical significance tests in marketing research. *Journal of Marketing Research*, *20*, 122–133.

Strube, M. J. (1985). Combining and comparing significance levels from nonindependent hypothesis tests. *Psychological Bulletin*, *97*(2), 334–341.

Triandis, H. C. (1977). *Interpersonal Behavior.* Monterey, CA: Brooks/Cole.

Veldman, D. J. (1968). *Fortran programming for the behavioral sciences*. New York: Holt, Rinehart & Winston.

Viana, M. (1980). Statistical method for summarizing independent correlational results. *Journal of Educational Statistics*, *5*, 83–104.

Wallis, W. A. (1942). Compounding probabilities from independent significance tests. *Econometrica*, *10*, 229–248.

Wilson, G. T., & Rachman, S. J. (1983). Meta-analysis and the evaluation of psychotherapy outcome: Limitations and liabilities. *Journal of Consulting and Clinical Psychology*, *51*, 54–64.

Wimsatt, W. C. (1981). Robustness, reliability and overdetermination. In M. Brewer & B. Collins (Eds.) *Scientific inquiry and the social sciences*. San Francisco: Jossey-Bass.

Winer, B. J. (1971). *Statistical principles in experimental design*. New York: McGraw-Hill.

Yu, J., & Cooper, H. (1983). A quantitative review of research design effects in response rates to questionnaires. *Journal of Marketing Research*, *20*, 36–44.

Zajonc, R. (1980). Feeling and thinking. *American Psychologist*, *35*, 151–175.

6
Social Interaction Data: Procedural and Analytic Strategies

DANNY L. MOORE

The purpose of this chapter is to provide an overview of procedural and analytic issues that arise in social interaction research. The chapter specifically focuses on the problem of uncovering sequences, patterns, and repetitive cycles of behavior based on observations of face-to-face marketing interactions. Historically, the popularity of observational techniques has varied with changes in the guiding models or paradigms in the behavioral sciences. With the advent of cognitive models, self-reports of behavior and thought processes have become the prevailing method of testing theoretical propositions. However, in social interaction research two general concerns have stimulated a re-emergence of observational studies (Parke, 1979). First, questions about the ecological validity of research findings have increased the perceived value of unobtrusive measures gathered in naturalistic settings. Second, theoretical or conceptual developments emphasizing the reciprocal, rather than unidirectional influence process have served as catalyst for research that examines the behavior of all participants in an interaction.

Although research on interpersonal influence in consumer behavior has been dominated by models of individual decision processes, ecological validity and reciprocal influence are latent concerns that periodically surface in discussions of buyer/seller interactions and family decision making. Olshavsky (1976), for example, concludes that we know little about how the salesperson enters into the consumer decision process in naturalistic settings. There is also a growing consensus that research is needed to determine how buyers and sellers synchronize or adjust the timing and content of their behavior over the course of an interaction (Holbrook & O'Shaughnessy, 1976; Weitz, 1981a). A similar concern can be found in the family decision-making literature. For example, Davis (1976) calls for research that examines how families make multiple purchase decisions over time rather than simply focusing on decision outcomes. Thus, the interest in naturalistic settings and the emergence of a reciprocal, dynamic view of interpersonal influence in marketing suggest that observational research on buyer/seller interactions and family decision making is likely to become more frequent in the near future.

Despite these concerns, few observational studies on buyer/seller interactions and family decision making have been reported. One factor contributing to this state of affairs is that the difficulties encountered in design, analysis, and interpretation frequently motivate a search for alternative research strategies. Observations of interactions based on even a simple coding scheme can produce massive quantities of data that violate the assumptions of standard statistical techniques. This technical complexity is often compounded by a lack of theory to guide the search through the data. The intent of this chapter is to discuss recent methodological developments that enhance the procedural and analytic capabilities of observational research. In the last decade, several articles and three edited volumes (Cairns, 1979; Lamb, Suomi, & Stephenson, 1979; Sackett, 1978) have been published on observational methods in social interaction research. These articles provide techniques for investigating sequential properties of social relationships such as dominance, reciprocity, and cyclical patterning of behavior.

To facilitate discussion, the chapter is organized around four global issues that represent stages in the research design process. The first section provides several examples of how observations of social interaction can be used to examine marketing and consumer behavior phenomena. In the second section the procedural problems encountered in developing and testing behavioral coding schemes, and the solutions to these problems offered by various researchers are discussed. The third section presents analytic techniques for social interaction research. The final issue discussed in this chapter concerns the use of social interaction data for theory development and testing.

Social Interaction Research in Marketing and Consumer Behavior

Before discussing methdological issues, it is useful to consider how interaction data can be used to investigate such problems as buyer/seller interaction and family decision making. Because there are several adequate reviews of research on buyer/seller interactions (e.g., Capon, Holbrook, & Hulbert, 1977; Davis & Silk, 1972; Holbrook & O'Shaughnessy, 1976; Weitz, 1981b) and family decision making (Davis, 1976), the present section will outline the types of research strategies used in previous research and discuss how measures of the interaction process can be incorporated to enhance our knowledge of marketing exchanges. The discussion is simplified further by focusing on buyer/seller interactions because the potential contributions of observational research in that domain are both easily identified and easily extended to other domains where interactions are central.

A taxonomy of variables relevant to interaction research is presented in Table 6.1. The taxonomy is not intended to be exhaustive; the variables listed merely illustrate properties of marketing exchanges that may be examined with interaction data. These variables are divided into three classes: (a) antecedent conditions, (b) interaction process variables, and (c) outcome variables. Antecedent conditions refer to factors that are either measured or manipulated prior to an

TABLE 6.1. Taxonomy of variables in social interaction research.

Antecedent (or Exogenous) Conditions	
Interactant characteristics	Situational characteristics
• Personality	• Physical Environment
• Similarity	• Social Environment
• Goals and Influence Strategies	• Cultural Environment
• Knowledge:	Communication Variables
—Product/Issue	• Source Credibility
—Previous Interactions	• Message Factors
Interaction Process Variables	
Aggregate features	Dynamic features
• Verbal Content	• Timing of Behavior
• Frequency of Behavior	• Interaction Stages
• Duration of Behavior	• Verbal and Nonverbal Behavior
• Noncontingent Reciprocity	• Dominance
	• Contingent Reciprocity
Outcome Variables	
• Attitudes	
• Interpersonal Attraction	
• Purchase Intention	
• Purchase	
• Decision Outcomes	
• Customer Satisfaction	

interaction. These factors include characteristics of the participants, situational characteristics, and communication variables, and are assumed to be causally related to either the interaction process or outcome of the interaction. Interaction process variables can be divided into aggregate features and dynamic features. Aggregate features are measures of behavior examined by summing across the entire interaction period (e.g., the frequency of closing offers or statements of concession limits). In contrast, dynamic features refer to behaviors that are considered to be variable during the interaction. Finally, Table 6.1 contains a list of outcome variables of interest to marketing and consumer behavior researchers.

Buyer-seller interaction studies have dealt with a wide assortment of applied and theoretical problems. These studies can be grouped into antecedent-outcome, process-outcome, and antecedent-process investigations based on the goals and research strategies of each study. Examples of these classes of research are given below and potential contributions of research on dynamic properties of interactions are identified for each area.

Antecedent-Outcome Investigations

Numerous antecedent-outcome investigations can be found in marketing and consumer behavior. These studies have been motivated by both practical and theoretical issues. For example, investigations dealing with the empirical relationship between personality variables and sales performance evolved from the need to develop effective selection instruments in sales management. Additional studies have attempted to verify hypotheses about the influence of buyer-seller similarity, source expertise, and social roles. While these investigations have contributed to knowledge about factors that influence marketing transactions, they often ignore process variables. In doing so, the interpretability of the findings may be weakened.

Salesperson Characteristics and Performance. Weitz (1981b) cites over 20 studies dealing with the relationship between personality, behavioral dispositions, or ability and performance in sales. This work is predicated on the assumption that characteristics of salespeople at least partially predict performance across a variety of situations and selling tasks. In general, this assumption has received little support; few studies report significant correlations, and the ones that find a significant relationship typically report only weak correlations. Weitz proposes that a more useful set of dimensions for predicting sales performance can be derived from a conceptual scheme that relates sales behaviors to performance in different circumstances. The behavioral dimensions in Weitz's "contingency framework" are closely related to interaction process variables. For example, the adaptive dimension of behavior represents the degree to which salespeople alter their behavior during the course of an interaction. This suggests that a more thorough understanding of how salesperson characteristics influence performance may be obtained by relating measures of adaptiveness to interaction process variables rather than simply examining outcome variables.

Similarity Effects in Buyer-Seller Interactions. Evans (1963), in one of the first discussions of social interaction research in marketing, hypothesized that the more similar buyers and sellers are, the more likely a sale or favorable outcome will result from the interaction. Presumably, similarity increases interpersonal attraction and establishes a basis for referent power. After numerous laboratory and field investigations of the similarity hypothesis, its empirical status is dubious. Wilson and Ghingold (1981) conclude that similarity may contribute to success in selling, but other factors such as expertise are more important. Implicit theories of selling seem to contradict this assertion; interviews with salespeople indicate that they consider developing good rapport and interpersonal attraction as important factors in obtaining a sale (Wilson & Ghingold, 1980). Wilson and Ghingold (1981) advance several speculative hypotheses to account for the apparent contradictions between experimental data and implicit theories of selling. One of their hypotheses is that similarity affects sales indirectly; similarity may establish rapport, and this, in turn, helps the seller to gather information that may be important later in the interaction. This hypothesis represents an interesting avenue for future research that incorporates interaction process variables and observational methodologies. For example, buyers or sellers who establish a basis for referent power may exert greater control over the interaction and obtain more favorable outcomes. One method of testing this hypothesis is to examine the patterns and sequences of behavior that develop in similar dyads compared to dissimilar dyads.

Interpersonal Communication. Marketing models of interpersonal influence have relied heavily upon persuasion theories that break the communication process into source, message, medium, and recipient components (e.g., Hulbert & Capon, 1972). This paradigm has been extremely useful for explaining the influence of noninteractive communications on consumers (e.g., advertising), but its usefulness for understanding interactive communications merits attention. Cognitive processes that determine yielding and attitude change are likely to be identical in both noninteractive and interactive settings (cf. Lutz & Kakkar, 1976; Sawyer, Deutscher, & Obermiller, 1980). However, the effectiveness of a message in interactive settings is likely to depend upon how the communicator responds to objections and questions during the interaction.

A study by Capon (1975) provides an excellent illustration of this point. Bales' (1950) interaction process analysis was used to design six messages by crossing an interactive-noninteractive dimension with task area (cognitive, affective, or socioemotional). The major finding in Capon's study was that a salesman by treatment interaction accounted for most of the variance in outcome variables. Some salespeople were most effective using interactive messages while other were more successful with noninteractive messages. Dynamic process measures could enhance the interpretability of this finding. For example, it would be useful to know how the timing and content of the salesperson and customer's behavior varied across messages and sales representatives.

Process-Outcome Investigations

Process-outcome investigations are typically correlational studies designed to describe the characteristics of successful and unsuccessful interactions. That is, comparisons between interactions resulting in a sale versus those resulting in no sale are made on some aggregate measure of buyer or seller behavior (e.g., the number of closing offers made). A frequently cited study by Pennington (1968) investigated the relationship between bargaining behavior and purchase of appliances. The results indicated that verbal bargaining behaviors of the salesperson and customer were significantly related to purchase behavior. A similar result has been obtained by Taylor and Woodside (1980).

Perhaps the most inventive study relating interaction process and outcome measures was an early study by Chapple and Donald (1947). In this study, department store sales personnel were observed during an interview about job-related problems. The observer recorded the amount of time the salesperson spent talking and the number of times the salesperson interrupted or initiated conversations. Chapple and Donald found that the more time a salesperson spent talking, the greater the average number of daily transactions obtained. However, initiating and interrupting conversation predicted success in some sales tasks and failure in others. The implication of this study is that interaction styles may be a good predictor of sales success.

While process-outcome investigations have uncovered a variety of interesting relationships, Holbrook and O'Shaughnessy (1976) noted that the focus on aggregate features has left two gaps in knowledge about the selling process. First, little is known about the temporal patterning of behavior. The problem in this case is that inappropriate conclusions may be drawn from aggregate data. Consider, for example, a hypothetical finding that the more closing offers made, the more likely a sale will be made. Clearly, timing is critical to closing, and therefore, it is possible that one closing offer following a particular cue from the consumer is just as effective as several offers distributed across the interaction. A second factor ignored in aggregate analyses is the synchronization of behavior. Sheth (1981), in a conceptual model of cross-cultural influences on buyer/seller negotiations, underscores the importance of synchronizing behavior by distinguishing between the content and style of interaction. Success or failure of a transaction depends upon synchronizing the content of communication (i.e., the reasons for which two parties interact) and the style of communication (i.e., the format, ritual, or mannerism which the buyer or seller adopt). Thus, understanding what patterns and sequences of behavior are related to interaction outcome variables should provide clues about the impact of content and style on the buyer/seller negotiation process.

Antecedent-Process Investigations

Investigations dealing with the relationship between antecedent conditions and process variables have been useful for examining the effects of such situational variables as the economic importance of the purchase decision or buying center characteristics on the evolution of multi-stage, protracted negotiations. Woodside and Taylor (1980), for example, tape recorded conversations of insurance salesmen and prospective buyers at various stages of the selling process. Buyers and sellers later listened to the tapes and provided retrospective reports of their thoughts and strategies. Based on these reports decision net models were constructed to examine the mental processes underlying the transaction. This technique has numerous applications and has been used in family decisions making research as well (Park, 1982).

A second class of antecedent-process studies has examined stages in the negotiation process. The common concern in these investigations is to explain how interactions evolve as a function of the buyer's task environment. Wilson (1977) provides a stage model that divides the negotiation process into source legitimization, information exchange-problem identification, attribute delineation, attribute value negotiation, and relationship maintenance. Depending upon the task environment, the concerns of the buyer may differ at each stage of the exchange process. When the buyer is faced with a straight rebuy task the problem identification, attribute delineation and attribute value negotiation steps may be skipped resulting in a different pattern of interaction compared to modified rebuys or new purchases. Support for this stage analytic approach has been obtained in studies of the structure of buyer/seller interactions for insurance policies (Taylor & Woodside, 1980) and for retail appliance sales (Olshavsky, 1973).

The Value of Observational Data for Social Interaction Research

The research reviewed in the preceding pages illustrates several potential applications of social interaction analysis in marketing. The research strategies in these studies vary from descriptive, correlational approaches to laboratory or field experiments. In each case, I have argued that observing the evolution of behavior during an interaction or across interactions can clarify and extend empirical knowledge of marketing and consumer behavior phenomena. Unlike other research strategies, the goal of observational research is to identify sequences, patterns, and repetitive cycles of behavior. This does not mean that observation is relevant only for correlational designs or field settings. Instead, observation can be incorporated into carefully controlled laboratory or field studies in which the dependent measures are sequences or patterns of behavior rather than individual acts or questionnaire responses. Thus, observational research can be viewed as one of several tools available to the researcher for examining marketing interactions. In this respect the value of observation depends upon how reliably the measurement procedure assesses properties of social behavior that other research approaches overlook.

Observational Coding Systems

The guiding assumption in observational research is that observing behavior can generate meaningful and verifiable statements about marketing and consumer behavior phenomena. This perspective differs from models of communication that focus on the cognitive processes involved in transmitting and decoding messages. In observational research the focus is on the content of verbal and nonverbal messages rather than the thought processes of participants in an interaction.

Kassarjian (1977) describes three criteria for assessing content-analytic systems. First, categories of behavior should be objectively and precisely defined. The objectivity criterion, if met, is necessary for establishing reliable measures; different observers applying the analytic scheme to the same interaction should agree on the content of the interaction. Second, content-analytic schemes should be systematic. Basically, the systematization criterion specifies that observations are ultimately linked to some theory that defines the domain of relevant behaviors and provides a substantive interpretation for the behaviors. Third, any content-analytic scheme should provide quantitative data that facilitate statistical inferences and comparisons across groups.

A fundamental problem encountered in designing an objective, systematic, and quantitative coding system is that the assignment of behavior to categories is based on inferences drawn by observers. Coding schemes that focus on verbal behavior often require the observer to infer the intentions of the communicator. For example, Gottman (1979a) finds that statements such as "yes, but. . ." are often viewed as a statement of agreement by the speaker, whereas the listener views it as a statement of disagreement. Inference problems are compounded when coding schemes include nonverbal behavior. In this case, the problem is that verbal labels must be assigned to gestures and facial expressions. Although these problems often detract from the interpretability of observational research, they are not insurmountable if the researcher has invested the effort necessary to define precisely the assignment rules for the coding system and to relate the categories to a theoretical system.

Designing a Coding System

Decisions regarding what behaviors to observe in an interaction are ultimately determined by the researcher's implicit or explicit theory of social interaction. Consider, for example, Wilson's (1977) conceptual model of dyadic interactions between buyers and sellers. This model views selling as a set of stages in which the objectives of each participant vary at each stage. In the first stage of the interaction, the objective of the salesman is to become a legitimate and credible source of information, whereas later stages involve determining the attribute set and exchange rate. Thus, a coding system designed to measure the early stages of the transaction might include different content categories (e.g., statement of agreement with an opinion, opinion giving or requesting) than coding systems designed to measure the bargaining process (e.g., Pennington, 1968). While there have been several attempts to design universal interaction coding systems (e.g., Bales & Cohen, 1979), the validity of these systems is not necessarily universal. The usefulness of any coding system ultimately rests upon assessment of the construct validity of the system.

Although the content of coding systems is not universal, there are two structural properties that characterize all coding systems: the unit and category of analysis.

Units of Analysis. The unit of a coding system is the basic element of behavior observed. Units of observation in social interaction research range from molecular units associated with one behavior to molar units representing a sequence of actions. The most basic unit in social interaction research is the *act*, which is a grammatical sentence that expresses a simple idea. Acts may also refer to nonverbal behavior. Gottman (1979a), for example, uses nonverbal signals to determine the affective nature of verbal messages and to describe the listener's response to the message. Molar level units include a speech (i.e., all words transmitted by one participant during a given time interval), an idea, or theme (see Kassarjian, 1977 for a more detailed discussion of molar units). Thus, the elementary decision that must be made when designing a coding system is to determine whether a molecular or molar unit of behavior is appropriate.

Both methodological and analytic factors enter into this decision. Methodologically, the more molecular a coding system, the more difficult it is to obtain consensus among observers. Observers must code behavior that unfolds rapidly in social interactions, and therefore, complex schemes may tax the observer's capacity to record the interaction accurately. To enhance reliability, complex coding schemes can be simplified by grouping semantically similar units together, by defining a unit with respect to conditional probabilities that one behavior will follow another (Gottman, 1979a), or by reducing the number of categories to an orthogonal set through principal components analysis (Gottman, 1978).

Analytically, the unit of observation should be consistent with the behavioral sampling strategy. When the analyst is interested in sequential patterns of behavior, behaviors should endure longer than the sampling interval, otherwise sequential changes may not be detected (Bakeman, 1978). Finally, the choice between molecular and molar units depends upon the level of inference to be drawn. For example, molar coding schemes are likely to be more appropriate than molecular schemes for investigations dealing with stages in a selling process involving multiple meetings, numerous parties, and long term relationships (cf. Woodside & Reingen, 1981).

Categories of Analysis. A category in observational research represents a grouping of units that share some common characteristic. As Kassarjian (1977, p. 12) notes, "(c)ontent analysis is no better than its categories, since they reflect the formulated thinking, the hypotheses, and the purpose of the study." Furthermore, because the category is the measure used to draw inferences, questions of reliability and validity rest primarily on the adequacy of category definitions. Thus, content analysis is no better than the consistency with which observers use specified rules to assign behavioral units to theoretically meaningful categories.

Pennington's (1968) study of customer-salesman retail transactions provides an interesting example of how theory enters into the definition of behavioral categories. A bargaining perspective was adopted in the study and four categories of verbal behavior were identified based on theoretical formulations of bargaining behavior. Concessions by the salesman, such as price reduction and extended credit, or the customer's offer to buy for concessions were classified as direct offers. Other categories included presentation of concession limits, determination of concession limits, and attempts to change concession limits. Alternative strategies for deriving analytic categories in buyer/seller interaction research are discussed by Holbrook and O'Shaughnessy (1976) and Olshavsky (1973).

Behavioral Sampling Strategies

Marketing and consumer behavior studies of social interaction traditionally rely on analyses of the verbal content of an interaction. When conversations are recorded it is feasible to transcribe the conversation for subsequent analyses. In such cases, it is possible to observe all behaviors of interest. However, when observations are collected on several facets of behavior or when the interaction cannot be recorded for later analysis, sampling behavior within fixed time intervals is a plausible alternative to exhaustive coding procedures.

Sackett (1978) identifies three different sampling strategies: (a) continuous, real-time samples in which the observer measures the onset and termination of behavior, (b) periodic probe measures of behavior, and (c) dichotomous measures of the occurrence or nonoccurrence of a behavior within some time interval. The choice of a sampling strategy depends upon the frequency with which various behaviors occur and whether the analytic procedures demand that no two behaviors can occur simultaneously.

Continuous, real-time measures permit the investigator to test hypotheses about the duration as well as frequency of behavior. More important, the probability that infrequently occurring behaviors will be detected is much higher in continuous measurement systems. There are difficulties, however, encountered in collecting continuous measures. When video or audio taping equipment is not available, it is often impossible to track the initiation and termination of a behavior. This problem has been greatly reduced by digital data acquisition devices, similar to calculators, that allow the observer to record the onset and termination of behavior (Holm, 1978). These devices store the sequence and duration of category codes allowing the investigator to transmit the data to a mainframe computer for analysis. A second problem encountered in continuous measures of behavior is that interactions last for different lengths of time, creating ambiguities in comparisons of the frequency and duration of behavior across interactions. Typically, adjusting for the length of the interaction reduces this problem.

Sampling strategies based upon recording behaviors within some specified time interval are relatively easy to execute and require less coding effort by the observer. For example, observations of a retail transaction may be made by simply checking whether a behavior occurred during each minute of the interaction. The major drawbacks to time sampling are that infrequent behaviors will often be overlooked and the duration of behavior is neglected. These problems are greatly minimized by utilizing short time intervals that allow behaviors to be repeated in successive intervals.

The final dimension that should be considered in selecting a sampling strategy is whether the analytic procedure requires that no two behaviors occur at the same time. This assumption is critical for Markov models of interaction, because these models attempt to describe the transition probabilities from one behavioral state to another. It is important to recognize that recording the occurrence or nonoccurrence of behaviors in a specified interval produces observations that are not mutually exclusive. Moreover, it may often be inappropriate to assume that the behaviors are actually mutually exclusive; for example, nonverbal messages are transmitted by the listener while the communicator conveys a verbal message.

Reliability Assessment

Assessing the reliability of social interaction data presents some unique problems not encountered in standard discussions of reliability. To illustrate these problems, a hypothetical set of observations from four customer-salesperson interactions is shown in Table 6.2 and three options for reliability analysis are given in Table 6.3. The codes in Table 6.2 represent the four bargaining categories used by Pennington (1968).

The key reliability question in observational research is whether observers are consistent in their use of assignment rules. While the principles governing relia-

TABLE 6.2. Hypothetical observations of customer-salesman interactions.

Dyad	Observer 1
1	CPC-CPC-SPC-CDC-SDC-CDC-CDO-SDO-CPC-CAC-SAC-CDO
2	SDC-CDC-SPC-CDC-SPC-CDC-SAC-CAC-CDO-SDO-CDO
3	SPC-CPC-SPC-CDC-SDC-CAC-SAC-CAC-SDO-CDO
4	CDO-SPC-CPC-SAC-CDC-SDC-CAC-SDO

Dyad	Observer 2
1	CDC-CDC-SPC-CPC-SPC-CPC-CDO-SDC-CPC-CAC-SAC-CDO
2	SDC-CAC-SDC-CDC-SPC-CAC-SAC-CAC-CDO-SDO-CDO
3	SPC-CDC-SDC-CPC-SPC-CAC-SAC-CAC-SDO-CDO
4	CDO-SDC-CDC-SAC-CPC-SDC-CAC-SDO

Code	Interpretation
CDO SDO	Direct Offer: A concession by the customer (CDO) or salesman (SDO), such as a discount
CPC SPC	Presentation of Concession Limits: Statement of expectations about negotiation
CDC SDC	Determination of Concession Limits: Attempt to determine the concession limits of others in a negotiation
CAC SAC	Attempts to change concession limits: Attempts to alter the expectations of others

bility analyses in observational research are identical to those found in standard psychometric treatments of reliability (e.g., Mitchell, 1979; Peter, 1979), demonstrating that observers agree on category assignments is the primary objective in assessing observational data quality. This objective can be accomplished in several ways, depending upon assumptions made about the data and the intended use of the data. Table 6.3 gives computational examples of three approaches to assessing the reliability of observations: (1) Cronbach's α, (2) an agreement index, and (3) Cohen's (1960) Kappa statistic.

Cronbach's α statistic assesses the extent to which one can generalize across observers (Cronbach, Gleser, Nanda, & Rajaratnam, 1972). In observational research, α is an appropriate estimate of reliability when inferences are to be drawn about aggregate features of the interaction. For example, if analyses are to be conducted on the number of times the customer presents concession limits, then assessment of the stability of these counts across observers is needed. The hypothetical observations shown in Table 6.2 illustrate a situation in which both observers agree on the total number of CPC statements occurring in each dyad. In this circumstance, a generalizability analysis conducted on the total number of CPC codes in each dyad would demonstrate perfect reliability, i.e., $\alpha = 1.0$ (see Table 6.3). However, closer inspection of Table 6.2 reveals that there is very little agreement on which statements constitute a presentation of concession limits by the customer (CPC). Therefore, in most consumer research settings when assess-

TABLE 6.3. Alternative reliability analyses for the data in Table 6.2.

Number of CPC observations by observer

	Observer	
Dyad	1	2
1	3	3
2	0	0
3	1	1
4	1	1

Agreement rates for customer behaviors

		Observer 2				
		CDO	CPC	CDC	CAC	Total
	CDO	6	0	0	0	6
	CPC	0	1	4	0	5
Observer 1	CDC	0	4	1	2	7
	CAC	0	0	0	4	4
	Total	6	5	5	6	22

(1) $\alpha = \dfrac{MS_d - MS_r}{MS_d - (\text{OBS-1})MS_r}$
$= 1.0$

(2) Proportion of Agreements

$P(A) = \text{Agreements}/(A + D)$
$= 12/22$
$= .545$

(3) Kappa $= \dfrac{P_o - P_t}{1 - P_c}$

$P_c = \Sigma\, (P_{i.} \times P_{j})$
$= (6/220^2 + (5/22)^2 +$
$(7/22)*(5/22) + (4/22)*(6/22)$
$= .248$

Kappa $= \dfrac{(.545 - .248)}{(1.00 - .248)}$
$= .395$

ing the reliability of observational data, it is also necessary to examine the extent of agreement among observers at a molecular level.

Assessment procedures (2) and (3) in Table 6.3 are standard measures of agreement reported in observational research. The proportion of agreement is easily computed by summing the diagonal for customer behaviors in Table 6.3 and dividing by the total number of behaviors. This statistic has a simple interpretation, and hence, is frequently reported as a reliability index. However, the agreement statistic varies as a function of the marginal probabilities of behavior. For example, if behavior A has a marginal probability of occurrence equal to .8 while the marginal probability of B is only .3, one would expect that "random" observers would agree approximately 64% of the time for behavior A and 9% of the time for behavior B. To adjust for chance agreement, most treatments of reliability in observational research recommend the application of Kappa (Johnson & Bolstad, 1973; Gottman, 1979a; Hollenbeck, 1978), which is generalizable to any number of observers (Fleiss, 1971).

Recently, Dillon and Mulani (1984) have developed a latent class model for assessing reliability. Their technique is analogous to confirmatory factor analysis for reliability assessment with continuous variables. Latent class models are extremely powerful and allow one to: (a) apply formal statistical tests to evaluate the significance of agreement and disagreement rates for observers, (b) evaluate the error rates for each observer and coding category, and (c) test for agreement for more than two observers. While an extensive treatment of the latent class is beyond the scope of this paper, Dillon and Mulani's procedure is likely to receive increased attention because it presents an interesting method for testing the measurement model underlying observational data.

Improving the Quality of Observational Data

The difficulties of designing a coding system that fulfill the requirements of scientific measurement are well-documented (e.g., Gottman, 1979a; Holbrook & O'Shaughnessy, 1976; Hollenbeck, 1978; Johnson & Bolstad, 1973; Yarrow & Waxler, 1979). Even when coding systems are closely linked to theory, in actual use they are frequently found to be unreliable and hence, of questionable validity.

Improving Reliability. The complexity of coding systems is a major source of unreliability in observational research. Complexity is determined by the number of coding categories, the breadth of a category (i.e., the number of behaviors that belong to the category), and the situation in which observations are collected (see Hollenbeck, 1978 and Johnson & Bolstad, 1973 for a more complete discussion). Several options are available for improving the reliability of complex coding systems. Gottman (1979a) describes an extensive training procedure that may facilitate observer agreement. The training sessions are progressive and require coders to learn the codes and category definitions, code transcripts of statements listed in random order, code a video tape with a trainer, and code a training tape to criterion. Perhaps the major drawback to extensive training is that observers may develop expectations about the research results that bias subsequent observations (cf. Johnson & Bolstad, 1973).

A second option for improving reliability is to reduce the number of categories in the coding system. Gottman's (1979) studies of marital interaction illustrate an interesting technique for accomplishing this goal. Summary codes were created by assessing the semantic relatedness of verbal statements; then, transition probabilities between statements were examined to determine whether the statements were contiguous. For example, a statement such as, "yeah, this does seem to be a good product, but it is priced too high for me" is not an uncommon sequence of thoughts in sales and might be considered as one thought rather than two separate statements.

Validity Issues. The quality of observational data also depends upon validity considerations. Johnson and Bolstad (1973), in an excellent discussion of validity problems in observational research, discuss three factors that often compromise data quality: (a) observer bias, (b) reactive effects of observation, and (c) the failure to relate observations to independent measures of a process. Although only a brief discussion of these issues is warranted in the present chapter, the interested reader may wish to examine Johnson and Bolstad's paper and Rosenthal's (1976) discussion of observer effects.

Observer bias refers to an overestimation or underestimation of the occurrence of specific behaviors. Rosenthal (1976) attributes observer bias to recording errors caused by beliefs about the phenomena under investigation or by expectations about the subject's behavior. This problem is seldom discussed in marketing studies. In studies where comparisons are made between "good" versus "poor" salesmen or where the observer serves as theoretician, it is difficult to determine the veridicality of the findings without independent replications. An often cited example of observer bias comes from a study by Kennedy and Upoff (1939) on extrasensory perception. Observers who believed in telepathy made 71.5% more errors that increased telepathy scores, while disbelievers made 100% more errors decreasing the telepathy scores. Thus, the lesson to be learned from investigations of observer bias is that controls should be included in any observational study to reduce the extent of bias.

The reactive effects of observation present a second threat to the validity of observation data. For example, the presence of an observer or recording device may alter the normal pattern of behavior in a sales transaction and produce results that do not generalize to other settings. There appear to be at least two ways of reducing the intrusiveness of observation. The fact that an interaction is being observed can be concealed or the conspicuousness of the observer can be reduced by collecting multiple samples of behavioral interactions. In the latter case the observer might accompany a salesman on several visits prior to the critical observation period in order to habituate the customer and salesman to his presence. A second method of dealing with intrusiveness is to measure its impact. For example, transcripts of customer-salesman interactions could be examined by an independent sample of buyers and sellers to determine how typical the interaction pattern is.

A final validity consideration in observational research concerns the construct validity of the coding system. Because direct observations of behavior present an overwhelming appearance of "face validity," construct validity is seldom examined. Nevertheless, the correspondence between categories in a coding system and theoretical constructs is an important issue meriting attention. Johnson and Bolstad (1973) propose that demonstrating convergent validity of behavioral measures with alternative measures is a minimal criterion for construct validation. When research conclusions are drawn on the basis of aggregate measures, assessing construct validity is relatively straight-forward. Consider, for example, a simple coding system in which the nonverbal affect expressed by buyers and sellers is categorized into positive, neutral, or negative behavior. Counts of these behaviors may be used as an index of the affective tone of the interaction and related to rating data collected from buyers and sellers; at a minimum one would expect some correspondence between these measures.

When dynamic, sequential aspects of interaction are of concern, an additional level of difficulty is added to validity assessment. Suppose that a theory postulates the existence of an attribute-value exchange process in which the buyer raises questions about the importance of product features and the seller responds to these inquiries by assessing the importance of each feature. Assuming that this sequence is embedded in a theory linking the process to other constructs, then at least one validation procedure can be identified. Specifically, the investigator could examine the relationship between either the duration or occurrence/nonoccurrence of the sequence to measures of theoretically related constructs, for example, consumer satisfaction. Thus, the complexity of validity questions greatly increases for dynamic, process measures, but these problems do not seem intractable.

In the following section analytic strategies for social interaction data are discussed. The assumption made in this discussion is that the investigator has taken the necessary steps to demonstrate that the behavioral observations are reliable and contain conceptually meaningful behavioral units. While these factors are frequently overlooked in studies using direct observations of behavior, acceptance of observational research strategies will hinge upon demonstrating that coding systems satisfy the standards of a good, scientific instrument.

Analytic Strategies for Social Interaction Data

Perhaps the major methodological achievement in social interaction research during the last decade has been the development of analytic procedures for identifying patterns, sequences, and cycles of behavior. This, in turn, has generated new conceptualizations of standard interaction concepts such as dominance and reciprocity. For example, in Table 6.1 I made a distinction between noncontingent and contingent reciprocity. Noncontingent reciprocity is an aggregate concept based on the notion that participants in an interaction may match each other in terms of the overall level of particular behaviors. Buyers and sellers, for instance, may make a similar number of concessions across a negotiation. Contingent reciprocity, however, is a dynamic concept that refers to the probability that one person's behavior influences subsequent behaviors of others (Gottman, 1979a). In this case, an investigator would be interested in determining whether a concession by a buyer at time t alters the probability of a concession by the seller at time t+k. As this examples illustrates, the primary analytic advances have come from framing interaction questions as time series and/or conditional probability problems.

Two classes of analytic techniques for dynamic interaction data have been discussed. Gottman (1979a, 1979b; Gottman & Ringland, 1981), who pioneered the move toward dynamic analysis models, describes the application of Box-Jenkins models and Fourier transforms to interaction data. These techniques (a) assume that the underlying measures are continuous and, (b) require a long series of data to insure stability of parameter estimates. Although scaling categorical data can produce the desired continuous measures, it is far more common to find analyses of categorical data in social interaction studies. Consequently, the present section limits the discussion to analytic techniques for categorical data.

Bakeman (1978) differentiates four types of categorial data sets produced by direct observations of behavior. The data types are derived from two orthogonal characteristics of the coding procedure: (1) event versus time base, and (2) sequential versus concurrent behaviors. Type 1 data sets are event based-sequential data in which the order of events is noted, but the duration is ignored, and only one event is permitted to occur at a time. Typically, observations of the verbal content in an interaction produce Type 1 data such as the hypothetical observations shown in Table 6.2. In Type 2 data sets (i.e., event-based, concurrent) multiple events are permitted to occur in the same time interval. Type 2 data are common when all behaviors occurring within some time interval are recorded. For Type 3 (time-based, sequential) and Type 4 (time-based, concurrent) the duration of each event as well as the occurrence of an event is noted.

A critical dimension affecting the selection of an analytic procedure is whether the data set is sequential or concurrent. Markov models of social interaction (e.g., Thomas & Martin, 1976) assume sequential data (Type 1 or Type 3) because the goal is to model the transition probabilities over time. When concurrent data are collected, it is possible to create a sequential data set by defining mutually exclusive codes. For example, a coding system consisting of two potentially concurrent codes (salesman talks or customer talks) can be transformed into four dyadic states (no conversation, salesman talks-customer silent, salesman silent-customer talks, and customer talks-salesman talks). This scheme is practical only when few behaviors are observed since the number of possible interaction states increases exponentially as more behaviors are observed. An alternative to the Markov procedures is to develop time series models of concurrent data sets. In this situation, the dyadic interaction data are treated as two potentially related time series, one string of observations for each participant, in which one or both series may show autocorrelations or cross-correlations suggesting a lead-lag relationship. Hence, the analytic problem with concurrent categorical data is similar to estimating the parameters of a transfer function or multivariate time series (Box & Jenkins, 1976).

The procedures discussed below are divided into exploratory and inferential techniques. The goal of exploratory analyses is to search for structure in a series of observations arrayed in time. Inferential procedures, on the other hand, either test for the presence of prespecified patterns of behavior or compare the patterning of behavior across two or more groups.

Searching for Patterns in Social Behavior

A preliminary goal in social interaction research is to identify sequential patterns of behavior. Conceptually, the solution to this problem rests on establishing a metric for uncertainty reduction; that is, how much information is gained about an individual's behavior by knowing the preceding behaviors of others? Altman (1965) and Gottman and Notarius (1978) formulate a metric based on information theory. Basically, the technique examines the average reduction in uncertainty resulting from the difference of the probability of consequent events conditioned on antecedent events and the unconditional probability of consequent events. This formulation has provided the conceptual basis for subsequent applications, but in practice, information theory estimates have proven unwieldy (cf. Gottman, 1979a). Consequently, a method referred to as lagged sequential analysis has been developed by Sackett (1979) to facilitate the search process.

Sackett's procedure tests for lagged dependency in behaviors by computing a z statistic based on the difference between the conditional, lagged probability of a behavior and the unconditional probability of the behavior. To demonstrate this procedure, suppose that an investigator observes a sequence of direct offers and attempts to change concession limits in a buyer-seller interaction. Determining whether there is some patterning in these behaviors can be accomplished by letting each behavior serve as an antecedent and examining the conditional probabilities of consequent behaviors at various lags. For each consequent behavior, the null hypothesis is: $\Pr(C_{t+k}|\, A_t) = \Pr(C_{t+k})$. Allison and Liker (1982) demonstrate that under the null hypothesis, a z statistic that is asymptotically distributed $N(0,1)$ is given by:

$$z = \frac{p_{C|A} - p_C}{\sqrt{\dfrac{p_C(1 - p_C)\,(1 - p_A)}{(n - k)\,p_A}}}$$

where p_C and p_A are the proportion of consequent and antecedent events, respectively, and $n - k$ is the number of total behavioral events minus the lag, k.

Table 6.4 gives an example of how the z-index can be used to identify *common patterns* in a buyer-seller negotiation. The first step in this process is to let each behavioral code serve as an antecedent and to compute the conditional probability of all other codes at various lags. For the example in Table 6.4 the analysis was

TABLE 6.4. Lagged conditional probabilities of direct offers and attempts to change concession limits for hypothetical buyer-seller interaction data.

Consequent behaviors	Antecedent behavior CDO at Lag 0				Unconditional probabilities
	Lag 1	Lag 2	Lag 3	Lag 4	
CDO	.10	.50*	.12	.65*	.25
CAC	.25	.25	.35	.10	.30
SDO	.15	.10	.45*	.10	.10
SAC	.50*	.15	.08	.15	.35
(MAX Z)	(2.56)	(4.69)	(12.16)	(7.47)	

Consequent behaviors	Antecedent behavior SAC at Lag 0				Unconditional probabilities
	Lag 1	Lag 2	Lag 3	Lag 4	
CDO	.60*	.25	.55*	.20	.25
CAC	.20	.20	.20	.30	.30
SDO	.05	.35*	.05	.15	.10
SAC	.15	.20	.15	.35	.35
(MAX Z)	(8.37)	(8.60)	(7.14)	(< 1.96)	

Note. The computations assume a sequence of 200 behaviors (i.e., n = 200). The conditional probabilities with an asterisk superscript have the highest z-scores at each lag; the value of this z is shown in parentheses at the bottom of each column.

initiated by selecting direct offers by the customer as the antecedent. The conditional probabilities of events following the CDO code suggest a simple pattern: A direct offer by the customer is followed by the salesman attempting to alter concession limits and then a series of counteroffers transpires. At each lag, the *z*-index indicates that the maximum conditional probability surpasses the arbitrary decision rule in which the null hypothesis of no dependence is rejected for *z*'s exceeding 1.96.

As a further test of the viability of this common pattern, we can examine the conditional probabilities of behaviors following a salesman's attempt to change the customer's concession limits. The bottom panel in Table 6.4 indicates a sequence of counteroffers similar to the sequence shown in the top panel, thus confirming the pattern found when direct offers by the customer were used as the antecedent event. This procedure could be repeated for additional lags until the *z* statistics for each consequent behavior are less than 1.96, indicating that the conditional probabilities do not sufficiently exceed the unconditional probabilities to warrant a conclusion of dependency between the antecedent and consequent behaviors. Further common patterns could be identified by examining the lagged conditional probabilities for each possible antecedent.[1]

Although the *z*-statistic provides a convenient metric for determining the predictability of future behavior from past interactive behavior, the significance levels associated with the *z* are not exact when short sequences of behavior are observed. The *z*-analysis is based on a normal approximation to the binomial (Sackett, 1979) and hypergeometric (Wampold & Margolin, 1982) distributions. It is well known that these distributions converge to a normal distribution more rapidly when events are equiprobable. Consequently, Gottman (1979a) uses the heuristic (previously stated by Siegel, 1956) that *z*-scores should be considered reasonable approximations when $NPQ > 9$; that is, the product of the total number of behaviors observed (N), the unconditional probability of an event (P), and $1-P$ (i.e., Q) must be at least nine. In practice this constraint limits the analysis of higher-order lags to data sets composed of long sequences of behavior—especially when infrequent behaviors are of interest. Since most dyads will not generate sufficient data, it is possible to consider the data from multiple dyads that share some common characteristic as a single sequence. The drawback to this procedure is that potential differences among dyads are ignored. When there is reason to suspect heterogeneity among dyads, the analyst should consider using variants of logit modeling that represent dyads as dummy variables (Allison & Liker, 1982; Budescu, 1984).

The interpretation of the *z*-scores from Sackett's procedure and subsequent modifications (Allison & Liker, 1982) assumes that there is no *autodependence*

---

[1]A program called Joint, written by Roger Bakeman (Georgia State University), is available for computing conditional probabilities and testing for lagged dependencies in social interaction data. The advantage of this program is that it allows the investigator to examine the patterns that arise when each behavior is considered as the antecedent in a chain of behaviors.

among observations. Autodependence refers to the dependence of each individual's behavior on previous acts by the person. The interpretive problems created by autodependence are most apparent for concurrent interaction data. For instance, suppose that one observes a significant z-score for the conditional probability of a customer making a direct offer following a salesman's attempt to alter a concession limit. If autodependence is present, it is possible that a behavior of the customer at time t influenced both the salesman's behavior at time t and the customer's subsequent behavior at time $t + k$. When event based data are collected, such interpretive problems are masked because no two behaviors are observed in the same time interval. However, autodependence may be present in the data if unobserved, concurrent events influence the observed behaviors or if autodependence arises for higher order lags. Therefore, the causal significance of observed antecedent-consequent relationships should be interpreted cautiously. As research on an interaction problem progresses beyond the exploratory stage, it is advisable to employ modeling procedures that incorporate tests for autodependence (see Allison & Liker, 1982, and Dillon, Madden, & Kumar, 1983 for a description of these methods).

Alternative approaches to exploring the structure of social behaviors have been described by Castellan (1979). Castellan's approach is derived from general analytic procedures for contingency tables that utilize chi-square as the test statistic. These techniques are useful for a variety of interaction questions. For instance, exploratory analyses of the stages in an interaction can be accomplished by testing the stability of event sequences at different points in the interaction. To test stability, Castellan recommends examining the marginal or transition probabilities at each of several time blocks. If stages in the interaction sequence are hypothesized, then this analysis should reveal that the conditional probabilities are not constant for all time blocks. An overall test of the stage hypothesis could be constructed by computing a chi-square statistic based on the sum of all antecedent-consequent analyses.

Two uses of exploratory analyses of social interaction data have been identified in this section. The first examines whether there is evidence of patterning in the behavior of individuals in a dyad, and the second deals with testing for stages in which particular patterns of behavior are more likely. These two goals are central to discovering the structure of buyer-seller behavior. Investigations concerning the patterning of interactive behavior are likely to facilitate identification of frequent antecedent-consequent chains. Similarly, Castellan's presentation of contingency table analysis provides statistical procedures for examining the phases in buyer-seller negotiations. However, if these techniques are to stimulate future research, it is necessary to consider how they can be used to test causal propositions about differences among groups.

Testing Interaction Hypotheses

Recent analytic developments in social interaction research have shifted attention from exploratory to confirmatory hypothesis testing techniques. Confirmatory

TABLE 6.5. Probability relationships implied by sequential interaction hypotheses.

Hypothesis	Conditional probablility statement
Dependence	$\Pr(C_{t+k} \mid A_t) - \Pr(C) \neq 0$
Contingent reciprocity	$\Pr(C_{t+k} = 1 \mid A_t = 1) - \Pr(C_{t+k} = 1 \mid A_t = 0) \neq 0$
Interaction stages	$\Pr(C_j \mid A_i)_t \neq \Pr(C_j \mid A_i)$
Dominance	$\Pr(B_{t+k} \mid A_t) \neq \Pr(A_{t+k} \mid B_t)$

analysis involves either a test for specific patterns of behavior or an examination of the equivalency of patterns among groups. In both cases, hypotheses are formulated by specifying the expected relationship between transition probabilities and some comparison standard. Table 6.5 shows the probability statements implied by common sequential interaction hypotheses discussed in the literature.

Dependence, Contingent Reciprocity, and Interaction Stages. The dependence and contingent reciprocity hypotheses are equivalent for dichotomous data. Both hypotheses assert that the presence of some antecedent event either increases or decreases the likelihood of a consequent event. For example, consider the hypothesis that a small concession by a seller will lead to concessions by the buyer at some future time, $t + k$. To test this hypothesis, a 2×2 contingency table could be constructed similar to the one shown in Table 6.6. The analysis of

TABLE 6.6. Artificial lag one frequencies of concessions by buyers and sellers.

	Buyer behavior at time $t+k$		
Seller Behavior at Time t	No Concession	Concession	Total
No Concession	90 (.692)	40 (.308)	130
Concession	20 (.285)	50 (.714)	70
Total	110	90	200
	Seller behavior at time $t+k$		
Buyer Behavior at Time t	No Concession	Concession	Total
No Concession	60 (.500)	60 (.500)	120
Concession	60 (.750)	20 (.250)	80
Total	120	80	200

Note. The numbers in parentheses are the conditional probabilities of each event at time $t+k$ given the preceding event at time t.

this table may involve two goals: (a) to state the degree of dependency, and (b) to test the significance of the relationship.

One analysis option for the data in Table 6.6 is to compute either a chi-square or normal approximation statistic. However, these tests are sensitive to marginal probabilities; when the probability of C_{t+k} approaches 0 or 1, the range of the difference between conditional probabilities is restricted (Allison & Liker, 1982). To overcome this problem, Allison and Liker recommend the use of a logit transformation, that is, logit(p) = $ln[p/(1-p)]$. The degree of dependency between behaviors coded as either present (1) or absent (0) can then be estimated by:

$$\beta = \text{logit}[\Pr(C_{t+k} = 1 \mid A_t = 1)] - \text{logit}\,[\Pr(C_{t+k} = 1 \mid A_t = 0)]$$

where exp(β) is equal to the ratio:

$$\frac{\Pr(C_{t+k} = 1 \mid A_t = 1)/\Pr(C_{t+k} = 0 \mid A_t = 1)}{\Pr(C_{t+k} = 1 \mid A_t = 0)/\Pr(C_{t+k} = 0 \mid A_t = 0)}$$

Thus, β represents the shift in the odds of the consequent event occurring given the antecedent event is present versus absent. For the data in the top panel of Table 6.6, β is estimated to be 1.73, which indicates that the ratio of the odds of a concession by the buyer are 5.64, given a previous concession by the seller, to 1, given no concession by the seller.

The principal advantage of the logit model is that it permits inclusion of dummy variables for comparisons among groups. For a two-group comparison the relevant model tests are:

$$H_0\text{: logit}[\Pr(C_{t+k} = 1 \mid A_t, X)] = \alpha + \beta A_t + \lambda X$$

$$H_1\text{: logit}[\Pr(C_{t+k} = 1 \mid A_t, X)] = \alpha + \beta A_t + \lambda X + \gamma A_t X$$

If H_1 provides a better fit to the data, then the conclusion is that the conditional probability of the consequent event given the antecedent is not constant across groups.

The logit procedure advocated by Allison and Liker can be extended to test the stability of antecedent-consequent relationships over stages of an interaction and to examine autodependence effects. Recently, Dillon, Madden, and Kumar (1983) developed a more general framework for testing these hypotheses based on latent structure analysis. Their technique is similar to confirmatory factor analysis in that the influence of categorical antecedent variables is assumed to be mediated by intervening or latent categorical variables. Latent structure analysis permits one to fit a variety of presumed interaction process models and to examine the adequacy of each model. When differences in interaction patterns between groups are of interest, latent classes are constructed to reflect the hypothesized interaction processes in each group. Thus, given adequate specification of theoretical models, latent structure analysis provides a general method of testing the viability of each model with respect to observed transition probabilities.

Dominance. Dominance and related concepts such as social power and control imply asymmetry in social influence. Consider the definition proposed by Gottman (1979a, p. 71):

> In a dyad, if B's future behavior is more predictable from A's past behavior than conversely, then A is said to be dominant.

The asymmetry suggested by this definition is that the probability of B's future behavior conditioned on past actions by A cannot be equated with the probability of A's future behavior conditioned on past actions of B (see Table 6.5).

Table 6.6 presents a simple example to illustrate the analytic considerations involved in testing dominance. The conditional frequencies and probabilities of concessions by buyers and sellers at time t+k given the other's concession behavior at time *t* are shown in the table. These hypothetical data indicate that the probability of a concession by the buyer increases dramatically when preceded by a concession by the seller. However, a concession by the buyer decreases the probability of a subsequent concession by the seller.

One analytic strategy for testing the significance of the asymmetry in Table 6.6 is to treat the data in the top and bottom panels as if they came from two independent groups. Allison and Liker (1982) note that a *Z* value for a two group comparison is given by:

$$z = \frac{\hat{\beta}_1 - \hat{\beta}_2}{\sqrt{\Sigma\ (1/f_i)}}$$

where $\hat{\beta}_1$ and $\hat{\beta}_2$ are coefficients derived from a logit dependency model for $\Pr(B_{t+k} \mid S_t)$ and $\Pr(S_{t+k} \mid B_t)$, respectively, and f_i is the cell frequency for the i-th cell in the three-way contingency table formed by merging the top and bottom panels of Table 6.6. Applying this test to the data in Table 6.6 yields:

$$z = \frac{1.73 - (-1.10)}{\sqrt{(1/90)+(1/40)+\ldots+(1/60)+(1/20)}} = 6.23$$

A simple interpretation of this comparison is that the seller exerts more control over the concession process than the buyer because the obtained z far exceeds what would be expected under the null hypothesis of symmetry in the influence process. Moreover, the negative weight for $\hat{\beta}_2$ indicates that the buyer's previous concessions harden the seller's negotiation stance.

The analytic model in this simple example is misspecified in two ways. First, autodependence effects are ignored and second, the standard error of the difference between estimators was calculated under the incorrect assumption that the estimates are independent. These problems have stimulated the development of more appropriate modeling procedures.

If autodependence is of concern, then it must be shown that the asymmetry in predicting an individual's behavior holds when the effects of the person's own previous behavior are partialled out.[2] Otherwise, the appropriate conclusion may be that past behaviors by one member of the dyad explain the other member's past behavior as well as the individual's own future behavior. Thus, a more precise statement of the dominance hypothesis is given by:

$$\mathrm{Pr}(\mathrm{B}_{t+k} \mid \mathrm{A}_t, \mathrm{B}_t) = \mathrm{Pr}(\mathrm{A}_{t+k} \mid \mathrm{B}_t, \mathrm{A}_t)$$

Allison and Liker (1982) recommend testing this hypothesis by a two-stage logit-linear modeling procedure. For the buyer-seller negotiation, expanded contingency tables could be constructed by considering the buyer's behavior at time t for the top panel of Table 6.6 and the seller's behavior at time t for the bottom panel of Table 6.6. Two logit models, one for each expanded contingency table, could be estimated:

$$(1)\ \mathrm{logit}[\mathrm{Pr}(\mathrm{B}_{t+k} = 1 \mid \mathrm{B}_t, \mathrm{S}_t)] = \beta_0 + \beta_1^*\mathrm{S}_t + \beta_2\mathrm{B}_t$$

$$(2)\ \mathrm{logit}[\mathrm{Pr}(\mathrm{S}_{t+k} = 1 \mid \mathrm{B}_t, \mathrm{S}_t)] = \beta_3 + \beta_4^*\mathrm{B}_t \ ^{\$}\ \beta_5\mathrm{S}_t$$

Following the estimation of each model, Allison and Liker suggest a z test for dominance based on the difference between coefficients 1 and 4 divided by the square root of the summed variances of the two estimators. Although this procedure accounts for autodependence, it ignores the covariance among the estimators; therefore, the standard error in Allison and Liker's statistic is biased.

Analytic models that consider both autodependence and the covariance among estimators have recently been developed by Budescu (1984), Wampold (1984), and Dillon, Madden, and Kumar (1983). Budescu (1984) proposes a weighted least squares procedure that simultaneously estimates the dependency models for both actors in a dyad. Basically, Budescu's procedure is a variant of the general linear model that represents logit transformations of the conditional probabilities

---

[2]Readers familiar with Box-Jenkins time series models will recognize that this condition is similar to demonstrating that two time series are cross-correlated when autocorrelations within each series are removed. Gottman and Ringland (1981) discuss how Box-Jenkins models can be used to test asymmetric and symmetric social relationships for continuous measures. Comparisons among four autoregressive functions are suggested for empirically defining dominance patterns in a dyadic interaction:

$$(1)\ A_t = \Sigma\alpha_k{}^*A_{t-k} + \epsilon_t{}^*$$

$$(2)\ B_t = \Sigma\beta_k{}^*B_{t-k} + \eta_t{}^*$$

$$(3)\ A_t = \Sigma\alpha_k A_{t-k} + \Sigma\lambda_k B_{t-k} + \epsilon_t$$

$$(4)\ B_t = \Sigma\beta_k B_{t-k} + \Sigma\gamma_k A_{t-k} + \eta_t$$

If models (1) and (2) best characterize the data, then neither A nor B influence one another's behavior. Asymmetric relationships would be implied by evidence that models (1) and (4) or models (2) and (3) fit the data. Accepting a symmetric hypothesis implies that models (3) and (4) provide the best fit and that the estimated coefficients for λ and γ are equal.

for each transition matrix as a function of linear combinations of parameters. Differences among any two parameter estimates are tested by a chi-square statistic with one degree of freedom. Wampold (1984), in contrast, recommends a test based on the hypergeometric distribution in which the difference between obtained frequencies in the transition matrices and expected frequencies are tested against a normal distribution. Currently, no substantive criteria are available for choosing between the weighted least squares and hypergeometric statistics. However, the compatibility between weighted least squares and standard analytic approaches eases the computational and interpretive demands on the user.

Latent structure models can also be used to test dominance (Dillon et al., 1983). In this procedure, a common factor model that represents observed behaviors of both actors at each time period as a function of a common factor is examined for fit. If the common factor model fits the data, then the researcher is justified in concluding that observed relationships between past and future behaviors are spurious, and therefore, no dominance pattern exists. If the common factor model does not fit the data, then constraints can be relaxed or imposed to test specific dominance hypotheses. The level of mathematical sophistication necessary for deriving latent structure models of dominance and the level at which the underlying model must be specified make latent structure analysis both a demanding and powerful tool for social interaction analysis.

Summary of Analytic Issues

The difficulties involved in selecting an appropriate analytic strategy for interaction data are related to two data characteristics seldom encountered by most researchers. Interaction process data sets are composed of discrete, categorical variables that are generated by a complex time series function. Exploration of such data involves the tedious task of sifting through a multitude of transition probabilities and determining whether there is sufficient evidence to conclude that a behavior can be represented as a function of past behaviors of others. When the goal is to draw inferences about the causal significance of previous behavior, the complexity of statistical assumptions and hypotheses compound the analytic problem. The logit and latent structure models described above are likely to prove helpful in distinguishing among alternative causal models. However, if social interaction research is to generate meaningful conclusions, then it is necessary to develop theoretical models that explain why certain patterns of behavior arise in marketing exchanges.

Using Social Interaction Data for Theory Development

Most discussions of theory development emphasize a staged approach. Presumably, phenomena are discovered through careful empirical investigations, untethered by theory; tentative models are developed to account for the data; and finally, the culmination occurs when some perceptive scientist pieces together the puzzle into a coherent system of axioms and postulates. While this is probably true to some extent, I do not believe that this protracted process will stimulate much interest in studying the dynamic features of marketing exchanges. If the methodological advances described in the preceding sections are to influence future interaction research, then it must be demonstrated that they provide the basis for altering current models of marketing interactions.

There are at least two important contributions that a dynamic conceptualization of interactive behavior can provide. The first is that it focuses attention on the reciprocal nature of social influence. In the last two decades, marketing scholars have underscored the importance of social exchange concepts for understanding marketing transactions (Bagozzi, 1975; Kotler, 1972). According to this perspective, success or failure in the marketplace is a joint function of a firm's influence on the consumer and the consumer's influence on the firm. The research strategies discussed in this chapter are consistent with this view and provide tools for investigating the marketing exchange process through direct observations of marketing transactions.

The second and perhaps most important contribution of dynamic interaction research is that it provides methods for a more detailed assessment of marketing phenomena. Social power, dominance, and control are constructs that have been defined both operationally and theoretically at a molar level. Consequently, the research strategies used to investigate these constructs have focused on self-reports of influence attempts and aggregate analyses of behavior. For example, Davis and Rigaux (1974), in a classic empirical investigation of couple decision making, found four influence patterns in economic decisions that varied across stages of the decision process. The data in this study were collected via an extensive questionnaire about the influence process. A recurring problem in such research is that spouses may not be accurate observers of their own behavior (cf. Jacobson & Moore, 1981). If so, then observations of the dominance patterns that evolve at various stages of economic decisions are more likely to provide detailed information about the joint decision process than are questionnaire data. There is also the possibility that dynamic analyses of social interaction data may contradict self report data. Dominance as defined in the present paper refers to asymmetry in the predictability of dyadic behavior. Self-report data provide little information about this asymmetry, and at worst, can be potentially misleading. Moreover, aggregate analyses of the frequency of influence attempts can be equally misleading. Dominant participants in an interaction may contribute little to the verbal exchange but when they do, subsequent behaviors of others are altered.

Although dynamic, observational research strategies have been advocated in this chapter, my opinion is that interaction research should not be limited to a single strategy. Ultimately, the usefulness of interactive research strategies depends on whether the design allows the investigator to draw inferences about how an individual's behavior is affected by other's behavior, his own behavior, and the context of interaction.

Acknowledgments. This chapter has benefited from comments and suggestions made by David Brinberg, Dipankar Chakravarti, William Dillon, Richard Lutz, and Cindy Moore.

References

Allison, P. D., & Liker, J. K. (1982). Analyzing sequential categorical data on dyadic interaction: A comment on Gottman. *Psychological Bulletin*, *91*, 393–403.

Altmann, S. T. (1965). Sociobiology of Rhesus monkeys. II: Stochastics of Social Communication. *Journal of Theoretical Biology*, *8*, 490–522.

Bales, R. F. (1950). *Interaction process analysis*. Chicago: University of Chicago Press.

Bales, R. F., & Cohen, S. P. (1979). *SYMLOG: A system for multiple level observation of groups*. New York: The Free Press.

Bagozzi, R. P. (1975, October). Marketing as exchange. *Journal of Marketing*, *39*, 32–39.

Bakeman, R. (1978). Untangling streams of behavior. In G. P. Sackett (Ed.), *Observing behavior volume II: Data collection and analysis methods*. Baltimore, MD: University Park Press.

Box, G. E. P., Jenkins, G. M. (1976). *Time series analysis: Forecasting and control*. San Francisco: Holden-Day.

Budescu, D. V. (1984). Tests of lagged dominance in sequential dyadic interaction. *Psychological Bulletin*, *96*, 402–414.

Cairns, R. B. (Ed.) (1979). *The analysis of social interactions*. Hillsdale, NJ: Lawrence Erlbaum.

Capon, N. (1975). Persuasive effects of sales messages developed from interaction process analysis. *Journal of Applied Psychology*, *60*, 238–244.

Capon, N., Holbrook, M. B., & Hulbert, J. M. (1977). Selling processes and buyer behavior. In A. G. Woodside, J. N. Sheth, & P. D. Bennett (Eds.), *Consumer and Industrial Buying Behavior* (pp. 323–332). New York: North-Holland.

Castellan, N. J. Jr. (1979). The analysis of behavior sequences. In R. B. Cairns (Ed.), *The Analysis of Social Interactions* (pp. 81–116). Hillsdale, NJ: Lawrence Erlbaum.

Chapple, E. D., & Donald, G. Jr. (1947). An evaluation of department store salespeople by the interaction chronograph. *Journal of Marketing*, *12*, 173–185.

Cohen, J. (1960). A coefficient of agreement for nominal scales. *Education and Psychological Measurement*, *20*, 37–46.

Cronbach, L. J., Gleser, G. C., Nanda, H., & Rajaratnam, N. (1972). *The dependability of behavioral measurements: Theory of generalizability for scores and profiles*. New York: John Wiley & Sons.

Davis, H. L. (1976, March). Decision making within the household. *Journal of Consumer Research*, *2*, 241–260.

Davis, H. L., & Rigaux, B. P. (1974, June). Perception of marital roles in decision processes. *Journal of Consumer Research*, *1*, 51–62.

Davis, H. L., & Silk, A. J. (1972, Winter). Interaction and influence processes in personal selling. *Sloan Management Review*, *13*, 56–76.

Dillon, W. R., Madden, T. J., & Kumar, A. (1983). Analyzing sequential categorical data on dyadic interaction: A latent structure approach. *Psychological Bulletin*, *94*, 564–583.

Dillon, W. R., & Mulani, N. (1984). A probabilistic latent class model for assessing interjudge reliability. *Multivariate Behavioral Research*, *19*, 438–458.

Evans, F. B. (1963, May). Selling as a dyadic relationship—A new approach. *The American Behavioral Scientist*, *6*, 76–89.

Fleiss, J. L. (1971). Measuring nominal scale agreement among many raters. *Psychological Bulletin*, 378–382.

Gottman, J. M. (1978). Nonsequential data analysis techniques in observational research. In G. P. Sackett (Ed.), *Observing Behavior Volume II: Data Collection and Analysis Methods* (pp. 45–62). Baltimore, MD: University Park Press.

Gottman, J. M. (1979a). *Marital interaction: Experimental investigations*. New York: Academic Press.

Gottman, J. M. (1979b). Detecting cyclicity in social interaction. *Psychological Bulletin*, *86*, 338–348.

Gottman, J. M., & Bakeman, R. (1979). The sequential analysis of observational data. In M. E. Lamb, S. J. Suomi, & G. R. Stephenson (Eds.), *Social interaction analysis*. Madison, WI: University of Wisconsin Press.

Gottman, J. M., & Notarius, C. (1978). Sequential analysis of observational data using Markov chains. In T. R. Kratochwill (Ed.), *Single subject research: Strategies for evaluating change* (pp. 237–286). New York: Academic Press.

Gottman, J. M., & Ringland, J. T. (1981). The analysis of dominance and bidirectionality in social development. *Child Development*, *52*, 393–412.

Holbrook, M. B., & O'Shaughnessy, J. (1976). Influence processes in interpersonal persuasion. In B. B. Anderson (Ed.), *Advances in consumer research: Vol. 3* (pp. 364–369). Ann Arbor: Association for Consumer Research.

Hollenbeck, A. R. (1978). Problems of reliability in observational research. In G. P. Sackett (Ed.), *Observing behavior volume II: Data collection and analysis methods*. Baltimore, MD: University Park Press.

Holm, R. A. (1978). Technique of recording observational data. In G. P. Sackett (Ed.), *Observing behavior volume II: Data collection and analysis methods* (pp. 99–108). Baltimore, MD: University Park Press.

Hulbert, J., & Capon, N. (1972, February). Interpersonal communication in marketing: An overview. *Journal of Marketing Research*, *9*, 27–34.

Jacobsen, N. S., & Moore, D. L. (1981). Spouses as observers of the events in the relationship. *Journal of Consulting and Clinical Psychology*, *49*, 269–277.

Johnson, S. M., & Bolstad, O. D. (1973). Methodological issues in naturalistic observation: Some problems and solutions for field research. In L. A. Hamerlynck, L. C. Handy, & E. J. Marsh (Eds.), *Behavior Change: Methodology, Concepts, and Practice* (pp. 7–68). Champaign, IL: Research Press.

Kassarjian, H. H. (1977, June). Content analysis in consumer research. *Journal of Consumer Research*, *4*, 8–18.

Kennedy, J. L., & Upoff, H. F. (1939). Experiments on the nature of extra-sensory perception: III. The recording error criticism of extra-chance scores. *Journal of Parapsychology*, *3*, 226–245.

Kotler, P. (1972, April). A generic concept of marketing. *Journal of Marketing*, *36*, 46–54.

Lamb, M. E., Suomi, S. J., & Stephenson, G. R. (1979). *Social interaction analysis*. Madison, WI: University of Wisconsin Press.

Lutz, R. J., & Kakkar, P. (1976). Situational influence in interpersonal persuasion. In B. B. Anderson (Ed.), *Advances in Consumer Research, Vol. 3* (pp. 370–378). Ann Arbor: Association for Consumer Research.

Mitchell, S. K. (1979, March). Interobserver agreement, reliability, and generalizability of data collected in observational studies. *Psychological Bulletin*, *86*, 376–390.

Olshavsky, R. W. (1973, May). Customer-salesman interaction in appliance retailing. *Journal of Marketing Research, 10*, 208–212.

Olshavsky, R. W. (1976). Consumer decision making in naturalistic settings: Salesman-prospect interaction. In B. B. Anderson (Ed.), *Advances in consumer research, Vol. 3* (pp. 379–381). Ann Arbor: Association for Consumer Research.

Park, C. W. (1982, September). Joint decisions in home purchasing: A muddling-through process. *Journal of Consumer Research, 9*, 151–162.

Parke, R. D. (1979). Interactional designs. In R. B. Cairns (Ed.), *The analysis of social interactions* (pp. 11–36). Hillsdale, NJ: Lawrence Erlbaum.

Pennington, A. L. (1968, August). Customer-salesman interaction in appliance retailing. *Journal of Marketing Research, 5*, 255–262.

Peter, J. P. (1979, February). Reliability: A review of psychometric basics and recent marketing practices. *Journal of Marketing Research, 16*, 6–17.

Rosenthal, R. (1976). *Experimenter effects in behavioral research.* New York: Irvington Publishers.

Sackett, G. P. (Ed.) (1978). *Observing behavior volume II: Data collection and analysis methods.* Baltimore, MD: University Park Press.

Sackett, G. P. (1978). Measurement in observational research. In R. B. Cairns (Ed.), *The analysis of social interactions* (pp. 25–44). Hillsdale, NJ: Lawrence Erlbaum.

Sackett, G. P. (1979). The lag sequential analysis of contingency and cyclicity in behavioral interaction research. In J. Osofsdy (Ed.), *Handbook of Infant Development.* New York: Wiley.

Sawyer, A. G., Deutscher, T., & Obermiller, C. (1980). Can seller/customer interaction and influence be studied in the laboratory. In J. Olson (Ed.), *Advances in consumer research, vol. 7* (pp. 393–399). Ann Arbor: Association for Consumer Research.

Sheth, J. N. (1975). Buyer-seller interaction: A conceptual framework. In B. B. Anderson (Ed.), *Advances in consumer research, Vol. 3* (pp. 382–386). Ann Arbor: Association for Consumer Research.

Sheth, J. D. (1981). Cross-cultural influences on buyer-seller interaction/negotiation process. In P. H. Reingen & A. G. Woodside (Eds.), *Buyer-Seller Interactions: Empirical Research and Normative Issues* (pp. 100–114). Chicago, IL: American Marketing Association.

Siegel, S. (1956). *Nonparametric statistics for the behavioral sciences.* New York: McGraw-Hill.

Taylor, J. L., & Woodside, A. G. (1980). An examination of the structure of buying-selling interactions among insurance agents and prospective customers. In J. C. Olson (Ed.), *Advances in consumer research, Vol. 7* (pp. 387–392). Ann Arbor: Association for Consumer Research.

Taylor, J. L., & Woodside, A. G. (1981). Exchange behavior among salesmen and customers in natural settings. In P. H. Reingen & A. G. Woodside (Eds.), *Buyer-Seller Interactions: Empirical Research and Normative Issues* (pp. 23–36). Chicago, IL: American Marketing Association.

Thomas, E. A. C., & Martin, J. A. (1976, March). Analyses of parent-infant interaction. *Psychological Review, 83*, 141–156.

Wampold, B. E. (1984). Tests of dominance in sequential categorical data. *Psychological Bulletin, 96*, 424–429.

Wampold, B. E., & Margolin, G. (1982). Nonparametric strategies to test the independence of behavioral states in sequential data. *Psychological Bulletin, 92*, 755–765.

Weitz, B. A. (1981a). Adaptive selling behavior for effective interpersonal influence. In P. H. Reingen & A. G. Woodside (Eds.), *Buyer-Seller Interactions: Empirical Research and Normative Issues* (pp. 115–123). Chicago, IL: American Marketing Association.

Weitz, B. A. (1981b, Winter). Effectiveness in sales interactions: A contingency framework. *Journal of Marketing*, *45*, 85–103.

Wilson, D. T. (1977). Dyadic interaction. In A. G. Woodside, J. N. Sheth, & P. D. Bennett (Eds.), *Consumer and industrial buying behavior* (pp. 355–366). New York: North-Holland.

Wilson, D. T., & Ghingold, M. (1980). Building theory from practice: A theory-in-use approach. In C. Lamb, Jr., & P. Dunne (Eds.), *Theoretical Developments in Marketing* (pp. 236–239). Chicago, IL: American Marketing Association.

Wilson, D. T., & Ghingold, M. (1981). Similarity-dissimilarity: A reexamination. In P. H. Reingen & A. G. Woodside (Eds.), *Buyer-seller interactions: Empirical research and normative issues* (pp. 88–99). Chicago, IL: American Marketing Association.

Woodside, A. G., & Reingen, P. H. (1981). Buyer-seller interactions: An introduction. In P. H. Reingen & A. G. Woodside (Eds.), *Buyer-seller interactions: Emprical research and normative issues* (pp. 1–10). Chicago, IL: American Marketing Association.

Woodside, A. G., & Taylor, J. L. (1980). Observations of buyer and seller transactions. In J. Olson (Ed.), *Advances in consumer research, vol. 7* (pp. 643–652). Ann Arbor: Association for Consumer Research.

Yarrow, M. R., & Waxler, C. Z. (1979). Observing interaction: A confrontation with methodology. In R. B. Cairns (Ed.), *The analysis of social interactions* (pp. 37–66). Hillsdale, NJ: Lawrence Erlbaum.

Part III Applications

7
Expanding the Ontology and Methodology of Research on the Consumption Experience

ELIZABETH C. HIRSCHMAN and MORRIS B. HOLBROOK

Introduction

Like any research tradition, the study of consumer behavior reflects certain ontological and methodological assumptions whose continual modification constitutes a necessary aspect of evolutionary progress (Laudan, 1977). Thus, Laudan (1977) defines the *ontology* of a research tradition as "the types of fundamental entities which exist in the domain" together with "the different modes by which these entities can interact" and its *methodology* as "certain modes of procedure which constitute the legitimate *methods of inquiry*" (p. 79):

> A research tradition . . . is a set of assumptions: assumptions about the basic kinds of entities in the world, assumptions about how those entities interact, assumptions about the proper methods to use for constructing and testing theories about those entities. (p. 97)

Laudan (1977) also emphasizes that changes in ontology and methodology are closely interconnected and are therefore likely to march together:

> the ontological and the methodological components of a research tradition . . . are often intimately related, and for a very rational reason: namely, that one's views about the appropriate *methods* of inquiry are generally compatible with one's views about the *objects* of inquiry. (p. 80)

In this chapter, we explore some proposed expansions in the ontology and methodology of consumer research. These comprise what Laudan (1977) calls "modifications in the core assumptions of the research tradition" (p. 98). We emphasize at the outset, however, that we intend these modifications *not* as revolutionary paradigm shifts, but rather as evolutionary aspects of progress in theory development (cf. Laudan, 1977, p. 98). Specifically, we wish to broaden our concepts of the elements involved in the consumption experience and of the interrelationships among these components and to extend our acceptance of the procedures and techniques appropriate for the systematic study of these consumption phenomena. These proposed ontological and methodological expansions reflect an emerging view of consumer behavior that enlarges the conventional decision-oriented approach to embrace a more experiential perspective.

In what follows, we begin by first disclosing some of the personal philosophical biases that inform our proposed redirection in the study of consumer behavior and lead us to our focus on the consumption experience. Reflecting these biases, we shall next suggest a broadened ontology in which consumption experiences involve complex reverberating networks composed of such components as thought, emotion, activity, and value. We shall then discuss some implications of this view for extending our methodology in the development and testing of theory beyond the traditional positivistic focus that has thus far characterized most consumer research toward more eclectic, creative, diverse, or even deviant pathways to theory development and more introspective, phenomenological, qualitative, or metaphysical approaches to validation.

The Consumption Experience

Background

Holbrook and Hirschman (1982) defined *the consumption experience* as "a steady flow of fantasies, feelings, and fun" and added that "this experiential perspective is phenomenological in spirit and regards consumption as a primarily subjective state of consciousness with a variety of symbolic meanings, hedonic responses, and esthetic criteria" (p. 132). In a related paper, dealing directly with hedonic aspects of consumer behavior, we discussed "the multi-sensory, fantasy, and emotive aspects of one's experience with products" (Hirschman & Holbrook, 1982, p. 92). Both papers developed a dialectical set of propositions and constructs in contrast with the then-prevailing cognitive or decision-making model of consumer behavior.

Where the dominant perspective viewed consumers exclusively as rational, information-seeking decision makers, we pointed to their accompanying tendencies toward arational, pleasure-seeking estheticism. Where the dominant view saw products as collections of functional, tangible attributes used for pragmatic ends, we viewed products as symbolic vehicles capable of creating strong emotive states in consumers and even capable of helping consumers to transcend their material surroundings (as, for example, during ecstatic states caused by music, dance, or art).

Since formulating those propositions, we have continued to evolve in our thinking about experiential consumer behavior (cf. Hirschman, 1983; 1984; 1985a,b,c), while others have also developed these notions in their own ways (Unger & Kernan, 1983; Ahtola, 1985; Spiggle, 1985). To date, however, it is probably fair to say that broad generalizations concerning the consumption experience have received the bulk of attention from researchers in this area, whereas more specific issues of ontology and methodology have received relatively less explicit thought. Indeed, much of the published research on experiential consumer behavior has continued to employ the conventional metaphysic of positivist science (cf. Anderson, 1983) and the traditional techniques of logical empiricism (e.g., rating scales, questionnaires, multivariate statistics).

To some extent this state of affairs has probably been unavoidable. Change in a pervasive scientific paradigm, such as the prevailing decision-oriented view of consumer behavior, is probably best accomplished by suggesting alterations in only one aspect of the world-view at a time (Laudan, 1984). Thus, we originally suggested modifications in the aims, values, and norms underlying that world-view (e.g., recognition of the importance of emotions and of the intangible aspects of products). Once such changes have been accepted, one can then venture to suggest that some alterations in ontology are also needed or that some changes in the methodology might also prove constructive. If all of these changes had been proposed simultaneously, they would doubtless have encountered far more resistance.

However, four years have now passed; the proposed redirections are no longer viewed as radical or dangerous; so it is now feasible to offer some additional suggestions for changes in the ontology and methodology of consumer research. In pursuing this objective, our task has been made substantially easier by a concurrent innovative movement within the discipline. This is the very palpable and arduously fought shift toward *relativism* in the philosophy of science utilized in marketing and consumer research (Anderson, 1983; Deshpande, 1983; Peter & Olson, 1983). Although relativism, per se, does not constitute an ontology or a methodology in the senses described earlier, the issues it raises concerning the socially constructed and context-bound nature of human knowledge permit the serious consideration of various philosophical traditions and methodological avenues that would earlier have been viewed as unacceptable within the boundaries of marketing science or consumer research.

Some Philosophical Biases Relevant to Consumers and Consumption

Before turning to more specific ontological and methodological questions, let us consider some broader philosophical issues relevant to research on experiential consumer behavior. Here, existentialism, humanism, Platonic idealism, phenomenology, subjectivism, and transcendentalism all have some aspects that relate, in various ways, to the consumption experience. Yet no one existing philosophy adequately captures all facets of this concept. Nor can we find any existing philosophy with all of whose tenets we would entirely agree. Thus, the most suitable revelation of our philosophical biases concerning research on experiential consumer behavior might enlist a series of statements outlining our basic beliefs about the nature of consumers and consumption. These statements encapsulate our personal ideology about consumers, the world, and life in general. While others have held similar beliefs before us, we can find no predecessors who have subscribed to the full set of convictions that we hold dear.

Consumers. Consumers are *people*. They are *not* merely decision makers, buyers, purchasers, owners, users, segments, numbers, probabilities, or data points. Each of these latter terms essentially de-humanizes consumers by reducing the consumer-as-person to the consumer-as-automaton. Consumers are complete, whole human beings, and we cannot tear one act or characteristic from that totality without irrevocably impoverishing the knowledge acquired.

Like many existentialists (e.g., Sartre, 1966, 1968, 1976) we view people as having a unique reality, an *existence* that precedes any specific acts they may undertake or any particular roles they may perform. This *totality*, not the simple sum of additive acts or roles, constitutes the human being. Further, each person, during the course of his/her life, is continuously *emerging into being*. There is no static end state, no final person; only a process of continuous emergence, continuous creation. Hence, statistics based on scales that measure one aspect of a consumer at one point in time may seem relatively meaningless within this philosophy. They are, at best, snapshots rather than movies and are dead numbers in that they capture bits of a person who is no longer there. This does not mean that we should abandon all quantitative measures, only that we should understand their limitations.

We believe, also, that human beings not only think, plan, and act; they also feel, appreciate, and react. Consuming, therefore, does not always (or even usually) involve *doing*; it can be responsive, reflective, and receptive. Humanistic psychologists like Maslow or Rogers and the transcendental or mystical philosophies of the East have most insistently recognized these human qualities (Pope & Singer, 1978; Tart, 1975). In this spirit, we believe that consumers display *spiritual* needs and yearnings, just as they exhibit "worldly" materialism. They possess *faith*, just as they do reason. They are moved by *passion*, just as they are also guided by intellect.

Further, not only do we regard spirituality, faith, and passion as important aspects of human life, we also hold them to be *desirable* aspects (cf. Cźikszentmihalyi & Rochberg-Halton, 1982). Far from viewing people as being "misguided" by their spirituality, "blinded" by faith, or "overcome" by passion, we see these phenomena as contributing to the depth, richness, and meaning with which they live their lives. Living without spirituality, existing without faith, and being without passion, we feel, leaves one in a cold, dry realm of pure intellect, facing one's mortality without hope and with no basis for reaching moral decisions other than the rationalist criteria of efficiency and effectiveness.

Consumption. The general view of consumers just espoused leads to a correspondingly subjective view of consumption. Consumption, we believe, is not something that people *do* to products (i.e., goods or services); rather consumption involves the experiences accumulating in consumers as they *interact* with products. This belief stems from two philosophical roots. First, it draws upon the philosophical tradition of extreme *subjectivism* (e.g., Berkeley, 1971; Bergson, 1902). To Bergson (1902), for example, no thing existed unless it was perceived. The presence of the sensory image within the mind of the perceiver constituted its reality; any objective reality of a thing beyond its perception was deemed unknown and unknowable. Berkeley (1971) went even further and questioned the existence of matter; the various images arising before our conscious minds and attributed to an external, objective world, he construed as a sort of elaborate cosmic joke. Kant (1982) posited that the human mind necessarily distorts reality in its attempt to make sense of external stimuli by fitting them into pre-existing cognitive structures (so that we may know the phenomenon but not the noumena), a position reiterated more recently by Bohm (1971, 1973), Ferguson (1980), and Watson (1979). This position posed the central challenge for phenomenology (e.g., Husserl, 1960, 1973).

Second, the subjective side of our view of consumption is tempered by the belief that it is an *interactive* phenomenon. Here our thoughts are closely tied to the philosophy of *phenomenology* (e.g., Husserl, 1960, 1973), which views human existence and the process of "becoming" as a continuous interplay between person and environment. Phenomenologists, it should be noted, do believe in a material world. In fact, they view the individual's reality as determined in large part by his or her objective environment. In essence, they posit (in contrast to the subjectivists like Berkeley) that a person is created or *made real* by interaction with the external world. Thus, the subjectivist would say, as Ulysses did in Tennyson's poem, "I am a part of everything I have met" (i.e., I have helped to create the world) whereas the phenomenologist would rephrase this passage, "Everything I have met is a part of me" (i.e., I have been created by the world).

In sum, we do not deny that there is a real world out there. In fact, we hold the interaction between that objective reality and subjective experience to be a topic of demonstrable importance. However, we also believe that the "reality" that matters most during consumption is that which is subjectively experienced, that which is in the consumer's mind. After all, that is what the consumer believes to *be real*. It, therefore, *is real* for the consumer. Thus, on this view, consumption consists fundamentally of experiences generated during interaction with products. The product may be a good or service, a sign or significate, a tangible or intangible, a thing or concept; in short, it may be any aspect of a person's environment. The consuming situation involves an interaction between that person and environment. The consumption experience responds to the nature of that person-environment interaction. The nature of this response provides the topic that we shall now address in our discussion of an expanded ontology in research on the consumption experience.

Ontology: An Expanded Model of the Consumption Experience

Some Ontological Modifications

The C-A-B-S Paradigm. For at least two decades, consumer researchers have tended to rely on a paradigm that can be traced back to Plato's distinction among cognition, affect, and conation. Specifically, the basic assumption guiding much or perhaps most research on consumer behavior is that cognition (C) determines affect (A) which in turn guides behavior (B). Generally, a feedback loop through some further variable such as satisfaction (S) is included to represent learning effects. We shall refer to this familiar representation as the C-A-B-S paradigm.

Holbrook (1985) has traced the development of the C-A-B-S framework from the early work of Howard and Sheth (1969), Andreasen (1965), Nicosia (1966), and Engel, Kollat, and Blackwell (1973) through the contributions of more recent writers such as Zaltman and Wallendorf (1979), and Assael (1981). Here, as in the continual revisions by Howard (1983), one finds a fundamental adherence to the C-A-B-S viewpoint. This faith in the basic schema receives support from related work in other disciplines. In communication research, for example, the familiar hierarchy of effects posits a forward flow of influence from cognition to affect to behavior (Lavidge & Steiner, 1961). Attitude models in psychology assume that cognitive beliefs and values combine to determine the affective responses that guide behavioral intention (e.g., Fishbein & Ajzen, 1975). This view coheres with the sociologist's concept of voluntaristic action systems (e.g., Parsons, 1937). Meanwhile, philosophers have proposed closely related theories of action such as Goldman's (1970) treatment of wants and beliefs (p. 74) of the desiring-intending-willing chain postulated by B. O'Shaughnessy (1980). Interestingly, this invisible college of writers from various traditions seldom cite one another. Nevertheless, generally, it probably would involve no great exaggeration to claim that some version of the C-A-B-S schema lies at the core of how most consumer researchers as well as many thinkers in other disciplines view the world.

Elaborations of the C-A-B-S Paradigm. Scientific progress may be characterized by the process wherein researchers notice anomalous deviations from the prevailing paradigm in a manner that eventually culminates in a crisis that can be resolved only by a paradigm shift or gestalt switch. Consumer research has not yet enjoyed its first such scientific revolution. Rather, most of us practice normal science and are still too wedded to the basis C-A-B-S schema to attempt anything really radical. We have instead concentrated on tinkering with the familiar framework and providing a series of elaborations and changes—all of which, implicitly or explicitly, take the C-A-B-S paradigm as their fundamental point of departure and proceed in the spirit of saving the underlying world view by making minor corrective adjustments in the theory. Holbrook (1985) describes such "epicycles" in some detail.

Expanding the C-A-B-S Paradigm Still Further. Our current belief is that previous modifications of the C-A-B-S schema, including our own, have not yet gone far enough toward expanding our conceptualization of the key variables and relationships involved. In other words, earlier elaborations have still not adequately transformed the ontology of our research tradition in consumer-behavior theory. In most applications, our view of the C-A-B-S model's components remains misleadingly narrow. "Cognition" almost always refers to beliefs, perceptions, or complex semantic networks composed thereof and stored in memory. "Affect" generally designates a simple bipolar continuum running from positive to negative, favorable to unfavorable, good to bad, pro to con, or like to dislike. "Behavior" usually includes the brand choices or purchase decisions of greatest interest in practical applications. "Satisfaction" tends to designate a comparison of actual against expected level of performance in a manner that rewards or reinforces the purchase event and thereby encourages brand loyalty. In short, though many psychologists have maintained broad views of these constructs, consumer researchers have built a tradition of regarding our key variables—cognition, affect, behavior, and satisfaction—in their most limited and narrow senses of "believing," "liking," "buying," and "learning." Moreover, we have stuck pretty tenaciously to the assumption of a forward flow of effects with a reinforcement feedback through satisfaction (C→ A→ B) ↔ S.

It appears that the vocabulary (variable names) and grammar (causal paths) built into the conventional C-A-B-S schema impose their subconscious influence on our thinking in a way that guides our ontology, whether we like it or not, in directions where we may not wish to have it pushed. We therefore propose to adopt a new vocabulary and grammar, a revised semantics coupled with a relaxed syntax, thereby to construct a language of consumer research that expands our conceptualization of its key components and extends our view of the relationships involved. In short, we attempt to replace the familiar C-A-B-S framework with what we call "An Expanded Model of the Consumption Experience." As noted earlier, we do not claim that this expanded model represents a paradigm shift, only that as one modification in the ontology of our research tradition (Laudan, 1977), it could form a link in the process leading toward progress if it were taken seriously as the basis for sustained attempts at validation.

An expanded model that embodies the proposed reorientation appears in Figure 7.1. Here, inputs from the person (motivation), the environment (information), and the person-environment interaction (situation) feed into the consumption process and are in turn affected by it. The consumption process itself involves thought (mental events), emotion (responding, interpreting, expressing, and feeling), activity (both action and reaction), and value (an interactive relativistic preference experience). These components (thought, emotion, activity, and value) interact and overlap among themselves and with the person and environment in a complex network of mutually interdependent relationships. In this view, then, the *consumption experience* may be defined as *an emergent property that results from a complex system of mutually overlapping interrelationships in constant reciprocal interaction with personal, environmental, and situational inputs.*

In the expanded model shown in Figure 7.1, we have replaced each of the familiar terms (cognition, affect, behavior, satisfaction) with a related but more broadly conceived component (thought, emotion, activity, value). Thus, the expanded model contains a broadened conceptualization of each building block in the consumption process (T-E-A-V). Moreover, it replaces the assumed linear flow of effects (C-A-B-S) with a system of overlapping, interdependencies. We shall return to the nature of these interrelationships and overlaps in a subsequent

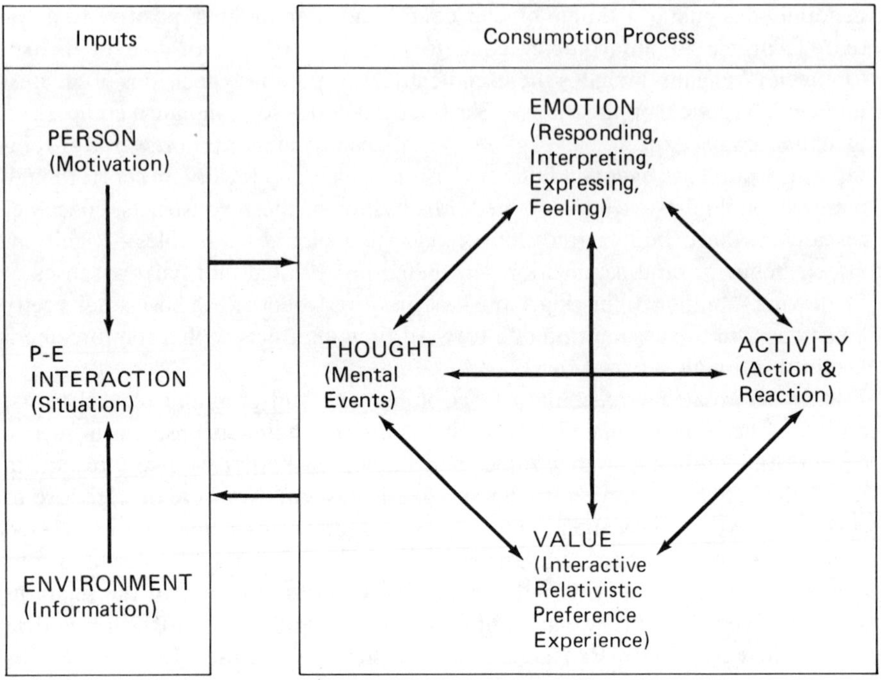

FIGURE 7.1. An expanded model of the consumption experience.

section. Here, we need only mention that T-E-A-V constitutes at most one of many possible causal paths through the model. Innumerable others exist (some of which, as discussed later, are probably not even causal in nature).

Model Inputs

Our conceptualization of model inputs draws upon the contrast often maintained between the *person* or agent and the *environment* or surrounding conditions (e.g., Lazarus, Averill, & Opton, 1970; Lewin, 1936, 1951; Mehrabian & Russell, 1974; Parsons, 1937). In addition, we follow several authors in regarding the consumption situation as a *person-environment interaction* (e.g., Ajzen & Fishbein, 1980; Denzin, 1984; de Rivera, 1977; Dickson, 1982; Drenan, 1983; Fennel, 1980; Kassarjian, 1973) and in viewing the resources, means, and abilities at the agent's disposal as part of that situational context (Harre & Secord, 1973; Parsons, 1937). Each of these model inputs now deserves more detailed comment.

Person (Motivation). We view the role of the *person* in consumer behavior primarily in terms of the *motivations* that people bring to the consumption experience. We use "motivation" to cover those explanatory factors that inhere within the person (as opposed to impinging from the outside). In this usage, "motivation" refers to the ends that guide purposive action and answer the question *why* some piece of behavior occurs. In other words, as used here, "motivation" involves internal mental states that explain consumer behavior.

Such mental states may be acute (e.g., desires and wants) or chemic (e.g., personality traits and values). They may be teleological (e.g., goals and objectives) or causal in nature (e.g., needs and drives). They may involve realistic expectations (e.g., purposes and aspirations) or unattainable longings (e.g., hopes and wishes). Moreover, their natures as answers to the question "Why?" depend on whether they are used retrospectively (to cover past action) or prospectively (to cover future action) and in the first person (regarding one's own action) or third person (regarding someone else's action). Thus, we may recast Von Wright's (1983) argument as a set of distinctions among intention (first-person prospective), prediction (third-person prospective), justification (first-person retrospective), and explanation (third-person retrospective). As modes of interpretation, all enrich our understanding of behavior. However, our view of motivation aligns most closely with the fourth category—namely, explanation.

Having defined motivation in consumption as a mental state that explains consumer behavior, we confront remaining questions concerning the nature of the different types of motivation that may come into play. Here, we encounter such widely used terms as needs, wants, wishes, hopes, desires, purposes, goals, objectives, ends, motives, drives, intentions, plans, reasons, and values (Davis, 1979). Some are near synonyms; some reflect key distinctions; and some belong elsewhere in our model of consumer behavior. Moreover, some authors blur concepts that others regard as fundamentally distinct. For example, as we shall see, Peters (1958) takes pains to distinguish between "reasons" and "motives," whereas Parsons (1937) treats the two as synonymous. Mitchell (1983) acknowledges the difference between "values" and "needs."

The basic concepts at stake are intimately bound up with the nature of means-ends relationships. For Parsons (1937), an end is "a future state of affairs . . . deemed desirable by the actor(s) but which differs in important respects from the state which they could expect . . . without active intervention" (p. 75). Philosophers concerned with the theory of action commonly refer to such ends in terms of "purposes" (Goldman, 1970), "desires" (Davis, 1979; B. O'Shaughnessy, 1980), or "wants" (Goldman, 1970; Hampshire, 1982). Such theorists generally argue that—when combined with beliefs about means-ends relationships—purposes, desires, or wants provide reasons for action. However, these thinkers are divided on the question of whether reasons should (e.g., Davidson, 1963; Goldman, 1970; B. O'Shaughnessy, 1980; Shaffer, 1968) or should not (e.g., Anscombe, 1957; Hampshire, 1982; Peters, 1958; Ryle, 1949; Von Wright, 1983) be regarded as causes of action. We shall return to this issue in a later section and shall suggest a resolution proposed by Thalberg (1977). Meanwhile, note the remarkable similarity of the philosophical theory of action to expectancy-value theory (e.g., Fishbein & Ajzen, 1975)—now called "the theory of reasoned action" (Ajzen & Fishbein, 1980)—in which beliefs are weighted by values to predict behavioral intention. Though Goldman (1970) acknowledges the work of some social scientists, explicit treatment of the parallels between psychology and the philosophy of action remains a fallow but fertile area for systematic exploration (Harre & Secord, 1973; J. O'Shaughnessy, 1980, 1985).

For guidance on the key relevant types of motivation, we may draw upon the careful distinctions made by Peters (1958) among wishes, reasons, wants, and motives:

> "motive"... is used in contexts where conduct is being assessed and not simply explained, where there is a breakdown in conventional expectations. (p. 35)
>
> The concept of "wish" is very like the concept of "motive" in that it always emphasizes directedness. But it... implies no grasp of the means necessary to attain what is wished for. (p. 63)
>
> At the consciousness level a wish becomes a reason for acting when logical and causal connections, together with norms of social correctedness, are grasped to connect what is wished for—the objective—with acts that lead on to it. (p. 65)

These distinctions emphasize the importance of the aforementioned means-ends connection and also bring social norms or conventions into play (another parallel with Fishbein's work). Specifically, Peters (1958) stresses contrasts between (a) *comprehending only an end* versus *understanding an efficient means-end relation* and (b) *conventional rule-following purposive action* (i.e., goal-directed behavior that conforms to social norms) versus *other unconventional goal-directed behavior* (i.e., purposive activity that falls outside social norms). Combining these distinctions, we may construct the classification shown in Table 7.1.

According to this scheme, a *reason* embodies understanding of an efficient means-end connection within the context of conventional rule-following purposive action. By contrast, in unconventional goal-directed behavior, the reason becomes a *motive*: We ask, "What was his 'motive' for doing that strange deed?" When deprived of clearly conceived means-ends relations, motives become *wishes* and reasons become *wants*. As already mentioned, other writers have referred to wants as "desires" or "purposes." For Peters (1958), wants differ from needs in that needs always imply a physical dependency wherein the absence of their fulfillment damages the individual. Clearly, not all needs result in corresponding wants (we may be oblivious to our own health and welfare), and not all wants reflect underlying needs (we may desire things beyond those physically required).

TABLE 7.1. A typology of motivation.

	Understanding an efficient means-end relation	Comprehending only an end
Conventional rule-following purposive action	Reason(s)	Want(s) (Desire(s)) (Purpose(s))
Other unconventional goal-directed behavior	Motive(s)	Wish(es)

Environment (Information). Readers who recall our earlier work (Holbrook & Hirschman, 1982), in which we criticized "the information-processing view" of consumer behavior, may be surprised to find us now defining the relevant *environment* by its capacity as a potential source of *information*. However, our earlier position attacked only a *narrow* information-processing perspective that views the consumer exclusively as a cognitively oriented decision maker concerned almost solely with making buying choices that result in purchase behavior. By contrast, we find a *broader* information-processing perspective entirely congenial and, indeed, virtually dictated by our aforementioned subjective-interactionist stance concerning the role of objective reality in the consumption experience. The external world plays a role in consumption only when it acts as a source of information with some subjective impact.

As often noted (see Holbrook, 1983a), information from the environment may reach a person in one of two *forms*: (a) as a *significate* (direct from some object such as a thing, event, or person) or (b) as *signs* (via symbols used to refer to that object, as in a promotional message or in some other communication from one's social environment). Further, the *source* of that information may be (a) *impersonal* (a thing or event) or (b) *personal* (other people). The latter distinction usually (though not necessarily) corresponds to a difference between one- and two-way communication according to whether the source does not or does respond to feedback from the receiver. Together, these contrasts suggest the classification of environmental information (with a partial set of examples shown parenthetically) in Table 7.2.

Information received direct from an *impersonal object*, such as a good or service, corresponds to the direct psychophysical effects of objective product characteristics or brand features mentioned earlier (Holbrook, 1981). By contrast, when the source is a *personal object*, such as a friend or family member, the transmission of information is likely to require some extrapolative or even speculative mediating inference—perhaps, for example, a guess concerning the norms or rules that govern that person's overt behavior (Von Wright, 1983). Such inferences benefit from the two-way nature of communication received from personal sources. Other people can answer questions. When they do or when they engage in attempts at persuasion, their messages become *personal signs*, such as

TABLE 7.2. Typology of environmental information.

	Impersonal source (Things or events)	Personal source (People)
Significate (Object)	Impersonal object (good or service)	Personal object (friend or family member)
Signs (Symbols)	Impersonal signs (ad or commercial)	Personal signs (salespeople or word of mouth or nonverbal communication)

those received from salespeople or in word of mouth from one's social contacts. Nonverbal social communication would also fall under this category. By contrast, when symbolic messages come from things or events like print ads or television commercials, such *impersonal signs* cannot aid interpretation by modifying their message in response to feedback from the receiver.

Our typology of environmental information retains much of the flavor of distinctions made many years ago by Howard and Sheth (1969). More recent treatments have further developed the contrasts (a) between significate and sign or direct and indirect experience (Fazio & Zanna, 1981; Holbrook, 1983a; Smith & Swinyard, 1983) and (b) between impersonal and personal or one- and two-way sources. In addition, one should recall a third distinction emphasized by Langer (1942) between *discursive* and *presentational* processes. Discursive information processing refers to experience in which elements occur separately as distinct units over time. By contrast, presentational experience involves the holistic apprehension of an entire pattern or configuration in the manner of a gestalt (Holbrook, 1983a). This distinction finds clear parallels in such related contrasts as verbal system/imagery system, successive/simultaneous, and left-brained/right-brained. However, Holbrook (1983a) argues that Langer's (1942) discursive/presentational duality is probably more fundamental than any of these more limited manifestations. As evidence of the venerable history of this basic distinction, we might recall Aristotle's ancient contrast between "aggregates" and "wholes," one long recognized by philosophers of art.

Person-Environment Interaction (Situation). We shall follow Lewin (1936, 1951) by defining the relevant *situation* as involving a *person-environment interaction* (cf. Ajzen & Fishbein, 1980; Denzin, 1984; de Rivera, 1977; Drenan, 1983; Fennell, 1980; Harre & Secord, 1973). Thus, for Lewin (1936, 1951), the "situation" or "life space" or "psychological field" comprises the relationship between person (P) and environment (E) that determines behavior (B):

> In summary, we can say that behavior and development depend upon the state of the person and his environment, B = F(PE). In this equation the person (P) and his environment (E) have to be viewed as variables which are mutually dependent upon each other. In other words, to understand or to predict behavior, the person and his environment have to be considered as *one* constellation of interdependent factors. (1936, pp. 239–240)

On this view, it follows that the consumption situation involves an interaction between a given consumer and his or her consuming environment (Dickson, 1982; Fennell, 1980; Kassarjian, 1973).

Among the many aspects of the consumption situation upon which we might choose to focus, we find some precedent for attending to the *resources* (or powers) that consumers bring to the consumption context (Harre & Secord, 1973; Parsons, 1937; Von Wright, 1983). For example, Harre and Secord (1973) view the individual's "personality" as "a cluster of . . . powers and liabilities" (p. 276) and see "circumstances" as "those conditions in the environment which are necessary for the exercise of a power" (p. 257).

TABLE 7.3. Typology of resources in the consumption context.

	Internal	External
Static	Ability	Money
Dynamic	Effort	Time

We shall distinguish among resources (or powers) in the consumption context according to whether they are (a) *internal* (originating in the person) or *external* (originating in the perceived environment) and (b) *static* (capable of measurement as a stock at any particular moment) or *dynamic* (observable as a flow in some process that unfolds longitudinally). Based on these two contrasts, we may derive the following classification of resources in the consumption context (with what we regard as one major example included to illustrate each).

As an easily observed and measured external static entity, *money* (and the expenditure thereof) has long preoccupied economists as a major resource deserving investigation in the study of consumer behavior. Recently, Becker (1976) has advocated a more dynamic approach to viewing consumption as a kind of productive activity in which *time* also serves as a key input. One internal static analogue of money might be construed as *ability*—a stock of knowledge, expertise, or prowess accumulated via experience, probably by reason of seeking competence (cf. White, 1959). A dynamic process by which this ability or competence gets invested in consumption activities involves *effort* or the expenditure of energy (cf. Parsons, 1937, p. 719).

The Consumption Process

As previously mentioned, our representation of the consumption process replaces the conventional narrow conceptions of cognition, affect, behavior, and satisfaction with four more broadly conceived constructs—namely, thought, emotion, activity, and value. Moreover, we shall view the latter as connected in a complex system of overlapping inter-relationships that together constitute the consumption process, with the consumption experience as a resulting emergent property. Let us therefore turn to a discussion of thought, emotion, activity, and value before proceeding to a consideration of systemic inter-relationships and overlaps in the consumption experience.

Thought (Mental Events). As noted earlier, "cognition" has generally been used by consumer researchers to refer to beliefs, perceptions, knowledge, or structure thereof stored in memory (e.g., Olson, 1980). However, this conventional usage of the term remains far too narrow to encompass the diversity of mental events that occur in the consumption process. Accordingly, we seek a term expansive enough to designate this broad spectrum of mental phenomena. Holbrook (1985) used the term "consciousness," but encountered problematic confusions when including *un*conscious phenomena under this heading. Another possibility, "mind," has been pre-empted by Ryle (1949) for special treatment in his sustained attack on the fallacies inherent in the dualistic assumption of a "ghost in the machine." Accordingly, we shall adopt Harman's (1973) use of "thought" to refer to the mental events of interest. *Thought* includes phenomena spread out at all positions along such dimensions as veridical/nonveridical (B. O'Shaughnessy, 1980), conscious/unconscious (Hilgard, 1980), waking/dreaming (Singer, 1966), and normal/altered (Pelletier & Garfield, 1976).

In loose correspondence with these continua, B. O'Shaughnessy (1980) has constructed what he calls "an epistemological-experiential map of the mind" (p. 167) in which he portrays mental events as a series of concentric circles, involving increasing degrees of cognizability/experienceability from the center out, as follows:

1. Neither experienceable nor cognizable (forgetting)
2. Possibly cognizable (believing, understanding, intending)
3. Experienceable conceptual consciousness (glimpsing, hearing, listening)
4. Experienceable alternative consciousness (imaging, emoting, dreaming)
5. Nonmental psychological (pain, kicking, bodily striving)

According to this schema, sensation occurs at the outermost periphery (nonmental psychological) via a mechanism remarkably like Brunswik's Lens Model in which an external object works through a sensation to affect an internal perception (Holbrook, 1981). The degree of perceptual veridicality/nonveridicality then depends on the extent to which the internal object (intentionality) corresponds to the external object (physical reality) (p. 270; cf. Holbrook & Bertges, 1981; Holbrook & Huber, 1983). As noted earlier, this view of perception confronts a host of epistemological difficulties of the type raised by Berkeley (1971) that open the door to a possibly devastating skeptical or solipsistic plunge into what Cameron (1983) calls "the pathos of epistemological solitude" (p. 168). Accounts that treat sensation and perception as inferential processes (e.g., Harman, 1973) still must deal with the problem of knowledge (Lewis, 1946). One approach proposed by Adler (1985) distinguishes "that which" we directly apprehend (e.g., sensations) from "that *by* which" we apprehend the public world of external reality (e.g., perceptions). Only the latter are subject to the aforementioned standard of veridicality. Within this sphere, hallucinations, illusions, and spectres may be regarded as nonveridical perceptions.

The concept of consciousness raises problems that have long troubled both philosophers and psychologists (Hilgard, 1980; Jaynes, 1976; MacIntyre, 1958; Shaffer, 1968). Hampshire (1982) defines consciousness in a manner that remains fairly close to the consumer researcher's conventional concept of cognition:

> A man's present intentions and his beliefs about his present situation and environment, taken together, constitute his present state of consciousness. (p. 101)

Farther down in B. O'Shaughnessy's (1980) series of concentric mental circles, one encounters unconscious phenomena. These include beliefs and wants below the threshold of awareness that constitute the mainsprings of the Freudian psychoanalytic theory and that have been accepted as important causal antecedents by many psychologists (Brody, 1983) and by some philosophers working on the theory of action (Goldman, 1970; Harman, 1973; Peters, 1958). After dominating much work on consumer behavior during the era of motivation research (Dichter, 1960), the psychoanalytic model has passed into an eclipse from which it must be rescued if we are to obtain a fully rounded understanding of the consumption experience (Holbrook & Hirschman, 1982).

B. O'Shaughnessy's (1980) concentric circles also encompass the difference between wakeful states and dreaming. This contrast parallels a third dimension that Lewin (1951) introduced into his life space to represent the difference between what he called "reality" and "irreality." In the extreme, dreaming or irreality involves uncontrollable nonveridical imaginative experience. At intermediate points on the wakefulness/dreaming or reality/irreality continuum, one encounters daydreams (Singer, 1966), free pictorial imagery (Richardson, 1969), and other aspects of fantasy (Klinger, 1971). Elsewhere, we have argued that such imaginative components play a key role in the consumption experience (Hirschman & Holbrook, 1982).

Finally, we may note the contrast between normal and altered states of consciousness (Pelletier & Garfield, 1976):

> An altered state of consciousness . . . differs from the normal conscious state in that ordinary stimuli are processed in a significantly different way, giving rise to experiences that are not normal in Western culture. (p. 3)

In other words, one should regard altered states *not* as nonveridical, unconscious, or dreaming but rather as qualitatively different from normal mental events (Tart, 1975). As such, altered states may serve as the basis for otherwise unobtainable consumption experiences (Hirschman, 1985b). Castaneda's (1968) detailed experiential accounts indicate the manner in which this "way of knowledge" or "world of non-ordinary reality" may occur. Another example, due to Huxley (1954) appears later in this chapter.

Emotion. Holbrook (1985) has recently provided a lengthy review of the role of *emotion* in the consumption experience (see also Holbrook & O'Shaughnessy, 1984). We shall therefore confine our present remarks to a brief account of the key components in the emotional process—physiological responses, cognitive interpretation, behavioral expression, and feelings—which we shall here refer to as "responding, interpreting, expressing, and feeling." Holbrook's (1985) treatment presents these four components as comprising an interlocking network of mutual interdependencies with no necessary causal priority among its constituent parts (cf. Denzin, 1984; Giorgi, 1970). This network of inter-relationships may therefore be construed as a microcosm within the more macrocosmic system shown in the representation of the consumption process that appears in Figure 7.2.

Responding. Virtually all theorists agree that emotion entails physiological responses of the autonomic and central nervous systems (e.g., Izard, 1977; Lyons, 1980; Mandler, 1975; Plutchik, 1980; Strongman, 1978). Good reviews

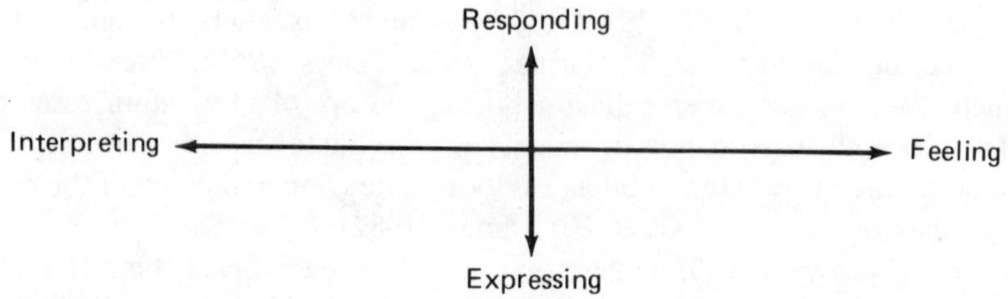

FIGURE 7.2.

of such psychophysiological measures on EKG, GSR, EMG, and EEG appear in work by Grings and Dawson (1978), Hassett (1978), Kroeber-Riel (1979), and Lang, Rice, and Sternbach (1972). However, though hopeful research continues (e.g., Ekman, Levenson, & Friesen, 1983), we still await the emergence of clear one-to-one correspondence between physiological states and subjective emotional experiences. Rather, though some investigators remain critical (e.g., Brody, 1983; Reisenzein, 1983), many accept Schachter's (1971) argument that, as a necessary but not sufficient condition, physiological arousal receives its emotional label via the cognitive interpretation of the surrounding situation. This cognitive labelling theory clearly points to the role of interpretation in emotional experience.

Interpreting. Numerous researchers have emphasized the role of cognitive interpretation in forming an emotional response (Arnold, 1960; Lazarus, Averill, & Opton, 1970; Lyons, 1980; Mandler, 1975; Thalberg, 1977). Though Zajonc (1980) argues that affective responses may happen independent of cognition or even recognition (Zajonc & Markus, 1982), simple logic convinces us that emotional responses rarely if ever occur without some interpreting, even if that thinking remains entirely at a subconscious or unconscious level (Lazarus, 1982; Thalberg, 1977). The most reasonable position appears to be that cognitive interpretation acts both as a cause (via appraisal) and as an effect (via attribution or labelling) of physiological responses (Dienstbier, 1979; Kleinginna & Kleinginna, 1981). In addition, both components (interpreting and responding) interact further with behavioral expression and feeling.

Expressing. Behavioral expression includes such overt manifestations as body postures, nonverbal gestures, facial mien, and vocalization (e.g., Bedford, 1981; Birdwhistell, 1970; Harre & Secord, 1973; Izard, 1977). These expressive movements communicate both externally (to significant others) and internally (as feedback upon which to base further interpreting, responding, and feeling). (For a detailed review, see Cacioppo, Losch, Tassinary, & Petty, 1985.) Indeed, in some cases, behavioral expression seems to serve not only as a concomitant but as the very target of the consumption experience. One clear example involves artistic creativity in which the artist in some sense consumes the creative process. Some theorists view artistic activity as synonymous with emotional expression (Langer, 1942; for a review see Holbrook & Zirlin, 1985). In this light, Sudnow (1978) provides an indispensible account of the experiential aspects of bodily participation in the expressive gestures required to play jazz piano. He analyzes the rule-following, way-seeking, course-running nature of improvisatory musical activity in a way that elucidates the experience of the behavioral expression and that clearly indicates the relation of creation to consumption.

Feeling. Responding, interpreting, and expressing generate feelings that belong to a subjective, phenomenological, experiential component of the emotional system. These aspects of lived consciousness, Lebenswelt, or the life-world—though potentially difficult to measure by the conventional precepts of positivistic science—cannot be ignored in an adequate account of the emotional process (Denzin, 1984; de Rivera, 1977). Indeed, any treatment of psychology that ignores feelings simply denies the humanity of its subject matter. In short, as noted by Rey (1980), feelings distinguish people from machines. Machines don't feel. Feelings make people human.

Activity. Behavioral expression forms one direct link between emotion and activity. Another link, running in the opposite direction, ties emotional responses to consuming activities. Here, we choose the term "activity" with some care. It includes both physical and mental events (B. O'Shaughnessy, 1980, p. 193) and corresponds to what Davis (1979) calls "doings" (pp. 4–5). In this usage, *activity* includes not only *action* (as described by the aforementioned philosophers concerned with the theory thereof), but also *reaction* (as embodied by relatively passive appreciative responses and other nonintentional behavior). We shall contend that these two facets of activity—action and reaction—constitute different circuits within the network of components in the overall consumption experience. In the active circuit, person and thought dominate. By contrast, in the *re*active circuit, environment and emotion play predominant roles.

One encounters the intended contrast between action and reaction in Ryle's (1949) distinction between reasons and causes (pp. 88–89), in Lewin's (1951) contrast between "directed action" and "emotional reaction" (p. 131), in Deci's (1975) emphasis on the difference between responses to inputs from memory or internal states and from the environment (pp. 122–128), and in Von Wright's (1983) related differentiation between internal determinants that shape intentions and external determinants to which the agent responds. However, the action/reaction contrast receives its most sustained attention from Harre and Secord (1973), who distinguish between "things done *to* a person" and "things done *by* a person" (p. 148) and who counterpose "a view of man . . . as a passive 'subject' who . . . reacts" with "a view of man as an active, self-directing, self-monitoring agent" (p. 297). These authors hasten to add that most behavior involves "enigmatic episodes" located somewhere between these two extremes, for which "adequate understanding may be reached only by an exploitation of both models" (p. 171). We shall therefore look briefly at the active and reactive formulations, with the understanding that a complete exploration almost always involves both.

A well-established stream of philosophical thought on the theory of action employs a type of logic called "practical reasoning" that Von Wright (1983) traces back to Aristotle by way of Anscombe (1957): In Von Wright's (1983) practical syllogism, (a) one wants to attain X (the first premise); (b) unless Y is done, X will not be attained (the second premise); (c) therefore, Y must be done (the conclusion). Thus, the steps are (a) a want, (b) a belief, and (c) an act. This corresponds to what Harman (1973) calls "common sense psychology" in which "the desire that P and the belief that Q *if* P . . . explain the desire that Q" (p. 56): In this view, wants and beliefs constitute reasons for action in the sense described earlier when discussing motivation. Action is defined as intentional if reasons operate in this manner so that "to know a primary reason why someone acted as he did is to know an intention with which the action was done" (Davidson, 1963, p. 689). Thus, intentions (Ajzen & Fishbein, 1980; Hampshire, 1982, p. 131)—or such related concepts as plans (Goldman, 1970), purposive rule-following (Harre & Secord, 1973) and volition (Davis, 1979)—become the distinguishing characteristics of action.

In B. O'Shaughnessy's (1980) hierarchy of desiring-deciding-choosing-intending-striving-willing, intention plays a mediating role comparable to its function in the model of consumer behavior proposed by Howard and Sheth (1969). J. O'Shaughnessy (1980, 1985) has further developed the role of practical reasoning in shaping consumers' intentional *actions*: "Goals, wants and beliefs . . . lead to the formation of an *intention* to buy. As such, they constitute the rules or reasons for buying" (1984, p. 211). Clearly, however, not all (and perhaps not even most) consumer behavior is intention in the manner just described. Rather, we must recognize a class of "sub-intentional" behavior (B. O'Shaughnessy, 1980, pp. 59–60; Von Wright, 1983, p. 58) that includes not only impulse purchases (buying behavior) but also the broad spectrum of consumption experiences (consuming behavior) that we have called "fantasies, feelings, and fun" (Holbrook & Hirschman, 1982). As a paradigm for intentional action, Anscombe (1957) chooses the example of a man making purchases in accord with a shopping list he has himself made (p. 56). But remarkably few consumption experiences hinge on the intentions implicit in that paradigm. Indeed, many lie entirely outside the scope of reasoned, purposive action. In the case of fantasies, we do not say that we "intend" to daydream; rather we say, "As I looked out the window at the snowflakes falling past the sooty icicles, I could not help daydreaming about a sunbath on a warm beach at Cancun." Similarly, with rare exceptions (Hochschild, 1983), we do not "plan" our feelings (Ryle, 1949, p. 214), but instead regard emotions as instances of being moved (de Rivera, 1977) wherein "Feelings . . . are things that happen to us" (Falk, 1983, p. 79). Similarly, we may learn the details of a work of art, but cannot necessarily force ourselves to appreciate it—as in Lewis' (1946) contrast between "knowledge imbued with the interests of action" and "esthetic apprehension . . . freed from the urge of doing" (p. 441). Finally, we do not necessarily "mean" to have fun, but instead may say, "I found myself enjoying the party immensely." In these and related instances, we may describe consumer behavior as reactive. It involves something that happens to us without our intention as opposed to something that we make happen intentionally. Many consumption experiences involve *reactions* in this sense.

It seems reasonable to conclude that, as contrasting types of activity, action and reaction involve different paths through the consumption experience or different circuits in the network of overlapping inter-relationships involved in consumer behavior. The action circuit involves a preponderance of inputs from the person (wants and beliefs) and engages one's thought processes (practical reasoning). The reaction circuit shows greater sensitivity to environmental inputs (symbolic meanings) and contains large emotional components (joy, love, anger, fear). The action circuit falls under the norms of rationality (B. O'Shaughnessy, 1980; Parsons, 1937) and is amenable to questions of the form "Why?" (Anscombe, 1957) which can provide explanations in terms of reasons (Davis, 1979) that fall primarily under the logical rules imposed by the Ego on secondary process thinking according to the reality principle (Hilgard, 1962; Peters, 1958). The reaction circuit bypasses rational means-ends relationships, often treating consumption activities as ends-in-themselves (Deci, 1975; Holbrook, Chestnut, Oliva, & Greenleaf, 1984) and is amenable to questions of the form "How?" which concern meanings or interpretations that may be illuminated through story telling (Davis, 1979) and that fall at least partially under the illogical control of the Id in primary process thinking according to the pleasure principle (Hilgard, 1962; Peters, 1958).

We hope that, in advocating the recognition of reactions along with actions as important types of activity in the consumption process, our remarks will not be interpreted as claiming the desirability of the former at the expense of the latter. Both contain much that is noble in human behavior. For example, reactions encompass esthetic responses and spiritual faith; actions embrace artistic creativity and moral virtue. Indeed actions constitute the domain for the exercise of volition or free will: "A person is more free . . . in proportion as his intentions are a reliable guide to his actions" (Hampshire, 1982, p. 285).

Value. Consumption activities—actions and reactions—result in value. Conversely, the perception or anticipation of value can lead to consumption activities. Buying involves an effect of value on activities; consuming involves an effect of activities on value. Therefore, because of its close interdependence with activity, value may be either active or reactive in the senses previously defined (a point soon to be developed further).

Though long neglected by consumer researchers, this topic has concerned a branch of philosophy known as axiology or the theory of value (Brightman, 1962; Frankena, 1967; Taylor, 1961). Reviewing work in this area, Holbrook (1984a) defines *value* as *an interactive relativistic preference experience*. It is *interactive* in that it entails a relationship between some person (subject) and some object (significate) or symbol thereof (sign) (Morris, 1964). It is *relativistic* in the three senses of being (a) *comparative* among objects (Lamont, 1955), (b) *personal* and differing among people, and (c) *situational* and dependent on the context in which an evaluative judgment occurs (Belk, 1975). Such evaluations result in *preference* and are therefore closely linked to the positive/negative affective polarities of emotion. These emotional components infuse value with an admixture of subjective *experience* (Baylis, 1958). Indeed, as previously mentioned, no product (good or service) can confer value except through its contribution to a consumption experience.

Notice the distinction that this definition implies between "value" (singular) and "values" (plural). The former, as just described, refers to an evaluative judgment that results in preference. The latter refers to the criteria or standards by which such evaluations are made (Baylis, 1958; Taylor, 1961). In our schema, such values (plural) underlie the motivations that a person brings to the consumption situation. They have, of course, been assessed by a wide variety of psychographic measures (e.g., Mitchell, 1983).

Holbrook (1984a) distinguishes among various types of value according to two major contrasts: (a) extrinsic/intrinsic and (b) self-oriented/other-oriented. *Extrinsic* value regards some object as a means toward some further end and is therefore instrumental, utilitarian, and practical; *intrinsic* value results from the appreciation of some experience for its own sake as an end in itself and is therefore self-justifying, autotelic, or ludic (Baylis, 1958; Brightman, 1962; Frankena, 1967; Goldman, 1970; Taylor, 1961). This contrast has recently received considerable attention in the psychological literature under the heading of extrinsic versus intrinsic motivation (e.g., Deci, 1975; for a review, see Holbrook et al., 1984). *Self-oriented* value depends on one's own response, whereas *other-oriented* value depends on the relationship of one's own self to the responses of other people or to some other significant aspect of the cosmos (Goldman, 1970; Morris, 1964; and especially Mukerjee, 1964). This contrast parallels the distinction between attitudinal and normative components in the extended Fishbein model (Fishbein & Ajzen, 1975). Combining the extrinsic/intrinsic and self/other distinctions produces the classification shown in Table 7.4.

Each type of value permits a further distinction based on whether it stems from an action or a reaction (as previously defined). Thus, *economic value* entails utility in the use of some means toward self-interested ends (Lamont, 1955) and may involve efficiency (active) or excellence (reactive). *Hedonic value* remains self-oriented but focuses on experiences enjoyed for their own sake as sources of pleasure (Baylis, 1958; Frankena, 1967), as in play (active) or esthetics (reactive). By contrast, *social value* maintains the extrinsic focus on means-ends relationships but hinges on the status-relevant responses of other members of society (Lamont, 1955), as in success (active) or esteem (reactive). *Deontological value*

TABLE 7.4. A typology of value in the consumption experience.

	Extrinsic	Intrinsic
Self-oriented	Economic value	Hedonic value
Other-oriented	Social value	Deontological value

implies larger aspects of the cosmos (e.g., society at large, the universe, or the deity) and deals with obligations or duties pursued as ends in themselves, as when moral virtue is its own reward (active) or religious faith expresses spiritual fulfillment (reactive).

Together, these types of value suggest categories of emotional responses to actions and reactions *any or all* of which may occur in a given consumption experience (Morris, 1964). Thus, we may appreciate a painting esthetically even while using it to cover a crack on the wall. We may gain social status from our most altrustic deeds. And so on. This copresence of different types of value and their variance across consumption experiences afford rich topics for research in an area where we have just begun to scratch the surface (Holbrook & Corfman, 1984).

Systemic Inter-Relationships and Overlaps in the Consumption Experience

Thus far, our proposed ontological modifications in the consumer-research tradition have dealt primarily with changes in our conceptualization of the entities involved in the consumption experience. However, we must also consider the relationships among these constructs. Here, our revised ontology suggests a system of interdependencies and overlaps that cause us to question the traditional causal scheme in favor of viewing the consumption experience as an emergent property or gestalt-like phenomenon.

The System of Interdependencies

As consistently maintained throughout the preceding discussion, we cannot reduce the consumption experience to any simple linear flow of effects from person and environment to thought to emotion to activity to value. Rather, these variables interact in a network of interdependencies to form a system of mutual inter-relationships. In Parsons' (1937) terms, this network or system constitutes an "organic" whole (pp. 31-32) composed of a " 'web of interwoven strands' " (p. 740). In Lewin's (1936, 1951) field theory, "the various parts of a given life space are to some degree interdependent" (1951, p. xii) so that "the state of any part of this field depends on every other part of the field" (1951, p. 25).

Conventional consumer research focuses on the forward flow of effects (a) from personal and environmental inputs to the consumption process and (b) within the consumption process from cognition to affect to behavior to satisfaction. Similarly, our discussion has shown (a) how model inputs from the person and environment affect the consumption process and (b) how thought shapes emotion to guide activity to generate value. We must also insist, however, on the *equally important* reverse causalities in which (a) the consumption process affects personal and environmental inputs and (b) activity and value affect thought and emotion. Presenting our variables in the sequence chosen (thought, emotion, activity, value) simply reflects the tradition of research on the C-A-B-S model. We could, with equal logic, discuss these constructs in any other order whatsoever. Where one starts in the interdependent system reflects nothing more than an arbitrary convention.

Overlapping Constructs. It should also be clear by now that, beyond their interdependence, the entities comprising our ontology of consumer behavior also overlap in various ways. Thus, emotion involves thought via the role of cognitive interpretation and activity via the role of behavioral expression. Action entails thought via the role of belief components. Value contains an emotional component associated with preference. Further examples could be constructed, but the general point should be transparent: thought, emotion, activity, and value overlap by virtue of the manner in which each includes aspects of the others.

This state of affairs suggests that, as a representation of our emerging ontology, the boxes and arrows that appear in Figure 7.1 to indicate mutual interdependencies in the consumption experience might better be replaced by a Venn diagram more suited to conveying the overlapping pattern of inter-relationships. In addition, such a diagram helps capture certain relevant aspects of Lewin's (1936, 1951) topological psychology. As already noted, Lewin regarded behavior as a function of the person-environment interaction contained in the "situation" or "life space" or "psychological field" (terms that he tended to use interchangeably). Drawing on principles from topology, he suggested that behavior could be described as *locomotion* along a *path* from one *position* into some other *region* of the life space. Regions differ in the *resistance* of their boundaries, some being easily crossed (*permeable*) and others being more difficult to penetrate (*solid*). Regions can *overlap* or *intersect*, thereby forming *sub-regions*, where movement between subregions may be easier than movement into entirely new regional areas.

Following this topological approach, Figure 7.3 presents an alternative view of our expanded model of the consumption experience. In this diagram, the situation consists of an environment that contains a consumer shown as a person positioned at a point located within the larger psychological field. The consumption process appears as a fan-leaf-clover pattern composed of three partially overlapping ellipses (thought, emotion, and activity) and a fourth donut-shaped region (value) superimposed on the first three. Notice that the value region must assume the donut shape with a hole in the middle in order to allow for the inclusion of all eleven types of two-, three-, and four-way intersections among the four major subfields. Consumer behavior may now be envisioned as a locomotion wherein the consumer follows a path indicated by the arrow drawn into the clover-shaped consumption process. Conceptually, the consumer's consumption experience might begin in any of the four subregions (thought, emotion, action, value) and might move rather freely among the various overlapping areas formed by their intersections. Locomotion within this particular consumption process would be more fluid than movement into some entirely different region of the life space involving some unrelated type of experience.

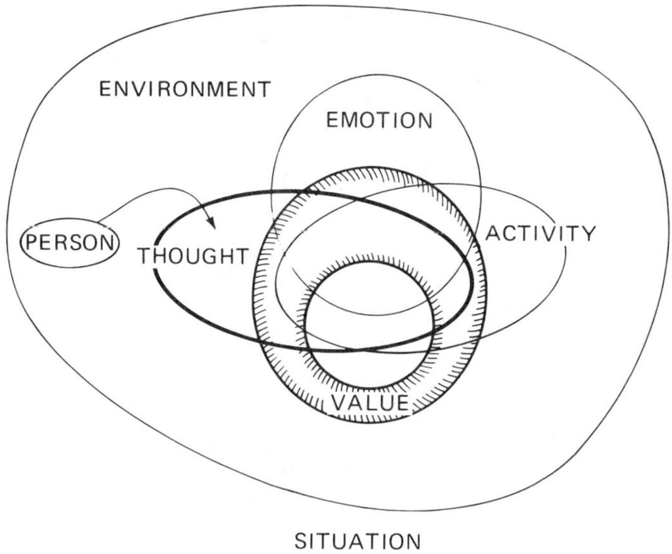

FIGURE 7.3. Alternate view of an expanded model of the consumption experience.

The Consumption Experience as an Emergent Property

Having recast the boxes and arrows of our original representation of the consumption experience into a Venn Diagram showing the configural pattern of overlapping regions, we must also reassess the role of causality in our ontology of consumer behavior.

Questions concerning the nature of causality in our view of the consumption experience stem from two sources. First, our points concerning the system of interdependencies suggest that everything depends on everything else; nothing is detached from these inter-relationships; all variables are endogenous and none is exogenous. For purposes of statistical modeling, such a system is not identified so that relative magnitudes and directions of causal links cannot be estimated. Those fond of systems of simultaneous equations and structural modeling will doubtless look askance at this conclusion. But we cannot resist the force of this basic truth; that, within any realistically rich representation of the consumption experience, true causal effects have been, are, and will continue to be extremely difficult or verging on impossible to estimate reliably.

Second, the fact that our constructs overlap casts further doubt on causal interpretations of their inter-relationships. Since Hume, philosophers have insisted that conceptual independence is a necessary condition for causality. If one construct logically entails another, it cannot be said to cause it. On these grounds, for example, many philosophers have refused to regard reasons as causes of actions because they view actions as logically entailing the conjunctions of beliefs and wants that are themselves defined as reasons (e.g., Anscombe,

1957; Peters, 1958; Ryle, 1949). Thus, according to this view, "a reason for an action is not logically distinct from the action; therefore, reasons are not causes of actions" (Davidson, 1963, p. 695, summarizing a perspective with which he disagrees). For our purposes, the force of this argument extends well beyond the sphere of reasons and actions because, on this construal, none of our constructs that overlap conceptually can affect each other causally.

Thalberg (1977) has attempted to rescue the causal connection between reasons and behavior by proposing a "component analysis" in which an event (e.g., action) may entail certain subevents (e.g., reasons and bodily movements) while still permitting a causal relation between the two components. This analysis may rescue some aspects of the consumption experience from causal oblivion. For example, if emotion entails both cognitive interpretation and physiological responses, it is possible in some circumstances for interpreting to cause responding (though not, of course, for interpreting or responding to cause the emotion). However, this move still leaves those parts of our model that do involve conceptual overlaps (most of Figure 7.2, for example) in a kind of causal limbo that further reinforces our doubts concerning the possibility of establishing firm causal links among the entities that compose our ontology of the consumption experience.

We arrive, then, at a view of the consumption experience as a complex system of mutually overlapping interdependencies where the distinction between entailment and causality may elude easy disentanglement. Such a view coheres with Lewin's (1951) view of "dynamic unity" in which "the state of one part within the whole depends upon the state of other parts of that whole" (p. 120), with Ryle's (1949) concept of "mind" as "one concatenation of events" (p. 167), with Shaffer's (1968) perspective a "mental phenomena" as "a large network of roads that crisscross, overlap, parallel each other at places and diverge at others" (p. 7), with Harre and Secord's vision of the "human being" as "a system of a different *order* of complexity from any other existing system, natural or artificial" (p. 87), and with McGuire's (1973) "nets of causally interrelated factors" involving "multivariate complexity,... parallel processing, bidirectional relationships, and feedback circuits" (but cf. Belk's 1984 warnings about such models). In short, like other aspects of human behavior, the consumption experience is a complex concatenation, a network, a web, an organic whole, a dynamic unity, a reverberating system of mutually overlapping interdependencies. It is a Gestalt in which "any part depends upon every other part." Thus, in the end, the long sought-after consumption experience must be viewed as *an emergent property that results from the inter-relationships and overlaps among person, environment, thought, emotion, activity, and value.*

Methodology: Some Extensions in Techniques for Studying the Consumption Experience

The ontology underlying our view of the consumption experience suggests a need for research methods that go beyond those common to positivistic science and logical empiricism. The rationale for positivism requires assumptions of researcher objectivity and personal distance from the phenomenon of investigation. But these assumptions contradict the spirit of experiential consumer behavior, whose very nature constitutes a subjective human process. Hence, to investigate and comprehend experiential consumption, a researcher must become as *personally involved* with the phenomenon as *humanly* possible. Thus, the humanity of researchers and their ability to think, to feel, to act, and to value as consumers do will facilitate their understanding of consumption experiences.

We must shift from our usual scientific posture of personal distance and the imposition of an a priori theoretical structure upon the consumer to a posture of greater personal *openness*. We must be receptive to structures and meanings as they flow *from* the consumer. We must strive to understand consumers' experiences in *their* terms and must refrain from forcing those experiences into some pre-existing structure that we have generated.

We shall distinguish two essentially humanistic methods that emerge from this viewpoint. The first, *role taking*, depends on the researcher's learning to take the role of the other. The second involves the researcher's use of self-cultivation and introspection.

Role Taking. The role-taking researcher conducts science by means of personal, emotional involvement with other humans, seeking insight into their lives, motives, and values. Mitroff and Kilmann (1978) describe this as an "intense concern with capturing and describing the uniqueness of individual human beings . . . [taking] to heart the dictum to treat everyone as a unique means, rather than an abstract, theoretical end" (p. 94).

The methodology followed by the role-taking researcher employs either the *case study*, as exemplified in clinical psychology, or *participant observation*, as exemplified in cultural anthropology (Mitroff & Kilmann, 1978). Both approaches seek to comprehend the life of another individual or group. To the role-taking researcher, all knowledge derives from personal contact and requires interpretation within the subjective context of both the observer and the observed.

Instead of reducing the individuals who serve as objects of inquiry to a set of data points or conceptual generalities, role-taking research tries to recreate them holistically. As Mitroff and Kilmann (1978) observe: "The preferred [scientific reporting] format is a personalized descriptive account of real human characters. Every attempt is made to capture the richness of detail of the lives of the characters: their strengths, weaknesses, hopes, dreams, and fears" (p. 97).

Personal Immersion. The methods employed in role-taking research align most closely with practices employed in ethnography, clinical psychology, and cultural anthropology. Although differences exist among these fields, the primary research procedure is the *immersion* of the investigator into the phenomenon under study. By "immersion," we mean the complete intellectual, emotional, and even locational involvement of the investigator with the object of study. In sharp contrast to the natural sciences, where researchers undertake elaborate steps to *distance* themselves from the objects of their investigations, the method of role taking *requires subjective involvement* on the part of the investigator.

Kaplan (1984) makes a similar point in his description of anthropological methods:

Effective observation of human affairs is virtually impossible without some degree of participation in what is being observed; without participation, data, even if somehow made visible, remain cryptic . . . Anthropologists . . . recognize that there is no substitute for actually *living* with a people, *participating* in their daily lives, learning their values from *personal contact* and *empathy*, and observing their *emotional reactions* at first range. (p. 33)

Interpretation via Empathy, Intuition, and Translation. The next step in the role-taking method is to provide an *interpretation* of the phenomenon in which one is participating. The investigator must rely upon two processes to arrive at an accurate interpretation—empathy and intuition.

Empathy is required because investigators must be able to project themselves into the others' reality, to see as they see, to feel as they feel, to believe as they believe. The process of empathy does not imply that the investigator must fully internalize the mind-set of the observed, but it does imply an ability to grasp the full implications of what that mind-set is.

An empathetic comprehension of the phenomenon must next be combined with *intuition* to arrive at an *interpretation*. In essence, intuition permits the investigator to *translate* personal comprehension of a phenomenon into propositional knowledge that can be communicated to the intended audience (for instance, other investigators). Levy (1981) provides a nice example of this interpretative process in his article on "Interpreting Consumer Mythology." Based on empathetic interviews with housewives, Levy constructed an intuitive interpretation of the meanings that various food items hold for consumers. He then communicated this interpretation to an audience of marketing researchers by using the diagrams and causal propositions that compose their "language." In essence, then, the role-taking method requires not only an empathetic participant-observer, but also an empathetic participant-*translator*.

Because the participant observer is a human being raised in a value-laden culture and not a tabula rasa, the role-taking method almost always poses interpretive difficulties. Within the method of role-taking, a consumer researcher's task is to unite the mental, emotional, (re)active, and evaluative aspects of the consumption experience through an interpretation of their human meaning. Because human thoughts, emotions, activities, and values are subjective, any interpretation that incorporates these entities must be subjective as well. Thus, to be complete, a humanistic interpretation must of necessity go beyond inherently fallacious attempts at mere objective quantification:

Data must be interpreted to serve as data; raw data is more likely to be indigestible than nourishing. It is sometimes supposed that the scientific value of research findings depends on a clear separation between observational data and theoretical inferences. A century ago Nietzsche condemned this belief as the "dogma of immaculate perception." There are always inferences in our observations. If facts speak for themselves it is inevitably in the accents of those who have uncovered and marshalled the facts. In the study of men, impersonal observation dehumanizes both observer and observed . . . what is to be avoided is not interpretation, but *projective* interpretation. Awareness that observer and observed are not identical need not deny to interpretation the resource of such sameness as does in fact exist. (Kaplan, 1984, pp. 34–35)

The interpretation of consumption experiences arrived at by role taking via the processes of empathy, intuition, and translation is analogous to the empirical findings generated within natural science, with one very important difference. The interpretation is recognized as *subjective* by both its creator and the audience of scholars to whom it is rendered. By contrast with the prevailing norm in the natural sciences, no pretense of impersonality, detachment, or distance is intended.

Problems of Validity. The role-taking investigator's stance as a subjective measuring instrument raises two issues not encountered so blatantly in logical empiricist science. The first concerns what has traditionally been termed the *internal validity* of the researcher's interpretation. That is, how do researchers "test" themselves to make sure that their interpretations are correct? How does one attempt to reduce the impact of the biases in one's perceptions so as to perceive honestly and openly? The second concerns traditional conceptions of *external validity*. That is, how do we contend with intersubjective conflicts among interpretations of the same consumption experience? If one empathetic consumer researcher sees one meaning in a particular set of behaviors or stimuli while a second observer sees a different meaning, how can we resolve this incongruence? Which interpretation is more appropriate?

Discussion of the first of these issues has been undertaken by anthropologists, by critics of literature and art, and by historians under the general heading of *the hermeneutic circle*. The basic premise of this argument contends that, if current perceptions depend on prior conceptions, then any interpretation or claimed observance of truth is always biased. Because conceptions are always reinforced by perceptions, truth remains unattainable.

However, the logical dilemma posed by the hermeneutic circle conceals an important oversight regarding human capabilities. Specifically, role-taking researchers are not necessarily trapped forever within their constricted worldviews. Despite their intrinsic biases and preconceptions, they do possess the mental capacity to expand, enlarge, and reconceive their views of reality. Hence, the hermeneutic circle need not turn inward upon itself, trapped in a vicious cycle of reinforcement. Rather, it can *spiral outward*, expanding its openness of comprehension as more and more personal experience is acquired.

Thus, the most effective way role-taking researchers can increase the appropriateness of their interpretations is through the *practice of interpreting*. As in the process wherein a novice pianist masters the instrument through early simple drills, followed by renditions of intermediate standard works, leading ultimately to interpretive playing of difficult pieces or even to composing, role-taking researchers master their investigative instrument—the self—by conditioned exposure to phenomena of interest. Empathetic vision, at first restricted by cultural dogma and ethnocentrism, will gradually give way to a redefined capacity to see life through the eyes of others and to translate the obtained vision back to one's own constituency.

The second issue of concern to role-taking research raises questions about how we can choose which of multiple interpretations most accurately reconstructs the phenomenon. This issue is very complex because, unlike natural science wherein some facts are viewed as unambiguous (e.g., the rate at which an object will fall in a vacuum) the phenomena of experiential consumer behavior give rise to multiple realities with multiple truths at different levels of abstraction.

One common reaction to this problem attempts to ascertain the *relative probability* or *likelihood* of a particular interpretation by means of evidence obtained from multiple sources external to the role taker. Thus, Ramsey (1973) concludes that, although the interpretive process is itself subjective, it does not differ in kind from the validation processes that occur in natural science:

> Intepretations and judgments (as other judgments involving value) are typically thought of as ambiguous, problematic, uncertain because it is the hard examples and not the easy ones which are chosen to discuss. [However], many judgments of "fact" are exceedingly problematical; many judgments of value are straightforward and sure. Some interpretations and judgments are certain, some highly likely, some dubious, some extremely eccentric. Interpretations and judgements are better or worse; to support them one can offer better or worse evidence, better or worse arguments. (p. 28)

Ultimately, just as with "facts" in the natural sciences, we must *choose* whether to accept or reject a particular interpretation of some phenomenon in the consumption experience. Because all "truths" are to some degree underdetermined by observable "facts," faith and personal conviction pose the same hurdles as in other research traditions.

Thus, the role-taking method seeks to establish the appropriateness of its interpretive findings through a logic quite similar to that employed in the natural sciences. However, there is one very important difference. The conclusions under assessment are explicitly acknowledged as *subjective* in origin. They are the products of human thought about human phenomena. They are recognized as relativistic and context-bound by both their creators and their evaluators—and herein lies their *strength*. Both the consumer researcher and the audience of evaluating scholars are aware of the subjective origin of an interpretation and its resulting potential for bias and distortion. Hence, knowledge acquired via role taking is always viewed as tentative and subject to reinterpretation. Ambiguity is accepted, embraced, and even lauded as an ineluctable aspect of scientific inquiry.

Example. To conclude this discussion of the role-taking method, we shall draw an illustration from a recent study by Hillery (1984), who clearly exemplifies one approach under consideration. Over the course of seventeen years, Hillery sojourned as a participant-observer in twelve Trappist monasteries where he attempted to discern the nature of the spiritual community and the types of communal love (especially sacrificial love or *agape*) found therein. Hillery utilized the *verstehen* approach of empathy—intuition—interpretation characteristic of role taking: "A subjective understanding of social action, which can be construed to mean an empathetic and intuitive interpretation as well" (Hillery, 1984, p. 313).

From his observations, Hillery discerned the significance of the activity of prayer within the sequestered religious communities under study:

> Understanding that prayer was central to monastic life was both a major breakthrough and a major difficulty. The breakthrough came in grasping the significance of prayer to monasteries. Ideally . . . monks pray because they love, particularly a form of sacrificial love known as *agape*. [However,] the difficulty in studying either prayer or agape is that neither can be [rationally] conceptualized; [rather they] must be *experienced*. . . . Thus, there were two basic phenomena which I *experienced* in studying monasteries: contemplative prayer and agapic love. I know without a doubt what these phenomena are. But I cannot *fully* . . . communicate this knowledge to anyone else. (p. 315)

At this point in the discussion, Hillery (1984) notes that his investigation must necessarily be based upon evidence obtained via human empathy and intuition and not through the instrumental/objective/intersubjective techniques common to the natural sciences:

> The problem I had encountered was this: what was true for monks, contemplative prayer, could not be assumed to be true or even real under conceptions of truth as employed, say, in classical physics. . . . One *assumes* the nature of truth. There is no way to prove (empirically) that any *experience* is *real*. (pp. 315–316)

However, Hillery (1984) notes that there is another form of truth derivable from human intuition and empathy with metaphysics different from those employed in the physical sciences: "The experience of prayer can yield a form of [subjective] truth" (p. 318). Hillery closes with a comment that aptly encapsulates the role-taking method:

> We must not assume that just because something is not fully observable in the scientific (i.e., empirical) sense, it does not exist. The human experience is too vast. There is much yet to be learned. (p. 331)

Self-Cultivation and Introspection

A second methodology for research on the consumption experience involves self-cultivation and introspection. As a guiding principle of this inquiry system, problems to be investigated are inevitably defined by reference to the investigator's own *self-concept* (Mitroff & Kilmann, 1978). In sharp contrast with the objective, distanced stance common to logical empiricism, the introspective researcher intentionally becomes personally, emotionally involved with the topics under investigation. This methodology views science as a value-laden enterprise into which one's own ethics and personal values are inextricably interwoven. In this sense, introspective researchers are often vocal advocates of a particular theory or intellectual position, especially when it has social, moral, or epistemic consequences they deem important.

Introspection and Evaluation. Much in keeping with the constructs of experiential consumer behavior, the practice of introspective investigation draws on processes of evaluation reminiscent of those found in esthetic philosophy, a source to which we shall therefore turn to develop this approach. Although it violates the democratic norms of logical empiricism to state that the conduct of introspective inquiry requires a certain *intrinsic nature* on the part of the investigator, this does appear to be the case. Introspective inquiry, perhaps more than any other type of inquiry system, is *self-generated*; its propositions and their evaluation are governed primarily by the *mind of the investigator.* Introspective outputs are less empirically-grounded than those of any other inquiry system. Hence, the quality of such research depends more than in other inquiry systems on the quality of the intellectual input devoted by the investigator.

Superficially, the research process for cultivated introspection begins in the same way as role-taking inquiry when the researcher exposes the self to a stimulus of interest and, using human responsiveness as the measuring instrument, insightfully records the impact of that stimulus on the self. In essence, such researchers *observe* their *own* consumption experiences—complete with thoughts, emotions, activities, and values—and then report these experiences as phenomenological output. In order to accomplish this effectively, like the role taker, the introspective investigator must possess diverse and deep human knowledge of all aspects relevant to the phenomenon under study.

However, two important differences distinguish the introspective and role-taking investigators. First, the objects of study in cultivated introspection are usually aspects of *material culture*—for example, paintings, advertisements, poems, novels, motion pictures, plays, music, automobiles, or television programs. In other words, they are the products with which the consumer interacts to acquire experiences. Second, the researcher interprets them not only in terms of what they meant to the artist (painter, poet, playwright, etc.)—which would be the role-taking approach—but rather focuses on what they mean to *the investigator* in terms of their intellectual content, emotional impact, appreciative reactions, and ethical value. Cultivated introspection thus goes *beyond* interpreting objects in terms of their significance to their creators or possessors and additionally provides personal commentary on their esthetic worth, social appropriateness, ethical value, and moral impact.

This latter point captures a very important distinction between cultivated introspection and the practice of logical empiricism or, for that matter, role-taking research. Whereas logical empiricism claims to exclude bias by the assumption of researcher distance and instrumental objectivity and even role taking strives for unprejudiced subjective interpretation of its phenomena, the method of cultivated introspection prescribes the *creation of an intellectual, affective, reactive, and normative critique of some experiential phenomenon*. Not only is the researcher's analysis subjective, it also encapsulates personal thoughts, values, and emotional reactions to the stimulus—thereby violating major operational taboos within logical empiricism.

It follows that the introspective investigator must possess an innate sensitivity to cultural phenomena and must combine this with knowledge obtained from other sources (e.g., exposure to historical data, philosophical schools of thought, diverse personal experiences, or artistic training) to provide a personal interpretation and evaluation of some object or phenomenon under study. To provide an interpretation of some consumption experience, the introspective researcher will attempt to "enter and dwell within it" much as does the role-taking researcher. However, having "entered" (personally responded to) the phenomenon, the introspective researcher will utilize two additional aspects of human responsiveness—namely, emotions and conscience.

Outputs. As the result of such an inquiry, the investigator will generate three types of *analytic outputs*: (a) a *cognitive interpretation* or *thought* (e.g., the object is a sonnet); (b) an *emotional reaction* (e.g., the object is expressing love) and (c) an *evaluative judgment* (e.g., the object is beautiful or morally inspiring). These three types of response are termed the "*Kantian Triad*"; i.e., cognition, emotion, and value (Kreiger, 1968, p. 26) and, of course, they combine aspects of the four central constructs in the consumption experience (thought, emotion, (re)action, and value).

We have already discussed the method used to develop the first of these (cognitive interpretation) in our previous discussion of role taking. Let us therefore turn to the second type of response—namely, emotion. Emotional response, though largely irrelevant to the physical sciences, is an essential ingredient of introspective inquiry, just as it is a central component of the consumption experience.

The third type of response provided by introspective inquiry is a judgment of value (esthetic appreciation, ethical contribution, social worth, epistemic importance, etc.). What does this object or phenomenon contribute to society? Is the world a better or worse place for the object's having been created or the phenomenon's having occurred? Is the object or phenomenon uplifting and inspiring or repulsive and debasing? Does it matter scientifically? Such assessments of normative value have sometimes been viewed as strictly extraneous to consumer research. Yet implicitly they pervade studies conducted to guide managerial decisions, public policy, consumer welfare, and the social impact of business. Cultivated introspection makes such value judgments overt and explicit so that they can be critically examined and rendered debatable by interested parties (cf. Holbrook, 1985).

All this does not mean that the audience of introspective researchers must accept all their value judgments concerning particular phenomena, issues, or consumption experiences. In the physical sciences, other investigators do not necessarily accept the conclusions drawn by a particular researcher regarding a given phenomenon; similarly, as individuals, consumer researchers need not accept the normative evaluations of an introspective colleague. But, whatever the cost in terms of intercolleagial friction, consumer research would be constructively broadened to include normative issues of importance to consumers and to those who study them.

The output format engendered by cultivated introspection will vary from one field to another. Within *journalism*, this type of output is usually labeled an *editorial*, to differentiate it from the news articles assumed to be factual. Within *philosophy*, such output might be termed an *essay*, as for example Locke's *Essay Concerning Human Understanding*. In *esthetics* such commentary is termed a *review* or *criticism*. In academic disciplines with a *social science* orientation—such as consumer research—such responses are typically termed *position papers*. In each case, however, the content of the output will contain intellectual, emotional, reactive, and evaluative components describing the author's response to a particular event or object. It is, in effect, a subjective reporting of one kind of consumption experience.

To use this method as an investigative technique, consumer researchers must be willing and able to record their own introspective reactions regarding consumption. They must be willing and able to report to their colleagues not simply an intellectual assessment of *someone else's* consumption behavior (the topic of traditional consumer research studies), but their own *thoughts, feelings, reactions* and *values* concerning personal consumption experiences. Further, the consumption experiences thus reported must not only be as authentically reconstructed as the researcher can manage, but must also be compelling and convincing to the intended audience.

Example. We close this discussion of cultivated introspection with an illustration of just such a report. Appropriately titled "The Doors of Perception," it recounts Aldous Huxley's (1954) first experience with mescaline consumption:

> I took my pill at eleven. An hour and a half later, I was sitting in my study, looking intently at a small glass vase. The vase contained only three flowers—a fullblown Belle of Portugal rose, shell pink with a hint at every petal's base of a hotter, flamier hue; a large magenta and cream-colored carnation; and, pale purple at the end of its broken stalk, the bold heraldic blossom of an iris. Fortuitous and provisional, the little nosegay broke all the rules of traditional good taste. At breakfast that morning I had been struck by the lively dissonance of its colors. But that was no longer the point. I was not looking now at an unusual flower arrangement. I was seeing what Adam had seen on the morning of his creation—the miracle, moment by moment, of naked existence. . . . What rose and iris and carnation so intensely signified was nothing more, and nothing less, than what they were—a transcience that was yet eternal life, a perpetual perishing that was at the same time pure Being, a bundle of minute, unique particulars in which, by some unspeakable and yet self-evident paradox, was to be seen the divine source of all existence. (p. 21)

Conclusion

This chapter offers, at best, a snapshot of one stage in an evolving view of consumer behavior. As a chapter in the present volume, it attempts to capture a momentary glimpse of a scenario that gradually unfolds in the authors' minds. Let us conclude with what we hope will prove a temporarily reassuring denouement.

In proposing certain ontological and methodological expansions in the consumer-behavior research tradition, we do not intend to foment any precipitous paradigm shift into metaphysical Never-Never land. Rather, in the sense proposed by Laudan (1977), we see our proposed modifications as part of an evolution in the existing tradition of research on consumer behavior. Toward this end, we have suggested a broadened set of central constructs (thought, emotion, activity, value) with an extended view of the overlaps and interrelations among those entities and have proposed some hitherto neglected methods for investigating some constructs and relationships.

We do not see these ontological and methodological modifications as a rejection of the prevailing paradigm. Rather, we see them as part of an evolutionary process that extends that tradition into new domains. Thus, for example, we retain an "action circuit" in which beliefs combine with wants to provide the reasons that underlie behavioral intention, but add a "reaction circuit" more in tune with subconscious, emotional, and appreciative responses to symbolic aspects of communication from the environment. One need not choose between these formulations. Instead, both are contained within the expanded approach. Our view of the consumption experience incorporates both aspects of consumer behavior. Hence, those inclined to be charitable may regard it as stretching our research tradition to accommodate the phenomena of interest so as to avoid impoverishing these phenomena to fit our philosophical prepossessions.

Acknowledgements. The authors thank John Howard and John O'Shaughnessy for ideas borrowed, extended, and possibly abused in this paper. They also thank Jim Bettman, Dave Brinberg, and Russ Belk for their helpful comments on an earlier draft. Morris Holbrook gratefully acknowledges the support of the Columbia Business School's faculty Research Fund.

References

Abbott, L. (1955). *Quality and competition*. New York: Columbia University Press.

Adler, M. J. (1985). *Ten philosophical mistakes*. New York: Macmillan Publishing Company.

Ahtola, O. T. (1985). Hedonic and utilitarian aspects of consumer behaviors: An attitudinal perspective. In E. C. Hirschman & M. B. Holbrook (Eds.), *Advances in Consumer Research: Volume 12*. Ann Arbor: Association for Consumer Research.

Ajzen, I. & Fishbein, M. (1980). *Understanding attitudes and predicting social behavior.* Englewood Cliffs, NJ: Prentice-Hall.

Anderson, P. F. (1983, Fall). Marketing, scientific progress, and scientific method. *Journal of Marketing*, *47*, 19–31.

Andreasen, A. R. (1965). Attitudes and customer behavior: A decision model. In L. E. Preston (Ed.), *New research in marketing*. Berkeley, CA: Institute of Business and Economic Research.

Anscombe, G. E. M. (1957). *Intention*. Ithaca, NY: Cornell University Press.

Arnold, M. B. (1960). *Emotion and personality.* New York: Columbia University Press.

Assael, H. (1981). *Consumer behavior and marketing action*. Boston: Kent Publishing Company.

Batra, R. (1983). Affective advertising: Role, processes, and measurement. In R. A. Peterson, W. D. Hoyer, & W. R. Wilson (Eds.), *The Role of Affect in Consumer Behavior: Emerging Theories and Applications*. Lexington, MA: D. C. Heath.

Baylis, C. A. (1958). Grading, values, and choice. *Mind*, *67*, 485–501.

Bayon, M. I. (1973). *A history of literary austhetics in America*. New York: Frederick Urgar.

Becker, G. S. (1976). *The economic approach to human behavior.* Chicago: University of Chicago Press.

Bedford, E. (1981). Emotions. In V. C. Chappell (Ed.), *The Philosophy of Mind* (pp. 110–126). New York: Dover Publications.

Belk, R. W. (1984). Against thinking. In P. F. Anderson & M. J. Ryan (Eds.), *Scientific Method in Marketing* (pp. 57–60). Chicago: American Marketing Association.

Belk, R. W. (1975, December). Situational variables and consumer behavior. *Journal of Consumer Research*, *2*, 157–164.

Bergson, H. (1902). L'effort intellectuel. *Revue Phisosophique de la France et de L'Etranger*, *53*, 1–27.

Berkeley, G. (1971). *A treatise concerning the principles of human knowledge*. Maston, England: Scholar Press.

Birdwhistell, R. L. (1970). *Kinesics and context: Essays on body motion communication* . Philadelphia: University of Pennsylvania Press.

Bohm, D. (1971). Quantum theory as an indication of a new order of physics, part a. *Foundations of Physics*, *1*, 359–381.

Bohm, D. (1973). Quantum theory as an indication of a new order of physics, part b. *Foundations of Physics*, *3*, 139–168.

Brightfield, M. F. (1968). *The issue in literary criticism*. New York: Greenwood Press.

Brightman, E. S. (1962). Axiology. In D. D. Runes (Ed.), *Dictionary of Philosophy* (pp. 32–33). Totowa, NJ: Littlefield, Adams & Co.

Brody, N. (1983). *Human motivation: Commentary on goal-directed action*. New York: Academic Press.

Cacioppo, J. T., Losch, M. E., Tassinary, L. G., & Petty, R. E. (1985). Properties of affect and affect-laden information processing. In R. A. Peterson, W. D. Hoyer, & W. R. Wilson (Eds.), *The Role of Affect in Consumer Behavior: Emerging Theories and Applications*. Lexington, MA: D. C. Heath.

Cameron, J. M. (1983). Autobiography and philosophical perplexity. In E. Schaper (Ed.), *Pleasure, preference, & value* (pp. 158–170). Cambridge: Cambridge University Press.

Czikszentmihalyi, M. & Rochberg-Halton, E. (1982). *The meaning of things: Domestic symbols and the self.* Cambridge, England: Cambridge University Press.

Davidson, D. (1963, November). Actions, reasons, and causes. *The Journal of Philosophy*, *LX*, 685–700.

Davis, L. H. (1979). *Theory of action*. Englewood Cliffs, NJ: Prentice-Hall.

Deci, E. L. (1975). *Intrinsic motivation*. New York: Plenum Press.

Denzin, N. K. (1984). *On understanding emotion*. San Francisco: Jossey-Bass.

de Rivera, J. (1977). *A structural theory of the emotions*. New York: International Universities Press.

Deshpande, R. (1983, Fall). Paradigms lost: On theory and method in research in marketing. *Journal of Marketing*, *47*, 101–110.

Dichter, E. (1960). *The strategy of desire*. Garden City, NY: Doubleday.

Dickson, P. R. (1982, Fall). Person-situation: Segmentation's missing link. *Journal of Marketing*, *46*, 56–64.

Dienstbier, R. A. (1979). Emotion-attribution theory: Establishing roots and exploring future perspectives. In R. A. Dienstbier (Ed.), *Nebraska Symposium on Motivation: Volume 26*. Lincoln: University of Nebraska Press.

Drenan, S. (1983). Personality factors. In L. R. Kahle (Ed.), *Social Values and Social Change* (pp. 277–260). New York: Praeger.

Ekman, P., Levenson, R. W., & Friesen, W. V. (1983, September). Autonomic nervous system activity distinguishes among emotions. *Science, 221*, 1208–1210.

Engel, J. F., Kollat, D. T., & Blackwell, R. D. (1973). *Consumer behavior.* Hinsdale, IL: Dryden Press.

Falk, B. (1983). The communicability of feeling. In E. Schapter (Ed.), *Pleasure, preference & value* (pp. 57–85). Cambridge, England: Cambridge University Press.

Fazio, R. H., & Zanna, M. P. (1981). Direct experience and attitude-behavior consistency. *Advances in Experimental Social Psychology, 14*, 161–202.

Fennell, G. (1980). The situation. *Motivation and Emotion, 4* (4), 299–322.

Ferguson, M. (1980). *The aquarian conspiracy.* New York: St. Martins.

Fishbein, M., & Ajzen, I. (1975). *Belief, attitude, intention and behavior.* Reading, MA: Addison-Wesley.

Frankena, W. (1967). Value and valuation. In P. Edwards (Ed.), *The encyclopedia of philosophy: Vol. 8* (pp. 229–232). New York: The Macmillan Company.

Giorgi, A. (1970). *Psychology as a human science: A phenomenologically based approach*. New York: Harper & Row.

Goldman, A. I. (1970). *A theory of human action*. Princeton, NJ: Princeton University Press.

Greene, T. M. (1952). *The arts and the art of criticism*. Princeton, NJ: Princeton University Press.

Grings, W. W., & Dawson, M. E. (1978). *Emotions and bodily responses: A psychophysiological approach*. New York: Academic Press.

Hamlyn, D. W. (1981). Behavior. In V. C. Chappell (Ed.), *The Philosophy of Mind* (pp. 69–73). New York: Dover Publications.

Hampshire, S. (1982). *Thought and action*. Notre Dame: University of Notre Dame Press.

Harman, G. (1973). *Thought*. Princeton, NJ: Princeton University Press.

Harre, R., & Secord, P. F. (1973). *The explanation of social behaviour.* Totowa, NJ: Littlefield, Adams & Co.

Hassett, J. (1978). *A primer of psychophysiology.* San Francisco: W. H. Freeman.

Hilgard, E. R. (1962). Impulsive versus realistic thinking: An examination of the distinction between primary and secondary processes in thought. *Psychological Bulletin, 59* (6), 477–488.

Hilgard, E. R. (1980). Consciousness in contemporary psychology. *Annual Review of Psychology, 31*, 1–26.

Hiller, G. A., Jr. (1984, December). Gemeinschaft Verstehen: A theory of the middle range. *Social Forces, 63* (2), 307–334.

Hirschman, E. C., & Holbrook, M. B. (1982). Hedonic consumption: Emerging concepts, methods and propositions. *Journal of Marketing, 46* (3), 92–101.

Hirschman, E. C. (1983). On the acquisition of aesthetic, escapist, and agentic experiences. *Empirical Studies of the Arts, 1*, 157–172.

Hirschman, E. C. (1984). Experience seeking: A subjectivist perspective on consumption. *Journal of Business Research, 12*, 115–136.

Hirschman, E. C. (1985a). Dual consciousness and altered states: Implications for consumer research. *Journal of Business Research, 3.*

Hirschman, E. C. (1985c). Sex roles and leisure motives. *Journal of Leisure Research.*

Hirschman, E. C. (1985b). Experiential cognitive processes. In J. N. Sheth (Ed.), *Research in Consumer Behavior: Volume I.* Greenwich, CT: JAI Press.

Hochschild, A. R. (1983). *The managed heart: Commercialization of human feeling*. Berkeley: University of California Press.

Holbrook, M. B. (1985). Emotion in the consumption experience; toward a new model of the human consumer. In R. A. Peterson, W. D. Hoyer, & W. R. Wilson (Eds.), *The Role of Affect in Consumer Behavior: Emerging Theories and Applications* (pp. 104–137). Lexington, MA: D.C. Heath.

Holbrook, M. B., & Bertges, S. A. (1981, October). Perceptual veridicality in esthetic communication: A model, general procedure, and illustration. *Communication Research*, *8*, 387–423.

Holbrook, M. B., & Corfman, K. P. (1984). Quality and value in the consumption experience: Phaedrus rides again. In J. Jacoby & J. C. Olson (Eds.), *Consumer Perception of Merchandise and Store Quality* (pp. 75–94).

Holbrook, M. B., & Huber, J. (1983). Detecting the differences in jazz: A comparison of methods for assessing perceptual veridicality in applied aesthetics. *Empirical Studies of the Arts*, *1* (1), 35–53.

Holbrook, M. B. (1981, February). Integrating compositional and decompositional analyses to represent the intervening role of perceptions in evaluative judgments. *Journal of Marketing Research*, *18*, 13–28.

Holbrook, M. B. (1983a). Product imagery and the illusion of reality: Some insights from consumer esthetics. In R. P. Bagozzi & A. M. Tybout (Eds.), *Advances in Consumer Research: Volume 10*. Ann Arbor: Association for Consumer Research.

Holbrook, M. B. (1983b, September). Using a structural model of halo effect to assess perceptual distortion due to affective overtones. *Journal of Consumer Research*, *10*, 247–252.

Holbrook, M. B. (1984a). Axiology in consumer research: The nature of value in the consumption experience. Working paper, Graduate School of Business, Columbia University.

Holbrook, M. B. (1985). Why business is bad for consumer research: The three bears revisited. In E. C. Hirschman & M. B. Holbrook (Eds.), *Advances in Consumer Research: Volume 12*. Ann Arbor: Association for Consumer Research.

Holbrook, M. B., Chestnut, R. W., Oliva, T. A., & Greenleaf, E. A. (1984, September). Play as a consumption experience: The roles of emotions, performance, and personality in the enjoyment of games. *Journal of Consumer Research*, *11*, 728–739.

Holbrook, M. B., & O'Shaughnessy, J. (1984). The role of emotion in advertising. *Psychology & Marketing*, *1* (2), 45–64.

Holbrook, M. B., & Hirschman, E. C. (1982, September). The experiential aspects of consumption: consumers, fantasies, feelings, and fun. *Journal of Consumer Research*, *9*, 132–140.

Holbrook, M. B., & Zirlin, R. B. (1985). Artistic creation, artworks, and aesthetic appreciation: Some philosophical contributions to nonprofit marketing. In R. Belk (Ed.), *Research in Nonprofit Marketing*. Greenwich, CT: J.A.I. Press.

Holbrook, M. B. (1985). The consumer researcher visits Radio City: Dancing in the dark. In E. C. Hirschman & M. B. Holbrook (Eds.), *Advances in Consumer Research: Vol. 12* (pp. 28–31). Provo, UT: Association for Consumer Research.

Howard, J. A. (1983, Fall). Marketing theory of the firm. *Journal of Marketing*, *47*, 90–100.

Howard, J. A., & Sheth, J. N. (1969). *The theory of buyer behavior.* New York: John Wiley & Sons.

Husserl, E. (1960). *Cartesian meditations: An introduction to phenomenology.* Atlantic Highlands, NJ: Humanities.

Husserl, E. (1973). *Experience and judgment.* Evanston, IL: Northwestern University Press.

Huxley, A. (1954). *The doors of perception.* New York: Harper & Row.

Izard, C. (1977). *Human emotions.* New York: Plenum Press.

Jaynes, J. (1976). *The origin of consciousness in the breakdown of the bicameral mind.* Boston: Houghton Mifflin Company.

Kant, I. (1982). *Critique of pure reason.* (N. K. Smith, Trans.). New York: St. Martin's Press.

Kaplan, A. (1984). Philosophy of science in anthropology. *Annual Review of Anthropology, 13*, 25–39.

Kassarjian, H. H. (1973). Field theory in consumer behavior. In S. Ward & T. S. Robertson (Eds.), *Consumer Behavior: Theoretical Sources* (pp. 118–140). Englewood Cliffs, NJ: Prentice-Hall.

Kleinginna, P. R., & Kleinginna, A. M. (1981). A categorized list of emotion definitions, with suggestions for a consensual definition. *Motivation and Emotion*, *5* (3), 345–379.

Klinger, E. (1971). *Structure and functions of fantasy.* New York: Wiley-Interscience.

Krieger, M. J. (1968). Literary *analysis* and evaluation—and the ambidentrous critic. In L. S. Dembo (Ed.), *Criticism: Speculative and analytical essays* (pp. 64–81).

Kroeber-Riel, W. (1979, March). Activation research: Psychobiological approaches in consumer research. *Journal of Consumer Research*, *5*, 240–250.

Krugman, H. E. (1965). The impact of television advertising: Learning without involvement. *Public Opinion Quarterly, 29*, 349–356.

Lamont, W. D. (1955). *The Value Judgment.* Westport, CT: Greenwood Press.

Lang, P. J., Rice, D. G., & Sternbach, R. A. (1972). The psychophysiology of emotion. In N. S. Greenfield & R. A. Sternbach (Eds.), *Handbook of Psychophysiology.* New York: Holt, Rinehart & Winston.

Langer, S. K. (1942). *Philosophy in a new key.* Cambridge, MA: Harvard University Press.

Laudan, L. (1977). *Progress and its problems: Towards a theory of scientific growth.* Berkeley: University of California Press.

Laudan, L. (1984). *Science and values: The aims of science and their role in scientific debate.* Berkeley: University of California Press.

Lavidge, R. J., & Steiner, G. A. (1961). A model for predictive measurements of advertising effectiveness. *Journal of Marketing*, *24*, 59–62.

Lazarus, R. S. (1982). Thoughts on the relations between emotion and cognition. *American Psychologist*, *37* (9), 1019–1024.

Lazarus, R. S., Averill, J. R., & Opton, E. M. Jr. (1970). Towards a cognitive theory of emotion. In M. B. Arnold (Ed.), *Feelings and Emotions.* New York: Academic Press.

Levy, S. J. (1981, Summer). Interpreting consumer methodology: A structural approach to consumer behavior. *Journal of Marketing*, 49–62.

Lewin, K. (1936). *Principles of topological psychology* (F. Heider & G. M. Heider, Trans.). New York: McGraw-Hill.

Lewin, K. (1951). *Field Theory in Social Science: Selected Theoretical Papers*, ed. Dorwin Cartwright, Chicago: The University of Chicago Press.

Lewis, C. I. (1946). *An analysis of knowledge and valuation.* La Salle, IL: Open Court.

Lyons, W. (1980). *Emotion.* Cambridge, England: Cambridge University Press.

MacIntyre, A. C. (1958). *The unconscious.* London: Routledge & Kegan Paul.

Mandler, G. (1975). *Mind and emotion*. New York: John Wiley & Sons.

McGuire, W. J. (1973). The Yin and Yang of progress in social psychology: Seven Koan. *Journal of Personality and Social Psychology, 26* (3), 446–456.

Mehrabian, A., & Russell, J. A. (1974). *An approach to environmental psychology.* Cambridge, MA: The MIT Press.

Mitchell, A. (1983). *The nine American lifestyles*. New York: Warner Books.

Mitroff, I. I., & Kilmann, R. H. (1978). *Methodological approaches to social science*. San Francisco: Jossey-Bass.

Morris, C. (1964). *Signification and significance*. Cambridge, MA: The M.I.T. Press.

Mukerjee, R. (1964). *The dimensions of values*. London: George Allen & Unwin.

Nicosia, F. M. (1966). *Consumer decision processes*. Englewood Cliffs, NJ: Prentice-Hall.

Olson, J. C. (1980). Encoding processes: Levels of processing and existing knowledge structures. In J. Olson (Ed.), *Advances in Consumer Research: Vol. 7* (pp. 154–160). Ann Arbor, MI: Association for Consumer Research.

O'Shaughnessy, B. (1980). *The will: A dual aspect theory.* Cambridge, England: Cambridge University Press.

O'Shaughnessy, J. (1980). A return to reason in buyer behavior: An explication of the rule-following paradigm. Working Paper, Columbia University.

O'Shaughnessy, J. (1985). *Why people buy.* Working Paper, Columbia University.

Parsons, T. (1937). *The structure of social action*. New York: The Free Press.

Pelletier, K. R., & Garfield, C. (1976). *Consciousness: East and west*. New York: Harper Colophon Books.

Peter, J. P., & Olson, J. C. (1983, Fall). Is science marketing? *Journal of Marketing*, *47*, 111–125.

Peters, R. S. (1958). *The concept of motivation*. London: Routledge & Kegan Paul.

Plutchik, R. (1980). *Emotion: A psychoevolutionary synthesis*. New York: Harper & Row.

Pope, K. S., & Singer, J. L. (1978). *The stream of consciousness*. New York: Plenum Press.

Ramsey, P. (1973). Literary criticism and sociology. In J. P. Strelka (Ed.), *Literary criticism and sociology.* University Park, PA: Penn State University Press.

Rey, G. (1980). Functionalism and the emotions. In A. O. Rorty (Ed.), *Explaining Emotions*. Berkeley: University of California Press.

Reisenzein, R. (1983). The Schachter theory of emotion: Two decades later. *Psychological Bulletin*, *94*, 239–264.

Richardson, A. (1969). *Mental imagery.* New York: Springer.

Russell, B. (1945). *A history of western philosophy.* New York: Simon & Schuster.

Ryle, G. (1949). *The concept of mind*. New York: Barnes & Noble Books.

Sartre, J. P. (1966). *Being and nothingness*. New York: Washington Square Press.

Sartre, J. P. (1968). *Search for a method*. New York: Vintage.

Sartre, J. P. (1976). *Critique of dialectical reason*. London: New Left Books.

Schachter, S. (1971). *Emotion, obesity, and crime*. New York: Academic Press.

Shaffer, J. A. (1968). *Philosophy of mind*. Englewood Cliffs, NJ: Prentice-Hall.

Singer, J. L. (1966). *Daydreaming: An introduction to the experimental study of inner experience*. New York: Random House.

Smith, R. E., & Swinyard, W. R. (1983, August). Attitude-behavior consistency: The impact of product trial versus advertising. *Journal of Marketing Research*, *20*, 257–267.

Spiggle, S. (1985). 7-Up art, Pepsi art, and Sunkist art. In E. C. Hirschman & M. B. Holbrook (Eds.), *Advances in Consumer Research: Vol. 12* (pp. 11–16). Provo, UT:
Strongman, K. T. (1978). *The psychology of emotion*. New York: John Wiley & Sons.
Sudnow, D. (1978). *Ways of the hand: The organization of improvised conduct*. New York: Harper Colophon Books.
Tart, C. G. (1975). *State of consciousness*. New York: E. P. Dutton.
Taylor, P. W. (1961). *Normative discourse*. Englewood Cliffs, NJ: Prentice-Hall.
Thalberg, I. (1977). *Perception, emotion and action*. New Haven: Yale University Press.
Unger, L. S., & Kernan, J. B. (1983, March). On the meaning of leisure: An investigation of some determinants of the subjective experience. *Journal of Consumer Research*, *9*, 381–392.
Von Wright, G. H. (1963). *The logic of preference*. Edinburgh: The University Press.
Von Wright, G. H. (1983). *Practical reason*. Ithaca, NY: Cornell University Press.
Watson, L. (1979). *Lifetide*. New York: Simon & Schuster.
White, R. W. (1959). Motivation reconsidered: The concept of competence. *Psychological Review*, *66*, 297–333.
Zajonc, R. B. (1980). Feeling and thinking. *American Psychologist*, *35* (2), 151–175.
Zajonc, R. B., & Markus, H. (1982, September). Affective and cognitive factors in preferences. *Journal of Consumer Research*, *9*, 123–131.
Zaltman, G., & Wallendorf, M. (1979). *Consumer behavior: Basic findings and management implications*. New York: John Wiley & Sons.

8
A Theory of the Inductive Learning of Multiattribute Preferences

ROBERT J. MEYER

Introduction

Overview

Much of the research in consumer decision making over the past 20 years has concerned the development of formal models of judgment and choice. Although the literature is a diverse one, most efforts have been joined by a common goal: to develop a parsimonious view of how consumers integrate stimulus information during the course of making a product evaluation or choice.

The most dominant modeling paradigm which has emerged in the area has been that of cognitive algebra, or the attempt to represent the processes of stimulus integration in terms of simple mathematical composition rules (cf. Anderson, 1981; Einhorn, Kleinmuntz, & Kleinmuntz, 1979; Fishbein & Ajzen, 1975). The approach is rooted in a rather simple postulate about how consumer judgments are made: Knowledge about the desirability of products is assumed to be organized in memory in terms of discrete product aspects or attributes. When a consumer is faced with a new product stimulus, knowledge about its features is presumed to be activated, and then cognitively combined to yield an overall impression. The goal of work in cognitive algebra, therefore, has been to infer the mathematical rules which govern this integration process.

The dominance of algebraic modeling accrues to its parsimony as a means of describing decision processes. While consumers may not literally execute algebraic rules—such as averaging—when forming evaluations, they often act *as if* they do. Models based on this assumption have been successfully applied to a wide variety of decision contexts, and have been instrumental in shaping the form of modern consumer choice and attitude research (e.g., Anderson, 1981; Fishbein & Ajzen, 1975; Wilkie & Pessimier, 1973).

Despite this success, the paradigm is not without a base of criticism. The focus of most concerns is that the paradigm has traditionally offered few insights into the origins or underlying determinants of observed preference structures. Given a product stimulus defined by an attribute profile, its goal has been simply to provide a static description of the relationship between scales defined on those attributes and some judgmental criterion. What determines the nature of this relationship in a given context, or how it evolved through learning, however, is left unaddressed.

To illustrate this problem, one of the most important findings which has emerged from the study of decision rules over the years is that there is no *one* cognitive algebra. Even subtle changes in decision context have been found to have a major impact on the way consumers integrate information, and individual differences have been the rule rather than the exception (e.g., Anderson, 1981; Johnson & Meyer, 1984; Payne, 1982). Although this result has been known for some time, we have surprisingly little progress toward explaining it in terms of a more general theory of judgment.

Rather than working toward a reconsideration of the paradigm, the thrust of most work in rule analysis has been taxonomic: noting the types of rules consumers seem to follow, and refining methods for differentiating them in applied contexts (e.g., Anderson, 1981; Montgomery & Svenson, 1976). The consequence is that while we have become technically skilled in describing decision strategies, we do not have a strong theoretic basis upon which to predict individual and contextual differences a priori.

The extent to which the lack of this primary explanation represents a real limitation of this research has long been a point of debate. If one's primary interest is in obtaining an understanding of the processes which underlie decisions, the limitation is straightforward. In this case, the algebraic rule is serving to summarize a set of decision outcomes, and few would argue that this summary is also sufficient as an explanation. If, on the other hand, one's goal is more applied, the limitation is not as clear. In the case of short-term prediction or cross-sectional description (such as in market segmentation analysis), static descriptions are probably sufficient. One can proceed without knowing how a given set of preferences or decision rules originally evolved. If, on the other hand, the goal is longer-term prediction or longitudinal description, the limitation is once again salient. Here, it is the evolution decision structures that one is faced with modeling. In such cases one needs to be supported by an analytic paradigm which is oriented toward characterizing the underlying determinants of change.

The purpose of this paper is to outline such a paradigm. A computational process model is proposed to represent the process by which consumers' impressions of products are formed over time during the course of learning about a product class. The model is advanced as a basis for unifying two, traditionally separate, literatures in the study of impression formation: the representation and evolution of knowledge in memory, and the cognitive algebra of impression formation. It is shown that through this unification a large number of empirical regularities which have surfaced in the study of impression formation—such as context effects, learning biases, and individual differences—can be explained in terms of a common theoretical structure.

The paper is partitioned into three sections. In the balance of this section I clarify the research problem, and review previous research. In Section Two the proposed theoretical model is described in detail. I conclude, in Section Three, with a discussion of the consequences of the model, and its implications for current research in product impression formation.

Background

This research is based upon a fundamental thesis: The key to expanding our understanding of how product impressions are formed lies in our ability to view impression formation as a *dynamic* rather than *static* process. A central postulate is that the variations in decision rules and preferences which we observe are not reflective of multiple processes, but rather of a single, dynamic, process evaluated in multiple states.

The dynamics which I focus on are those of product information storage and retrieval. Specifically, the recursive process by which product experiences are recorded and organized in memory, and then retrieved and integrated to form impressions at a later point in time. Through a model of such a process, it is shown to be possible to explain differences in preferences and impression-formation rules in terms of one primary function: the changing structure of memory.

Over the past ten years the field of consumer research has shared this recognition of the potential importance of work in memory (e.g., Bettman, 1979; Olsen, 1978; Mitchell, 1981). It has been only recently, however, that steps have been taken to formally link models of memory organization with findings in impression formation (e.g., Brucks & Mitchell, 1980; Smith, Mitchell & Meyer, 1981; Sujan, 1985). Although a number of results have been made available (e.g., Sujan, 1985), our knowledge of this linkage remains highly fractional.

To illustrate, a rather natural point upon which we might begin to blend these research streams would be to investigate the relationship between the organization product knowledge at one point in time and the rules which seem to characterize how this knowledge is integrated to form product judgments at later points in time. At issue would be the fundamental concern of whether the structure of knowledge drives the impression-formation rule, or whether the rule drives the structure of memory. Although the first of these hypotheses seems to be the more intuitively plausible, I should note that the second is inherent in much of the work in multiattribute judgment modeling. Specifically, theorists such as Anderson (1981) and Fishbein and Ajzen (1976) posit the existence of generic value functions defined for attributes, with the presumed role of knowledge acquisition being only to better refine these functions. In other words, none of these formulations explicitly recognizes a recursive link between decision outcomes and integration rules.

The work which would seem to bear closest relevance to this problem is that in multiple-cue probability learning (MCPL), a paradigm of judgment analysis which emerged in psychology during the 1960s (cf. Castellan, 1977). The goal of this work has been to examine our ability to learn, through induction, the rules of this data generated by multiattribute sources. In the usual approach a subject is given feedback about the overall value of a complex stimulus, and is then asked to use this information to infer the likely value of later, novel, stimuli. The mapping of such experiments to the present problem is clear: They would seem to provide a direct basis for observing how the process of memory and impression formation interact over time during learning.

Unfortunately, most of the work in multiple-cue learning has tended to focus on learning *achievement* rather than *process*. For example, one of the major results is that we seem capable of learning additive generating rules quickly and accurately, but have a more difficult time adapting to configural rules, or rules in which the predictive value of one attribute is conditioned by the observed level of another (e.g., Brehmer, 1969; Hammond & Summers, 1965; Mellers, 1980). Exactly why this is the case has not been fully established. One presumes the explanation lies in how additive versus configural data are treated in memory, but no formal explanation in these terms has appeared.

Similarly, another major result which has emerged from this literature is that learning achievement tends to be superior for cues or predictors that are positively correlated with criteria rather than negatively (e.g., Brehmer, 1973; Muchinsky & Dudycha, 1975; Naylor & Clark, 1968). The normal rephrasing of this result is that subjects tend to think in terms of what leads *to* a particular result or state (for example, a high criterion value, or a desirable stimulus), rather than what leads *away* from it. Once again, although the result is intriguing, the MCPL literature has not yielded a consistent theoretical explanation for the finding.

When exploring potential process explanations for such results, researchers in the MCPL area have tended to look to traditional theories of concept learning (cf. Restle, 1962; Levine, 1975). The dominant paradigm of explanation for how we induce concepts or the rules underlying phenomena—be they defined by single or multiple attributes—is that of hypothesis testing (cf. Restle, 1962; Kellogg, 1980). The essence of the explanation is that, given the task of predicting the criterion value associated with a stimulus, the individual samples an explanation which is used as the basis of evaluation. This explanation—be it a hypothesis about which of several nominal categories a stimulus belongs in, or an algebraic classification rule—is then retained until, at some point, rejected by data. Hence, individuals are viewed as intuitive hypothesis testers: The more often a given hypothesis is supported, the stronger the belief in the explanation. Variations in decision rules would be explained within this paradigm, therefore, in terms of such a learning process: We observe a mix of rules which have been found to "work" in some context but not others.

Most recent developments in concept learning have focused on systematic biases in hypothesis selection and rejection. Probably the most well known is that the learning asymmetry found in MCPL studies noted above seems to be quite general: Individuals are most efficient in learning from positive or confirming instances of a hypothesis rather than negative ones. Beginning with the experiments of Wason (1960), it has frequently been reported that individuals do not seek out disconfirming evidence when searching for causes of phenomena (e.g., Einhorn & Hogarth, 1978; Huber & Elrod, 1980; Shaklee & Fischoff, 1982;

Schustuck & Sternberg, 1981), and do not efficiently learn from disconfirming instances when they are presented (e.g., Brehmer, 1980; Crocker, 1981).

Although a variety of rationales for this finding have been offered (e.g., Crocker, 1981; Einhorn & Hogarth, 1978; Klayman, 1984; Wyer & Scrull, 1981), perhaps the most parsimonious lies in a second consistent empirical finding in research in concept learning: Hypothesis selection seems to be tied to hypothesis salience in memory. Manipulations which have served to enhance the salience availability of particular categorization rules—such as frequency, recency, and imaginability—all have been found to increase the likelihood of that hypothesis being adopted as an inference (e.g., Kahneman & Tversky, 1973; Kellogg, 1980; Nisbett & Ross, 1980). The failure of individuals to seek and learn from disconfirming evidence might thus be explained in these terms. Because more recent hypotheses will tend to be more salient in memory (by the lack of interference or time decay), there is a stronger likelihood of their being resampled. If this is the case, information seeking would naturally be guided toward recent hypotheses, and hypotheses might often persist in the face of disconfirming evidence (e.g., Hoch, 1983). Taylor and Crocker (1981), for example, use such an explanation to rationalize the emergence and persistence of social stereotypes.

Based on these insights, an emerging view among researchers in both marketing and social cognition is that the process which guides impression and inference formulation may be closely tied to that which guides the schematic organization of knowledge in memory (Cohen, Minard & Dickson, 1979; Hoch, 1983; Shank & Abelson, 1977; Taylor & Crocker, 1981; Wyer & Srull, 1981). The basic suggestion is that when we observe contextual variations in inferences, we are not observing differing heuristics being activated, but rather a single process of stimulus recognition and recall being executed on differing data. Models of the organization and evolution of knowledge in memory, therefore, are thought to offer a natural blueprint for a more general theory of impression formation.

While the possibility of such a general explanation is an exciting one, no formal architecture detailing this process has appeared to date. The consequence is that the link between our knowledge of how information is stored in memory and how judgments are made remains largely informal. As an example, one hypothesis which has emerged from this view is that evaluations may be modeled as a pattern-matching process: If a stimulus matches a configuration stored in memory, it will be evaluated by referral to any available affectual associations. If such associations do not exist, the evaluation may be constructed from the associations of partial matches (e.g., Fiske, 1981; Sujan, 1985). Unfortunately, because this search and integration process has not been modeled with any precision, it is currently impossible to predict the exact outcome of an evaluation given a particular knowledge structure.

In the next section, I describe such a memory-based model of impression information. The model is one which represents the dynamics of consumer evaluation processes in terms of a computational analog of the views of schema evolution and evaluation previously outlined by Fiske and Taylor (1984), Hoch

(1984), Smith, Mitchell, and Meyer (1981), and Taylor and Crocker (1981), among others.

Theory

Overview

The model I describe focuses on how consumers form judgments of expected value or affect during the course of learning about the elements of a product class. My specific goal is to characterize how generalized preferences evolve over time from affective responses to sequential product experiences. A consequence is a number of predictions about the likely evolutionary and contextual properties of multiattribute preference structures.

The model is developed within a limited domain: I focus on the problem of how consumers form independent judgments of product desirability given an assumption about the structure of knowledge in memory. As such, I do not examine the process of product *choice*, per se—that is, how consumers select options from complex competitive arrays. This is done in the immediate interest of parsimony; in the discussion I will outline how the proposed architecture might be expanded to recognize a broader domain of decision problems.

Conceptualization

A central thesis underlying the model is that the process of product evaluation and preference formation is inseparable from that which guides the more general principles of information recognition, storage, and retrieval. The evolution of preference structures is viewed by close analogy to several classical models of knowledge generalization and learning, in particular, those of Anderson (1983), Hayes-Roth (1977), and Rumelhart and Ortony (1977). The model is one which attempts to explain the way in which preferences evolve and vary in terms of the structure and dynamics of long-term memory.

At its root, the approach is quite simple. I follow closely the work of Anderson (1983) by assuming that when an individual engages in a stimulus experience, such as a product purchase, the trace of its individual aspects or features is stored in memory in logically organized schemata or *associative sets*. These packets summarize the objective features of the experience (such as what was ordered at a restaurant), its subjective features (such as how the meal tastes), and the pattern of association with other associative sets (such as the conversation and atmosphere).

The model I describe is built around two algorithms: a pattern-matching algorithm and an evaluation algorithm. The matching algorithm, which I describe first, is a formal hypothesis about how product information is organized in and retrieved from long-term memory. When an individual views a product, a set of expectations is posited to be primed or activated, which defines a hypothesis about its most likely schematic location in memory. This hypothesis triggers a feature matching process; if the hypothesis matches the product in view, the product is declared recognized, and coded vis-a-vis the hypothesized schema. The process of product recognition, storage, and retrieval is viewed as being recursive: The pattern of priming at one point in time dictates the pattern of recognition which, in turn, shapes the template by which new information is stored at later points in time.

I posit that evaluations are formed by a process in which differing levels of affect associated with a product's features are averaged in memory. If a product is fully recognized, then this process corresponds to the "affect referral" model of judgment suggested by Fiske (1981), Sujan (1985), and Wright (1975). If only *elements* of the product are recognized—for example, a given shape and taste that are familiar, but not their combination—the process corresponds to a multi-attribute averaging model, similar to that suggested by Anderson (1981).

Generalized preferences for product attributes are thought to evolve as consumers begin to experience differing products with overlapping features. The level at which preferences are generalized—for example, whether preferences are defined for independent attributes or remain defined only for unique configurations—is driven by both the diversity of product types the consumer has been exposed to and the natural independence of attribute effects.

The Pattern-Matching Algorithm: The Representation and Evolution of the Knowledge Base

Theory. Preliminaries. The matching algorithm is a hypothesis about how knowledge related to alternative brands or offerings in a product class is organized and retrieved from long-term memory. I begin the presentation with two fundamental definitions: (a) How the features of products or experiences with products are represented in the algorithm, and (b) how recollections of these features may fade through memory decay.

I assume that experiences with respect to products are represented in memory in terms of associative networks. The basic structure follows closely a representation proposed by Bower (1981) and Bower and Cohen (1982): The features of products and associated levels of affect are represented as nodes in these networks, and their associations by families of arcs.

The product experiences contained in a schematic map may be represented in set notation as follows: Let $i = 1,\ldots,m$ subscript the total set of offerings or brands a consumer has encountered in a product category, and $j = 1,\ldots,n$ the set of discrete features which characterize these offerings—that is, the number of different feature nodes in a schematic map. For example, i could refer to a particular brand in a food category, and j an ingredient of that brand. In addition, let α_{ij} be a 0–1 measure of whether or not offering or experience i possesses feature j, and let ϱ_i be a measure of the intensity of affect or liking with i.[1] ϱ_i is assumed

[1]In the present work I focus on a unidimensional representation of affective responses to stimuli (i.e., degree of liking). This is done for the sake of development; in future work I may wish to consider the consequences of multidimensional representations (e.g., Bower & Cohen, 1982; Simon, 1982).

to be zero-centered, such that pleasurable associations with i would be reflected in *positive* values of ϱ_i, while unpleasurable associations would be reflected in *negative* values.

Any given string of connected features in a schematic map which describes a product experience is termed as *associative set*, and is expressed in the general form

$$A_i = \{\alpha_{i1}, \alpha_{i2}, \ldots, \alpha_{ij}, \ldots, \alpha_{in}; \varrho_i\}$$

The purpose of these sets is to permit mathematical comparisons of products with differing nominal characteristics—a property necessary for recognition operations. Specifically, each product in a semantic net is represented as an $n \times 1$ vector, whose elements are binary indicators of its features.

Central to the model's view of memory dynamics is the idea that within a given associative set each node is characterized by a differential *memory strength potential*, or the strength of a given node conditional upon its activation or recall. This value is defined by an operator, $s(\alpha_{ij})$ or $s(\varrho_i)$, which serves to:

1. Amplify or deflate the degree to which j is recalled as a feature of experience i; and
2. amplify or deflate the intensity of affect associated with i.

Following Anderson (1983), I define the strength operator associated with a given aspect (α_{ij}) or affect (ϱ_i) as an additive power function of the time since its last recall in the cumulative number of such recalls. Specifically:

$$s(\alpha_{ij}) = \alpha_{ij}(\sum_{k=1}^{p} t_{jk}{}^{-\beta}) \tag{1a}$$

$$s(\varrho_i) = \varrho_i(\sum_{k=1}^{p} t_{ik}{}^{-\beta}) \tag{1b}$$

$$0 < \beta\ 1,\ t_k > 0.$$

Where t_k is the time-lapse since the kth activation of a given node, p is the number of such activations, and β is a memory decay parameter. As an operator on an aspect node, α_{ij}, Equation la implies that the probability that aspect j will be recalled as a feature of a stimulus approaches zero as the time since its last activation increases and/or the total number of activations decreases. Similarly, as an operator on an affect node, ϱ_i, Equation 1b implies that the level of affect will approach neutrality (zero) as the incidence of recall similarly decreases.

The Evolution of the Knowledge Base. I assume that the organization of the knowledge base evolves through a recursive process of stimulus recognition and storage. The algorithm, summarized in Appendix One, follows in the spirit of the recognition models of Wescourt and Atkinson (1976) and Gillund and Shiffrin (1984). I assume that recognition follows an interative process of feature sampling and pattern matching. Initial exposure to a product primes a categorization hypothesis, defined as an associative set. The probability that a given set will be sampled is posited to be a function of the strength of its features in memory. Recognition proceeds iteratively, with sets being sequentially sampled until the product is declared fully recognized or partially recognized; that is, having all generalized features or some generalized and some unique features.

I illustrate the algorithm through an example of the development of a Knowledge base given two initial (previously stored) product experiences. Assume that the memory system is characterized by two product experiences, defined by the associative sets A_1 and A_2:

$$A_1 = \{s(1), s(1), s(1), 0, 0, 0; s(\varrho_1)\}$$

$$A_2 = \{s(1), 0, 0, s(1), 0, 0; s(\varrho_2)\}$$

As before, "1" denotes possession of a given aspect (such as a particular food ingredient), ϱ_1 and ϱ_2 associated affective reactions, and $S(\cdot)$ the memory strength of a given node at the time of observation. For simplicity, I assume that all strengths are initially equal; that is,

$$s(\cdot) = t^{-\beta} .$$

Assume that the individual is exposed to a new, similar product (A_3), which is defined by the associative set

$$A_3 = \{1, 0, 1, 0, 1, 1; \varrho_3\}$$

Note that because A_3 is being observed (rather than recalled from memory), all feature strengths are set at unity. The modeling problem I address is how this new product will initially be recognized, and then encoded in the memory base.

I postulate that recognition and categorization proceeds as an automated process following the five iterative steps formalized in Appendix 1:

1. All or a subset of the features of an associative set stored in memory are sampled for comparison with those of the new product. This defines an initial categorization template or *hypothesis set*.

   The associated sets of nodes which forms an initial hypothesis set is that whose average strength is the largest at the time of observation. Formally, I assume that the probability that a given subset $G_k\{\alpha_{11}, \alpha_{12}, \ldots \alpha_{1q}\}$; $q < n$ will be sampled as a hypothesis is given by:

$$P(G_k) = \frac{S(G_k)}{\sum_{k=1}^{N} S(G_k)} \qquad (2)$$

   where:

$$S(G_k) = \frac{1}{q}\left(\sum_{j=1}^{q} s(\alpha_{ij})\right),$$

   N is the number of feasible hypothesis sets (defined below) and q is the number of aspects in set G_k. A feasible hypothesis is any group of product aspects which: (1) is contained within a common associative set; and (2) shares a memory strength greater than or equal to a minimum value. The first condition conveys the idea that a group of aspects which form a hypothesis must be formally linked in memory. For example, in the present case, hypotheses containing just aspect 1, aspects 1, 2, and 3, and aspects 1 and 4 are feasible, but not hypotheses containing aspects 1, 2, and 4, or 1, 3, and 4 (as they are drawn from different product experiences). The second condition conveys the idea that if a hypothesis contains an aspect which is of one strength level, all associated aspects of the same or greater strength levels are also implicitly contained in that hypothesis. For example, if the aspect "high price" and "high quality" are part of a common associative set and are of equal salience, any hypothesis containing high price implies the joint presence of "high quality."

In the current example, because all memory strengths are equal, all subsets of A_1 or A_2 will be equally probable as hypotheses. In general, of course, this will not be the case; by the definition of set strength expectation, $S(G_k)$, the model implicitly favors the sampling of smaller, more generalized, associative subsets as hypotheses. The most likely hypothesis sets will be those with the highest average feature strengths.

2. Once a hypothesis set has been defined, its elements are compared to the observed features of the new product, A_2. Elements which match define a matching feature set, Z, and are strengthened in memory by Equations 1a and 1b. Formally, A_3 is defined as matching the hypothesis set G_1 on aspect j if, for any aspect of j of i,

$$s(\alpha_{ij})\ \alpha_{3j} > T_1, \tag{3}$$

where T_1 is a non-negative heuristic cutoff. In words, Equation 3 says that A_3 matches G_1 on aspect j if j is a feature of both G_1 and A_3 and the strength of j in memory is at least T_1.

3. The overall degree of similarity between the hypothesis set and the new product is considered. Formally, let A_i be the associative set defining a new product, and let A_{G_k} be a corresponding associative set defining the hypothesis set G_k. The general element of A_i is a_{ij}, a binary indicator of whether aspect j is possessed by i, while the general element of A_{G_k}, $s(\alpha_{G_k\,j})$, is a continuous measure of the extent to which aspect j can be recalled as a feature of hypothesis G_k. The overall similarity between i and G_k, C_{iG_k}, is defined as the vector product

$$C_{iG_k} = (A_i' A_G)/q$$

or equivalently,

$$C_{iG} = \frac{1}{q}\,(\sum_{j=1}^{n} \alpha_{ij} s(\alpha_{ij}))/q\ , \tag{4}$$

where q is the number of features in the hypothesis set G_k.

4. The comparison statistic C_{iG} is compared to a heuristic threshold, T_2. If C_{iG_k} is above this bound, A_2 is considered recognized as an example of the hypothe-

sis G_k and is encoded in memory in the same schematic location. In this case, none of the unique or unmatched aspects of the new product are assumed to be encoded; the new product is recognized as a strict replicate of the hypothesis. The encoding of unique features is assumed to require successive recognition *failures*, or the explicit "noticing" of unmatched features (Step 6).

5. In the more general case where C_{iG_k} falls below T_2, A_2 is considered either partially recognized or unrecognized and a new hypothesis set is sampled. A stimulus is said to be partially recognized if the overall comparison statistic (C_{iG_k}) is below the recognition threshold, however there are individual elements or aspects which *do* match those of the hypothesis set (the matching feature set Z is nonempty). If such is the case, I postulate that the resampling of hypothesis is not independent of the initial sample, but is rather restricted to those associative sets (instances) which share these originally matched aspects. Hence, the process of recognition is one of logical focusing: the pattern of partial recognition at one stage sequentially restricts the set of potential recognition hypotheses for the next state.
6. The new hypothesis set is then compared with the product in view following steps (2), (3), and (4). This process continues until either C_{iG} exceeds a recognition threshold or a continuation operator expires. If the last comparison statistic executed prior to the expiration of this operator falls below T_2, those aspects of A_2 (the new stimulus) which remain unsuccessfully matched are declared unrecognized and stored as unique features.

Note that throughout the recognition algorithm I do not assume that the aspects of the target stimulus itself are ever sampled; the process of recognition is postulated to flow from memory to the stimulus, with reverse causality being only indirect. While factors such as the order in which a stimulus is perceived and its physical make-up (such as some elements being larger than others) will affect recognition, it is only by altering the input description—something which is exogenous to the recognition system itself. In other words, I do not assume that there is such a thing as an "inherently recognizable" stimulus.

To illustrate the algorithm in the case of our simplified example, assume that the first hypothesis for the categorization of A_1 is

$$G_1 = \{s(1), s(1), s(1), s(0), s(0), s(0)\}.$$

Following Step 2 of the algorithm, this hypothesis will be perceived as matching the new produce (A_3) on two aspects: the first and third. Both of these nodes will thus be strengthened in memory, by Equations 1a and 1b. Because G_1 matches A_3 on only two aspects, however, the overall comparison (Step 3) will likely indicate that only partial recognition (C_{iG_k} will be below T_2).

Recognition failure will induce the sampling of a new hypothesis (Step 4). As the first and third aspects have been matched, the new hypothesis would be drawn from only those instances possessing these features—in this case, A_1 alone. Because A_3 shares no other aspects with A_1, the recognition process would stop at this point, or after several successive recognition failures.

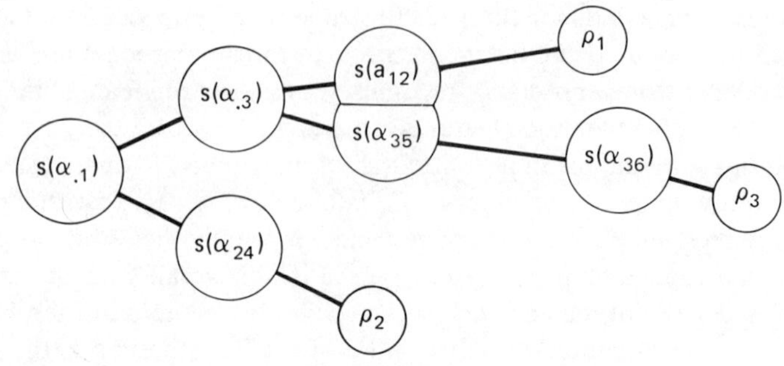

FIGURE 8.1.

By assuming that product instances are stored hierarchically in memory by order of feature (node) strength, the resulting schematic representation of A_1, A_2, and A_3 in memory is shown in Figure 8.1. I derive this graph by assuming that the memory strengths of aspects 1 and 3 will be greater than those of 2, 4, 5, and 6 by virtue of their strengthening by recognition.

As a final note, it should be emphasized that while I assume that product knowledge is stored in memory via associative networks, arcs or links between nodes do not play a formal role in the calculus of recognition and storage. Specifically, in contrast with, for example, the spreading activation models of Anderson and Bower (1980), node or feature strength is not formally modeled as a function of the strength of associated nodes. This is done largely for the sake of parsimony; although a complex spreading activation model is more appealing theoretically, it is possible to represent the key dynamics of knowledge generalization and hierarchical storage through a rather simple frequency-of-recognition model, as is done here. I illustrate this principle more fully next.

Implications. A central consequence of the recognition algorithm is that it provides a characterization of how hierarchical structures of knowledge or schemata evolve over time. Such structures are viewed as evolving through a rather simple stochastic process. Given that products follow a natural hierarchy of features, hypothesis sets which contain those features which are more general will be more often satisfied by recognition than those which contain less general features. Because recognition implies the termination of hypothesis sampling, nodes which are members of "successful" hypothesis probes are rewarded by an increase in memory strength not shared by unactivated nodes. Hence, over time, aspects which are shared by more products will be: (a) associated with greater memory strengths (be more salient); and (b) by virtue of (a), be more likely to be used as a probe in *future* recognition tests. Thus, the algorithm is one which uses feature strength as the central mechanism by which it infers natural structure of stimuli as well as improve the efficiency by which it searches for new structures.

An important element of the model which should be stressed is that knowledge generalization and efficient structuring arise only through an explicit recognition and storage process: if a product is not recognized as sharing properties with another, knowledge generalization cannot occur. One consequence is that, under some conditions, it may give rise to storage inefficiencies and/or classification errors.

For example, sampling hypotheses based on memory strength is an efficient method for stimulus categorization or recognition only if the basic rules of categorization do not change. A natural property of the model is that existing schemata tend to perpetuate themselves; they provide the "most likely" hypothesis for the proper representation of new data. If an individual is exposed to new products following a *differing* set of organization laws, however, learning would be predictably slow and error-prone; recognitions would take longer (as false hypotheses are repeatedly resampled) and there would likely be frequent instances of recognition or categorization failure (e.g., Hoch, 1983).

Failure to correctly categorize stimuli may arise in the model by any one of three potential means: (a) by memory decay in the existing LTM information base; (b) by the setting of improper match and recognition thresholds (for features, T_1, and, for hypotheses, T_2); and/or by early termination of feature sampling by the continuation operator. Recall that the overall value of the comparison statistic Equation 3 is driven by both the number of features in the hypothesis set which are shared by a new product, and the salience of those features in memory. Within this framework it is possible to show that variations in memory strength can induce the false recognition of a product which is, in fact, unprecedented, and the false lack of recognition of a previously viewed stimulus. The first case arises when a new product corresponds to the hypothesis set on a few highly salient, probe aspects. Even though the product may share few other features with the hypothesis, if the features of the hypothesis which *are* matched are highly salient, the comparison statistic will take on a large value—suggestive of a match. The second case is the opposite extreme: Even if a stimulus is, in truth, matched on every aspect with a hypothesis, if the strength of the template is insufficiently large this match may not be recognized.

Both of these tendencies will be inflated or deflated depending on the nature of the match and recognition thresholds (T_1 and T_2), and the continuation operator. Although these terms are left exogenous to the model, one might presume that they will vary as a function of competing cognitive demands, time pressure, and the historical efficiency of various categorizations. For example, increases in time pressure might be reflected in a shortened continuation operator and lower recognition thresholds. The former would encourage false rejections of recognition by constraining the duration of search. The latter would encourage false acceptances by allowing recognition based on weaker hypothesis-to-stimulus matches.

If recognition failures arise, the long-term consequence is that information will be inefficiently represented in long-term memory. For example, overlapping stimuli being represented in an unassociated fashion, or one stimulus being mistakenly represented as an instance of another. Both of these possibilities have potential implications for why stimulus evaluations may be sensitive to judgmental context. We explore this issue next.

The Evaluation Algorithm

In this section I advance a hypothesis about the process by which consumers form evaluations of the level of affect likely to be associated with a newly recognized product or stimulus. The central assumption is that the process of evaluation is closely tied to that of recognition: given a goal to evaluate a new product, the consumer conducts a search of his or her knowledge base for a matching precedent. Evaluations are then formed either by referring to the affects associated with several, partially matching, precedents.

Following this notion, I assume that the basic representation of affectual information in memory is by the episode; that is, attributes themselves do not initially hold generalized (independent) affect associations (cf. Smith, Mitchell, & Meyer, 1981). I assume that attributes can *acquire* such associations—that is, generalized attribute preferences can evolve—but only through a controlled process whereby affect integrations which are performed at one point in time are recorded for referral at later points—a heuristic useful when an individual is likely to make numerous evaluations of partially matched stimuli. Discussion of this process will be deferred to the next section.

My representation of the evaluation process formalizes a set of general hypotheses previously proposed by Bettman (1979), Fiske (1981), Sujan (1985), and others. Given exposure to a stimulus and an evaluation goal, a recognition hypothesis is primed which may include a unique affect association. Given recognition, the evaluation is a mapping of this affect level—a process Fiske (1981) terms "schema-driven affect," and Wright (1975), "affect referral." Complete recognition failure leads, by definition, to a neutral affect expectation. From a modeling perspective the more difficult process—and the one which forms the center of our interest—is that of evaluation under partial recognition. Here, I assume that evaluation follows a process in which overall affect are sequentially constructed through an averaging of expectations associated with partially matched feature groups.

The formal algorithm describing this process is presented in Appendix Two. I will review it by way of illustration. Assume at some initial point in time an individual has experienced three products in a class, represented by the schematic graph in Figure 8.2. As before, $s(\alpha_{ij})$ is the memory strength associated with aspect j of product experience i, and $s(\varrho_i)$ is the recalled level of affect asocciated with i. The dot subscript $(\alpha_{.j})$ is used to denote an aspect possessed by all lower-order instances in a graph. Specifically, aspect 1 is common to all product experiences, and aspect 2 is shared by the first and second.

Assume that an individual is asked to evaluate a new product which possesses three recognizable features—1, 2, and 3—and a new feature—7. I assume a neutral prior affect, hence the product would be represented by the associative set:

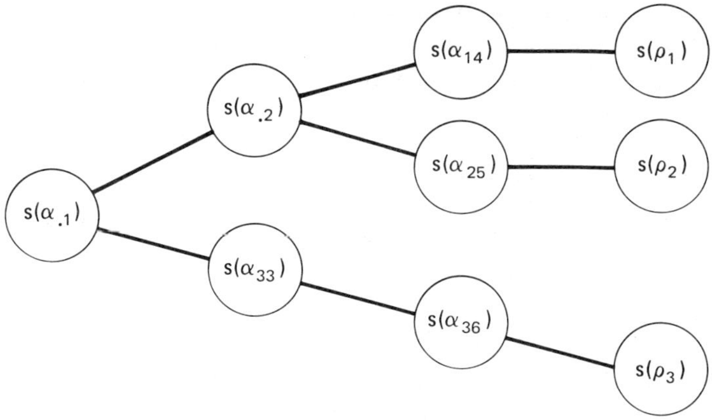

FIGURE 8.2.

$$A_4 = \{1, 1, 1, 0, 0, 0, 1; 0\} .$$

Evaluation is thought to proceed by way of a four-step iterative process represented in Appendix Two:

1. An initial categorization hypothesis set is primed and compared to the features of the new stimulus. For development, let this initial set contain features 1 and 2, and $A_{G_1} = \{s(1), s(1), 0, 0, 0, 0, 0\}$.
2. If the comparison statistic (Equation 3) exceeds the recognition threshold, the new product is declared recognized and the evaluation is the value of any unique affect node associated with that hypothesis set. If there is more than one affect node associated with a successful hypothesis—as would be the case in our example—the individual is thought to sequentially sample product experiences which share the aspects contained in the hypothesis set, and average their associated affects (ϱ_i) in working memory to yield an overall evaluation. As in the recognition algorithm, I assume the existence of a continuation operator which sets a limit on the number of such experiences which may be recalled or sampled. For example, if the new product has been recognized in terms of the first hypothesis set (features 1 and 2), and both product experiences sharing these features are sampled, the evaluation would be $(s(\varrho_1) + s(\varrho_2)/2$.
3. If the product is declared only partially recognized, then evaluation proceeds iteratively, with evaluations constructed in a sequential fashion. Specifically, given a partial match, the affect expectation of the first set of matched features is temporarily stored. This expectation is derived as in Step (2) above; it is either implied by direct referral to a stored instance or global value, or computed by averaging the sampled instance-based affect nodes. Following the recognition algorithm, a new hypothesis set is then drawn, and the expected affect associated with the second set of matched features is averaged

with the first, weighted by the normalized number of aspects in each set (relative size).

In the present example, if the knowledge base is exhaustively searched without recognition, we would conclude that the new stimulus shares features 1 and 2 with experiences 1 and 2, features 1 and 3 with experience 3, and aspect 7 is unique. The predicted complete evaluation would thus be:

$$E(1, 2, 3, 7) = 2/5(\varrho(1) + \varrho(2)/2) + 2/5(\varrho(3)) + 1/5(0).$$

In general, the evaluation of a new product $i(E(i))$ is given by:

$$E(i) = \sum_{k=1}^{m} \left(\left(\frac{n_k}{\sum_{k=1}^{m} n_k}\right) s(\varrho_{k'})\right) \tag{5}$$

where k=1,...m subscripts groups of aspects of the new product which are either unique or match differing product experiences (in the above sample, there were three such groups), $s(\varrho_{k'})$ is the average level of affect associated with group k, and n_k is the number of product aspects in group k. Note that (5) implies that if no aspects of the stimulus are matched (all features are unique), it has a neutral affect expectation (0).

4. Because the evaluation process outlined in Step (4) is potentially lengthy, it is again necessary for us to assume the existence of a continuation operator. As an example of how such an operator may function, if the decision goal is to find the best stimulus while minimizing effort, the operator may terminate the process if the expected affect associated with one set of matched features of the stimulus falls below some threshold value. Hence, the overall evaluation of a partially recognized stimulus is a weighted average of those partial expectations that were processed prior to the expiration of the continuation operator.

Implications. The evaluation algorithm is based on a rather simple hypothesis about how evaluations are formed. Its essence is that evaluations or impressions are formed through a pattern-matching process: Given a stimulus, the individual attempts to recognize it vis-a-vis previously viewed (and judged) stimuli. The algebraic integration of previously stored information arises when this basic process fails, due either to a stimulus being new (a failure to match on physical aspects) or having ambiguous affects (a failure to match with a unique affect association). If such is the case, evaluations are posited to be formed by an averaging process defined over those affect associations which were triggered during the unsuccessful pattern search.

An initial point-of-departure between the present view of impression formation and more classic approaches is that processing is defined at the *instance* or *episode* level rather than of the generic attribute level. One advantage of this approach is that it provides a consistent framework for representing both instance-based evaluation processes (such as affect referral) *and* constructive (algebraic) processes.

To illustrate, central to most traditional algebraic representations of information integration is the assumption that overall impressions can be decomposed in terms of attribute *weights* (or importances) and *scale values* (Anderson, 1981). Although the present formulation is not built at the attribute level, it nevertheless holds a direct link to models based on these ideas.

Consider a problem where a product defined by N aspects is to be evaluated. Let m be the number of independent sets of features which have been partially matched with the product, n_k be the number of elements (aspects) in the set k, and let $s(\varrho_{k\cdot})$ be the expected scale value (affect) of set k. The present model posits that the evaluation (E) of the product is given by

$$E = \sum_{k=1}^{m} ((\frac{n_k}{\sum_{k=1}^{m} n_k})s(\varrho_{k\cdot})) \qquad (6)$$

These partially matched feature sets can correspond to either a group of generic attributes—such as a car's style—or a single such attribute—such as its size, mileage or cost. In the limiting case where m = 1—that is, the product is matched with one prior experience—Equation 6 reduces to an affect referral model. In particular, the evaluation of the product is simply the affect value of the experience with which it is matched in memory. If, in contrast, there are multiple, partially matched, sets, then (6) expands to a weighted additive utility model where the weight or importance of each attribute is driven by the number of minor aspects it captures (n_k), or generality.

When viewed in this light, the present model can be thought to offer a primary explanation for the two constructs central to algebraic information integration theory. The scale value of an attribute level corresponds to the average affect associated with product experiences sharing that level ($s(\varrho_{k\cdot})$). The empirical weight of an attribute would be a manifestation of its generality as a stimulus descriptor ($n_k/\sum_{k=1}^{m} n_k$) and the range of associated affect values (its natural regression effect). Thus, for example, an empirically "important" attribute would be one which serves as a broad basis of categorization (such as type of food served at a restaurant) and/or for which there is considerable affective variance in the scale value of past experiences (such as the extent to which the restaurant's enjoyableness varied greatly with type of food).

Two important contributions of the model vis-a-vis more traditional approaches is that it yields explicit predictions about how evaluations may be affected by recognition and memory decay. First, the model implies that the particular product experiences which drive a given evaluation will be dictated by the hypothesis sets used for recognition.

Specifically, changes in the way a new product is recognized—for example, from a match with one past experience to another, or from a general to specific level of recognition—will all induce changes in the set of affect nodes which underlie a predicted evaluation. Likewise, such evaluations will also be driven by the relative frequency and recency with which these affect nodes have been recalled. Consistent with the hypothesis of Tessier, the more salient a given affect node in memory, the more polarized its value will become.

One feature of the model which merits closer scrutiny is the assumption that the aggregation algebra is one of averaging. A technical rationale for this assumption is that it is the simplest of a number of functions which insure a bounded affect scale. Specifically, the algebra must be bounded to avoid the problem of affect expectations becoming infinitely large or small with growth in the knowledge base—the drawback of simple adding or multiplying models. While other, bounded, forms could be considered (such as a differentially-weighted averaging form), none are as parsimonious.

The assumption of averaging is also encouraged by the empirical work of Linville (1982), who reports that affective responses toward stimuli tend to be less polarized as their description becomes less specific. She interprets this as a type of "affective interference" effect: As a stimulus description became more general, its triggered affect becomes mollified as if by an averaging of associations.

I should also emphasize that while the integration of information is assumed to follow averaging, the algorithm as a whole can yield data consistent with a variety of more complex (configural) rules, such as differentially weighted averaging and multiplicative models. First, because individuals are postulated to form evaluations by attempting to refer to examples, the model implicitly favors the configural processing of data. Judgments generated by configural matches, therefore, will appear to be best modeled by interactive forms of value functions. Secondly, when processing is by independent attribute, judgments may appear generated by a nonadditive source if the algorithm is halted by the continuation operator before all pattern matches have been completed. As an example, if the operator truncates the evaluation algorithm after encountering a single bad subset, the process could be modeled as one which differentially weights negative information or is conjunctive in form (cf. Einhorn, 1970).

Finally, I might add that the model also offers a framework for analyzing how evaluations will proceed given ecologically implausible stimulus combination—such as, for example, a subject being asked to judge the desirability of a small house with twenty-three bedrooms. In such a case if both features are implicitly linked in memory—that is, for example, "small house" is always implied by "small number of bedrooms"—a partial pattern match based on only one of the features would never be permitted (by the definition of feasible hypotheses). Hence, the evaluation would be indeterminant (we would predict neutrality). An important feature of the model, therefore, is that it predicts that individuals will reveal additive sensitivity to attributes only to the extent that those attributes are logically independent in memory.

Completion of the Integrated Model: The Dynamics of Preference Structures

Theory. In the previous sections I outlined two algorithms which form the core of the proposed computational process theory of impression formation: pattern recognition and evaluation. Although each holds independent implications for the processes underlying judgment, the view they provide remains incomplete without an explicit consideration of their integration: how the evolution of the knowledge base affects the evaluation process, and how evaluations affect the evolution of the knowledge base. In this section I complete this development.

I examine dynamics in the context of an inductive learning problem similar to those studied by researchers in multiple-cue probability learning. An individual is exposed to a complex product stimulus, provides an evaluation of its likely desirability, and then receives feedback concerning its "true" value. My interest centers on how these evaluations will be formed during a sequence of such events, and how generalized evaluation policies may evolve.

The application of the model to this problem is not as straightforward as it might first appear, as it requires one to deal with the issue of representing feedback from expectations—something not implicit in either the recognition or evaluation algorithms. My approach is as follows: Given exposure to a new product, I assume that a search is first conducted across memory for a categorization hypothesis which matches or partially matches the product. The evaluation is either the unique level of affect associated with that hypothesis or some average of the affect associations of its aspects. I posit that the decision maker encodes in memory, as an associative set, the features of the new product, its overall evaluation, and any partial averages of affects (within aspects) which led to that evaluation. Such partial or part-worth evaluations form the seeds of *generalized affects* which may, if strengthened, be referred to in future evaluation tasks.

The nature of subsequent processing is posited to be contingent upon whether the true or experienced affect associated with the new product matches the decision maker's expectation. If there is correspondence, the evaluations associated with the new product (both overall and part worth) are strengthened in memory. The memory base at this time would be defined by a mix of affects associated with product instances or experiences *and* generalized affects associated product features. If there is *not* correspondence, the experienced affect is encoded, however the features associated with the previous evaluation are not strengthened.

The notion that overall and part-worth expectations of products are not reinforced given correspondence failure allows the model to be consistent with a large body of empirical work which suggests that individuals usually fail to learn from negative instances (e.g., Brehmer, 1980) and fail to recognize rejected hypotheses (e.g., Kellogg, Robbins, & Bourne, 1983). Specifically, overall and part-worth evaluations can be thought of as hypotheses about the level of affect likely to be associated with particular products and aspects of products, respectively. Given a lack of confirmation, such hypotheses are not recalled as failed explanations, but rather simply fade through memory decay. Hence, it is quite possible for a previously rejected hypothesis to be resampled, or not recognized if presented again.

We illustrate the evolution of preferences via the following example. Assume that memory is characterized by four associative sets, arrayed in the associative network shown in Figure 8.3. As before, α_{ij} is a binary indicator of the jth aspect

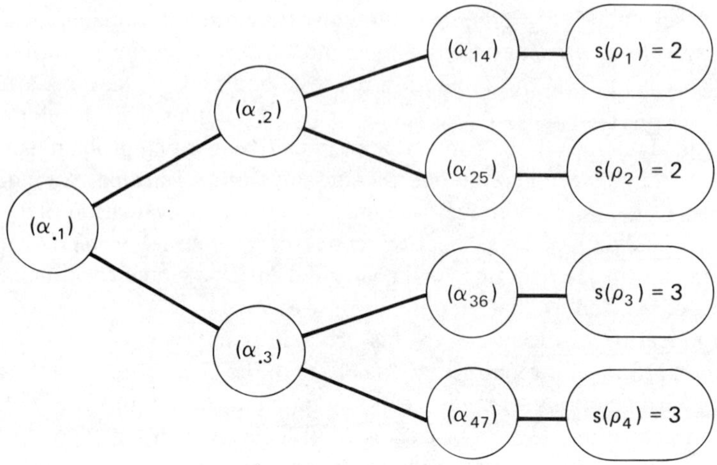

FIGURE 8.3.

possessed by associative set or experience i. $(\alpha_{\cdot j})$ refers to an aspect possessed by all lower-order experiences, and $s(\varrho_i)$ is affect associated with experience i.

In the example the affect levels of 2, 2, 3, and 3 are assumed to have been generated by the averaging model

$$E(i) = 1/3 \, \Sigma \, E(\alpha_{ij}),$$

where $E(\alpha_{ij})$ is the part-worth expectation of a given aspect. The following part-worth expectations are assumed: $E(\alpha_{\cdot 1}) = E(\alpha_{14}) = E(\alpha_{25}) = 3$; $E(\alpha_{\cdot 2}) = E(\alpha_{36}) = E(\alpha_{47}) = 0$; $E(\alpha_{\cdot 3}) = 6$.

Assume that a decision maker is exposed to a new product possessing aspects 1, 3, and 5, and is asked to predict its overall value or utility. By the generating model, its truth value is $(3+6+3)/3$ or 4. The evaluation algorithm assumes that the subject will approach the problem by attempting to match the new product with experiences in memory and then integrate available response associations. Assuming no memory decay, one would predict the evaluation to be the average of the affects associated with the two partial matches, $\{\alpha_{\cdot 1}, \alpha_3\}$, and $\{\alpha_{\cdot 1}, \alpha_{25}\}$, or

$$\begin{aligned} E &= 1/2\ (3) + 1/2\ (2) \\ &= 2.5 \end{aligned}$$

The decision maker is then postulated to encode the features of the new product, the overall evaluation, and the two part-worth evaluations ("3" for $\{\alpha_{\cdot 1}, \alpha_3\}$, and "2" for $\{\alpha_{\cdot 1}, \alpha_{25}\}$) in memory as a new associated set.

If the 2.5 prediction is judged not to match the subsequently-viewed 4.0 truth value, these encoded evaluations will not be reactivated, hence will fade for future prediction problems (by $t^{-\beta}$). Any new product involving aspects 1, 3, and 5, therefore, will be evaluated in the same manner as before: a set of nodes (ϱ_1, ϱ_2, ϱ_3, and/or ϱ_4) will be averaged. If, on the other hand, 2.5 and 4 *were* judged to match, both the overall and part-worth evaluations would be strengthened. These part worth affects then become available for direct reference in future evaluation problems involving aspect-sets $\{\alpha_{\cdot 1}, \alpha_5\}$. It is such generalized (part-worth) evaluations which are posited to form the basis of generalized preference structures.

Generalized preferences are thus viewed in the model as evolving through a process of hypothesis sampling and testing. The important requirements which preceed the formation of such preferences are that: (a) they be associated with a successful hypothesis test; and (b) they be explicitly strengthened (reactivated) by recall both upon formation and through subsequent referral.

Perhaps the most intriguing consequence of these conditions is that they allow one to define the circumstances under which generalized preferences are most likely *not* to evolve. The first condition implies that set-level preferences will exist only if the data generating source is additive in structure. Specifically, because the postulated internal integration model is additive, hypotheses generated by such a process in a configural or nonadditive world will rarely be confirmed. Hence, one would predict that configural data would favor the retention of an episodic representation of affects, with judgments being arrived at almost exclusively through a precedent-searching process.

In general, the model offers a rather straightforward view of how judgment processes for partially-recognized products are likely to evolve over time. Initially, evaluations should be entirely episode-based; evaluations will be drawn from the information provided by closest-matching episodes stored in memory. As the knowledge base expands, evaluations of novel products may switch from being primarily instance-based to generalization-based. The extent to which this occurs will depend upon whether the experienced affect associated with a product can be reliably predicted from simple averages of the affect associated with product features. The more configural the data-generating rule, or the more strict the decision-maker's criterion for successful prediction, the less likely the decisions will be based on generalized values for attributes.

Discussion

Summary

The past several years have witnessed a sizable growth in interest within consumer research on the relationship between consumer judgments and knowledge structures (e.g., Bettman, John, & Scott, 1984; Bettman & Park, 1980; Cohen, Minard, & Dickson, 1979; Johnson & Russo, 1984; Brucks & Mitchell, 1981). Much of the motivation for this work stems from a desire to derive primary explanations for the wide diversity of processes which seem to characterize how consumers make choices and form judgments in differing contexts. One hope is that by understanding how evaluations are formed vis-a-vis the organization of knowledge in memory, a consistent view of the determinants of preferences will emerge.

The present research followed in this stream of investigations. The goal was one of understanding how multiattribute preference structures evolve through induction from expanding episodic knowledge bases. Toward this end, I presented a computational process model of evaluation which presented how multiattribute preferences may be induced through experience.

The model formalized the ideas of a number of previous authors concerning how schematic knowledge structures evolve, and how evaluations are formed vis-a-vis those structures (e.g., Fiske, 1981; Rumelhart & Ortoney, 1977; Taylor & Crocker, 1981). The central thesis was that the way in which a product was judged in a given context conditioned by both the way in which it was recognized and the types of affect associations that recognition pattern triggers. Formally, exposure to a stimulus induced a pattern-matching process which defined recognition vis-a-vis existing product traces in memory. The particular trace which was sampled for matching—the categorization hypothesis—then primed a set of associated features—among which being historical levels of affect. If there was a unique affect association, a product evaluation was defined as a direct mapping of this expectation. If the affect association was not unique, or if the stimulus only partially matched an existing trace, evaluations were defined vis-a-vis an averaging process defined across activated affect nodes.

Implications

Overview. A central feature of the proposed model is that it offers a consistent framework for explaining a wide range of empirical findings which have surfaced in studies of consumer impression formation, inference, and concept learning. To illustrate, I explore its implications for three traditional research areas in judgment analysis: priming or availability effects, framing biases, and multiple-cue probability learning.

Availability Biases. As I have previously stressed, the central point of departure of the present model from more traditional approaches to the study of impression formation is that evaluations are viewed in terms of the affect associations of particular instances or episodes stored in memory rather than global value structures. One consequence is that it provides a natural vehicle for explaining how instance priming or availability can serve to affect the outcome of evaluations.

Instance priming may be defined as the activation of a particular associative set or episode in memory. By Equations 1a and 1b, such activations serve to increase the strength of each aspect and affect within a given associative set. The consequence of priming, therefore, is to: (a) increase the probability that the primed set is used as a hypothesis in a subsequent recognition or evaluation task; and (b) increase the effective salience (modality) of the affect associated with the primed set in any integration of affect nodes.

As an example, consider an experiment in which an individual is asked to recall the last time he or she had to wait an excessive length of time to be served in a restaurant. After an intervening task, the subject is asked to evaluate the desirability of a number of aspects of restaurants, one of which includes a long waiting time. I would predict that this latter evaluation would likely be strongly influenced by the affect associated with the primed instance by virtue of its recent strengthening in memory. Specifically, the strength operator for an associated primed node would be given $\sum_{k=1}^{p} t_k^{-\beta}$, where p would be one larger than that associated with any other episode. This strengthening would thus increase both the probability that the primed episode will be among the set of sampled instances which is used to compute the global evaluation, as well as the relative salience of that episode in the computation (through the strengthened extremity of the affect level).

I should also added that such a priming effect would *not* arise if the task itself—judging the value of a generic attribute—had been rehearsed. In this case, because evaluations at one point in time would be encoded as a generalized feature—we would observe simple referral to the previous evaluation, with no processing of instance-based information. An implication of this is that availability effects may be permanently ingrained in generalized knowledge bases; as long as the episodic information upon which a general evaluation is based is not reexamined, the biases which entered this evaluation will never be corrected—as long as the generalized evaluation remains salient in memory (hence is referred to) (e.g., Read, 1983).

Framing Biases. An area of traditional interest in research in judgment and decision making is the issue of problem framing: The empirical result that the outcome of an evaluation is often dependent upon the semantic context of a problem, or the way in which it is "framed" (e.g., Hoch, 1983; Kahneman & Tversky, 1979; Lichtenstein & Slovic, 1971; Tversky & Kahneman, 1980). The usual explanation is that they are suggestive of an evaluative process in which problem-solving rules or heuristics are keyed in memory to problem types. Specifically, patterns of problem recognition dictate the pattern of evaluation heuristics (cf. Tversky & Kahneman, 1981).

The present model offers a formal representation of this process for the case of affective expectations, similar to that suggested by Hoch (1983, 1984). In our case we would view a frame as a particular hypothesis set or recognition pattern. Because the pattern of recognition dictates the set of affective associations which are integrated during evaluation, variations in recognition patterns imply variations in evaluation outcomes.

Recognition patterns can be externally influenced through one of two means: (a) by altering the set of salient features of the observed stimulus (upon which match comparisons are based); and/or (b) by strengthening various associative sets or strings in long-term memory which will influence hypothesis sampling. The first corresponds to the usual experimental paradigm in background framing. It characterizes the case, for example, where the evaluation of a product appearing in an ad is found to vary depending upon the desirableness of the background (cf. Edell & Staelin, 1983; Mitchell & Olson, 1981). Although the two are normatively independent, recognition will be defined on those associative sets which include both the product aspects and background aspects. Hence, the integration will be over that, more limited, set of affective nodes in long-term memory associated with sets containing both sets of features. For example, a beach scene in a camera ad will encourage the sampling of instances which contain both elements—recollections of both beach and camera episodes.

The second manipulation—strengthening subsets of memory—is a carryover or prior context effect. Those nodes in memory which have most recently been activated through a recognition/recall process provide the most likely hypothesis candidates in a new recognition task, by virtue of their recent strengthening. The pattern of recognition—or the frame—thus can depend upon the proceeding processing task. Hence, I would expect that the evalution of a product in an ad will depend upon both the background material in the ad *as well as* the nature of any ad or task which preceded it. A good example of this in the context of mood settings has been provided by Johnson and Tversky (1983).

As a final note, I should add that the domain of the model does not formally extend to the role of framing in *problem-solving tasks*, such as gambling preferences (e.g., Tversky & Kahneman, 1980). In the present research, we assume the existence of only one computational heuristic (averaging of affect nodes). The extension to problem solving would require the model to recognize *procedural knowledge*—a generalization which I elaborate below.

Multiple-Cue Probability Learning. A systematic finding which has emerged from multiple-cue learning studies is that while individuals can learn a wide variety of data-generating rules, simple additive ones are learned most quickly and accurately. Configural or non-additive rules, in contrast, are acquired only slowly and with less accuracy (e.g., Hammond & Summers, 1965; Castellan, 1977; Mellers, 1980). The proposed model would seem to offer a natural explanation for this result. Given an additive data source, cognitive addition across generalized aspects will rapidly be confirmed as a hypothesis. Because such generalization greatly reduces the amount of feature sampling which must be conducted prior to recognition and evaluation, the model is inherently adapted to "learning" additive generating rules.

When data are generated by a *non*additive source, the model postulates that individuals do not literally learn the more complex rule; rather they approximate its consequences through the heuristic of matching stimuli with idiosyncratic precedents. Because extensive searches across episodic data bases are both time consuming and potentially error-prone, the model is thus less adapted to learning configural rules. For configural rules to be accurately captured by the model, a rather large episodic data base is demanded—consistent with the finding of longer learning times. Given such a base, the more extensive the required search, the higher the likelihood of a recognition error—which is consistent with lower accuracy rates.

The model also yields predictions which may be used to explain the findings of work rule switching, or changing the generating rule during multiple-cue learning tasks (e.g., Edgell, 1983). A frequent finding is that while rule changes can be learned, delay is often substantial, and performance after delay is often asymptotically poorer than it was before it (e.g., Dudycha, Dumoff, & Dudycha, 1973; Edgell, 1983; Summers, 1969). Within the model such delayed adaptation would follow naturally. Given a new rule—or the sudden failure of an existing hypothesis—would predict that the hypothesis would simply not be strengthened, and evaluations, if based on generalized response nodes, would eventually revert to their episodic bases and then gradually be regenerated. If existing hypotheses are quite strong, the absence of a single new strengthening will likely be insufficient to cause it not be immediately resampled. Hence, it may take several failures in prediction before the memory strengths associated with a given hypothesis decay to the point where it no longer drives evaluations.

Limitations and Future Directions

In many respects, the model presented here must be viewed as offering a foundation for a theory of consumer judgment rather than a completed architecture. While its empirical domain is argued to be large, it is nevertheless restricted to the explanation of simple problems of consumer impression or attitude formation.

For example, as an automated system, the model does not allow for explicit control of cognition—something which will be needed when approaching problems of consumer problem solving. This would require recognition of procedural knowledge: heuristics for controlling the input of information, its processing, and translation into an action heuristic. Following the model set by Anderson (1983), such an extension might be achieved by nesting the present associative network model within a formal production or condition-act system. For example, a pattern match might be posited to trigger an instruction for subsequent processing in addition to an affectual response. These instructions, in turn, might be driven by an externally-specified goal system (e.g., Anderson, 1983; Smith, Mitchell, & Meyer, 1981).

An issue which will complicate this extension, however, is modeling the evolution of the productions themselves. It will clearly be insufficient to presume they are static, as has been the case in previous production-system models of consumer choice (e.g., Johnson, 1981). Toward this end, future research may wish to explore the applicability of learning algorithms recently developed for this purpose in Artificial Intelligence (e.g., Cohen & Feigenbaum, 1982).

Beyond the model's immediate limitations, however, a more general question which may arise with respect to this work is whether a formal, data-based, model of evaluation vis-a-vis knowledge structures is actually needed in the development of theory in the area. For example, most of the predictions we derived might well have been deduced by calling on several existing verbal theories of schematic judgment. A central tenant of this research is that formal models *are* needed—and future work should be guided in this direction—for two reasons: (a) they offer a theoretical framework which can be rejected by data; and (b) they offer a framework which can be systematically refined by both induction and deduction. The key is that if we are to have any hope of unifying the wide diversity of paradigms which currently characterize research in schematic judgment, it must be by working toward a common mathematical structure. Only within such a structure can comparisons of theoretical views be made, and alternative explanations formally integrated.

Acknowledgments. The author is indebted to John Lynch and Wes Hutchinson for comments and suggestions made on an earlier draft of this chapter.

Appendix 1. The Pattern Recognition Algorithm

Assume that product experiences are stored in memory in terms of associative sets of features. Let G_k be a subset of features which are shared by one or more associative sets, termed a *hypothesis set*. Let U be the universe of feasible hypothesis sets, and let $U|\,(a_{i1}, a_{i2},\ldots, a_{im})$ be that subset of U which shares the features a_{i1} through a_{im}. For example, $U|\,(a_{i1}, a_{i2},\ldots,a_{im})$ might refer to those products which share a similar shape, color, and price.

Assume that a consumer is exposed to a new product A_i described by the set of features $A_i=(a_{i1}, a_{i2},\ldots, a_{ij},\ldots, a_{im})$. The recognition and storage algorithm proceeds as follows:

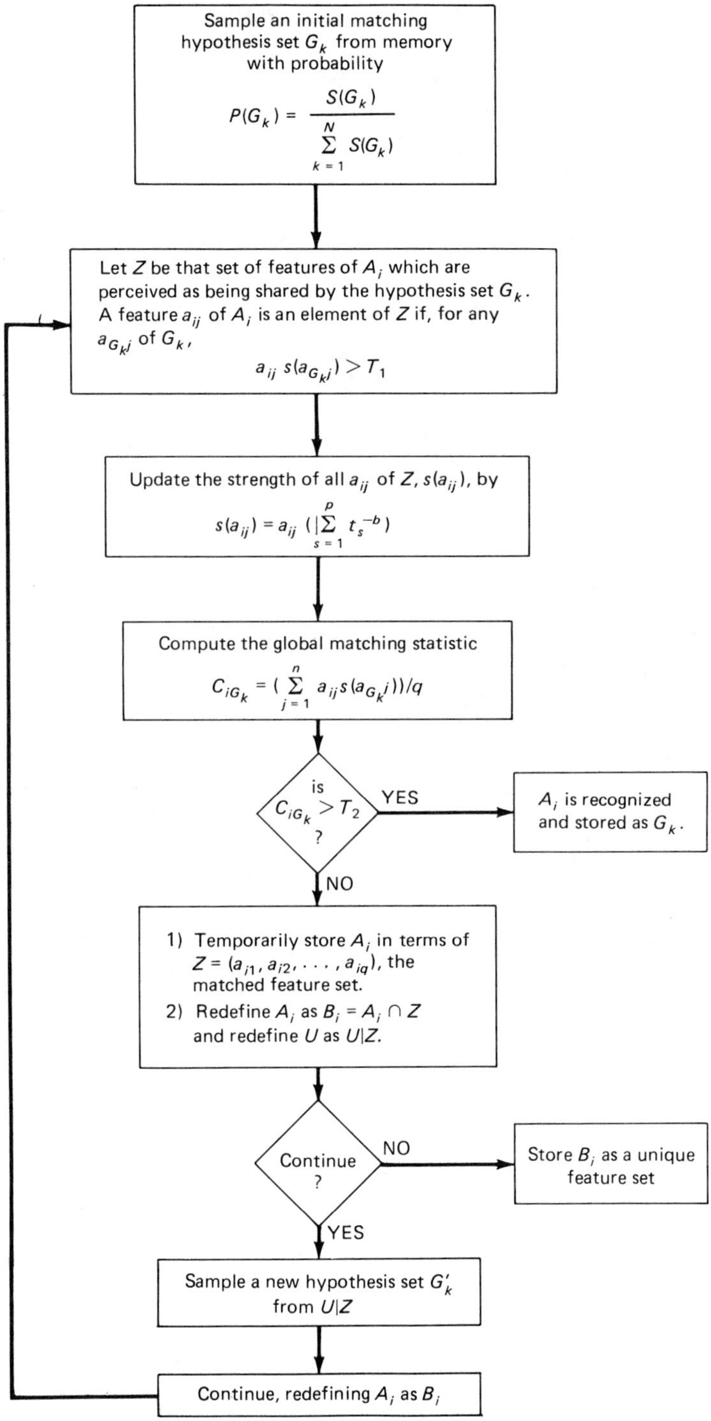
Sample an initial matching hypothesis set G_k from memory with probability
$P(G_k) = \frac{S(G_k)}{\sum_{k=1}^{N} S(G_k)}$
Let Z be that set of features of A_i which are perceived as being shared by the hypothesis set G_k. A feature a_{ij} of A_i is an element of Z if, for any $a_{G_{kj}}$ of G_k,
$a_{ij}\ s(a_{G_{kj}}) > T_1$
Update the strength of all a_{ij} of Z, $s(a_{ij})$, by
$s(a_{ij}) = a_{ij}\ (|\sum_{s=1}^{p} t_s^{-b})$
Compute the global matching statistic
$C_{iG_k} = (\sum_{j=1}^{n} a_{ij} s(a_{G_k j}))/q$
is $C_{iG_k} > T_2$?
YES
A_i is recognized and stored as G_k.
NO
1) Temporarily store A_i in terms of $Z = (a_{i1}, a_{i2}, \ldots, a_{iq})$, the matched feature set.
2) Redefine A_i as $B_i = A_i \cap Z$ and redefine U as $U|Z$.
Continue ?
NO
Store B_i as a unique feature set
YES
Sample a new hypothesis set G'_k from $U|Z$
Continue, redefining A_i as B_i

Appendix 2. The Evaluation Algorithm

We follow the general notation developed in Appendix 1, with $s(r_i)$ being the value of the affect node associated with product experience i. We assume that a consumer is asked to provide an evaluation of the desirability of a new product A_n, defined by the features $A_n=(a_{n1}, a_{n2}, \ldots, a_{nj}, \ldots, a_{nm})$. We denote this response dimension as $E(A_n)$. The process of recognition and partial feature matching is assumed to follow the first algorithm.

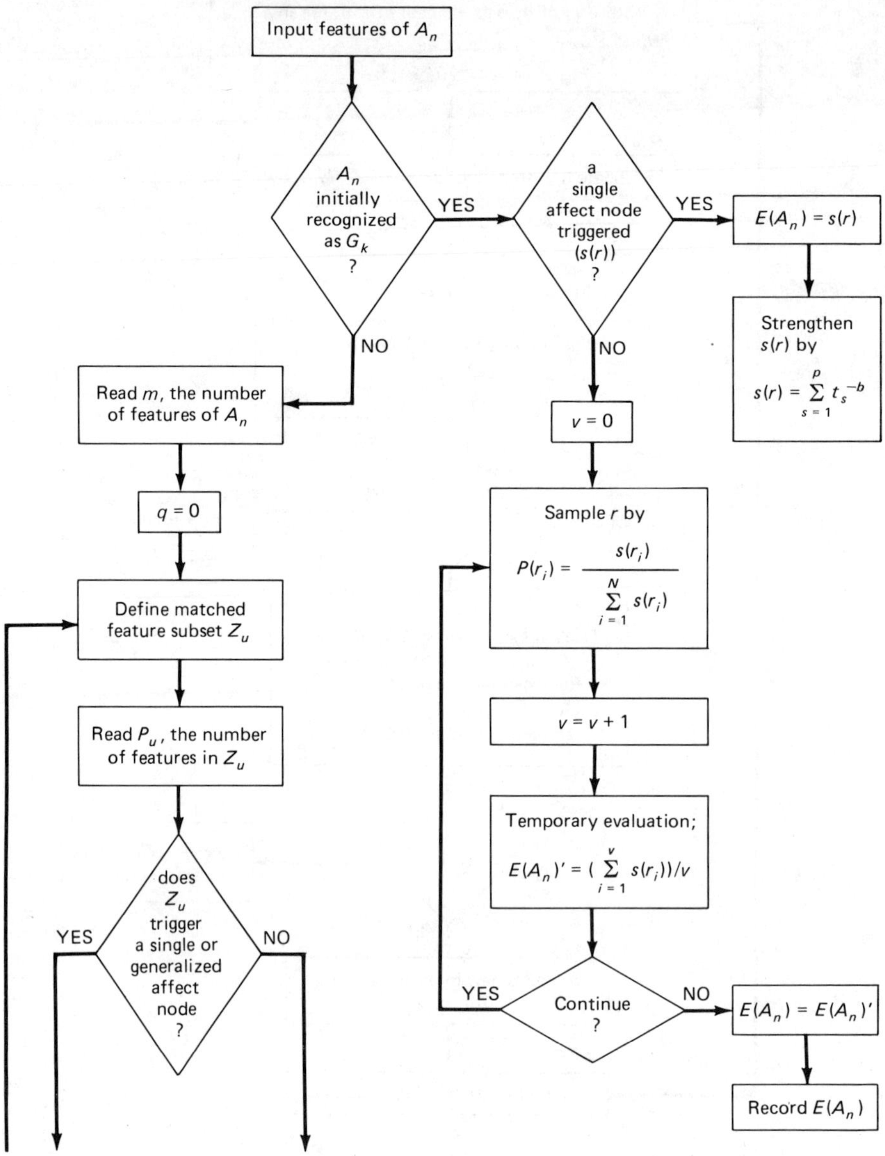

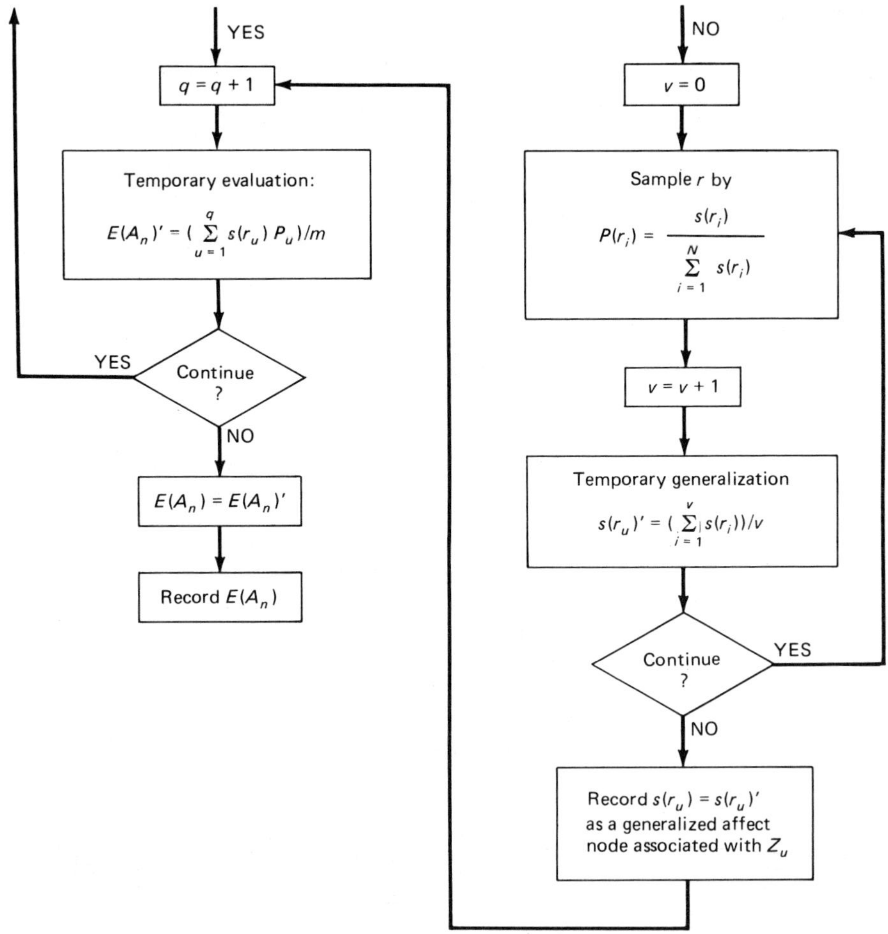
YES
q = q + 1
Temporary evaluation:
E(A_n)' = (Σ_{u=1}^{q} s(r_u) P_u)/m
YES
Continue ?
NO
E(A_n) = E(A_n)'
Record E(A_n)
NO
v = 0
Sample r by
P(r_i) = s(r_i) / Σ_{i=1}^{N} s(r_i)
v = v + 1
Temporary generalization
s(r_u)' = (Σ_{i=1}^{v} s(r_i))/v
Continue ?
YES
NO
Record s(r_u) = s(r_u)'
as a generalized affect
node associated with Z_u

References

Adelman, L. (1980). The influence of formal, substantive, and contextual task properties and the relative effectiveness of different forms of feedback in multiple-cue probability learning tasks. *Organizational Behavior and Human Performance*, *27*, 423–427.

Anderson, J. R. (1983). *The architecture of cognition*. Cambridge, MA: Harvard University Press.

Anderson, J. R., & Bower, G. H. (1980). *Human associative memory: A brief edition*. Hillsdale, NJ: Lawrence Erlbaum.

Anderson, N. H. (1981). *Foundations of information integration theory*. New York: Academic Press.

Bettman, J. R. (1979). *An information processing theory of consumer choice*. Reading, MA: Addison-Wesley.

Bettman, J. R., John, D., & Scott, C. (1984). Consumers' assessment of covariation. In T. C. Kinnear (Ed.), *Advances in Consumer Research*, *11*, 466–471.

Bettman, J. R., & Park, C. W. (1980). Effects of prior knowledge and experience and phase of the choice process on consumer decision processes: A protocol analysis. *Journal of Consumer Research*, *7* (3), 234–248.

Bower, G. H. Mood and memory. *American Psychologist*, *36*, 129–168.

Bower, G. H., & Cohen, P. R. (1982). Emotional influences in memory and thinking: Data and theory. In M. S. Clark & S. T. Fiske (Eds.), *Affect and cognition* (pp. 291–331). Hillsdale, NJ: Lawrence Erlbaum.

Brehmer, B. (1969). Cognitive dependence on additive and configural cue-criterion relations. *American Journal of Psychology*, *82*, 490–503.

Brehmer, B. (1973). Single-cue probability learning as a function of the sign and magnitude of the correlation between cue and criterion. *Organizational Behavior and Human Performance*, *9*, 377–395.

Brehmer, B. (1980). In one word: Not from experience. *Acta Psychologica*, *45*, 223–241.

Brucks, M. & Mitchell, A. (1980). Knowledge structures, production systems, and decision strategies. In K. B. Monroe (Ed.), *Advances in Consumer Research*, *8*, 750–757.

Castellan, J. J. (1977). Decision making with multiple probabilistic cues. In N. J. Castellan, N. B. Pisoni, & G. R. Potts (Eds.), *Cognitive Theory: Vol. 2* (pp. 117–147). Hillsdale, NJ: Erlbaum.

Cohen, J. B., Minard, P. W., & Dickson, P. R. (1979). Information integration: An information processing perspective. In J. C. Olson (Ed.), *Advances in Consumer Research*, *7*, 161–170.

Cohen, P. R., & Feigenbaum, E. A. (1982). *The handbook of artificial intelligence: Vol. 3*. Stanford, CA: Heuristiech Press.

Crocker, J. (1981, February). Judgment of covariation by social perceivers. *Psychological Bulletin*, *81*, 95–106.

Dudycha, A. L., Dumoff, M. G., & Dudycha, L. W. (1973). Choice behavior in dynamic environments. *Organizational Behavior and Human Performance*, *9*, 328–338.

Edell, J. A., & Staelin, R. (1983). The information processing of pictures in print advertisements. *Journal of Consumer Research*, *10* (1), 45–61.

Edgell, S. E. (1983). Delayed exposure to configural information in nonmetric multiple-cue probability learning. *Organizational Behavior and Human Performance*, *32*, 55–65.

Einhorn, H. J. (1970). Use of nonlinear, noncompensatory models in decisionmaking. *Psychological Bulletin*, *73*, 221–230.

Einhorn, H. J., & Hogarth, R. M. (1978). Confidence in judgment: Persistence of the illusion of validity. *Psychological Review, 85*, 395–416.

Einhorn, H. O. J., Kleinmuntz, D. N., & Kleinmuntz, B. (1979). Linear regression and process tracing models of judgment. *Psychological Review, 86* (5), 465–485.

Fishbein, M., & Ajzen, I. (1975). *Belief, attitude, intention and behavior.* Reading, MA: Addison-Wesley.

Fiske, S. T. (1981). Schema-triggered affect: Applications to social perception. In M. S. Clark & S. T. Fiske (Eds.), *Cognition and Affect: the 17th annual Carnegie symposium on cognition* (pp. 55–78). Hillsdale, NJ: Erlbaum.

Fiske, S. T., & Taylor, S. E. (1984). *Social cognition*. Reading, MA: Addison-Wesley.

Gillund, G., & Shiffrin, R. M. (1984). A retrieval model for both recognition and recall. *Psychological Review, 91* (1), 1–35.

Hammond, K. R., & Summers, D. A. (1965). Cognitive dependence on linear and nonlinear cues. *Psychological Review, 72*, 215–224.

Hayes-Roth, B. (1977). Evolution of cognitive structures and processes. *Psychological Review, 84* (3), 260–278.

Hayes-Roth, B., & Hayes-Roth, F. (1977). Concept learning and the recognition and classification of exemplars. *Journal of Verbal Learning and Verbal Behavior, 16*, 321–338.

Hoch, S. J. (1983). *Availability and interference in predictive judgment*. Working paper, Graduate School of Business, University of Chicago.

Hoch, S. J. (1984). Hypothesis testing and consumer behavior: If it works, don't mess with it. In T. C. Kinnear (Ed.), *Advances in Consumer Research, 11*, 478–483.

Hoffman, P. J., Earle, T. C., & Slovic, P. (1981). Multidimensional functional learning and some new concepts of feedback. *Organizational Behavior and Human Performance, 27*, 75–102.

Huber, J., & Elrod, T. (1980). Consumer learning through experience: A study and experimental paradigm. In K. B. Monroe (Ed.), *Advances in Consumer Research, 8*, 66–70.

Johnson, E. J. (1981). DECIDER: A production-system model of choice. Paper presented at the meetings of the Association for Consumer Research, St. Louis, MO.

Johnson, E. J., & Meyer, R. J. (1984). Compensatory models of noncompensatory choice processes: The effect of varying context. *Journal of Consumer Research, 11* (1), 528–541.

Johnson, E. J., & Russo, J. (1984). Product familiarity and learning new information. *Journal of Consumer Research, 11* (1).

Johnson, E. J., & Tversky, A. (1983). Affect generalization and the perceptions of risk. *Journal of Personality and Social Psychology, 45*, 20–31.

Kahneman, D., & Tversky, A. (1973). On the psychology of prediction. *Psychological Review, 80*, 237–251.

Kellogg, R. T. (1980). Feature frequency and hypothesis testing in the acquisition of rule-governed concepts. *Memory and Cognition, 8* (3), 297–303.

Kellogg, R. T., Robbins, D., & Bourne, L. E. (1983). Failure to recognize previous hypotheses during concept learning. *American Journal of Psychological, 96* (2), 179–199.

Klayman, J. (1984). Learning from feedback in probabilistic environments. *Acta Psychologica, 56*, 81–92.

Levine, M. A. (1975). *A cognitive theory of learning*. Hillsdale, NJ: Erlbaum.

Linville, P. (1982). Affective consequences of complexity regarding the self and others. In M. S. Clark & S. T. Fiske (Eds.), *Affect and Cognition* (pp. 79–109). Hillsdale, NJ: Lawrence Erlbaum.

Lichtenstein, S., & Slovic, P. (1971). Reversals of preference between bids and choices in gambling decisions. *Journal of Experimental Psychology, 89* (1), 46–55.

Mellers, B. A. (1980). Configurality in multiple-cue probability learning. *American Journal of Psychology, 93* (3), 429–443.

Mitchell, A. (1981). Models of memory: Implications for measuring knowledge structures. In A. Mitchell (Ed.), *Advances in Consumer Research, 9*, 15–51.

Mitchell, A. A., & Olson, J. C. (1981, August). Are product attribute beliefs the only mediator of advertising effects on brand attitudes? *Journal of Marketing Research, 18*, 318–332.

Montgomery, H., & Svenson, O. (1976). On decision rules and information processing strategies for strategies for choices among multiattribute alternatives. *Scandinavian Journal of Psychology, 17*, 283–291.

Muchinsky, P. M., & Dudycha, A. L. (1975). Human inference behavior in abstract and meaningful environments. *Organizational Behavior and Human Performance, 7*, 377–391.

Naylor, J. C., & Clark, R. (1968). Human inference behavior as a function of validity magnitude and sign. *Organizational Behavior and Human Performance, 3*, 378–399.

Nisbett, R. E., & Ross, L. (1980). *Human inference: Strategies and short-comings of social judgment.* Englewood Cliffs, NJ: Prentice-Hall.

Olsen, J. C. (1978). Theories of information encoding and storage: Implications for research. In A. A. Mitchell (Ed.), *The Effect of Information on Consumer and Market Behavior* (pp. 49–60). Chicago: The American Marketing Association.

Payne, J. W. (1982, September). Contingent decision behavior. *Psychological Bulletin, 92*, 312–402.

Read, S. J. (1983). Once is enough: Causal reasoning from a single instance. *Journal of Personality and Social Psychology, 45* (2), 323–334.

Restle, F. (1962). The selection of strategies in cue learning. *Psychological Review, 69*, 329–343.

Rumelhart, D. E., & Ortoney, A. (1977). The representation of knowledge in memory. In R. C. Anderson, R. J. Spiro, & W. E. Montague (Eds.), *Schooling and The Acquisition of Knowledge.* Hillsdale, NJ: Erlbaum.

Schustack, M., & Sternberg, R. (1981). Evaluation of evidence in causal inference. *Journal of Experimental Psychology: General, 110*, 101–120.

Shaklee, H., & Fischhoff, B. (1982). Strategies of information search in causal analysis. *Memory and Cognition, 10* (6), 520–530.

Shank, R., & Abelson, R. (1977). *Scripts, plans, goals, and understanding: An inquiry into human knowledge structures.* Hillsdale, NJ: Erlbaum.

Simon, H. A. (1982). Affect and cognition: Comments. In M. S. Clark & S. T. Fiske (Eds.), *Affect and Cognition* (pp. 333–342). Hillsdale, NJ: Lawrence Erlbaum.

Smith, T. R., Mitchell, A. A., & Meyer, R. J. (1981). A computational process model of evaluation based on the cognitive structuring of episodic knowledge. In A. Mitchell (Ed.), *Advances in Consumer Research, 9*, 136–146.

Sujan, M. (1985). Consumer knowledge: Effects on evaluation processes mediating consumer judgments. *Journal of Consumer Research, 12* (1), 31–46.

Summers, D. A. (1969). Adaptation to change in multiple probability tasks. *The American Journal of Psychology, 32*, 235–240.

Taylor, S. E., & Crocker, J. (1981). Schematic bases of social information processes. In E. T. Higgins, P. Herman, & M. Zanna (Eds.), *Social cognition: The Ontario symposium: Vol. 1* (pp. 89–134). Hillsdale, NJ: Erlbaum.

Tversky, A., & Kahneman, D. (1980). Causal schemas in judgments under uncertainty. In M. Fishbein (Ed.), *Progress in social psychology.* Hillsdale, NJ: Erlbaum.

Wason, P. C. (1960). On the failure to eliminate hypotheses in a conceptual task. *Quarterly Journal of Experimental Psychology, 12*, 129–140.

Wescourt, K. T., & Atkinson, R. C. (1976). Fact retrieval processes in human memory. In W. K. Estes (Ed.), *Handbook of learning and cognitive processes: Vol. 4* (pp. 363–413). Hillsdale, NJ: Lawrence Erlbaum.

Wilkie, W. L., & Pessemier, E. A. (1973, November). Issues in marketing's use of multiattribute attitude models. *Journal of Marketing Research, 10*, 428–441.

Wright, P. R. (1975). Consumer choice strategies: Simplifying vs. optimizing. *Journal of Marketing Research, 11*, 60–67.

Wyer, R. S., & Srull, T. K. (1981). Category accessibility: Some theoretical and empirical issues concerning the processes of social stimulus information. In E. T. Higgins, C. P. Herman, & M. P. Zanna (Eds.), *Social Cognition: The Ontario Symposium (Vol. 1)* (pp. 161–197). Hillsdale, NJ: Erlbaum.

Author Index

Subject Index